How to access the supplemental web resource

We are pleased to provide access to a web resource that supplements your textbook, *Physical and Health Education in Canada.* This resource offers activities, examples, and templates that in-service teachers can use in their efforts to organize and deliver quality physical and health education experiences.

Accessing the web resource is easy! Follow these steps if you purchased a new book:

1. Visit **www.HumanKinetics.com/PhysicalAndHealthEducationInCanada**.

2. Click the <u>first edition</u> link next to the book cover.

3. Click the Sign In link on the left or top of the page. If you do not have an account with Human Kinetics, you will be prompted to create one.

4. If the online product you purchased does not appear in the Ancillary Items box on the left of the page, click the Enter Key Code option in that box. Enter the key code that is printed at the right, including all hyphens. Click the Submit button to unlock your online product.

5. After you have entered your key code the first time, you will never have to enter it again to access this product. Once unlocked, a link to your product will permanently appear in the menu on the left. For future visits, all you need to do is sign in to the textbook's website and follow the link that appears in the left menu!

→ Click the Need Help? button on the textbook's website if you need assistance along the way.

How to access the web resource if you purchased a used book:

You may purchase access to the web resource by visiting the text's website, **www.HumanKinetics.com/PhysicalAndHealthEducationInCanada**, or by calling the following:

800-747-4457 . . . . .U.S. customers
800-465-7301 . . . . .Canadian customers
+44 (0) 113 255 5665 . . . . European customers
217-351-5076 . . . . .International customers

For technical support, send an email to:
support@hkusa.com . . . . U.S. and international customers
info@hkcanada.com . . . . Canadian customers
academic@hkeurope.com . . . . European customers

HUMAN KINETICS

6-2018

HUMAN KINETICS WEB RESOURCE

Product: Physical and Health Education in Canada resource

Key code: BARRETT-LWDLT2-OSG

This unique code allows you access to the web resource.

Access is provided if you have purchased a new book. Once submitted, the code may not be entered for any other user.

Physical and Health Education in Canada

Integrated Approaches for Elementary Teachers

EDITORS

Joe Barrett, EdD
Brock University

Carol Scaini, MEd
Tyndale University College
and Peel District School Board

HUMAN KINETICS

Library of Congress Cataloging-in-Publication Data

Names: Barrett, Joe, 1976- editor. | Scaini, Carol, editor.
Title: Physical and health education in Canada : integrated approaches for
  elementary teachers / Joe Barrett, Carol Scaini, editors.
Description: Champaign, IL : Human Kinetics, [2019] | Includes
  bibliographical references and index.
Identifiers: LCCN 2018005860 (print) | LCCN 2018006842 (ebook) | ISBN
  9781492569824 (e-book) | ISBN 9781492520429 (print)
Subjects: | MESH: Physical Education and Training | Health Education | School
  Teachers--standards | Physical Fitness | Canada
Classification: LCC GV363 (ebook) | LCC GV363 (print) | NLM QT 255 | DDC
  613.7071/271--dc23
LC record available at https://lccn.loc.gov/2018005860

ISBN: 978-1-4925-2042-9 (print)

The web addresses cited in this text were current as of May 2018, unless otherwise noted.

Acquisitions Editor: Diana Vincer
Developmental Editor: Jacqueline Eaton Blakley
Managing Editor: Kirsten E. Keller
Copyeditor: Tom Tiller
Indexer: Nan N. Badgett
Permissions Manager: Dalene Reeder
Graphic Designer: Dawn Sills
Cover Designer: Keri Evans
Cover Design Associate: Susan Rothermel Allen
Photograph (cover): Caiaimage/Robert Daly/OJO+/Getty Images
Photographs (interior): © Human Kinetics, unless otherwise noted
Photo Asset Manager: Laura Fitch
Photo Production Manager: Jason Allen
Senior Art Manager: Kelly Hendren
Illustrations: © Human Kinetics, unless otherwise noted
Printer: Data Reproductions Corporation

Printed in the United States of America   10   9   8   7   6   5   4   3   2   1

The paper in this book is certified under a sustainable forestry program.

Human Kinetics
P.O. Box 5076
Champaign, IL 61825-5076
Website: www.HumanKinetics.com

In the United States, email info@hkusa.com or call 800-747-4457.
In Canada, email info@hkcanada.com.
In the United Kingdom/Europe, email hk@hkeurope.com.

For information about Human Kinetics' coverage in other areas of the world,
please visit our website: **www.HumanKinetics.com**

E6685

Contents

Preface **ix** ■ Acknowledgments **xi**

Part I Preparing to Teach Physical and Health Education 1

1 A Sociocultural Perspective on Teaching Health and Physical Literacy   3

Teresa Socha and Erin Cameron

What Is Health Literacy? 4
What Is Physical Literacy? 5
Health in the Context of Physical Literacy 6
Common Practices and Alternatives 8
Infusing HPE Curriculum With a Sociocultural Perspective 9
Summary 9
Voices From the Field 11

2 Long-Range Planning   13

Joe Barrett and Daniel B. Robinson

Definitions and Meaning 15
Long-Range Planning 16
Backward Design Model 16
Step 1: Identifying Provincial or Territorial Learning Outcomes 17
Step 2: Considering the Scope of the PE Program 17
Step 3: Sequencing Potential Unit Topics Across the Calendar 18
Step 4: Planning Unit Overviews 19
Step 5: Considering the Culminating Unit Task 19
Step 6: Selecting an Evaluation Tool 19
Step 7: Determining Criteria for Success 19
Step 8: Calculating Teaching Time 20
Step 9: Reviewing the Unit and Incorporating Outcomes 22
Step 10: Completing Daily Info 23
Summary 24
Voices From the Field 25

3 Promoting Safe Practices   27

Greg Rickwood

Space and Facilities 28
Equipment 29
Safety Rules 30
Summary 33
Voices From the Field 36

4 Including Everyone 37

Carol Scaini and Jeannine Bush

Instructional Supports 39
Teaching Methods and Instructional Strategies 41
Modifying the Environment and Equipment 46
Building Partnerships 47
Modifying Games and Sports 48
Summary 50
Voices From the Field 51

5 Addressing Diversity 53

Erin Cameron

Creating Sociocultural Connections 54
Social Justice Education 55
Addressing Diversity: Becoming Aware of the Water 56
Race and Ethnicity 56
Disability 57
Gender 57
Body Size 58
Summary 58
Voices From the Field 60

6 Infusing Indigenous Games and Perspectives Within HPE 61

Mary Courchene, Blair Robillard, Amy Carpenter, and Joannie Halas

Creating a New Narrative for Turtle Island 62
Mino' Pimatisiwin: Living a Balanced Life 63
Teaching Active Life and Learning 64
Playing It Forward With Games and Activities: The Original Intent of Play 64
The Circle We All Share as a Way of Being 65
Affirming Indigenous Pathways to Health and Wellness 66
Balancing the Four Directions: *Mino' Pimatisiwin* as Formative Assessment 67
Summary 67
Voices From the Field 68

Part II Teaching Health Education 69

7 Recommendations for Quality Health Education Teaching 71

Joe Barrett, Chunlei Lu, and Jillian Janzen

Why Do We Teach Health Education in Our Schools? 72
Relationship Between Health Literacy and School Health Education 75
Improving Health Literacy 76
Recommendations to Support Quality Health Education 76
Summary 80
Voices From the Field 82

8 Promoting Positive Mental Health   **85**

Susan Rodger

Developing Mental Health Literacy. 86
Understanding Mental Health and Resilience. 87
Understanding Resilience 87
Noticing Student Mental Health and Behaviour 88
Helping Students Manage Stress. 89
Adverse Effects on Well-Being. 91
Normalizing Mental Health Discussion 93
Summary. 93
Voices From the Field 94

9 Comprehensive School Health   **95**

Rebecca Lloyd, Joanne G. de Montigny, and Jessica Whitley

What Is Comprehensive School Health? 96
World Health Organization. 97
Joint Consortium for School Health. 98
Physical and Health Education Canada 98
Whole School, Whole Community, Whole Child 99
Becoming a Champion of CSH: Forming a Community of Practice 99
Creating Partnerships Between Schools and Communities 100
Becoming a Champion of CSH: A Mindfulness Example 103
Creating Ongoing Opportunities to Promote CSH 106
Concluding Exercise 106
Summary. 107
Voices From the Field 109

Part III Teaching Physical Education **111**

10 Teaching Team Building Activities   **113**

Carol Scaini and Catherine Casey

Organizing Teams 115
Summary. 117
Voices From the Field 118

11 Teaching Movement Skills and Concepts   **119**

Helena Baert and Matthew Madden

Movement Education. 120
Motor Development and Learning 123
Phases and Stages of Motor Development 123
Movement Skill Posters. 124
Summary. 129
Voices From the Field 130

12 Teaching Games Using a TGfU Approach 131

Nathan Hall and Brian Lewis

Defining Games in Physical Education. 132
Strategies for Selecting and Designing Games in Physical Education 136
Teaching Games for Understanding. 137
Summary. 141
Voices From the Field 142

13 Incorporating Activities for Functional Fitness 143

Brian Justin

Starting With Why. 144
Components of Physical Fitness 144
Implementing Physical Fitness Activities. 145
Fitness Variables 148
Focused Fitness Qualities by Age. 150
Guide to Using Activities 150
Summary. 152
Voices From the Field 154

14 Designing Games 155

Carol Scaini and Catherine Casey

Designing Cooperative Games. 157
Designing Tag Games 158
Designing Games Through TGfU 159
Summary. 166
Voices From the Field 167

15 A Wellness Approach to Teaching Physical Education 169

Michelle Kilborn and Kim Hertlein

Rethinking Physical Education. 170
A Wellness Way of Being a Teacher. 171
Mindfulness. 171
Interconnectedness: Kindness and Compassion 172
Balance 173
Summary. 173
Voices From the Field 174

16 Education for Sustainability and Well-Being 175

Thomas Falkenberg, Michael Link, and Catherine Casey

Physical Well-Being in Complex Systems 176
Appreciation for the Natural Environment 176
Guide to Using Activities 177
Summary. 177
Voices From the Field 178

17 **Curricular Integration** **179**

Carol Scaini and Carolyn Evans

What Does It Mean to Integrate?...180
Potential Benefits of Integration in Health and Physical Education 180
Integrating Academic Subjects Into Physical Activities 181
Integrating Physical Activity Into Academic Subjects 183
Summary...184
Voices From the Field 185

18 **Taking Physical Education Outside** **187**

Andrew Foran

Three Teachers in the Outdoors...188
Scope and Benefits of Outdoor Education 189
Planning and Preparation...190
Planning Phase 191
Site Assessment 191
Preparing Students 192
At-a-Glance Checklist...193
Student Medical Form 193
Assessing and Managing Risk...194
Equipment and Instructional Resource Checks 195
Managing Groups Outside..196
Locations...197
Activities 199
Summary...199
Voices From the Field 201

19 **Teaching Dance and Movement Education** **203**

Michelle Hillier

Why Teach Dance? 204
Who Can Teach Dance?...205
What Does Dance Look Like in HPE?..205
1. Move It 206
2. Learn It 207
3. Live It..211
Summary...212
Voices From the Field 213

20 **Enhancing Teaching With Technology** **215**

Camille Rutherford

Tech-Enabled HPE 216
Aligning HPE With 21st-Century Competencies....................................217
Collaboration 218
Creativity 219
Communication 221
Critical Thinking..222
Citizenship 223
Summary...224
Voices From the Field 225

References **227** ▪ Index **239** ▪ About the Editors **245** ▪ About the Contributors **247**

Preface

In Canada, there is no federal or integrated education system. Rather, the ten provinces and three territories are individually responsible for the organization, delivery, and assessment of K-12 education. As such, each of our provincial and territorial jurisdictions approach physical and health education curriculum and teaching in a way that is uniquely reflective of the needs, characteristics, and understandings recognized within each province and territory. Beyond our differences, across Canada we have much more in common that binds our efforts to improve the lives of children through the provision of quality physical and health education teaching.

Physical and Health Education in Canada: Integrated Approaches for Elementary Teachers is a comprehensive resource specifically for Canadian elementary (K-8) teacher candidates preparing for responsibilities associated with physical and health education teaching. This practically oriented text is also useful for practicing elementary teachers responsible for physical and health education teaching. It's also a valuable evidence-based tool for reinforcement, review, and study toward additional qualifications.

It is well understood that youth spend a large amount of time in schools between the ages of four and seventeen. It is also well understood that during K-12 school years, Canadian youth face a barrage of health-related challenges affecting, for example, students' mental well-being, safe and healthy behaviours, and lifestyle choices associated with sustained physical inactivity. Elementary teachers, through the provision of physical and health education teaching, can play a vital role in helping students find their way to make informed, healthy choices that may lead to improved behaviours affecting learning, learning outcomes, psychosocial coping strategies, engagement in physical activity, and understandings and experiences that may lead to lifelong healthy habits. We strongly believe that this resource can serve as a teacher's foundation and guide to support efforts to deliver quality physical and health education experiences for students.

The chapters in this book constitute a collection of integrated evidence-based approaches and strategies to relevant topics in physical and health education teaching. We believe the strength in these approaches and strategies lie not just in the underlying research and theories but in the synthesis of research and theories with the years of field-related experience that our authors possess.

These chapters are contributed by a distinguished group of physical and health education teachers, researchers, and field leaders from across Canada. The contributors have been selected from coast to coast, capturing the spirit and expertise of health and physical education in Canada. They have synthesized relevant research and field experience to provide evidence-based and practically oriented strategies and approaches to support your emerging or established physical and health education pedagogies.

In addition to contributions from leading teachers, researchers, and field leaders, this book features insights from outstanding classroom teachers across Canada. A special sidebar at the end of each chapter called Voices From the Field profiles physical and health education teachers who experience daily the practices outlined in that particular chapter. These profiles illuminate the connections between chapter theory and practice and will inspire you to pursue the modeled excellence in your own classroom.

To further help teacher candidates and teachers translate content into practice, we offer access to an online web resource full of ready-to-use templates, examples, activities, and other tools that will give you a head start in applying best practices. Our contributors have hand-selected the components of the web resource to complement chapter learning. The ample collection of web resource activities used alongside chapter content may help you more immediately test and thoughtfully integrate the various strategies and approaches shared in each chapter. To access the web resource, go to www.Human Kinetics.com/PhysicalAndHealthEducationInCanada and follow the instructions on the key code letter at the front of this book.

We have divided the book into three main categories. The first section, Preparing to Teach Physical and Health Education, provides insights and considerations related to the concepts of health and physical literacy, long-range planning, promoting safe practices, inclusion, diversity, and indigenous perspectives. In the second section, Teaching Health Education, our authors share approaches and considerations related to health education teaching and promotion of positive mental health and comprehensive school health. In our final section, Teaching Physical Education, chapter authors share approaches and considerations for a variety of topics, including team-building activities, teaching movement skills and concepts, fitness, teaching games using a Teaching Games for Understanding (TGfU) approach, designing your own games, a wellness approach to PE teaching, educating for sustainability and well-being, infusing literacy and numeracy into physical activities, leading physical activities outside, teaching dance and movement education, and enhancing teaching with technology,

We encourage physical and health education teachers, teacher candidates, and practicing teachers to use the chapters as they see fit. Chapters may be read in any order and are interrelated where applicable by cross-references. All chapters begin with an overview of the learning outcomes to set teachers and teacher candidates on the right track. Discussion questions have been provided at the end of each chapter. These questions can serve as a way for elementary teachers and teacher candidates to reflect on and consolidate learning related to particular chapter topics.

This book and web resource do not offer *the* way to teach physical and health education, but rather it is our hope that our contributors' integrated approaches and strategies will serve to support elementary teacher candidates' and elementary teachers' efforts in finding *their* way to informed and evidence-based ways to teach aspects related to the various topics present within this text.

Reflecting back upon our time in teacher education and through the early part of our careers, we had wished to have a Canadian resource, such as this, to help guide our emerging pedagogical approaches to planning, teaching, and assessing student learning in physical and health education. May it serve you well.

Acknowledgments

We are sincerely thankful to the entire team at Human Kinetics for their enthusiasm, patience, and dedication to our book.

Special thanks to Jake Rondot, our managing director, who listened to our ideas and saw the value in a book designed to support elementary teacher candidates and teachers responsible for physical and health education teaching. We thank you for your efforts and support in making our dream become a reality.

Thank you, Diana Vincer, our acquisitions editor, for your expertise and support with setting our dream in motion, helping us establish the foundations of our text, and keeping us moving forward on this wonderful journey.

Thank you, Jackie Blakley, our developmental editor. You have been instrumental in moving this book to completion. Your support and expertise is greatly appreciated. Of equal importance, we thank you for your patience and good humour throughout the process—all of which made fine tuning the book a real pleasure.

A special thank you to Dr. Catherine Casey for your contributions to our initial thoughts of this book.

We would like to thank all of our chapter authors, whose expertise, leadership, and passion have enriched a text that we believe will inspire elementary teacher candidates and teachers in the area of physical and health education across Canada. We also thank our authors and Dr. Albert W. Taylor who served as peer-reviewers. Your efforts and expertise helped further strengthen and clarify content and direction throughout the book.

We thank our Voices From the Field educators, who serve as an inspiration through the sharing of their experiences as they work to improve the lives of Canadian students.

To all those physical and health educators working in the far corners, the margins, the spaces between: We honour and recognize your efforts to help improve the lives of Canadian children through the provision of quality physical and health education teaching. Thank you.

I would like to express my deepest gratitude to my co-editor, Carol Scaini, for your perseverance, sense of humour, patience, and friendship. Over the course of our collaboration, life found a way to throw a variety of trials and adversity your way. You set the bar high and served as an example for all of us by handling these challenges with grace, strength, steadfast optimism, and poise—you are one-of-a-kind. It has been an honour working with you.

I wish to thank Brock University and my colleagues in the Department of Teacher Education. I continue to aspire toward the high standards, originality, and integrity evident in all that underpins your research, teaching, and service efforts. It has and continues to be an absolute privilege to represent our great university while working alongside all of you.

A special feeling of gratitude to my loving parents, Bill and Marlene Barrett. You taught me the value of hard work, dedication, and the importance of family. You instilled in me a passion for education as well as the inspiration to set lofty goals and the confidence to go out and achieve those goals...thank you.

Finally, I wish to thank the three most important people in my life: my wife, Dr. Kate Coulson, my daughter, Layne, and my son, Roan. Your infinite belief in me continues to drive my efforts to be better. Your unconditional love and support give me the confidence and courage to pursue my goals and dreams. You shared in the risks and sacrifices required to complete this text. Again, I dedicate this book to you. I love you and thank you.

Joe Barrett

First and foremost, I would like to thank my co-editor, Joe Barrett. Your dedication, expertise, insights, and passion for quality health and physical education have challenged our thinking and inspired all of us. I appreciated your collaborative spirit, caring nature, laughter, and friendship. It has been an honour working with you and I look forward to future projects.

Thank you to my family at Tyndale University College, in particular, our director, Dr. Carla Nelson, and the preservice teachers, for allowing me to share my passion for health and physical education. It has and continues to be an honour to work with all of you as we seek to prepare teachers with the utmost commitment to professionalism, excellence, collegiality, equity, and service.

To all of my students, your smiles and laughter are what drives me to be a better teacher! I am grateful to the many administrators and colleagues whom I have worked with and who have supported me during my career with the Peel District School Board.

In remembrance of my dear colleague, mentor, and friend, Dr. Andy Anderson. As a preservice teacher, Andy took me under his wing and provided me with opportunities to teach alongside him at the University of Toronto and develop health and physical education resources within Ontario and Canada. I will carry in my heart forever his words of wisdom, guidance, support, and his wonderful laugh.

I am blessed to have a dear friend who has always been there with me. Thank you, Jeannine Bush, for your friendship, your support, and for being "my person."

To my nieces and nephews: Emily and Sarah d'Entremont and Shaelynne, Colleen, Griffin, and Emerson Bush. You have brought such joy and love to my life. Enjoy each day and always eat ice cream!

When I count my blessings, my parents are at the top of this list. Thank you, Armand and Joan Scaini, for being great role models and for your love and support. Those many times spent on the tennis court, or playing catch, or cycling, instilled in me a love of physical activity and started my journey to an incredible career and life! Thank you for always supporting my dreams and for providing me with the knowledge and confidence to achieve them. I love you both.

Carol Scaini

PART I

Preparing to Teach Physical and Health Education

A Sociocultural Perspective on Teaching Health and Physical Literacy

Teresa Socha ■ **Erin Cameron**

After studying this chapter, you will be able to

- describe health and physical literacy,
- summarize the characteristics of a sociocultural perspective on health and physical education,
- examine your own beliefs about teaching health and physical education and how they align with a sociocultural perspective,
- appreciate the role that a sociocultural perspective can play in health and physical education, and
- use a sociocultural approach to teaching for health and physical literacy.

In Canada, *literacy* is a ubiquitous term that is seemingly understood by all, yet its meaning differs across people and circumstances. Traditionally, it has been described as the ability to read and write, but in recent years it has taken on a more comprehensive meaning. Here is one such definition: "Literacy is the ability to identify, understand, interpret, create, communicate and compute, using printed and written materials associated with varying contexts" (United Nations Educational, Scientific and Cultural Organization, 2004, p. 13). Today, of course, literacy plays a key role in society in numerous ways, for different purposes, and in varied contexts that extend well beyond print to include various kinds of audiovisual media. This plural notion of literacy has led to a proliferation of literacy concepts—for example, critical, cultural, digital, financial, legal, and of course health and physical.

Notions of literacy vary because they are shaped by sociocultural values, history, language, religion, socioeconomic conditions, research, institutional agendas (including those of schools), local and national contexts, and personal experiences (United Nations Educational, Scientific and Cultural Organization, 2006). Paulo Freire, an influential educational thinker and theorist, has described the practice of literacy as reading not just the word but also the world (Freire & Macedo, 1987). This view posits learning as a process not only of acquiring knowledge and skills but also of contextualizing those assets and applying and adapting them in an increasingly complex world. The idea is that enhancing literacy enhances learning "in ways that contribute to socio-economic development . . . [and] to developing the capacity for social awareness and critical reflection as a basis for personal and social change" (United Nations Educational, Scientific and Cultural Organization, 2006, p. 147). In this way, health and physical literacy is not merely something to teach, or a kind of content to cover in class; rather, it provides a foundation or framework for teaching and learning that is integral to one's approach in health and physical education (HPE).

What does this approach look like in practice? It could mean paying attention and being sensitive to the multiliteracies of all students. It could mean creating and developing safe, inclusive learning environments for everyone. It could mean incorporating thought-provoking multimedia and multimodal approaches into teaching. And it could mean prompting students to think critically about the historical, social, political, and cultural contexts of health and physical education. This list is not meant to be exhaustive but to help you start thinking about what literacy means in health and physical education. This contemplation is particularly important given that many Canadian provincial and territorial curricula make reference—either explicitly (e.g., Saskatchewan, Ontario, and Prince Edward Island) or implicitly—to health and physical literacy.

In this chapter, we explore health and physical literacy from a sociocultural perspective—one that views knowledge as socially constructed and shaped by cultural, historical, economic, and political factors. A sociocultural perspective creates opportunities to articulate, explore, and critique ways of thinking and acting that are shared by members of a particular group, as well as the power and social relations among dominant and subordinate groups (Cliff, Wright, & Clarke, 2009). In other words, it is concerned primarily with Freire's practice of "reading the world." Thus the chapter includes reflective activities to nudge you to explore your own ideas, values, beliefs, and behaviours related to health and physical literacy in order to open doors to new possibilities for your own health and physical education teaching practice.

We begin by providing some contexts for health and physical literacy and drawing attention to the words and phrases used to define the distinct constructs of health literacy and physical literacy. We then explore various teaching practices that use a sociocultural lens focused on health and physical literacy. We conclude with a vignette or case study of a practicing teacher's experience using a sociocultural approach to health and physical education.

What Is Health Literacy?

Most of us acknowledge that being healthy is a desirable goal, but why? What does it mean to be healthy? Is health a state to be achieved or a resource or capacity for everyday living? How does one achieve or maintain health? How does one know when health has been achieved? In trying to respond to these questions, we might each be tempted to take stock of certain well-known health behaviours related to factors such as nutrition, physical activity, sleep, and stress. In fact, we would likely each come up with a very similar list of behaviours. But why?

In North America, understanding of the term *health* has been deeply influenced by the World Health Organization (WHO), which defined it some decades ago as a "state of complete physical, mental, and social well-being, and not merely the absence of disease or infirmity" (1946, n.p.). Since then, ideas of health have evolved to be both more multidimensional in scope (including spiritual and environmental health) and multifactorial (including such factors as social support, income, education, food, employment, and peace) (Public Health Agency of Canada, 2008). This shift led to the emergence of the field of health promotion in the late 1980s, as well as the creation of the Ottawa Charter for Health Promotion (World Health Organization, 1986). The charter posited health as a resource for everyday life that enables people to "live, love, work, and play" (Kickbusch, 2006, p. 6). This focus on everyday health created an environment in which settings such as schools could become sites for health promotion. As a result, more comprehensive approaches to school health have emerged, such as that of the health-promoting school (HPS), which is "constantly strengthening its capacity as a healthy setting for living, learning, and working" (World Health Organization, 1995, n.p.) and bases its program aims on the five components of the Ottawa Charter for health promotion (World Health Organization, 1986):

- Building healthy public policy
- Creating supportive environments
- Strengthening community actions
- Developing personal skills
- Reorienting health services

To learn more about this approach, see chapter 9 (Comprehensive School Health).

Although Canadian youth are familiar with school and public health messages (Rail, 2009), many admit to not taking action on the very messages associated with being healthy (Burrows, Wright, & Jungersen-Smith, 2002; Rail, 2009). For instance, in 2012-2013, an estimated 91 percent of Canadian children and youth between the ages 5 and 17 did not accumulate at least 60 minutes of moderate-to-vigorous activity per day (Statistics Canada, 2015); and, an estimated 62 percent of Manitoba youth (in grades 7 through 12) did not eat vegetables or fruit seven or more times per day (Partners in Planning for Healthy Living, 2014). Additionally, in 2011, an estimated 23.4 percent of youth aged 9-19 were living with a mental illness.

Bridging this gap between knowledge and action among Canadian youth is at the forefront of educators and health professionals' concern. As a result, health educators, researchers, and practitioners have moved beyond the goal of merely providing health information and begun to focus on helping young people develop health literacy. This approach views health literacy as a concept, outcome, goal, and asset of effective health education programming (Nutbeam, 2000, 2008). In practical terms, according to the Canadian Public Health Association (CPHA; 2008), health literacy involves the skills needed to get, understand, and use information in order to make good decisions for health. More formally, CPHA's Expert Panel on Health Literacy defines health literacy as "the ability to access, understand, evaluate, and communicate information as a way to promote, maintain, and improve health in a variety of settings across the life-course" (Canadian Public Health Association, n.p.). In other words, for both individuals and communities, health literacy involves possessing not only knowledge of healthy behaviours but also the ability and willingness to translate that knowledge into everyday realities.

> *For both individuals and communities, health literacy involves possessing not only knowledge of healthy behaviours but also the ability and willingness to translate that knowledge into everyday realities.*

As school health continues to emerge as a focus for policy makers, health practitioners, educators, and the general public, greater emphasis is placed on the importance of health literacy. This focus not only encourages health education in schools but also addresses the diversity and complexity of student populations and the fact that health is not just an area of information to be learned but a vital part of students' lives.

What Is Physical Literacy?

Many provinces and territories in Canada have embraced the concept of physical literacy as they engage in physical education curricular reform that emphasizes the whole child. For example, Physical and Health Education Canada (PHE Canada) posits that "individuals who are physically literate move with competence and confidence in a wide variety of physical activities in multiple environments that benefit the

"Individuals who are physically literate move with competence and confidence in a wide variety of physical activities in multiple environments that benefit the healthy development of the whole person."

healthy development of the whole person" (n.d., n.p.). In an example from abroad, Margaret Whitehead, one of the leading researchers on physical literacy in England—and the person credited for coining the term—defined it in 2001 as follows: An individual who is physically literate "moves with poise, economy, and confidence in a wide variety of physically challenging situations. Furthermore the individual is perceptive in 'reading' all aspects of the physical environment, anticipating movement needs or possibilities and responding appropriately to these, with intelligence and imagination" (p. 131). Whitehead (2007, 2010) has gone on to refine this definition, and her pioneering work has provided a language of possibility in which literacy includes movement, creativity, and diversity.

Though some observers have characterized physical literacy as "the new kid on the block" (Tremblay & Lloyd, 2010, p. 26), it grows from deep historical roots. Indeed, a critical examination of the history of physical education reveals an interest in reading bodily movements beginning in the mid to late 1800s. François Delsarte is often identified as the first person to articulate certain ideas of movement, which he termed "applied aesthetics." His work focused on the arts, but he was generally interested in combining mind, body, and spirit to convey emotion (Abels & Bridges, 2010). Inspired by this work, Rudolf Laban studied movement in both its expressive and functional forms and identified four factors—weight, space, time, and flow—as crucial factors in what he later referred to as "movement education." His work became the foundation of physical education, wherein physical educators used the major movement concepts of body, space, effort (energy), and relationship to ensure that learners not only knew how to move but also when, why, where, and in what form (Abels & Bridges, 2010).

Movement education fell out of favour in the 1970s, which saw the introduction of other curricular models based more on fitness and sport (Forsberg & Chorney, 2014). However, over the last 10 years—and particularly given the growing attention to the term *physical literacy*—interest has been renewed in movement education, wherein students are now encouraged both to

learn how to move and to understand why they move. The focus on understanding why invokes a sociocultural perspective that accords with growing awareness of whole-person development—physical, mental, emotional, social, and spiritual.

In Canada, Whitehead's concept of physical literacy has been highly influential. For example, in PHE Canada's position paper titled *Physical Literacy for Educators*, Mandigo, Francis, Lodewyk, and Lopez (2009) extend the definition of physical literacy by describing physically literate individuals as those who

consistently develop the motivation and ability to understand, communicate, apply, and analyze different forms of movement. They are able to demonstrate a variety of movements confidently, competently, creatively, and strategically across a wide range of health-related physical activities. These skills enable individuals to make healthy, active choices that are both beneficial to and respectful of their whole self, others, and their environment. (pp. 6-7)

The definitions of physical literacy presented in this section share the fact that they identify and incorporate aspects of moving that go beyond just the physical dimension of movement. Whitehead's definition addresses the aesthetic aspects and suggests that movement is not merely physical activity but constitutes an art form in which one understands and responds to the environment, thus showing creativity of both mind and body. Meanwhile, the PHE Canada position paper speaks to the need to develop the whole person by engaging the social and emotional elements of movement. It also suggests that the benefits of physical literacy extend beyond the person to include the health and well-being of surrounding people and places. By using Whitehead's and PHE's definitions, we move beyond the physical and draw attention to how the social, emotional, and cultural environments all play a role in our moving selves.

Health in the Context of Physical Literacy

As you can see, the Canadian definition of physical literacy uses many of the concepts promoted by Whitehead; however, it also makes an interesting departure. As you look back at the health and physical literacy definitions, consider the terms and phrases *healthy, health-related, make healthy, active choices,* and *make good decisions for health.* Why do you think this language is included when physical literacy is intended to be a holistic way of looking at child development that results in wellness? What do the phrases *healthy choices* and *good decisions* add or change? What might they reflect about the current sociocultural context?

Physical educator and scholar Michael Gard (2008) suggests that contemporary conceptions of health tend to focus on personal responsibility and presume that the *correct choice* or *right decision* is easy to make, as in the following examples:

- Be active every day.
- Eat more fruits and vegetables.
- Eat more whole grains and less added sugar.
- Eat foods that are low in saturated fat and free of trans fat.
- Strive for a healthy weight.

Increasingly, however, scholars argue that this way of thinking ignores many social determinants of health that have been shown to carry far greater consequences. For instance, the following list was provided by Raphael (2016, p. 11):

- Indigenous ancestry
- Disability
- Early life
- Education
- Employment and working conditions
- Food security
- Gender
- Geography
- Health care services
- Housing
- Citizenship status
- Income
- Social safety net
- Social exclusion
- Unemployment and employment security

Definitions of health, then, are both personal and complex. As a result, if we let individualistic definitions of health determine how we approach health education, we do so at the expense of valuing and starting from the lived experiences of our students. Moreover, if we simply assume a given meaning of the word *healthy*, demanding no explanation, then both curriculum and teacher expectations are likely to reflect traditional

healthy lifestyles messages based on notions of personal responsibility. Yet the intended benefits of *healthy activity* and *healthy eating* messaging have proved very difficult to realize in children, and they remain controversial in health research (Gard, 2008; McDermott, 2008).

As stated earlier, Canadian youth are well versed in health messaging but often choose not to engage in "healthy behaviours." Why? What if we moved away from teaching students to be healthy and toward helping them learn health? That is, what if we took account of "the different ways in which students 'do' health" and "how they learn to make sense of themselves as healthy (or not)?" (Quennerstedt, Burrows, & Maivorsdotter, 2010, p. 98). What might this approach look and feel like? What are the possibilities? Or, what if we focused on learning about the place of food in our lives rather than on which foods to eat and how much? Such a shift in curriculum would move away from a focus on individual decisions—and whether or not they are *good* or *correct* ones—and toward a focus on factors such as why, where, and with whom we eat food; where food is obtained; and social and cultural differences in food preferences, preparation, and contexts of eating.

> *Canadian youth are well versed in health messaging but often choose not to engage in "healthy behaviours." Why? What if we moved away from teaching students to be healthy and toward helping them learn health?*

This type of shift would require a completely different way of approaching health education—one that is more in line with evidence suggesting that socioeconomic circumstances, not lifestyle behaviours, play the biggest role in a person's health. To illustrate such a shift, the following examples of potential societally oriented health messaging (adapted from Raphael, 2016, p. 19) assume that the most important determinants of health lie beyond students' control:

- Don't be poor.
- Don't have poor parents.
- Don't work in a stressful, low-paying manual job.
- Don't live in damp, low-quality housing.
- Be able to afford going on a foreign holiday.
- Don't live next to a busy road or near a polluting factory.

This messaging may sound absurd, but research continues to show that these determinants of health exert far greater influence on health than do lifestyle behaviours. As a result, we may be doing a disservice to our students by making health seem simple when in fact it is complex. Therefore, though it can be challenging to take a sociocultural perspective in health and physical education, the following section provides you with some ideas about how to begin making the shift.

Common Practices and Alternatives

Physical education is said to offer the best opportunity to foster the development of health and physical literacy. Yet it also has a long history of perpetuating inequality and alienation by excluding, marginalizing, or shaming members of certain groups as being "other" on the basis of criteria such as race, ability, weight, gender, and sexual orientation. Think back to your own school experiences in physical education. What is your story? Is it one of glory and enjoyment, or of shame and exclusion, or of indifference? How might this question be answered by some of your classmates? If your own experience of physical education was (thankfully) free from public shaming, consider the following tweets: "PE doesn't stand for physical education, it stands for public embarrassment" (Popik, 2013, n.p.). "PE is 5% exercise and 95% embarrassment" (Common White Girl, 2014, n.p.). What are some other forms of exclusion found in schools?

Another way to get at the question is to consider what image comes to mind when you think of a physical education teacher, or of physical education students. A teacher's dress code, norms, and routines—along with curriculum content and instructional activities—all affect students' participation and, ultimately, their overall physical education experience. With that power in mind, let's explore some often-unquestioned practices in physical education and look at alternatives for your own practice.

For instance, have you ever wondered why some teachers have students sit in "squads" as soon as they enter the gym, while the teacher stands in front of the class? Though some educators view this approach as an effective strategy for classroom management and grouping, it stems from physical education's roots in military training and its early focus on calisthenics and physical training. In other words, it provides a means for maintaining order in the gymnasium. What hidden messages might this practice deliver to students? For one thing, the use of squads positions the teacher as an all-powerful figure who makes all decisions and leaves little if any room for choice by students. Thus it does not fit with a sociocultural approach to teaching that seeks to fully engage students in their learning.

What alternatives exist? When gathering students together after an activity, one possibility is to invite them to sit in a circle and then seat yourself among them, as part of the circle. Indeed, in some Indigenous cultures, the circle symbolizes equality and interconnection among all things—"all peoples, all animals, all spirits, all perspectives" (chapter 6, p. 65). Thus the physical arrangement of the circle is important and requires that everyone be able to see every face without having to lean forward. You might also ask your students why they think you have chosen to use a circle. Then stand up and ask them how they feel now as compared with when you were sitting with them. Notice whether students seem to detect a shift in the balance of power in the teacher–student relationship. Chapter 6 describes the circular world view and how talking circles can be used to give each member an opportunity to share thoughts, feelings, perspectives, and questions—in other words, to be valued.

Another common practice in physical education that we have come to take for granted is the use of a whistle to get students' attention. Think back to your early physical education days. Did your gym teacher use a whistle? If so, how did you feel when you heard it blow? Did it evoke a feeling of obedience, lack of control, nervousness? Have you ever questioned its use? Emitting 100 decibels or more with each blow, a whistle can produce a sound as loud as a motorcycle or rock concert. Used in excess, it can even damage hearing, and for some students it conjures up the image of a drill sergeant in boot camp. It may also evoke feelings of anxiety or even shame based on previous negative experiences in physical education.

One alternative practice is to use your voice to communicate through words such as *stop*, *hold*, *look*, *listen*. You can teach the children what each instruction means: **stop** what you are doing, **hold** the equipment you are using, **look** at the person speaking, and **listen** for instructions or feedback. Students can practice following these instructions in a game-like activity. This is only one alternative; no doubt you can come up with others!

In another common practice, in health classrooms, students are often required to sit and be quiet during an entire lesson. Here again, think back to your own early days, this time in health education rather than physical education. Did you sit while learning about health? If so, did you learn the names and parts of the human body? Did they have much relevance to your life as a student? As Halas and Kentel (2008) have questioned, "Do we consider how painful it can be when we hold young people back from the movement their bodies crave, particularly in schools?" (p. 214). This question is especially poignant when applied to students who are learning about health.

Despite growing support for health education, research has shown that health in schools continues to be taught in ways that are outdated, didactic, and reductionist (Begoray, Wharf-Higgins, & MacDonald, 2009; Lu & McLean, 2011). In other words, whereas physical education is movement oriented, health education continues to be taught in a teacher-centred and physically inactive manner. What can we change to make health education experiential, active, and fun? For example, rather than simply teaching dry facts about specific body parts—say, the human heart—perhaps students could *embody* the cardiovascular system, thus learning by acting out how it works. In another example, rather than just learning *about* food groups and the Canada Food Guide, perhaps students could also involve their bodies in completing tasks that help them remember the learning. For example, first- to third-grade students could work alone or in pairs to retrieve various food cards that are placed on the perimeter of a large circle at the centre of the gym or field. They would travel to the perimeter of the playing area and place the card in the correct designated food group (e.g., fruit, vegetable, root vegetable, tuber vegetable, grain products, meat and eggs, legumes, dairy, nuts and seeds) location (e.g., a hula-hoop). While traveling, students could explore various locomotor skills and movement concepts at the same time. As the old saying goes, "Tell me and I'll forget. Show me and I may remember. Involve me and I'll learn."

Whereas physical education is movement oriented, health education continues to be taught in a teacher-centred and physically inactive manner. What can we change to make health education experiential, active, and fun?

Infusing HPE Curriculum With a Sociocultural Perspective

In order to infuse a sociocultural perspective into your health and physical education curriculum, you must first create a class community in which students feel included, respected, and safe while participating in a culture of playfulness that is fostered through opportunities to be playful. Characteristics of playfulness include humour, cheerfulness, expressiveness, curiosity, imagination, creativity, and freedom from inhibition (Chang, Hsu, & Chen, 2013; Proyer & Jehle, 2013). For example, willingness to make fun of yourself and your mistakes goes a long way toward creating an environment in which students feel free to risk being vulnerable. Other examples of ways to infuse your teaching with a sociocultural perspective are provided in the activities included in the web resource for this chapter.

Ultimately, developing your ability as a health and physical educator requires critical self-awareness—knowing who you are, what assumptions you bring to the classroom, and how those assumptions affect your students. To gain further insight, ask your students about their experiences in your class. Pay particular attention to the silent voices or those from the periphery; these students have much to contribute but may feel devalued and marginalized or be too shy to share their experiences and have their voices heard.

Summary

This chapter provides a sociocultural perspective on health and physical literacy and addresses the context in which these concepts originated and how they are evolving. A sociocultural perspective encourages us to better understand historical, social, political, and cultural knowledge so that we can better understand our attitudes, behaviours, and practices. We hope that you take away from this chapter the following key learnings: First, we hope that you have a better understanding of health literacy and physical literacy and of how they can be used synergistically. Second, we hope that you have a better understanding of what a sociocultural perspective means, not only for discussions about literacy but also for the field of health and physical education. To this end, we have provided examples and descriptions of teaching and learning practices to illustrate what this approach might look like in the classroom.

Third, we hope that you find value in examining your own attitudes, beliefs, and behaviours related to health and physical literacy. As is stated over and over again in the literature, *who* a teacher is (in terms of identity, values, and personality) determines *what* a teacher will reinforce in the classroom. Thus, the more we can be aware of who we are as teachers, the better and more reflective teachers we can become.

DISCUSSION QUESTIONS

1. How would you describe the similarities and differences between health literacy and physical literacy?

2. How does a sociocultural perspective on health and physical education differ from a more traditional approach?

3. How do your own beliefs about health and physical education influence or inform your teaching?

4. How can a sociocultural perspective on health and physical education improve student outcomes?

5. How might a sociocultural approach to teaching change health and physical education in your classes or in your school?

6. How might a sociocultural approach to teaching improve health and physical literacy?

 Visit the web resource for activities that encourage reflection for students and critical reflective practice for teachers.

Voices From the Field

Kellie Baker

Teacher (Grades 5, 7, and in the Faculty of Education at Memorial University of Newfoundland)

Over the past 20 years in public education, I have taught K-8 physical education, grades 5 through 7 in the classroom, and postsecondary classes on both a part-time and a full-time basis. Presently, I teach eight subject areas (in grades 5 and 7, with 10- through 13-year-olds) at two schools in St. John's, Newfoundland. I also teach in the faculty of education at Memorial University of Newfoundland.

Building a caring class community with students provides the basis for the ways in which I provide a fun and educational environment for all. Teaching personal and social responsibility (TPSR; Hellison, 2011) has been a pedagogical approach that has enhanced the teaching and learning environment in multiple schools and contexts in which I have taught. TPSR is an educational model that promotes the building of caring relationships and a safe environment in which knowledge can be co-constructed (for more information, visit www.tpsr-alliance.org). The goal of TPSR is to increase instructional effectiveness by supporting student empowerment to take and accept responsibility for self and others. The model emphasizes a daily lesson format that includes five components: relational time, awareness talk, physical activity, group meeting, and reflection time (RAP-GR for short).

- *Relational time* supports students' development of relationships both with peers and with the teacher. For this component, I always arrive early so that there is time to mingle with students one-on-one and in groups once everything is set up. I specifically plan to touch base with each student each week during this time and also to check back with students as needed.

- *Awareness talks* provide opportunities to focus on concepts of personal and social responsibility. Guided discussions are used to explore and discuss personal and social responsibility strategies that can be incorporated both in and outside of class.

- Applying these concepts lies at the heart of the *physical activity* lesson, which is used for responsibility and skill development.

- *Group meeting* provides the opportunity for the class (or small groups) to reflect on personal and social responsibility and on their collective learning during the lesson. I often begin with a structured question and then try to let the students lead the discussion.

- *Reflection time* supports individualized reflection on the learning experience. I often use exit slips or reflective writing to give students the opportunity to reflect on personal and social responsibility and how to apply it to their lives outside of the classroom. There are also times when this reflection remains private where they don't have to hand in anything, thus providing students an opportunity to reflect without fear of being judged.

This model applies to all games, activities, and interactions during a physical education lesson. To me, the TPSR model supports the development of health and physical literacy in that it moves beyond just focusing on the development of students' physical confidence and competence. It does so by drawing attention to the importance of developing students' social, emotional, and mental confidence and competence through physical activity.

For example, during sport lead-up games, we can use small groups to question the concept of baserunning in relation to differing abilities and discuss what is fair or equal. Constructing strategies together to make an activity fair for everyone is one way to support a caring and safe environment. Another way to build a caring class community is to engage in class-constructed games and activities, which also support students' learning of course concepts and personal and social responsibility. For example, if peer pressure is a topic in the health curriculum, groups can construct a game that incorporates learning about ways to resist peer pressure both individually (e.g., running away; making an excuse and leaving; finding a safe place, person, or peer group) and collectively (e.g., celebrating differences and diversity, working together, team-building).

(continued)

(continued)

Co-constructing this type of game allows learning on the part of both students and the teacher. Students experience the concept of peer pressure in a different context, apply what they understand, and are exposed to what they need to learn in order to accomplish the task. For teachers, this activity not only provides a means of summative assessment in multiple learning domains—cognitive, affective, and perhaps physical—but also provides an assessment of their teaching: How are students showing understandings of major concepts? What major concepts are (or are not) apparent in the activity? Why? What improvements can be made, both now and next time, to support learning?

It takes time and effort to support the development of a class community that provides a safe, warm, welcoming environment in which learning is co-constructed. The first time I used TPSR, I thought I had made a monumental mistake. When I began teaching at a new school, however, it was easy to identify the need for an environment that was safer—physically, emotionally, and socially—for both the students and myself. After the first unit of physical activity using a TPSR approach, only two students were working at the necessary level of self-responsibility for creating a student-directed class—that is, one in which the student chooses the activity, the space, when to change the equipment and game, and when to go in and out of the equipment room. The other students had to have one-on-one conferences with me in order to strategize ways to increase their self-responsibility during the next unit so that they could safely participate in the next student-choice day. I wasn't trying to take activity time away, but that was exactly what had happened. At the end of the second unit, however, only two students had to have the one-on-one conference while the others participated safely, respectfully, and responsibly in student choice.

CHAPTER 2

Long-Range Planning

Joe Barrett ■ Daniel B. Robinson

LEARNING OUTCOMES

After studying this chapter, you will be able to

- define key terms relevant to planning and assessment in Canadian K-12 education,
- describe the relationship between effective long-range planning and quality PE experiences for students,
- explain the physical education long-range plan (PE-LRP) approach,
- summarize the steps of the PE-LRP approach, and
- use the PE-LRP approach to create quality PE units.

Classroom teachers are central to the provision of quality physical and health education opportunities in Canadian elementary schools. Whether generalist or specialist by training, all Canadian elementary teachers play a crucial role in providing opportunities for children to develop physical literacy. Happily, evidence continues to indicate that classroom teachers understand the important role played by quality physical education in the healthy development of children and youth (Alberta Education, 2008; Barrett, 2011, 2014; Morgan & Hansen, 2008). Yet despite their strong belief in the value of physical education, elementary teachers face considerable barriers related to student motivation, teaching self-efficacy, instructional time, curricular tensions, inadequate resources, and a perceived lack of training and preparation (Barrett, 2011; Hill & Brodin, 2004; Morgan, 2008; Morgan & Bourke, 2005).

Several of these perceived challenges have been associated with elementary teachers' perceptions of PE and low self-efficacy about their ability to plan and deliver quality PE instruction (Barrett, 2015; Doolittle, Dodds, & Placek, 1993; Gurvitch & Metzler, 2009; Morgan, 2008). These realities indicate a need to state outright that there is no single, catch-all solution for the challenges faced by elementary teachers of PE. Rather, our elementary teachers will need to employ a variety of strategies to address the barriers and other factors that negatively influence PE planning, teaching, and student participation (Barrett, 2015). With this recognition, they can explore and experiment with potential solutions and strategies. This chapter presents one such solution—specifically, a systematic approach for developing long-range plans for quality physical education. An overview of this step-by-step process is shown in figure 2.1.

Preparing teacher candidates (TCs) to plan for meaningful PE teaching experiences constitutes a fundamental pedagogical task in all teacher education programs. Accordingly, it is especially important to see planning habits develop and underpin PE teaching practices in training and beyond. This particular long-range planning approach was developed in part from our lengthy experience in working as PE teacher education (PETE) faculty members charged with both teaching and research, as well as our observations of PETE

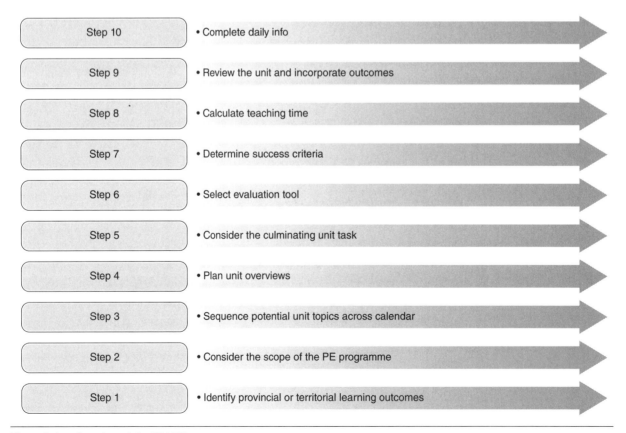

Figure 2.1 Overview of the PE-LRP process.

teacher candidates' planning practices during practicum experiences. The approach is enhanced by our understandings and interpretations of the backward design approach put forth by Wiggins and McTighe (1998).

We have seen our own PETE students unevenly apply approaches to planning that resulted in misguided, and sometimes disjointed, PE teaching. This teaching relied heavily on sterile or generic PE resources that often failed to account for individual student needs and interests. With practice, our TCs had little difficulty in preparing daily lessons and unit plans, but they lacked a deep understanding of how and why individual lessons and units were situated within and across a full-year PE program. Therefore, we wanted to equip our TCs not merely with a long-range plan but with an approach to long-range planning. We firmly believe that when teachers possess the necessary tools and understandings to design meaningful experiences for PE students, they gain power, confidence, and competence. In response to these concerns and beliefs, we developed an approach that can be used as part of a comprehensive set of planning strategies designed to simplify the planning process into stages. Though our emphasis here focuses on planning practices in PE, the underlying structures and steps are certainly transferable; thus they can be adapted very easily by teachers who are responsible for health education teaching and learning.

Definitions and Meaning

This chapter uses a number of terms related to planning and assessment in physical education. In order to fully understand those terms, we need to distinguish definition and meaning. Quite simply, a definition is a precise description of something; it is intended to provide clarity and eliminate uncertainty. Meaning, on the other hand, may not be expressed explicitly, and it involves understanding in context. With this distinction in mind, we offer the following definitions of key terms and their ascribed meanings in the context of PE planning and assessment.

- *Criterion-referenced assessment.* This type of assessment "focuses on whether a student's performance meets a predetermined standard, level, or set of criteria rather than on the student's performance [as] measured in relation to the performance of other students" (Ontario Ministry of Education, 2010, p. 145). *Meaning in the PE context:* PE

teachers are responsible for constructing or co-constructing, with students, measurable and achievable success criteria with which to assess student learning. Assessments that account for the student's progress toward achieving the defined success criteria provide the basis for the feedback provided by the teacher to the student.

- *Assessment for learning.* Assessment *for* learning "is the process of seeking and interpreting evidence for use by learners and their teachers to decide where the learners are in their learning, where they need to go, and how best to get there" (Assessment Reform Group, 2002, p. 2). *Meaning in the PE context:* This type of assessment can be used for both diagnostic and formative purposes. Whereas diagnostic assessment provides teachers with understanding of students' skills and abilities, formative assessment involves a two-way conversation between teacher and student about the student's progress toward meeting established success criteria. This type of assessment can be used to inform both teacher planning and feedback on student progress; more specifically, it can help the teacher identify student strengths and gaps in knowledge, skills, and experience.

- *Assessment of learning.* Assessment *of* learning is "assessment that becomes public and results in statements or symbols about how well students are learning. It often contributes to pivotal decisions that will affect students' futures" (Earl & Katz, 2006, p. 55). *Meaning in the PE context:* In this type of assessment, which is often summative in nature, the teacher—and only the teacher—passes judgment on the student's level of achievement in terms of the established success criteria.

- *Assessment as learning.* Assessment *as* learning "focuses on the explicit fostering of students' capacity over time to be their own best assessors, but teachers need to start by presenting and modelling external, structured opportunities for students to assess themselves" (Earl & Katz, 2006, p. 42). *Meaning in the PE context:* The use of peer and self-assessment strategies can help promote students' independence and ownership of their learning. In this approach, students provide meaningful feedback to others or monitor and reflect on their own progress by identifying strengths, gaps, and next steps for learning.

■ *Scope of learning.* This term refers to the range of skills to be acquired or the knowledge to be demonstrated in a particular grade level or course. In the Canadian context, it is understood in terms of learning outcomes or expectations set by each provincial or territorial department or ministry of education. *Meaning in the PE context:* Scope involves the "what" and the "why" that guide our PE planning practices at specific grade levels and in particular courses.

■ *Sequence of learning.* This term refers to a key logical orientation of learning experiences that provides students with a wide variety of opportunities to achieve desired course or program outcomes. *Meaning in the PE context:* Sequence of learning involves the "when" and the "how" of building a PE program that helps students achieve desired grade-level or course outcomes.

■ *Physical literacy.* This term refers to "the motivation, confidence, physical competence, knowledge, and understanding to value and take responsibility for engagement in physical activities for life" (Whitehead, 2016, n.p.). *Meaning in the PE context:* Physical literacy is a goal of PE—not a subject area that is taught in school curricula (Whitehead, 2013). For an in-depth overview of the conceptualization of physical literacy, please refer to chapter 1.

Long-Range Planning

Long-range plans (LRPs) help teachers and teacher candidates identify program and curricular focuses, scope and sequence, and a time frame for program or subject delivery. Using a systematic approach to long-range planning helps teachers of PE and PETE candidates set aside potentially unreliable intuitive tendencies and tacit understandings as they prepare and teach engaging, relevant, and meaningful school-based PE experiences. In turn, such experiences meet the needs of learners, meet all the requirements of provincial and territorial curricular guidelines, and are both developmentally appropriate and fun.

In thinking about what to offer TCs in this chapter on planning and assessment, we decided quite intentionally to focus on the big picture. In our work with PETE candidates, we have often seen TCs spend a disproportionate amount of time thinking about unit structures and daily plans.

Although these aspects of planning are critical, we have found that TCs often situate a unit or lesson haphazardly, without clearly understanding where it belongs in the context of a grade level or course program. In contrast, using long-range planning practices to step back and look at the big picture allows TCs to address the following key considerations:

■ What does my provincial or territorial education authority hope that students will achieve in my PE course or grade level?

■ What do I want my students to experience or achieve in my PE course?

■ Am I providing a wide variety of PE experiences and learning opportunities that help students succeed in terms of desired provincial or territorial outcomes?

■ Have I considered my own students' interests and motivations, as well as their effects on participation and achievement across the grade level or course?

■ How do I determine how much time to allocate to specific units and daily lessons in my PE teaching?

Backward Design Model

The backward design model was proposed by Wiggins and McTighe (1998) in an effort to help teachers synthesize relevant planning and curricular theory and find ways to identify, understand, and meet student learning needs. Wiggins and McTighe (n.d.) describe this approach as purposeful task analysis: Given a worthy task to be accomplished, how do we best get everyone equipped? We might also think of the process as one of using a map to build a wise itinerary: Given a destination, what is the most effective and efficient route for getting there? Or, we might think of the process as one of planning for coaching: What must learners master if they are to perform effectively? What will count as evidence on the field—not merely in activities—that they really "get it" and are ready to perform with understanding, knowledge, and skill on their own? How will the learning be designed so that learners' capacities are developed through use and feedback?

As you might guess, since the model was introduced, its proponents have attempted to shift teachers' thinking toward a focus on the end or desired result; at the same time, the model has been criticized by some observers as leading teachers to "teach to the test." In our view, planning practices inspired by backward design lead to learning experiences that are purposeful because they place assessment of student learning at the core; as a result, all decisions are made to help students best achieve the desired results. The backward design model comprises three stages:

1. Identification of desired results
2. Determination of acceptable evidence of learning
3. Design of learning experiences and instruction

As we move through the approach in this discussion, we will lean on the work of Wiggins & McTighe (1998) in order to help you think systematically with the end in mind—that is, make informed choices that are based on the model and refined by your reflections, student input, and your ongoing professional development.

As you learn about the long-range planning process described here, take care to be present and mindful of each stage. It can be daunting to consider the task of creating a plan for an entire year, and the magnitude of the challenge can lead teachers to get ahead of themselves. Resist this urge and focus on each stage of the planning exercise while you are in it. This systematic and stepwise approach will help you set aside anxieties in favour of a clear, focused, and mindful approach to long-range planning for quality PE experiences.

This systematic and stepwise approach will help you set aside anxieties in favour of a clear, focused, and mindful approach to long-range planning for quality PE experiences.

Step 1: Identifying Provincial or Territorial Learning Outcomes

Before you can begin planning per se, you must examine the desired grade-level outcomes for your province or territory; doing so will provide you with insight into local requirements for each particular grade. In other words, your planning efforts cannot get under way until you understand what the province or territory expects you to help students achieve in physical education.

To illustrate how to structure your review of the curriculum, let's consider one example from *The Ontario Curriculum, Grades 1-8: Health and Physical Education* (Ontario Ministry of Education, 2015). We begin by reviewing the Movement Competence and Active Living strands, which pertain specifically to PE. The aim of the review is to answer the following questions:

- What PE knowledge and skills will students acquire by the end of this grade level?
- What key concepts or big ideas are included in the grade-level strands?
- Can I clearly articulate—to students and parents—the skills, concepts, strategies, and tactics that provide the focus for the selected grade level?

Now, take 5 to 10 minutes to examine the desired PE outcomes for a particular grade level. Then outline the key focus for your selected grade level by drawing a concept map; to review concept map examples, see the web resource for this chapter.

Before you move on to the next stage of planning, you should be able to clearly answer the following questions:

- After my review of the curriculum, can I clearly answer the three questions that guided my exploration?
- Do I have a quick access resource (e.g., concept map) that I can keep ready and available during my planning efforts?

Step 2: Considering the Scope of the PE Program

Once you understand the focuses and the complexity of the desired outcomes for a particular grade level, you can move on to considering potential program activities or units to make up your PE program at that level. Here, the word *might* is a powerful tool. In this stage of the process, you are simply brainstorming activities or potential unit topics that *might* help students succeed in physical education. As part of this stage, you are invited to consider the particular interests that may be present in the classroom. Of course, as teachers, we all have a wide variety of activities that we would like our students to experience. In some cases, these activities relate to personal biography—for instance, our own student experiences in elementary and secondary PE; in other instances, they may derive from our physical activity (PA) interests as adults. In order to teach most effectively, however, we must approach these choices with our students in mind. Specifically, we must consider what activities or units may be of interest to them. Indeed, the more involved students are in making program choices and decisions, the more likely they are to participate willingly in a wide variety of physical activities, rather than only the ones in which they are most interested.

Now, take about 10 minutes to brainstorm age- or grade-appropriate unit topics for PE and PA. For guidance, see the template included in the web resource. In addition, keep your concept map (from step 1) with you for reference. During your brainstorming, consider the following questions:

- What activities would I like to introduce to my PE students?
- What activities or unit topics would my students be interested in experiencing or learning more about?

Put yourself in your students' shoes and imagine whether they can see themselves in the activities you are considering.

Next, review your list of potential unit topics and consider revisions. Specifically, consider the list *from the perspectives of your students.* Put yourself in your students' shoes and imagine whether they can see themselves in the activities you are considering. Now, take a moment to revise, add to, or eliminate activities from your brainstormed list. The aim here is to end up with a variety of developmentally appropriate activities. Ask yourself the following questions:

- Does my list include a wide variety of physical activities across a range of domains (e.g., games education, dance, fitness, relaxation and stress management, Indigenous games, sport, cooperative games)?
- What proportion of my activities would be classified as sport? How many of my students enjoy sport? Sometimes we need to think outside the box in order to help our students develop healthy and wide-ranging physical activity habits. PE is not sport; rather, sport is an important part of a comprehensive and wide-ranging elementary PE program.
- Have I revisited my concept map for grade-level outcomes? Doing so can help you keep students at the centre of your planning

efforts. Are your selected activities and unit topics interesting to your students? Are they age appropriate and developmentally appropriate based both on what you know of your students and on provincial or territorial focuses? Returning continually to your concept map will help ensure that you provide sufficient challenge and growth opportunities, take into account student interests, and remain mindful of your responsibilities in regard to desired provincial or territorial outcomes.

Step 3: Sequencing Potential Unit Topics Across the Calendar

In this step, think about each month as a basket that needs filling. Using your brainstormed list, assign PE activities or unit topics to each calendar month in which you are responsible for PE teaching. Then, when it's time to make your unit and daily plans, you can open the appropriate basket and find a list of potential items to include in your PE programming for that month. Thus you have a ready-made starting point in your planning efforts.

How often should you schedule PE in your weekly and monthly plans? There is no single correct answer; just try to include PE as often as possible. We advocate strongly for providing regular and consistent opportunities for students to learn and reach physical literacy goals through physical activity.

Before moving on to the next step, take a moment to reflect on your progress thus far. You began by reviewing expectations—that is, what the province or territory is looking for you to achieve with your students at this particular grade level. Next, you created a concept map to aid your planning efforts by highlighting both the desired provincial or territorial outcomes and the complexity of those outcomes (i.e., focuses that are age appropriate and developmentally appropriate). Then you brainstormed a list of potential PE program activities and unit topics, including items that appeal to you personally, after which you reviewed the list with an eye toward the following considerations:

- Student interests
- Proportion of activities considered to be sport
- Revisiting of desired provincial or territorial outcomes (developmentally appropriate)

Finally, you revised the list to ensure that it includes potential activities and unit topics that offer wide-ranging variety.

Step 4: Planning Unit Overviews

After you have slotted all potential activities and unit topics into specific months across the teaching calendar, you can get down to the business of long-range planning by developing high-quality unit overviews based on a clear and well-defined approach. At this point, you may wonder how many days to plan for each of your units. To answer this question, continue to immerse yourself in a narrow, step-by-step, mindful approach to planning—you are still not far enough along in your planning efforts to address timing within potential unit structures. Long-range planning can be overwhelming if it is approached as a collection of big-picture tasks that need to be addressed all at once. However, if you have substantively implemented the preceding steps—and therefore arrived at this point in the planning process ready to develop your first unit for your long-range plan—then all the hard work is behind you. The message, then, is this: You possess the autonomy, training, and emerging skills to make quality PE planning decisions for your students!

When developing unit overviews for your PE-LRP, you do *not* write out full unit or lesson plans. Rather, in this approach, you identify core components that will enable in-depth unit and daily planning in the future. Think of the PE-LRP as a skeleton—a framework that provides the foundation for the body's systems (unit plans) and their constituent parts (daily lessons). Here are the core components to address in the unit days of your PE-LRP.

Think of the PE-LRP as a skeleton—a framework that provides the foundation for the body's systems (unit plans) and their constituent parts (daily lessons).

- Unit topic
- Provincial or territorial outcomes on which the lesson focuses
- Learning goals crafted from success criteria (to be established in step 7)
- Teaching and learning focus for the day
- Assessment and evaluation: what is being assessed and how

Now, take a moment to review your concept map and familiarize yourself with the grade-level PE foci. As we move forward with this discussion, see yourself in the process, examining your potential list of activities for a selected month. Remember not to get ahead of yourself as you use the PE-LRP approach; plan and think about only one unit at a time. Be mindful and remain in the moment, concerning yourself only with your efforts to plan for a high-quality unit. For the remaining discussion, let's imagine that you have chosen to plan a yoga unit for students in grade 3.

Step 5: Considering the Culminating Unit Task

In this step, we begin by considering a task that could be used to evaluate student learning and progress in our chosen unit on yoga. Again, be mindful. You are doing nothing more than coming up with a culminating task that you believe you could use to evaluate student learning. For illustrative purposes, we have selected the following culminating task that will guide the rest of our planning for the yoga unit: Students will work in groups of two or three to create a yoga sequence.

Step 6: Selecting an Evaluation Tool

In this step, consider what tool or strategy you will use to evaluate student progress—for example, a checklist, rubric, or checkbric. You are not creating the tool at this point; you are simply noting what tool you *will* use. Eventually, of course, you will craft the tool and use it, both to help you provide rich formative feedback to your students and to guide your judgments of student learning and progress in terms of the culminating task. Specifically, you will create the tool during your in-depth unit and daily planning and preparation.

Step 7: Determining Criteria for Success

In this crucial phase of the approach, the key is specificity. This is where you establish the success criteria that you will use to evaluate student learning in the culminating task. What do you want your students to demonstrate, say, or do in the culminating task? Success criteria can be co-constructed with students or developed by you without student input; either way, they will guide your assessment or evaluation of student learning through the unit and within the culminating task. For example, here is a set of success criteria for a culminating task in our yoga unit:

- Students include at least five different positions in their yoga sequence.
- Students demonstrate smooth and controlled transitions between selected poses.
- Students include poses and transitions from multiple levels (e.g., low, medium, high).
- Students can identify at least two personal benefits associated with participating in yoga.
- Students can describe how they safely perform the various poses and their developed yoga sequence (e.g., "I never lock my elbows or knees because . . . ," "I don't twist my body or overreach because . . . ," "I stay an appropriate distance away from my classmates because . . .").

To ensure fidelity to developmentally appropriate outcomes for your students' grade level, keep your concept map available for quick reference.

Step 8: Calculating Teaching Time

In this step, use your success criteria to determine how much time you will need in the unit to do all of your important work with your students: teaching, assessing, refining, embedding opportunities for practice, and evaluating student learning. Here are a few guidelines to inform your choices and decisions.

1. The first day of every unit must be diagnostic and explorative. If we are truly to evaluate student learning, we must first understand what our students bring to physical education. Moreover, students' fundamental movement skill proficiency and demonstrations of physical literacy will differ across unit topics and tasks. Thus we suggest that you begin the first day of every unit with a diagnosis of learning through games, play, fun, and plenty of teacher-managed social interactions—all of which can yield a contextualized understanding of your students' abilities, motivations, and interests.

2. What you teach in a particular PE unit should be derived *only* from your established success criteria for the unit's culminating task. This point is critical: *All* that we teach in a particular unit should be based on what we expect students to say or do in the unit's culminating task.

> All *that we teach in a particular unit should be based on what we expect students to say or do in the unit's culminating task.*

3. Less is more. We strongly encourage you to keep units relatively short. Why? Consider the following potential outcomes associated with shorter units:

- With fewer success criteria, the emphasis on teaching and assessing multiple or broad-range aspects within a shorter-duration unit are lessened. This helps narrow the teaching focus within a unit and may lead to the provision of more meaningful refinement and feedback.
- Shorter-duration units can provide students with multiple opportunities to demonstrate new learning across a wide range of physical activities (e.g., learning associated with sending and receiving of objects as well as the demonstration of that learning may look very different across a wide range of physical activities: baseball, handball, ultimate Frisbee, badminton, soccer).
- The use of shorter-duration units across a PE program may lead to a shared sense of novelty, interest, and ongoing challenge by both teachers and students alike.
- Shorter-duration units help the teacher ensure he or she is truly providing a broad range of learning opportunities for students across a wide range of PAs and domains.
- The use of short-duration units may serve as a teaching strategy to tackle challenges associated with student motivation (e.g., students may be more inclined to engage and participate knowing they can see a time horizon within reach where they will move on to something new).

4. Trust your judgment and your emerging pedagogical content knowledge. There are no hard-and-fast reference points or resources that will tell you how much time to spend

teaching, assessing, refining, and evaluating within your unit structures. Fortunately, you have the autonomy to make planning decisions in the best interest of your students.

In our sample yoga unit, we can use our crafted success criteria for the culminating task to systematically determine the number of days needed for the unit. What we teach in the unit will be derived exclusively from the success criteria. Specifically, we think about our students and consider the following vital question in relation to each criterion: How much teaching time will I need to help my students find success?

- *Students include at least five different positions in their yoga sequence.* Given this expectation, we must ensure that we spend some time teaching students about multiple poses and their significance, as well as breathing patterns and effects on the body. For instance, we might decide to teach 10 poses in one PE lesson through a variety of instructional strategies (e.g., stations, teacher-led activity, peer teaching).
- *Students demonstrate smooth and controlled transitions between selected poses.* To address this criterion, we might decide to allocate half of a PE class to practicing learned poses. Our teaching focus will be directed toward helping the students find ways to combine poses using a variety of smooth and controlled transitions.
- *Students include poses and transitions from multiple levels (e.g., low, medium, high).* Here again, we might allocate half of a PE class to addressing this criterion—specifically, exploring and emphasizing the various levels used in selected yoga poses and transitions.
- *Students can identify at least two personal benefits associated with participating in yoga.* We might decide to address this criterion across the unit both through inquiry-based discussions in each class and through question-and-answer activities at the start or finish of each lesson leading up to evaluation day.
- *Students can describe how they safely perform the various poses and their developed yoga sequence (e.g., "I never lock my elbows or knees because . . . ," "I don't twist my body or overreach because . . . ," "I stay an appropriate distance away from my classmates*

because . . ."). We believe that the teaching of safe practices should be infused into each class. In this case, we might decide to set aside half of the class time for students to practice teaching the various poses to each other in partner or small-group activities. This work should include opportunities to engage in peer feedback and to identify and describe safe practice recommendations for each pose and transition.

Based on this analysis, let us now consider how much time is needed for our sample yoga unit—that is, the number of classes required. ·

- *Day 1.* Diagnostic focus—intro to yoga (what, why, safety, use of games and activities that emphasize participation, play, and enjoyment)
- *Day 2.* Teaching of specific poses (infusion of safety and exploration of benefits through questioning)
- *Day 3.* Combination of activities that emphasize controlled, smooth transitions and learning about levels (low, medium, high) and exploring benefits of participation in yoga (questioning)
- *Day 4.* Combination of opportunities for students to practice teaching poses to each other and to form groups and begin developing their yoga sequence
- *Day 5.* Practice of yoga sequence and opportunity to teach it to another group (emphasis on highlighting two benefits of yoga participation)
- *Day 6.* Participation in and evaluation of student-developed yoga sequences (no new teaching on this particular day; evaluation of student learning guided by tool developed using success criteria)

Once you have estimated the time required to address each success criterion in your teaching, consider the following questions before moving on. If you answer no to any of them, take a moment to review and revise your time allocations as needed.

- Am I teaching everything necessary that is outlined in the evaluation success criteria?
- Will I have enough time to assess my students' progress through the unit?

■ Am I providing my students with sufficient practice opportunities during the unit?

■ Have I given myself enough time to evaluate student learning at the conclusion of the unit?

Before moving on to consider the planning for another unit, reflect on the outcome of this unit-planning effort and consider alternatives. For instance, rather than the six-day structure outlined here, you might decide—based on the culminating task's success criteria (the absolute must-haves that are to be evaluated in that task)—that either fewer or more days are needed. If you decide that the unit is too long, then the only choice in this approach is to remove one or more success criteria from the culminating task requirements. Of course, doing so will mean that you spend no time in the unit on teaching associated with the removed criterion material.

Thus, as you move through your teaching, you will review, reflect on, and revise your PE-LRP—a necessary and important part of good reflective PE teaching practice.

What if you are reluctant to alter the number of teaching days? In that case, there are options for you to think outside the box—for example, by structuring the unit so that students participate in yoga lessons once a week for six weeks. This type of solution can help you manage challenges associated with student motivation and engagement across your elementary PE program.

How will you know if the amount of time allocated to each criterion is enough or too much? You will find out by teaching the unit to your students! Indeed, you will sense it very early in the unit if you require more or less time for given tasks. Thus, as you move through your teaching, you will review, reflect on, and revise your PE-LRP—a necessary and important part of good reflective PE teaching practice.

Step 9: Reviewing the Unit and Incorporating Outcomes

In order to add outcomes to the unit, you should begin by reviewing the unit day by day. For each day, read the focus and connect it with relevant outcomes in your grade-level PE curriculum. List only the outcomes that are directly in focus in your teaching; do *not* list any that you are simply touching on in a given day. At this point in your review, you can adjust your plan based on your assessment of your unit plans. You may find, for instance, that you are spending too much time in one particular area of the PE curriculum. To illustrate the process, let us now add Ontario grade 3 expectations to our yoga unit (Ontario Ministry of Education, 2015):

■ *Day 1.* Diagnostic focus—intro to yoga (what, why, safety, use of games and activities that emphasize participation, play, and enjoyment)

• A1.1 Actively participate in a wide variety of program activities, according to their capabilities, while applying behaviours that enhance their readiness to take part.

• A1.2 Demonstrate an understanding of factors that contribute to their personal enjoyment of being active as they participate in a wide variety of individual and small-group activities.

• A3.1 Demonstrate behaviours and apply procedures that maximize their safety and that of others during physical activity.

■ *Day 2.* Teaching of specific poses (infusion of safety and exploration of benefits through questioning)

• A1.3 Describe the benefits of participating in physical activity every day.

• A3.1 Demonstrate behaviours and apply procedures that maximize their safety and that of others during physical activity.

• B1.1 Perform controlled transitions between static positions, using different body parts and shapes and different levels, with and without equipment.

■ *Day 3.* Combination of activities that emphasize controlled, smooth transitions and learning about levels (low, medium, high) and exploring benefits of participation in yoga (questioning)

• A1.3 Describe the benefits of participating in physical activity every day.

• B1.1 Perform controlled transitions between static positions, using different body parts and shapes and different levels, with and without equipment

• B1.3 Perform a variety of locomotor movements with and without equipment, alone and with others, moving at different levels, using different pathways, and traveling in different directions.

■ *Day 4.* Combination of opportunities for students to practice teaching poses to each other and to form groups and begin developing their yoga sequence (emphasis on practice and not the teaching of new concepts)

- A1.1 Actively participate in a wide variety of program activities, according to their capabilities, while applying behaviours that enhance their readiness to take part.
- A1.3 Describe the benefits of participating in physical activity every day.

■ *Day 5.* Practice of yoga sequence and opportunity to teach it to another group (emphasis on highlighting two benefits of yoga participation)

- A1.1 Actively participate in a wide variety of program activities, according to their capabilities, while applying behaviours that enhance their readiness to take part.
- A1.3 Describe the benefits of participating in physical activity every day.

■ *Day 6.* Participation in and evaluation of student-developed yoga sequences (no new teaching on this particular day . . . evaluation of student learning guided by tool developed using success criteria);

- A1.1 Actively participate in a wide variety of program activities, according to their capabilities, while applying behaviours that enhance their readiness to take part.

In the province of Ontario, measures of student learning in a given curricular area are based on students' achievement of Ontario's overall expectations. In other words, specific expectations are tied directly to a particular overall expectation. These specific expectations guide elementary teachers' PE teaching in an effort to help students achieve success based on overall grade-level expectations. The following list presents the overall expectations related directly to evaluation of the yoga-sequence culminating task (Ontario Ministry of Education, 2015).

■ A1. Participate actively and regularly in a wide variety of physical activities, and demonstrate an understanding of the value of regular physical activity in their daily lives.

■ A3. Demonstrate responsibility for their own safety and the safety of others as they participate in physical activities.

■ B1. Perform movement skills, demonstrating awareness of the basic requirements of the skills and applying movement concepts as appropriate, as they engage in a variety of physical activities.

Step 10: Completing Daily Info

In this final step, use the success criteria and outcomes to complete the core elements for each day of the unit. As a reminder, the following core elements should be addressed for each day of your PE-LRP:

- ■ Unit topic
- ■ Provincial or territorial outcomes on which the lesson focuses
- ■ Learning goals crafted from success criteria
- ■ Teaching and learning focus for the day
- ■ Assessment and evaluation: what is being assessed and how

A crucial relationship exists between the outcomes, learning goals, and success criteria established for each day. The success criteria that guide your PE teaching describe for students what success looks like in your class. The criteria also help you craft learning goals, which characterize the skills and knowledge required for success. For instance, in our yoga sample, the learning goals for day 2 would be based on the success criteria and outcomes that guide the day 2 teaching in the unit. Because day 2 includes multiple PE teaching focuses, we would craft more than one learning goal for that day (see the sample at the end of this section). In your own planning, some days will address one learning goal and other days will address more than one. Either way, the key is to list only the outcomes and learning goals that are directly in focus for the day in question.

A crucial relationship exists between the outcomes, learning goals, and success criteria established for each day.

No hard-and-fast rule dictates how long your description of planned activities should be for a given day. Some teachers find comfort in providing greater detail, whereas others provide just enough to clarify the focus for the day. As you move through your first PE-LRP planning efforts, you will quickly find what works for you—for instance, jotting notes, writing verbatim instructional cues, or using a full sentence or paragraph structure.

Unit Topic: Yoga

■ Outcomes (taken directly from day 2 planning):

• A1.3 Describe the benefits of participating in physical activity.

• A3.1 Demonstrate behaviours and apply procedures that maximize . . . safety.

• B1.1 Perform controlled transitions between static positions.

■ Learning goals:

• I can demonstrate my understanding of how to move my body while exploring 10 yoga poses and controlling my breathing by teaching poses to my peers and practicing poses taught to me by my peers and teacher (e.g., animal-picture poses, video poses, word-cue poses).

• I can describe how and why yoga practice is good for managing my stress (e.g., when my neck and shoulders get tight, my tummy feels upset, or my heart beats too fast).

• I can demonstrate understanding of what it means to modify movements in order to achieve *my* safe range of motion in each pose (e.g., I stretch only to the point where my muscles feet tight).

■ Planned activities:

1. Introduction: Exploring and experimenting with breathing by using familiar analogies (e.g., balloon breathing, foggy winter windows, choo choo breathing)

2. Five core stations, each with a skills chart for two poses and sticky notes on which students can share benefits and modification suggestions for participating safely

   1. Tablet station

   2. Peer-to-peer teaching

   3. Animal theme photo poses

   4. Word cues

   5. Poses with a prop

3. Movement in teacher-selected groups of two or three

4. Consolidation: gallery walk and class discussion (benefits, modifications, safety, enjoyment)

■ Assessment and evaluation:

• Refinement and feedback (while walking about during station activity): safe range of motion, breathing, management of on-task behaviours that support student learning

• Questioning during class discussion: modifications, benefits, safe range of motion, safe spaces

Summary

This chapter presents a step-by-step mindful approach to PE long-range planning practices that can be used to develop high-quality, student-centred programs for elementary physical education. The PE-LRP approach helps you set aside intuitive PE planning practices that rely on subjective perceptions, inferences, and personal experiences. It also provides a foundation on which you can build detailed unit and daily plans. Your PE teaching will thrive when it is supported by and built on this informed, tangible, and systematic planning approach.

DISCUSSION QUESTIONS

1. Take a moment to reflect on your own experiences as a student in elementary or secondary physical education. Brainstorm a list of activities included in your PE courses. Why do you think these activities were chosen? Explain.

2. Consider more deeply the effect of your student experiences in PE on your current PE planning choices and decisions. Explain.

3. What is the relationship between long-range planning and assessment of student learning? Explain.

4. Describe your perceptions of the potential advantages and disadvantages of crafting units of shorter duration. Provide examples.

5. What relationship exists between wide-ranging PE program offerings and physical literacy?

6. "I make the decisions about what activities and unit topics will be included in my elementary PE programs." How do you feel after reading this statement? Explain.

 Visit the web resource for sample concept maps, a daily information template to use in developing long-range plans, and a template for brainstorming content for health and PE units.

Voices From the Field

©Joe Barrett

Joseph Forte
Health and Physical Education Teacher, Grades JK-6
St. Mary's Catholic School, Ontario

Variety is central to my planning efforts. Variations in my program offer needed change and opportunities for students to build confidence and competence across a wide variety of physical activities. From year to year, my students appreciate the novelty infused into the HPE program. I want my students to know that I know their interests vary. As often as I can, I introduce new games, activities, and units that we have never experienced before.

Throughout a crafted unit, I try to consider each student's progress. I also ensure that I am always providing a safe and fun learning environment. Consideration of safety, fun, and each student's needs often leads to learning that helps my students develop transferable skills and self-confidence. I try to help my students see their skill competencies across a wide variety of activities; for example, learning to throw can open the door to fun in a variety of games.

Every student has the ability to learn, and I recognize that my students learn in different ways. Having taught the same students over multiple years, I have watched them progress socially, emotionally, psychologically, and physically. So I think I have a good idea of students' particular needs across both health and physical education teaching and learning. All of this student information drives my long-term planning for the year. I try to balance students' needs by considering activities and topics that help build students' strengths while ensuring that I also include teaching and learning opportunities to foster growth in other areas. These decisions also fuel how I assess. I have paid greater attention to students' living skill development over the last few years.

I often make changes in my long-range planning based on students' growth or emerging areas that require more improvement (e.g., critical thinking, intrapersonal skills, interpersonal skills). As I progress through each year, I am constantly changing gears and straying from initial long-range plans to adjust and meet student needs. I look at my long-range plan as a living document. Often, my teaching decisions are also driven by big-picture themes. For example, I want my students to demonstrate and use skills and strategies and to understand how to move, how to solve problems, how to work with others, and how to care for equipment and for the facilities we use together. I like to frame these big ideas in advance, along with the daily and unit plans that guide what we are doing.

In my early years of HPE teaching, I had a number of students who stood on the side and would not participate because they "didn't know how to do it." Those early experiences served as important lessons for me. In my long-range planning practices, I remind myself of the many students who feel this way in our classes, and I try to consider their needs in my planning. Considering all of my students' needs makes me better prepared to handle challenges proactively rather than reactively, which is better for me and for all of my students.

I try to remember that I need to be ready to change directions. Over my many years of teaching, I have learned the value of changing plans based on students' motivation, enjoyment, and progress. I always consider age-appropriate skill development. Over the years, I have watched my students gain great confidence through developmentally appropriate teaching. A student needs to be able to practice in class and participate confidently. I readily make changes to long-range planning based on student progress and confidence. I often rely on previously developed assessment tasks and current observations to make appropriate decisions for my students in my long-range planning practices. Finally, I recognize that, like my students, I need to change. My ever-evolving long-range planning process is vital to my effective teaching in HPE, and it guides my efforts to meet my students' needs.

CHAPTER 3

Promoting Safe Practices

Greg Rickwood

After studying this chapter, you will be able to

- describe standards of reasonable care and concern for student safety;
- summarize safety guidelines to follow before and during physical activity in elementary school;
- devise and implement appropriate safety practices for school-based physical activities;
- explain equipment safety, space and facility awareness, appropriate clothing and footwear for students, and mandatory supervisory conditions for school-based physical activities; and
- articulate the rationale for implementing and enforcing safety rules.

Mr. Barton divided his grade 4 health and physical education (HPE) class into four teams of six students each. In preparation for participating in floor hockey, each team was asked to designate two defenders, one goaltender, and three offensive players. Mr. Barton allowed one minute for the teams to assign roles, gather the appropriate equipment, and take their individual positions in the assigned game space. However, as teams and students were taking their positions, Mr. Barton noticed that one of the four goaltenders was not wearing the mandatory safety equipment—helmet, face mask, pads, chest protector, blocker, glove, and stick. With only three sets of goalie equipment available, how can Mr. Barton modify the goaltender position or the activity itself to make the game safe for this particular goalie?

In order to be effective, role modelling must be ingrained into student learning across subjects and grade levels. As teachers, it is particularly important for us to model approved safety policies and practices when motivating students to engage in physical activity opportunities (e.g., daily physical activity sessions, HPE classes, intramural and intermural activities, nutrition breaks). Beyond modelling, we must consistently remind students of approved safety policies and teach them their role in creating and maintaining safe spaces and activities. This chapter outlines strategies that establish and support a culture of student safety in elementary physical activity contexts.

Student safety is at risk in HPE and physical activity settings due to the physical movement that occurs outside of desk areas—often in large, open spaces—and is defined by equipment and rules that may be foreign to some elementary students. Because safety risks exist in any school-based physical activity, we must ensure that activity environments are safe for all elementary students both before and during activity.

The term "safety" is multidimensional and includes both physical and emotional elements. For example, a lack of appropriate safety rules for physical activities can evoke fear in students. In addition, if some students fail to abide by safety rules, their peers may "check out" or lose motivation for playing the game. In a health-related example, trouble can arise when students are not safely guided through topics related to sexuality and healthy relationships; specifically, students may experience negative emotional responses and disassociate from the content. Similarly, students who feel unsafe either before or during

school-based physical activities often withdraw or reduce their level of participation. However, when an activity is perceived as safe (both physically and emotionally), students engage fully and learn more. The following sections address key characteristics of safe, school-based physical activities.

Space and Facilities

It can be challenging to fully define what constitutes a safe and suitable space or facility for physical activity that is available to students when they need it. The preferred setting is often the school gymnasium, but when it is booked for other classes or activities we must seek out alternative spaces and facilities, whether on or off school grounds. On-campus possibilities include, for example, open spaces on a school field, paved surfaces on the school grounds, empty classrooms, the school's basement, and the school stage. Examples of off-site possibilities include local recreational facilities, fields, pools, and parks.

A space or facility is generally safe if you can answer yes to the following questions:

- Is it large enough to accommodate the intended activity for the number of students involved? If the space is small, avoid games that include throwing for distance, as well as end-to-end games such as soccer and tag.
- Does it allow for safe and proper use of required equipment?
- Is it free from features that might injure students? Consider both permanent features (e.g., trees, walls, doors, cars) and nonpermanent ones (e.g., broken glass, needles, cans, large rocks). If such features are present, can they be padded or blocked off without affecting the integrity of the activity and the safety of the students?
- Is a first aid kit easily accessible in or near the space or facility?
- Is a phone or school intercom system available nearby in case of injury?

Let's consider an example of a game setup that promotes safety. Figure 3.1 illustrates a soccer skill activity that reinforces proper kicking motion and target accuracy. Note the variations in goal width and kicking distance. Organizing the equipment and students in this configuration promotes safety because it ensures that students are not kicking

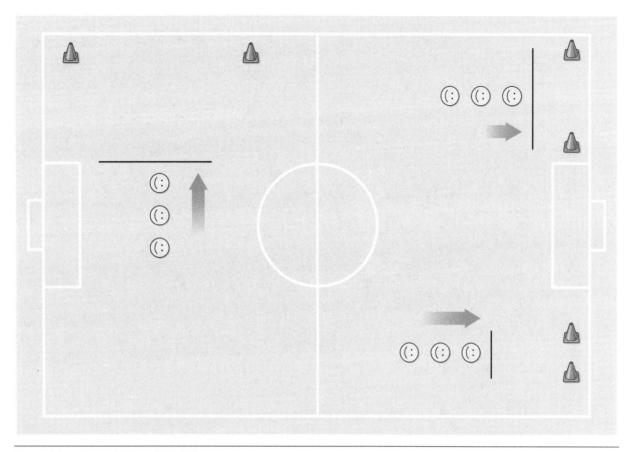

Figure 3.1 Soccer kicking skill activity.

toward one another; moreover, the space is large enough to accommodate the required equipment and the intended number of students. In addition, students are encouraged to select the station that best suits their skill level in order to reduce anxiety and increase their effort level and success. If the space was even larger (e.g., an outdoor soccer field), then a fourth station could be added—for instance, to enable students to practice using their nondominant foot to kick a soccer ball into a hoop placed on the ground at a specified distance.

This activity can be modified to practice throwing rather than kicking. Replace the soccer balls with tennis balls or the like and instruct students to throw their object between the cones. You can also place a student between the cones to catch the ball when it is thrown to them; then they switch roles, and the activity continues. This organization of space and students can be easily adjusted to practice other movement skills, concepts, and strategies.

To maximize student safety, implement this activity in a gymnasium or a large, smooth outdoor space on school grounds. Attempting to use this activity in a school hallway or on a school stage is *not* recommended, because the lack of sufficient space between participants increases the risk of ball and body contact with other students.

Equipment

Safe, modern equipment plays a key role in enabling students to participate successfully in physical activities. As a result, students can be more active in schools that possess up-to-date equipment, and enough of it, to support curricular and extracurricular physical activities. It is also essential to have access to equipment when it is needed. Unfortunately, as school budgets decline, funding may not be available for equipment updates; therefore, the quality and number of activities may diminish over time. Solutions for these financial restrictions include equipment donations from students, parents, and alumni; charitable donations from sports equipment chains; and school upgrade grants.

To maximize student safety, teachers in elementary schools should regularly maintain physical activity equipment, inspect it semiannually, and record their findings in a checklist similar to the one presented in table 3.1. Students must also learn how to use equipment properly and report any damaged or broken equipment immediately for replacement or removal from active use.

The pedagogical procedure for teaching students how to use equipment safely depends on the activity and the needed equipment. For example, students must learn how to manipulate a floor hockey stick before practicing skill activities or participating in modified floor hockey games. In order to teach safe stick usage in this context, you can use the following steps:

- *Grip pattern.* The dominant hand is placed at the top of the stick shaft (the knob); the other hand is placed at the middle of the shaft (i.e., halfway between the top of the stick and the stick blade). The top hand controls the majority of stick movements, whereas the bottom hand is used for strength and to determine puck direction.
- *Stick blade.* The blade should remain on the ground at all times except when a player passes or shoots on the net; in these situations, the stick may follow-through to knee or waist height.

- *Stickhandling.* The stick blade should be placed half a stick length in front of the body. To help control the puck, the player can move the bottom hand up or down the shaft; both hands will turn over as the puck travels from one side of the stick to the other.
- *Shooting and passing.* The stick will start on the ground but follow through to knee height for passing and to waist height for shooting.
- *Stick height.* The top of the stick shaft (i.e., the knob) should be no higher than the student's chin when the student stands flat-footed. A stick that is too short or too long makes it more difficult to handle and shoot the puck; it also decreases passing accuracy and can lead to more unintentional fouls due to poor stick control.
- *Goalie stick.* The goalie stick should be gripped with the dominant hand where the shaft meets the stick blade. Only one hand is placed on the stick; the other hand is the glove hand used for catching.

Safety Rules

Though necessary, proper space and equipment are insufficient to ensure safety if students do not follow safety guidelines. For example, a plastic floor hockey stick is currently considered the safest option for the game, but if a student raises the stick above the waist for any reason, it may injure an opponent. The stick can also

■ TABLE 3.1

Sample Equipment Checklist

Equipment item	Yes	No	Follow-up
Badminton racquets: usable (no splinters or broken strings)			
Floor hockey: plastic hockey sticks free of cracks and broken edges or ends; stick blades secured to shaft			
Emergency equipment: first aid kit fully stocked and accessible; emergency phone numbers posted			
Tumbling mats: no holes (okay if rips are taped); uniform thickness and compaction; fasteners in good condition			
Track and field: high-jump mat in good condition; fiberglass crossbars free of cracks and splinters			
Volleyball: nets free of exposed or frayed wires along poles and free of tears and holes; posts (hooks, pulls, and ratchet) in good condition			

Adapted from Ontario Physical Education Safety Guidelines. http://safety.ophea.net/sites/safety.ophea.net/files/docs/appendices/E_C/E_C_AppendixI2_16.pdf cause serious injury if it is used illegally against an opponent, as in cross-checking, slashing, and hooking. Thus, even safety-approved equipment can lead to unsafe playing conditions if you do not manage it effectively.

When designing and implementing safety rules for physical activities, consider the following guidelines for maximizing student safety and participation:

- Implement a "no body contact" rule for all physical activities.
- Structure activities to provide as much organization as possible.
- Ensure that teams are equally competitive and include both boys and girls.
- Ensure that consequences for rule infractions are relevant to the action and are imposed immediately after the infraction.

- Post the consequences for excessive intensity or illegal play in readily visible locations on gymnasium walls
- Students who continuously and intentionally break safety rules should be removed from the activity.
- Increase the emphasis on participation and decrease the focus on winning or on a specified outcome.
- Reinforce the importance of technique.
- Provide both competitive and recreational activity options and allow students to choose.

The following floor hockey activity demonstrates how space, students, and equipment can be organized to reduce the risk of injury and maximize student participation. Consider how the activity framework could be transferred to practice skills in soccer, running, tag games, and basketball.

Gated Community

Equipment

Plastic floor hockey sticks, pinnies (two colours), felt hockey pucks (or tennis balls or the like), pylons (or poly spots), gymnasium or paved outdoor surface. Note: The required equipment depends on student numbers. For instance, if you have 24 students, then you should create 8 gates (2 pylons or poly spots per gate) to maximize opportunities for scoring and provide 24 sticks (one for each student) and 12 pucks (one puck per student pairing).

Setup

See figure 3.2.

How to Play

1. Students play in pairs, with one player trying to stickhandle the puck (or ball) through the defined gates in any direction while the other player protects the gates.
2. If the defender gains possession of the puck, he or she shoots it into an area where there are no gates.
3. A goal is awarded whenever the puck is stickhandled through any gate by the offensive player.
4. A player is not permitted to score consecutive goals through the same gate.
5. After one minute, the players reverse roles.
6. The winner is the player with the most goals after four rotations.

Variations and Differentiation

- Play without sticks. The offensive player runs through the gates with a beanbag (or balloon or no-sting ball) while the defending player tries to touch the offensive player before he or she scores.
- Reduce or increase the number of gates.
- Reduce or increase the size of the playing area.

Figure 3.2 Gated Community activity setup.

- Have the defensive player turn over his or her stick so that the knob is touching the floor
- Have students play keep-away. The student with possession of the puck is on offense; if the defender gains possession, then she or he plays offense.
- Have each pair join with another pair for 2v2 play (reduce the number of gates by half).
- Adapt the activity for soccer, flag football, rugby, or field hockey.

Assessment "Look-Fors"

- Head up, with and without the puck
- Two hands on the stick
- No more than stick-length distance between the defender and the player with the puck
- Efficient control of the puck—for example, stickhandling kept close to the body and puck protected from the defender by the stickhandler's body
- Variety of tactics used to gain scoring position—for example, change of pace and invasion of open space
- Variety of tactics used to prevent scoring—for example, keep the stick in front of your body, position your body between the puck and the gate
- Puck possession time (Who has the puck more, and why?)

Teaching Tips

- Space out the gates so that students do not collide with each other while traveling through or around them.
- Position the gates safely away from walls and any other permanent features in the playing area.
- Gates should be about one and a half stick lengths wide to allow for safe travel through them.

- Hockey stick blades should remain on the ground at all times.
- No body contact or checking is allowed; both hands should remain on the stick at all times.
- Students should play to an open gate in order to avoid unnecessary collisions.
- Keep sequences to one minute in order to minimize player fatigue and maximize the level of competition.
- After traveling through a gate, students are not permitted to return to it. This restriction helps prevent the collection of several students in a small area, which can lead to collisions.

This activity can be integrated across game and activity contexts. For example, the puck and stick could be replaced with a basketball. In that case, each pair of students shares a ball, and one player takes the offensive role by trying to dribble the ball through the gates while the partner takes the defensive role by trying to prevent passage through any gate. After a specified amount of time, the players switch roles. This version can also be expanded into a 2v2 activity in which one pair of students works, by dribbling and passing, to move through the gates while the defensive pair tries to prevent it.

You can also consider organizing the space, equipment, and students in the same formation as for a game of tag or chase. Designate half the class as "predators" (wearing pinnies) and the other half as "prey" (no pinnies). On your cue, the predators begin pursuing the prey. If an individual designated as prey is touched by a predator, then he or she is frozen, However, if a prey student who is free runs through any of the gates, all tagged prey are released to roam the space again. Both groups receive two opportunities to act as predators and as prey. The purpose of the game is to tag all the prey in the shortest time possible.

Such variations may require modifications in equipment and safety rules. For examples, the safety practices for the basketball and chase activities would require minor modifications of the safety rules for the original floor hockey activity. Even so, if safety guidelines are generally consistent across games and activities, then students are more likely to adhere to them and self-manage for player safety. Even when such modifications for safety are required, the organization of the space can often remain the same. In this way, you can take advantage of the same space for multiple activities, thus reducing transition time.

Let's return now to the vignette discussed at the start of the chapter. To review, Mr. Barton organized his grade 4 class to play floor hockey but was short one set of goalie equipment. Rather than place a goalie in net without proper safety equipment, he could eliminate the use of goaltenders altogether. For example, he could place a large cone or set of cones on the goal line of each net to act as a shooting target for the players. Another possible modification is to use tires for goals; in this case, players score a goal by hitting the tire with the puck or ball. A third solution would be to turn four wooden benches over and challenge players to hit the opponent's bench with the puck or ball in order to score.

Lack of proper goalie equipment for floor hockey is common in elementary schools. Instead of risking player injury for the sake of the game, modify the game to make it safe and inclusive for all students. Use the equipment available to play safe games and organize safe PE lessons in your specific school context. Table 3.2 presents a safety-first checklist that you can use to promote and sustain student safety during school-based physical activities.

Summary

This chapter demonstrates how student safety can be enhanced during school-based physical activities by ensuring safe equipment, providing appropriate spaces and facilities, and instituting necessary safety rules. As stated in Ontario's *Health and Physical Education Curriculum, Grades 1-8*, "Following procedures, using equipment as instructed, wearing appropriate attire, and using thinking skills to assess risk and take appropriate precautions are some ways in which students can contribute to their own safety and the safety of others while participating in physical activity" (Ontario Ministry of Education, 2015, pg. 27). Thus, teachers and students have dual ownership of the process of creating and managing safe and interactive physical activities. As part of ongoing safety measures, both parties should reflect after an activity and determine whether modifications are needed in equipment, space or facility, clothing or footwear, or supervision or safety rules.

Safety-First Checklist for Physical Activity in Elementary Schools

Safety considerations	Yes	No	Action required
1. Is a fully stocked first aid kit accessible?			
2. Do you have access to a working communication device?			
3. Have you determined that all equipment is safe for use?			
4. Have students been given time to inspect the equipment and report any deficiencies?			
1. Are students properly dressed (layered if necessary), including appropriate footwear for the activity?			
2. Have students removed all jewelry and tied back any long hair?			
3. Have long scarves or oversized jerseys or pants been removed or replaced with appropriately sized clothing?			
1. Is there adequate space for all students to participate actively and safely?			
2. Are turning points and finish lines located safely away from permanent features (e.g., walls, trees, holes)?			
3. Have proper boundaries been defined for physical activities in large areas?			
4. Have you inspected the space or facility for any potential hazards to students?			
5. Does the playing surface allow for safe footing and traction?			
6. Have immovable hazards been brought to the students' attention and marked by pylons?			
7. Have all doors into and out of the playing area been closed or secured?			
1. Has a call person (other than you) been designated in case of student injury?			
2. Are you certified and current in first aid?			
3. Are you NCCP-certified* at a level to responsibly coach intermural teams?			
4. For intermural games, have certified officials been allocated to supervise the activity?			
5. For off-site activities, has the minimum standard been met for student–teacher (or student–supervisor) ratio?			
1. For tag games, have you clearly defined which areas of the body can be tagged (i.e., arms, legs, back)?			
2. Do students know that a tag is a touch—not a push or punch?			
3. Have safety zones been clearly delineated (e.g., with pylons or poly spots)?			
4. Is a wall, stage, fence, or other immoveable barrier used as a finish line or safe zone?			
5. In relay games and races, does each student or team have a definitive lane?			
6. Are students aware of how the game or activity will stop or end (e.g., whistle blowing, music stopping)?			
7. Has the game or activity been modified as needed based on student skill levels, ages, facilities, and equipment available?			

*NCCP denotes the National Coaching Certification Program.

Adapted from Ontario's Physical and Health Education Association (2015).

DISCUSSION QUESTIONS

1. Why is taking risks important while participating in health and physical education classes or playing on a school sport team?

2. In what areas of life do you take risks despite the potential negative consequences?

3. Before you take a chance, do you weigh the advantages and disadvantages of taking a risk (i.e., staying out past curfew)?

4. Are some risks *not* worth taking because the consequences outweigh the advantages? Explain.

 Visit the web resource for safety case studies and questions, as well as blank printable versions of the checklists from this chapter.

Voices From the Field

Courtesy of Greg Rickwood.

Lynne Vokes-Leduc

Vice Principal (Elementary), Health and Physical Education Teacher (Grade 7), and Education Professor, Faculty of Education, Nipissing University, Ontario

Many of my teacher candidates are apprehensive about being in the gymnasium, and I ask them only to participate to the best of their ability. At the same time, I ask them to challenge themselves. One of my assignments asks them to teach a skill in the gymnasium. Knowing that they will be teaching many skills, most of them choose to teach one with which they are not comfortable. The response to this assignment has always been positive. Before we leave it, I ensure that my teacher candidates understand how to evaluate student success during skill acquisition; specifically, the focus should be on process, not product. For example, if I were teaching the skill of shooting a basketball, we would discuss the acronym BEEF (balance, eyes, elbow, follow-through). I am not concerned about whether the ball goes into the basket; instead, I want them to shoot the ball correctly.

In another example, I have used the following daily physical activity with my teacher candidates to promote healthy lifestyles and learning about the effects of smoking. The activity impresses on participants some of the physical effects of smoking and leads into activities that help students learn about the social and emotional effects of smoking.

Introduction

- We need to reinforce the importance of making good choices. Education is critical. Outside agencies may be able to help you with resources (e.g., Lung Association).
- When presenting this material, role playing and real life scenarios may be useful.
- Review effective decision-making skills for primary and junior students.
- Discuss ways of saying no—for example, changing the subject or giving an excuse to escape the situation.
- The hook: Smoking is the primary cause in Canada of preventable illness, disability, and premature death.
- The curricular expectation (grade 7) is for students to understand the social, emotional, and physical effects of smoking.

Materials

- Straws
- Aerobic steps
- Cue cards with trivia
- Zippered storage bags with numbered instructions
- Treats
- Stopwatch (or watch)

Description

1. Using aerobic steps, ask students to complete a two-minute routine that increases their heart rate.
2. Prompt students to measure the number of heartbeats in 10 seconds and multiply by 6 to get the per-minute heart rate. A healthy resting heart rate usually falls between 72 and 75 beats per minute.
3. Have students perform the same routine again, at the same pace, but this time while breathing through a straw. This restriction simulates how a smoker feels during physical activity by restricting oxygen flow to the peripheral blood system and lungs.
4. Calculate heart rate.
5. Discuss the differences in heart rate and perceived level of exertion.

CHAPTER 4

Including Everyone

Carol Scaini ■ **Jeannine Bush**

After studying this chapter, you will be able to

- explain the importance of building an inclusive classroom community where all students participate in physical activities;

- describe the differences between modifications and accommodations in curriculum;

- modify and accommodate an activity, environment, or equipment set to suit the needs of all students; and

- challenge students to effectively support each other so that all can achieve success.

Inclusive education is based on the principles of acceptance and inclusion of all students. Students see themselves reflected in their curriculum, their physical surroundings, and the broader environment, in which diversity is honoured and all individuals are respected.

Government of Ontario (2009, p. 4)

Inclusive education means more than just involving students in activities and games. An inclusive philosophy accommodates and values all individuals and challenges educators to revamp the ways in which they structure and implement tasks for all students. The key to establishing a quality inclusive physical education program is to create an environment in which students are accepted for the skills and abilities they have, appreciated for their differences, and given opportunities to be active and achieve success. Although barriers may exist that influence individuals' involvement in physical activities, there are many ways to overcome them and maximize participation. Thus we must be open to deconstructing traditional ways of knowing and doing and constructing a program where all participants are valued and respected. This approach focuses not on the word *disability* but on the word *ability*; moreover, it emphasizes learning to appreciate that the health benefits of being active are important for everyone. If this seems like a challenging task, fear not—this chapter outlines teaching methods and instructional strategies that you can implement to make physical activity engaging and fun for all (L. Kasser & Lytle, 2013).

What is an inclusive environment? Figure 4.1 highlights an inclusive approach in contrast to exclusion, segregation, and integration. In *exclusion*, students with disabilities are denied the chance to participate in physical activities; for example, while a regular physical education classroom is in session, these students would be sitting on the side. In a *segregated* classroom, students with special needs are separated from the rest of the class, or isolated, during physical activities. In other words, while mainstream students participate in one activity, students with special needs participate in a completely different one. When *integration* is used, students with special needs remain with the class and participate at whatever level they are able to achieve. For example, while mainstream students work on shooting basketballs at regulation goals, students with special needs might shoot into a lower target. This approach might also mean that a student in a special needs classroom would join a mainstream classroom for the physical education program and then return to the special needs classroom.

In contrast to all of these approaches, an *inclusive* physical education classroom includes all students, regardless of their abilities or disabilities. In a successful inclusive classroom, the teacher modifies content, methods, and strategies so that all students can experience success. In the example of shooting basketball, all students would rotate through stations offering targets at multiple levels so that everyone is included in the full activity. As a result, all students would feel that they belong in this classroom.

Students who have a diagnosis must be seen as children or students first. They are not defined by their disability or challenge; rather, the diagnosis is merely a part of who they are. Moreover, just as every child is different in general terms, so too are those who are identified with the same diagnosis. With this reality in mind, if you approach each student as a whole child and learn about his or her individual strengths and needs, then you can begin building an inclusive, engaging physical education program for all. Table 4.1 provides a

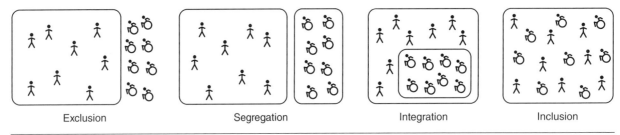

Figure 4.1   There are four classroom models for educating students with disabilities: exclusion, segregation, integration, and inclusion.

■ TABLE 4.1

Exceptionalities and Challenges

Exceptionalities	Challenges
Physical disabilities	Hearing, vision, or physical impairment; significant medical conditions; head injuries
Autism and pervasive developmental disorder (PDD)	Issues with communication (verbal and nonverbal) and social interaction (including leisure or play activities)
Developmental disabilities	Significant delays in learning rate, social interaction, and life-skill acquisition
Emotional and behaviour challenges	Difficulty in developing and sustaining relationships (with both adults and other students); challenges in social skills, self-regulation, self-care, and classroom behaviour
Giftedness	Need for differentiated learning experiences, beyond what is typically provided in a regular school program, in order to satisfy educational potential
Learning disabilities	Difficulty with learning academic or social skills due to disorder in one or more of the processes needed to use spoken or written language
Syndromes (e.g., fetal alcohol, Williams, fragile X, Prader-Willi)	Difficulty with learning academic or social skills due to disorder

©Peel District School Board

glimpse of some of the exceptionalities you may encounter in a physical education program, as well as their challenges.

Let's begin by addressing some of the special needs you may encounter in a physical education program. There are three main categories: students with physical challenges, students with cognitive challenges, and students with both physical and cognitive challenges. Students who experience physical challenges may have hearing, vision, or physical impairments or medical conditions that limit their motor skills. Those who experience cognitive challenges may have delays or issues with rate of learning, depth of understanding, verbal and nonverbal communication skills, or social interactions.

Most students who receive a diagnosis have an individual education plan (IEP), which is developed to address the student's curriculum goals and life skills. The IEP may not be specific to physical education, but you still have a legal responsibility to become familiar with it. In addition, doing so will help inform you about the student's expectations and acknowledge activities that the student may be restricted from, whether due to a medical condition or another type of limitation. Be aware, however, that many students who have a diagnosis can participate in activities without modifications or adaptations.

Once you understand your students' needs, you can work with the educational assistants or special education staff at your school or school board to adapt or modify equipment, environments, and activities. You can also connect with staff members who have worked with your students previously in order to identify successful strategies. Students should never be separated from the class community simply because they have an exceptionality. In pursuing this goal, you can turn to specialists, educational resources, and relevant equipment that can help you enable all students to participate in all aspects of a physical education program. Set up meetings with specialists—both at your school (e.g., special education support teacher) and within your school board (e.g., itinerant special education resource teacher, psychoeducational consultant, social worker)—who can provide you with these supports.

Students should never be separated from the class community simply because they have an exceptionality.

Instructional Supports

Various instructional supports are available to help you meet the diversity of student needs. These supports, presented in figure 4.2, include

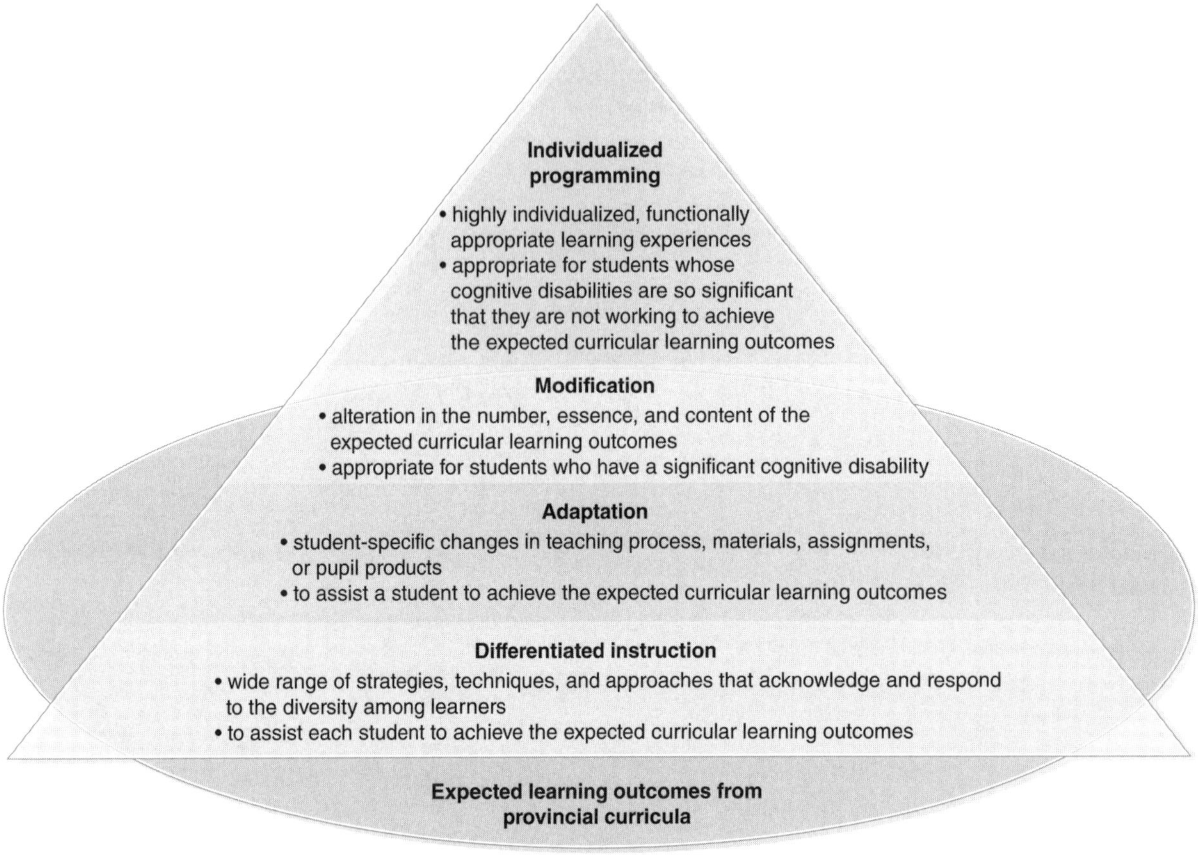

Figure 4.2 Instructional supports for addressing student diversity.

Source: Manitoba Education. *Student-Specific Planning: A Handbook for Developing and Implementing Individual Education Plans (IEPS)*. Winnipeg, MB: Manitoba Education, 2010. Available online at www.edu.gov.mb.ca/k12/specedu/iep/.

differentiated instruction, adaptation, modification, and individualized programming. Let's consider each in a bit of detail.

As the term suggests, *differentiated instruction* acknowledges and responds to differences among learners. When planning and providing daily instruction, educators who take this approach use a wide range of intentional strategies and techniques, as well as ongoing formative assessment, to support student learning and help the broadest student population achieve the expected curricular learning outcomes (Manitoba Education, 2010, p. 15). In physical education, this approach may incorporate a Teaching Games for Understanding model, wherein teachers offer a variety of minigames focused on a specific skill or technique to improve game play. For example, if you were teaching volleyball, one court might focus on serve accuracy by using hoops as targets while another court might focus on bumping in a keep-up game.

Adaptation, or *accommodation*, can involve the use of special teaching and assessment strategies, human supports, and individualized equipment to enable a student to both learn and demonstrate learning. Adaptations do not alter the provincial curricular expectations for the grade (Ontario Ministry of Education, 2004, p. 25), but they do allow you to adjust the teaching process and materials. For example, students might use a rubber chicken to play an adapted game of basketball; since the object does not bounce, students will focus on the specific skill of passing.

In contrast, *modification* involves changing the age-appropriate grade-level expectations for a subject or course in order to meet a student's learning needs. The changes may involve developing expectations that reflect knowledge and skills required in the curriculum for a different grade level or increasing or decreasing the number or complexity of the regular grade-level expectations (Ontario Ministry of Education, 2004, p. 25). In a physical education class, students might focus on developing basic skills through a simplified game. For example, when teaching the game of bowling, you might use a larger target or focus on knocking down a reduced number of pins in order to achieve success.

Individualized programming is intended for students whose cognitive disabilities are so significant that they do not benefit from participating in provincial curricula. It identifies highly individualized learning experiences that are functionally appropriate (Manitoba Education, 2010, p. 16), thus allowing you to focus on student needs by identifying specific expectations toward which a particular student is working. These expectations will differ from those of the provincial curriculum. For example, in a physical education class, to learn the social skill of waiting, students might play a game of bocce, which requires one student to roll a ball toward a target while the other person waits; thus the alternative goal for this activity is not to hit the target but to develop students' ability to wait appropriately.

In figure 4.2, the circle indicates three instructional supports—differentiated instruction, adaptation, and modification—that use the expected learning outcomes from provincial curricula. Individualized programming, on the other hand, uses specifically developed outcomes that will differ from provincial expectations.

Teaching Methods and Instructional Strategies

Before you begin a class, think about how you will conduct it. The tried-and-true methods and strategies presented in this section are meant to be flexible and evolving; instructional approaches may change based on your experiences of using them with students. Remember that no two students are alike; rather, each student has unique individual needs. Therefore, it is crucial to adjust your teaching methods and instructional strategies to suit each student's needs, or to suit all students.

This approach includes adapting or modifying an activity when necessary. Do so judiciously. If you introduce too many adaptations too early based on presumed understanding of students' abilities, the changes may have the opposite effect of what you intend; that is, they may *reduce* student involvement and inhibit students from achieving their full potential. Focus on adapting for students' levels of skill and ability. Consider introducing a few games or modified mini versions of the same game, running at the same time, to engage all students' abilities. In addition, allow students who acquire the necessary skills to demonstrate those skills or take on mentorship roles in the class.

To help you decide whether to implement any adaptations or modifications, use the following steps. As you begin teaching, consider reflecting on whether your student in question can achieve the task. If the answer is no, then try implementing different strategies and reevaluate how the student is doing. If the student continues to struggle, you may need to identify whether he or she possesses the underlying skills to accomplish the activity. For example, if a student has a hard time throwing a ball toward a target, you might initially try a number of strategies. If none of them help, then perhaps the student does not have the requisite skills to succeed at the task. In that case, in order to support the student's learning, you may need to begin by teaching her or him how to release an item, then proceed to the original target goal. Possible adaptations and modifications include having the student drop coins into a bowl, then drop a ball into a bowl, and then roll a ball without a target—all leading up to the original task of hitting a target.

In addition to implementing adaptations or modifications, consider your thoughts and words when teaching your students. Begin by focusing on thinking and speaking positively and in a caring manner to your students. Imagine being a student in a classroom who is constantly told "No, don't do that" or "No, stop that." This negative manner of speaking focuses on what you don't want a student to do instead of what they should do. Instead, consider using words to highlight the positive behaviour you want to see. For example, you could say "I like how you are waiting your turn" or "Great job! I like how you are working on rolling the ball to the target." To illustrate this point even further, let's examine driving a golf ball toward the hole in a game of golf. You step up to the ball, ready to take your swing, but you see a bunker a few meters from the hole. You begin to think negatively: "Don't hit the bunker, don't hit the bunker." As you make contact with the ball, you watch it travel through the air and right into the bunker—exactly where you did not want it to go. Now let's look at this same situation but with positive thinking: "Aim for the hole, aim for the hole." By using this positive self-talk and a growth mind-set, you can change the outcome for yourself and your students. The web resource includes a growth mind-set and inclusion template that provides questions and comments to help remind you of the importance of thinking positively.

Beginning Class With Routines

The first step in ensuring a safe environment is to establish a clear set of rules and routines to follow when students enter the gymnasium. Begin each class by having students meet you in the centre circle of the gym so that you can take attendance and provide instructions for the task or activity of the day. If you like, provide poly spots (rubber mats) for them to sit on. During this time, students are expected to listen and pay attention; students may need to be supported in this process by having you review what it looks and sounds like. For example, you might say that listening to instructions means that their legs are crossed, their hands are in their lap, their eyes are looking at you, their mouths are closed, and their ears are listening to you. Consider that listening may look different for students with special needs. For instance, a student with autism spectrum disorder may not look at a speaker but may still take in what the speaker is saying; another student may need to sit on the outside of the circle in a chair, whereas another may need to hold something in their hand to fidget with while instructions are provided. During this routine, any equipment should be kept out of the way to avoid potential distraction.

Using a Visual Schedule

Many students, particularly those with developmental delays, appreciate knowing the structure of a class, when an activity or task will begin, and when it will end: "We have only 10 more minutes to play. . . . We have only 5 more minutes to play. . . . It is now tidy-up time." Such cues enable students to be prepared to stop playing without being suddenly disappointed that the class has ended.

To facilitate students' understanding, you can also provide a visual schedule, or visual outline, summarizing what will happen in today's class. A visual schedule presents a series of images representing the various parts of a class session. For example, the first photo might show the class sitting in the designated area when students enter the gymnasium. The second photo might show a warm-up activity or the game or activity in which your students will participate (e.g., bowling, bocce). The third photo could show students putting away the equipment used for the activity, and the final photo could show students lining up at the door to return to class. The photos can be generic, or you can take photos of your own students involved in the activities (Alexander & Schwager, 2012).

Figure 4.3 shows a sample of a very detailed visual schedule that gives a step-by-step outline of an entire physical education class. The visuals on the left indicate what students will do to begin the class, whereas those on the right depict the activities in which students will participate.

Try to keep your visual schedule to 5 or 6 steps so that it does not overwhelm your students. Included here are many more pictures than you should use with your visual schedule to give you a sense of what you can include in your own visual schedules. Review the schedule before beginning the class so that students are aware of how it works; in addition, try to use a similar format each time in order to make it easier for your students to know what to expect. At the beginning of the year, you may teach the visuals on the left and then keep them up as a standard format for each physical education class. The visuals on the right may be changed to match the activity you are introducing to each class. If you use photos of your own students, they may feel more connected to your class.

Providing Instructions for the Activity

Once you have outlined the class for students, it is time to provide instructions for the activity. To maximize students' understanding, use simple words and visual demonstrations of the actions to be performed. Consider posting keywords and visuals of the skills to reinforce the activity's requirements. For instance, figures 4.4 and 4.5 show how students can learn the underhand throw and then use that skill in the game of bocce.

Figure 4.3 Sample visual schedule.

Grade Three
The Underhand Throw

Good throwers:

1. Look at their target.
2. Point their toes at the target.

3. Swing their arm back like an elephant's trunk.

4. Step forward as they throw (step with the foot opposite to their throwing hand).

To throw a grounder: Control the underhand throw so the ball rolls smoothly.

Figure 4.4 Images and words can serve as powerful supports in teaching skills such as the underhand throw.

©2001 Heart and Stoke Foundation of Canada. Reproduced with permission.

These simple diagrams, along with simple wording, explain how the skill is executed and how the game is played. Figure 4.6 shows how a complicated skill, such as the overhand throw, can be broken down using simple words and actions to help students learn the skill. Posting such visuals around the gymnasium allows students to review game instructions and game activities by quietly reading the text and reviewing the visuals. As part of an inclusive classroom, these supports—both pictorial and language based—allow all students the opportunity to review skills and procedures as needed.

Creating Groups

Many physical activities involve working with a partner or small group. When creating such groupings, take care that no student is marginalized or excluded. Or, to put it in positive terms, "Well-designed groups support positive interactions and have the power to help students become part of an environment in which they feel respected, included, and connected to one another" (Peel District School Board, *Character Attributes*, n.d., p. 4).

Consider creative ways of selecting teams to help all students feel included. For instance, you might hand out playing cards or coloured beanbags and have students find other students with the same card number or suit or beanbag colour. You might also use name cards to select teams

ahead of time. Consider also using the various team-building methods identified in chapter 10 for promoting an inclusive environment.

Introducing an Activity

When introducing an activity, consider modifying it to suit the individual needs of your students and thus help them experience greater success. Examples include altering the movement required (e.g., walking instead of running, kicking instead of throwing in bocce), limiting the movement (e.g., using scooter boards), adjusting the playing area (e.g., using a quarter of the space and setting up minigames), and allowing additional time or attempts to achieve a task. More examples are provided a bit later, in the section titled Modifying the Environment and Equipment.

You can also consider introducing basic games to develop a particular skill before students play a sport. Such games may use a simplified version of key tasks and limit the number of skills required to play. For example, a modified version of basketball might involve only passing and shooting.

Assessing Success

When assessing, reflect on the success of the accommodations or modifications you have implemented to address the needs of your students. Did the adjustments to the environment, equipment, or game optimize success for all students? If the answer is no, consider whether additional or different changes should be made in order to encourage success. It is not necessary to focus your assessment on whether the student has achieved the game task or goal. Instead, focus on participation and celebrate all successes. Encouraging a positive experience, both socially and physically, encourages lifelong participation in physical activities.

> *Although physical education classes typically focus on engaging students in the physical aspect of games, they also provide a natural way to help students develop and practice a number of social skills.*

Teaching Social Skills

Although physical education classes typically focus on engaging students in the physical aspect of games, they also provide a natural way to help students develop and practice a number of social skills. Common examples include taking turns, standing at an appropriate distance while talking, rec-

Power Skills

BOCCE

Set!

- Mark off boundaries (use a jacket, hats, chalk, etc.).

Go!

Scoring

- At the end of each round, the player with the ball closest to the marker ball wins ONE point for every ball closer to the marker ball than their opponent's.
- Play the game to 11 points

Marker ball

← 10 gaint steps →

Learn the game

- Find some different colour or different types of balls (e.g., tennis balls croquetballs, golf balls). You need two sets of four balls that are the same colour/type and one ball that is different from all the others.
- Kevin wins the coin toss, so he will throw the marker ball past the mid-line.
- The marker ball needs to be a ball of a different colour or size than all the others.
- Monica throws her ball to try to get as close to the marker ball as possible.
- Kevin now throws his ball, trying to get it resting closer to the marker ball than Monica's.
- Each takes a turn until all their balls are thrown.
- Another round starts, but this time Monica throws the marker ball.

Add a rule!

You can hit the marker ball (accidentally or intentionally) and its new position now becomes the new targeted spot. Play bocce again and see if this rule changes how you play the game.

Which technique makes the ball roll more?

a) A low toss.
b) A high toss.
c) Tossing the ball with topspin (palm up release).
d) Tossing the ball with a back spin (palm down release).

Experiment with getting the ball to "break right" or "break left" **Hint: Spin the ball.**

Add a challenge!

- Bounce the ball off a wall and use the rebound angles to your advantage.
- Create an "obstacle zone" halfway down the court. Before each throw, opponents can place a shoe strategically to make the shot more difficult.

Heart Leaders!

Can you think of a way to include four players? Invite friends and family members to try it out.

Figure 4.5 Simple illustrations and words can help students see how skills are applied in a game.

Grade Three
The Overhand Throw

Good throwers:

1. Stand sideways to the target.
2. Look at the target.
3. Make a big "J" with their arms.
4. Feel a stretch in their shoulder.
5. Rock back on their back leg.
6. Step forward as they throw on their front foot.
7. As you step, twist your hips underneath you (think about taking a picture of the target with your tummy).
8. The throwing arm finishes down and across the body (pretend to scratch the opposite knee).

Helpers say:

"Turning the hips is tricky to learn, but WOW, it really makes a difference!"

Figure 4.6 Simple words and actions may help break down a complicated skill such as the overhand throw to make it easier to learn.

©2001 Heart and Stoke Foundation of Canada. Reproduced with permission.

ognizing and using appropriate voice tones and volumes, listening to others, sharing equipment, asking for help, dealing with mistakes and the ups and downs of winning and losing, following the rules of the game, and using appropriate touch during tag games or activities (Alexander and Schwager, 2012, p. 108).

Physical education class is often seen as a fun environment in which these and other social skills can be taught casually, often without students even realizing that it is happening. However, if you take a moment to discuss and demonstrate appropriate cues for the targeted social skills, you will enable your students to play and learn to work together in a healthier way. For example, if you are teaching students to guard in a game of ultimate, you can use the example of a stretched-out arm with the disc in your hand as an appropriate distance from which to guard an opponent; it also happens to be an appropriate distance from which to speak with someone.

You can also incorporate various social skills in a game focused on a specific physical skill. For example, if your class is focused on dribbling a basketball, you can have students move from one student to the next while asking each individual they encounter a question to learn a new fact about that person. In this way, while working on

dribbling and social skills—for example, making eye contact, standing at an appropriate distance, staying on topic, asking questions, and using appropriate voice volume—students also learn ball control (Alexander & Schwager, 2012, p. 109). Thus you can introduce games and activities that allow your students to develop both physical and social skills in a fun and realistic manner.

Modifying the Environment and Equipment

At this point, you have been provided with a variety of teaching methods and instructional strategies. Let us look now at further modifications that can be made in both environment and equipment.

Environment

The gymnasium can be an overwhelming place for any child, with its loud whistles, screams of excitement, equipment noise (e.g., balls bouncing), and echoes—and of course the many students moving around! The combination of such inputs can cause students to experience sensory overload, some examples of which are presented in table 4.2. Minimizing the risk of sensory overload may be as simple as changing the way you capture students' attention. For example, instead of using a traditional whistle, you might implement a "red light–green light" system in which a red card is used to stop students and a green card is used to allow them to engage in activity.

Equipment

Adapting or modifying equipment to suit individual needs is essential to the task of enabling all students to succeed. Whether it means using a softer ball or a longer hockey stick, we must be creative in order to be inclusive. Useful items for this purpose can be purchased from various sellers or developed on your own; either way, it is vital to take a few minutes to ensure that equipment is safe before it is used. If the needed equipment is expensive, additional funding may be available through your school board or community organizations.

Here are some examples of modifications used in physical education classes:

- Large rubber ball for bouncing
- Ball with holes in it to facilitate catching

■ TABLE 4.2

Sensory Overload in Physical Education

Sound	Shrieking whistles, bouncing balls, yelling kids ("gym voices"), blaring music
Sight	Bright sunlight, glare from gymnasium lights, bright posters, general motion of many people running around
Touch	Contact with other kids, pinnies, ball textures, sensation of sweating, grass (possibly moist from dew or long and touching ankles if not mowed)
Smell	Rubber balls, body odor, deodorants used in the changing room
Proprioception and vestibular aspects	Tumbling, jumping, climbing, spinning, movements that require going up and down (e.g., touching toes)

Reprinted by permission from M. Alexander and S. Schwager, *Meeting the Physical Education Needs of Children with ASD* (United States: Human Kinetics, 2012).

- Textured ball for added grip when sending and receiving
- Fleece ball for throwing and catching
- Beach ball or lightweight trainer for keep-up games (e.g., volleyball)
- Oversized racquet for net and wall games
- Scooter boards for easy movement around the gymnasium
- Balls with bells inside to facilitate identification of ball location
- Foam or lighter-weight equipment (e.g., soccer balls, flying discs, bats)
- Extended hockey or ringette sticks
- Oversized targets (e.g., bowling pins, basketball hoop)
- Oversized objects to be struck (e.g., larger foam ball instead of baseball or hockey ball)
- Baseball tee to stabilize the ball for batting
- Ball that is slightly deflated to slow it down
- Bowling ramp that can extend up to a wheelchair or standing height
- Equipment to extend a student's reach (e.g., foam noodle for tag, hockey stick for manipulation of a soccer ball)
- Pool noodles for striking objects (e.g., softball, larger hockey ball)
- Equipment to improve balance and coordination (e.g., stability balls, balance discs, bumpy massage yoga balls)
- Resistance bands to improve strength
- Mini-trampolines for fitness and core strength
- Textured (sensory) balls
- Weighted compression vest for calming and steady proprioceptive input
- Alternative method for indicating activity starts and stops (e.g., green and red flags, lummi sticks hit together, lower-pitched whistle)

Building Partnerships

Your success with your students may be determined by the connections you make with families and local community organizations. If at all possible, invest the time to meet your students' parents during school open houses—or, if necessary, phone them—not only to share what you are teaching (social, fundamental, and game skills) but also to learn about each child's abilities and the various strategies used at home or in therapy. Many students with special needs have benefited from recommendations given by occupational therapists or physical therapists. If reports about a student have been shared with the school, you should be able to find them in the student's school record. This partnership will allow you to teach more effectively by tailoring your program so that the student can be more active in class.

Another way to help students with special needs be physically active is to reach out to community centres and organizations. Take a look around your local community and identify recreational centres and other organizations

> *Your success with your students may be determined by the connections you make with families and local community organizations.*

that provide support and physical activities for students. These connections can help socialize your students in the community at large by providing fun opportunities for social interaction beyond the school and home settings. Suggest that the student choose an activity that he or she enjoys—for instance, a sporting activity, games group, reading club, cooking group, or arts and crafts club. Such connections also provide great opportunities for parents to share experiences and support each other.

One such community organization, located in the greater Toronto area, is Variety Village, which promotes appreciation, interaction, empowerment, and inclusion (Variety Village, n.d.). The organization's staff facilitates the achievement of life goals by people with disabilities through sport, fitness, wellness, awareness, education, training, and skill development. By offering specialized programs and services, the staff creates a level playing field without barriers, intimidation, or other obstacles. The goal is to improve quality of life and integration into society by all people, regardless of ability. Thus it is a great place to get fit and have fun.

Variety Village also offers Ability in Action programs dedicated to educating individuals, groups, and community organizations about the importance of providing opportunities for people of all abilities. The programs use inclusive and integrated hands-on activities (e.g., adapted games, wheelchair activities, rock wall climbing) to help participants learn the value of welcoming, accepting, and understanding that we are all able. The program is available both at Variety Village and as an outreach program delivered at schools across Ontario.

Another community organization, Special Olympics Canada, uses the transformative power of sport to enrich the lives of Canadians with intellectual disabilities. Operating in 12 provinces and territories across Canada, Special Olympics programs cater to all ages and a wide range of abilities. From two-year-olds to mature adults, more than 40,000 athletes with intellectual disabilities are registered in the group's year-round programs. Special Olympics is a catalyst for social change, helping to instill confidence, self-esteem, and other life skills in individuals with intellectual disabilities; help participants develop lifelong physical fitness habits; and create a more inclusive society while strengthening communities across Canada.

Special Olympics Canada offers an array of programs, such as the following:

- *Active Start* is a family-centred activity program geared toward children with intellectual disabilities from age 2 to age 6 (Special Olympics Canada, 2004a). It helps children learn basic motor skills such as walking, running, jumping, and throwing in a fun and safe environment.

- *FUNdamentals* is a continuation of the Active Start program for individuals with intellectual disabilities from age 7 to age 12 (Special Olympics Canada, 2014b). It facilitates the transition from basic movement skills to basic sport skills, thus providing participants with an in-depth introduction to sport-related motor skills, along with training and competition, while maintaining an atmosphere of fun and meaningful interaction. This program also promotes specific sport education, proper nutrition, and social inclusion through participation in positive sport experiences.

- *Long-term athlete development* (LTAD) is a framework for developing physical literacy, physical fitness, and competitive ability through a stage-by-stage approach. The LTAD model recognizes physical literacy as the foundation both for being active, healthy, and engaged in physical activity for life and for achieving personal-best performances at all levels of competition.

These programs for young people with intellectual disabilities provide great opportunities for parents and caregivers to expand their networks and support systems. They also act as gateways for long-term athlete development. Additional information about stage-specific development, objectives, and programs can be found on the Special Olympics Canada website.

Modifying Games and Sports

In this section, we provide an example of how a traditional game can be broken down to suit the functional capabilities of all participants by altering the equipment, the environment, and the game itself. We then present a few simple and fun modified versions of traditional games and activities. Finally, we discuss how you can make changes that focus specifically on the needs of students in your class.

All activities, games, and sports can be redesigned by simply adjusting equipment, players, movement, organization, and rules to create optimal challenges and successful experiences for all.

All activities, games, and sports can be redesigned by simply adjusting equipment, players, movement, organization, and rules to create optimal challenges and successful experiences for all (L. Kasser & Lytle, 2013, p. 197). For each game or activity you teach, consider how you can make changes to ensure that all students are able to succeed in it. A simple change in one or more of the elements can make a huge difference in creating optimal game experiences for students. The following example explores how the elements of foursquare can be changed to suit students' needs. Table 4.3 shows how this game might be varied.

Foursquare

Purpose: eye–hand coordination

Equipment: playground ball

Players: four (one in each square)

Movement patterns: striking, sliding

Organization: playing area measuring 2.4 meters square and divided into four equal subsquares

Rules

1. One person plays in each square.
2. Players can hit the ball on the fly or after one bounce.
3. Players can hit to any square other than their own.
4. A fair hit bounces in an opponent's square.
5. A ball hitting a line is considered to be in play.

Note: A determination of "fair hit" will also be declared before the game (e.g., contact time with ball, spins, use of body parts).

■ TABLE 4.3

Foursquare Game Elements and Variation Possibilities

Game elements	Variation possibilities
Equipment	• Use lighter or heavier balls. • Increase or decrease ball size or use an extension (e.g., racquet, hockey stick). • Increase or decrease base of support (e.g., with use of a chair, walker, or wall). • Use equipment with a bell or other sound.
Organization	• Increase or decrease the size of the playing space or change the shape of the space. • Increase or decrease the number of squares. • Rotate team members or partners after each hit. • Play twosquare.
Players	• Assign a pair or team to each square. • Increase or decrease the number of players.
Movements	• Play while sitting on the ground or in a chair. • Try variations: touch and push, catch and throw, or strike and volley. • Allow rolling, catching, or striking or use an extension.
Rules	• Catch or hit from a range of variations, including rolling, multiple bounces, and no bounces. • Rotate out for rest if fatigued. • Increase or decrease the number of rules. • Play for a short time, then rotate. • Increase duration of the activity.

Adapted by permission from L. Kasser and R. Lytle, *Inclusive Physical Activity: Promoting Health for a Lifetime* (Champaign, IL: Human Kinetics, 2013), 197.

Now that you understand how to adapt and modify activities, check out the activities presented in the web resource for this chapter. You can use them to activate your students and teach basic fundamental and social skills. The resource also includes a blank version of table 4.3 to help you plan variations for any other game you might choose.

Summary

An inclusive environment focuses not on winning but on growing and developing needed skills (both social and physical), learning about and respecting each other and our differences, and participating in a physical education program that is engaging and fun. Take a moment to reflect on your teaching practices from the perspective presented in this chapter. Don't be afraid to connect with other staff, support staff, and parents for advice and support.

DISCUSSION QUESTIONS

1. How might you address and balance individual student needs in large-group games?
2. What is the importance of inclusive education in physical activities?
3. How will you encourage students to help and support each other in game situations?
4. What does an inclusive physical education program look like?
5. What steps can you take if you have a concern or question about a student's abilities?
6. How will you structure your classroom—in terms of environment, activities, teaching style, and assessment—to enable all students to succeed?
7. Why is it important to involve community partners in your planning?

Visit the web resource for ready-to-use activities that help develop physical and social skills and are appropriate for all levels of ability, a template for planning variations to any activity, as well as a growth mindset poster.

Voices From the Field

Lindsay LaMorre

*Course Director/Community Practicum Coordinator; Seconded Faculty
York University*

*Teacher, Toronto Catholic District School Board
Ontario*

I am currently seconded to York University, where I teach teacher candidates in the Faculty of Education. As a teacher with the Toronto Catholic District School Board, my teaching included health and physical education in primary, junior, and intermediate grades. I was also a professional learning network lead teacher for the north region of Toronto.

I challenge my students to reframe health and physical education from an endeavour oriented strictly toward competition and achievement to one focused more on participation and lifelong active living. I emphasize fun, participation, challenge, and competition in a nonthreatening environment. I get to know my students, which enables me to make connections, build relations, and create a culturally relevant curriculum. Through games, I assess their entry level, which helps me plan learning engagements to motivate them and respond to their needs. I use nontraditional equipment to emphasize play and to support students in discovering activities that they enjoy. In addition, I believe strongly in role modelling and sharing my narrative of health as life practice, thus encouraging students to think of their everyday experiences and the effects on their health. I try to facilitate a health and physical education class in which students leave with smiles, wanting more. I challenge students to take their learning beyond the four walls of the gym—to apply and promote health as the foundation of who they are and everything they do.

In practice, this approach involves either reinvigorating health and physical literacies or developing new ones—that is, either recalling forgotten knowledge related to movement or challenging received wisdom in order to create new ones. Along the way, the intrinsic qualities of motivation, physical competence, and confidence are woven together with more extrinsic aspects such as environmental contexts and cues, interpersonal communication, plural notions of embodiment, and multiple knowledge traditions.

Because students' needs differ, I regularly use a variety of activities to promote inclusion in the classroom. Examples include the use of pool noodles in tag to increase reach and modify the relational field of the activity, the use of a chair or other guide for support in movement activities, rule changes in games to include passing to students on the outside of boundaries, deflation of balls to increase the probability of a successful catch, stations that allow students to work at their own pace, game modifications that emphasize students' abilities (e.g., sitting volleyball), and unconventional approaches or unexpected equipment (rubber chicken, anyone?).

In connection with these activities, I focus assessment on whether the student is participating actively and safely and on the student's individual growth in terms of personal goals. This type of assessment incorporates and promotes living skills, such as self-awareness, active listening, cooperation, relationship with others, communication, goal setting, and decision making. When focusing on a specific movement skill or concept, I emphasize the student's ability to demonstrate understanding in multiple ways. What might the student say, do, or write to meet the expectation? How might we highlight the student's ability to communicate his or her thinking and comprehension of the movement skill or concept, as well as game strategy?

For me, an inclusive classroom comes down to getting to know each student (both on an individual basis and in the broader context of the class), getting to know students' abilities and potentials for success, and building trust in the relationship. How can we recognize and reduce barriers and advocate and communicate with and for all students? I focus on ability rather than on disability, and student voices are essential to this process, particularly in regard to any accommodation or modification that needs to be made in consultation with a student. One of the greatest lessons I've learned came about when I thought of a set of wonderful accommodations I could make to include a student—and the student didn't want any of them. I had forgotten to include in the pedagogical discussion the very person who was affected most, and this realization changed my definition of success. I also try to create safe environments for learning, both physically and affectively. If we want to promote diversity and inclusion in the greater community, how do we begin those teachings and model them authentically in the school environment?

CHAPTER 5

Addressing Diversity

Erin Cameron

After studying this chapter, you will be able to

- explain the meaning and benefits of diversity,
- express a new way of thinking about diversity in health and physical education,
- explain the major diversity issues in health and physical education teaching,
- describe the role of inclusion in building and strengthening diversity in health and physical education,
- discuss opportunities for creating inclusive environments in health and physical education, and
- create inclusive activities in health and physical education.

A growing number of educators, administrators, and researchers are calling for more to be done to promote diversity in the field of health and physical education. Many suggest that we need to move beyond simply acknowledging diversity and adopt the attitudes, values, and belief systems of inclusiveness. This approach celebrates student diversity and enables every student to feel supported in living a healthy and active life. In other words, inclusion cannot be achieved by simply using guest speakers or adapting games and equipment. Instead, it needs to be viewed in terms of the sociocultural contexts of a classroom, school, and society (for more on developing a sociocultural framework, see chapter 1). To achieve true inclusion in health and physical education, we need to work together to use teaching and learning strategies that are contextual and inclusive of and for everyone.

Creating Sociocultural Connections

I have always felt that the action most worth watching is not at the center of things but where edges meet. I like shorelines, weather fronts, international borders. There are interesting frictions and incongruities in these places, and often, if you stand at the point of tangency, you can see both sides better than if you were in the middle of either one. This is especially true, I think, when the apposition is cultural.

Fadiman (2012, p. viii)

Consider for a moment how members of different cultures might view health and physical education differently, or how they might give it different meanings than you would. For example, think about your own culture and ask yourself the following questions:

- What sets of beliefs, values, and attitudes are common in my culture regarding health and physical education?
- How does my culture influence how I approach teaching in health and physical education?
- How is my culture different from or the same as my students' cultures?
- How might a student's culture influence how he or she prioritizes health and physical education? How might it influence the types of activities to which the student has been exposed outside of school?
- How do I address cultural differences in my teaching in health and physical education?

Such questions are often used to enable reflection to help us see new meanings and better understand how diversity might influence our perspectives and practices. With that in mind, here is another set of questions, adapted from Fadiman (2012), that can challenge how we see, think, and "do" health and physical education.

- What do you call health and physical education?
- What do you think about health and physical education?
- Why do you think it is a school subject?
- What do you think health and physical education does?
- What is the role of health and physical education?
- What do you hope to achieve in health and physical education?
- What are the problems related to health and physical education?
- What do you fear about health and physical education?

We must ask such questions about cultural context if we want to meet students where they are and build on their existing knowledge and experiences. In this approach, often referred to as scaffolding, we support students cognitively, motivationally, and emotionally while helping them further develop their autonomy (Meyer & Turner, 2002). It is a particularly useful strategy for building inclusiveness in a diverse classroom because it is a student-centered approach.

While there is increasing awareness for the need to promote diversity in the field of health and physical education (Robinson & Randall, 2016), health and physical education classes are still often taught with a teacher-driven, sport-focused skills and drills approach that prioritizes certain team sports. Such an approach privileges students who like or have been exposed to the chosen sports while alienating many other students in the class. This effect is undesirable for various reasons, including the fact that student participation is one of the major issues faced by many

To ensure that students are not marginalized in health and physical education, we need to be culturally responsive by asking ourselves questions and taking the time to learn about the different cultures of our students, their families, our communities, and the contexts in which we all live.

teachers and identified as a challenge in the field of health and physical education. To ensure that students are not marginalized in health and physical education, we need to be culturally responsive by asking ourselves questions and taking the time to learn about the different cultures of our students, their families, our communities, and the contexts in which we all live.

What is needed, then, is a sociocultural approach that aims to engage all students in meaningful ways. For example, Kozub, Sherblom, and Perry (1999) argue that teachers who use a sociocultural approach are more likely to see the similarities between students with and without physical disabilities; as a result, they are able to create activities that develop fundamental movement skills essential to *all* students. In other words, becoming aware of individual and societal perceptions about ability—or any other social or human difference, such as race, ethnicity, socioeconomic class, gender, sexual orientation, or body size—is critical to a sociocultural approach because it acknowledges that one's identity frames how one experiences the world. In fact, we need to go beyond merely acknowledging identity and difference and move toward actively asserting and confronting issues of power and privilege in society. This work involves challenging cultural biases, as well as inequitable practices and policies, with the understanding that culture can be important to student success but can also impede it if cultural issues are not viewed through the lens of diversity and inclusion. In other words, making explicit sociocultural connections in teaching health and physical education can help us create opportunities to build inclusive environments in which everyone feels safe to participate.

Social Justice Education

In order to understand how a sociocultural approach can help us address diversity in health and physical education, we need to situate this chapter within the field of social justice education. The past century has seen the development of a growing number of educational approaches committed to addressing diversity and inclusiveness in educational settings. This work has been described with various labels, such as education for liberation, transformation, empowerment, anti-oppression, and social justice. By any name, it pursues the goals of inclusion, equity, and fairness (in distribution of resources and recognition of human potential) and embodies a process focused on democracy, participation, and change

(Adams, Bell, & Griffin, 2007; Darder, Baltadano, & Torres, 2009). Broadly speaking, then, this growing field of social justice education is not only *about* justice and fairness but is also part of a larger effort to ensure that we will *live* in a more socially just world in the future (Giroux, 1997).

Social justice education involves four key components (Nieto & Bode, 2012). First, it challenges stereotypes, misconceptions, and assumptions that lead to unequal and unfair treatment of individuals. In this approach, teachers consciously include activities and topics that encourage students to engage actively in equality and fairness. Second, social justice education supports all learners in realizing and achieving their full potential. To do so, teachers use resources that address the unique needs and diversity of all learners; for example, material resources are important (e.g., books, curriculum, financial support), but so are emotional resources (e.g., belief in students' ability and worth). These resources must be used to make visible the diversity in student populations so that all students can see themselves in the learning rather than merely being talked at. Third, social justice education draws on students' unique talents. Here, teachers seek to discover what students bring in terms of knowledge, skill, and interest and use that as a foundation for their learning. Last, social justice education promotes critical thinking; in other words, teachers focus not necessarily on what students learn but on how they learn to think. In summary, then, social justice education is about

> *In summary, then, social justice education is about challenging harmful stereotypes and assumptions, helping all learners realize their full potential, engaging learners' talents and perspectives, and promoting critical thinking in learners.*

- challenging harmful stereotypes and assumptions,
- helping all learners realize their full potential,
- engaging learners' talents and perspectives, and
- promoting critical thinking in learners.

The health and physical education context is home to many specific issues of social justice and diversity. With that fact in mind, this chapter offers you a base from which to begin thinking about diversity through inclusive teaching. That is, in addition to offering an overview of what social justice education means in health and physical education, the chapter addresses the question "What should I do?" Fortunately, this topic is the focus of a growing body of resources in Canada (e.g., Casey, Kentel, & Cameron, 2014; Singleton & Varpalotai, 2006; Robinson & Randall, 2016). The more resources we have—and the more we critically reflect on diversity issues stemming from social inequity, marginalization, and oppression—the better we will be prepared in the field of health and physical education to bring about change in classrooms and to improve the experiences of *all* our students.

In *Against Common Sense: Teaching and Learning Toward Social Justice,* Kumashiro (2009) writes, "Now more than ever, we need to redefine what it means to be a teacher. . . . We need to reshape how we prepare and support teachers in contexts that actively hinder social justice education" (p. xxvi). Kumashiro has studied the teaching practices used in social justice education and highlights four areas commonly used to address inclusion:

- Improving the experiences of students who are perceived as different
- Changing our knowledge about students who are labeled as different
- Challenging the social dynamics of difference in society
- Addressing reasons that social justice education is challenging

The following sections of the chapter situate social justice issues related to race, ability, gender, and body size and use Kumashiro's work to identify ways to address specific social justice and diversity issues in the context of health and physical education.

Addressing Diversity: Becoming Aware of the Water

Before addressing specific diversity issues in health and physical education, we must acknowledge the multiple axes of diversity—that is, the intersectionality of social identities. In other words, our social identities are not often unitary but rather tend to be multiple. For example, I am a white, thin, cisgender, able-bodied, heterosexual female. Therefore, some of my social identities afford me a great deal of privilege and social capital, whereas others do not. Here, *privilege* refers

not to fortunate happenstance but to the rights, advantages, and protections available to a person due to being part of a dominant group.

In the book *Is Everyone Really Equal: An Introduction to Key Concepts in Social Justice Education,* Sensoy and DiAngelo (2012) offer a helpful analogy for understanding privilege—it's like being a fish in water. When the fish moves, the water moves around the fish. When the fish floats, the water continues to move around the fish and affect its movement. When the fish swims upstream, the effort is enormous. When the fish swims downstream, the effort is minimal—like privilege. Thus privilege is like having a current pushing you through life.

> Privilege—it's like being a fish in water. When the fish moves, the water moves around the fish. When the fish floats, the water continues to move around the fish and affect its movement. When the fish swims upstream, the effort is enormous. When the fish swims downstream, the effort is minimal—like privilege. Thus privilege is like having a current pushing you through life.

In human life, of course, the analogy gets complicated because privilege is socially constructed, meaning that it does not occur naturally but is produced and enacted within society to benefit dominant groups. Still, the first step in social justice education is to become aware of privilege. Together, we need to acknowledge the water—the sociocultural contexts in which we work, live, and play—and begin to act in ways that promote a more just society. The following sections highlight some specific ways to begin thinking and acting differently to help address diversity and create more inclusive environments.

Race and Ethnicity

When talking about social justice issues, racism is often the first topic to come up. Like the ideas of gender and disability, race is a socially constructed concept that exerts profound social influence on aspects of life ranging from where people live to what schools they attend. It has been argued that teachers in health and physical education lack the expertise and confidence to talk about the issues of race that normalize the presence and experiences of the white racial majority (Casey et al., 2014; Douglas & Halas, 2008). However, bringing forward issues of race can help us address the social inequalities that shape health and physical education contexts for ethnic minority youth.

Here are some suggestions for reflection and action:

- *Improving the experiences of students.* Ensure that all students can see themselves in the course materials (e.g., textbooks, handouts, videos). Ask students what activities they like to do outside of school, then make a point to include their preferences among a range of activities that resonate with *all* of your students. If students aren't participating in class, try to find out the underlying reason—you may be surprised.
- *Changing the knowledge about students.* Ask various students to lead or plan class activities. Encourage them to share games and activities that they know well and that are specific to their culture.
- *Challenging the social dynamics.* It is best never to let students pick teams so as to avoid students being excluded but to give them lots of choice in other matters. Encourage students to consider the social, political, historical, and cultural contexts for various games and sports.
- *Addressing reasons why.* Initiate class discussions about white privilege. For example, engage students in discussions about who has access to physical activity and sport programs, or ask them who the general managers tend to be in professional sports.

Disability

There is a rich historical context in North America of including people with disabilities in health and physical education. This history began sometime after the Second World War, a period which saw an emphasis on health and sports and a push for all children to have access to physical activity. In Canada, there has also been a particularly strong adapted physical activity movement. Even so, children with disabilities continue to be marginalized in physical education contexts because teachers are often not well equipped to address issues related to disability (Harvey, 2014a, 2014b). Furthermore, the idea of disability continues to be viewed through socially constructed standards of normality, which locates the problem in the person rather than in society's understanding of ability. Although efforts have been made to

"normalize" participants so that they can engage in mainstream activities, there has *not* been a concerted effort to critically examine the conceptualization, delivery, and evaluation of how we teach students with disabilities in health and physical education (Harvey, 2016).

Here are some suggestions for reflection and action:

- *Improving the experiences of students.* Use person-first language that begins by considering the whole person and identifies the disability secondarily. Get to know your students and ask them what they can and cannot participate in.
- *Changing the knowledge about students.* Plan activities that don't depend on ability or disability. For example, sitting volleyball, wheelchair basketball, and bocce are excellent activities for any student.
- *Challenging the social dynamics.* Ask students to do an inventory of the school to assess how accessible it is. Invite a guest speaker or connect with a community organization focused on accessibility to expose students to people who live with various disabilities.
- *Addressing reasons why.* Ask students why they think it is so difficult to make society more accessible.

Gender

Health and physical education has a long and gendered history (Penney, 2002). For example, early researchers studying physical education found that different activities were taught to boys than to girls, that girls were socialized into "female" activities (e.g., gymnastics, dance), and that boys were socialized into "male" activities (e.g., football, baseball, hockey). Researchers have also pointed out differences in the origins of physical education teacher training for males and for females. Specifically, the training of male teachers was informed by militarism and competitive team games, whereas the training of female teachers was informed by physical activities such as dance, gymnastics, and games.

It has been argued that these historical differences continue to powerfully influence ideas about masculinity, femininity, and physicality in health and physical education (Flintoff & Scraton, 2004). For example, such ideas influence cultural norms about behaviour (e.g., violence in sport), attitudes (e.g., "girls don't sweat"), language (e.g., "playing like a girl"), and clothing (e.g., differential clothing standards). Although many efforts have been made to shift this culture, gender stereotyping remains largely unchallenged and is often reproduced. Fortunately, an increasing number of people are calling attention to the need for health and physical education to move beyond binary constructions of "male" and "female" and toward allowing students the opportunity to live in their diverse and multiple subjective identities (Sykes, 2011).

Here are some suggestions for reflection and action:

- *Improving the experiences of students.* Ask students what activities they like and don't like, whether competitive or noncompetitive. Build your curriculum around their preferences. Ask them what motivates them. Use different ways of evaluating course engagement.
- *Changing the knowledge about students.* Include role models of all genders in your class. Include activities that highlight gender similarities and differences. Discuss the differences between the terms *gender*, *sex*, and *sexual orientation*.
- *Challenging the social dynamics.* Have students check school policies to ensure that they are gender neutral. Pay attention to language and language preferences.
- *Addressing reasons why.* Engage students in discussions about gender and sport. Examine assumptions and stereotypes about gender. Explore ways in which physical activity and sport continue to be gendered and how they could be made more inclusive.

Body Size

Just as students come in many heights, they also come in many different shapes and sizes. Unfortunately, despite this diversity, schools are permeated with a Western cultural ideal that privileges thinness and shames fatness (Cameron et al., 2014). This culture is driven by a way of thinking that equates body size and shape with negative lifestyle behaviours such as irresponsibility and lack of willpower but fails to include other, more serious social determinants of health. Increasingly, researchers are highlighting how this ideal has led not only to harmful attitudes toward and

judgments of larger body sizes but also to a shadow epidemic of weight bias expressed as fat bullying (Cameron & Russell, 2016). Research has shown that fat bullying occurs most often in physical activity settings and that health and physical education teachers are significantly influenced by this culture (Tinning, Philpot, & Cameron, 2016).

Here are some suggestions for reflection and action:

This culture is driven by a way of thinking that equates body size and shape with negative lifestyle behaviours such as irresponsibility and lack of willpower but fails to include other, more serious social determinants of health.

- *Improving the experiences of students.* Take time at the beginning of a course to develop a class contract that addresses how to create a supportive environment. Institute a policy of zero body-based bullying. Create an environment in which all students feel safe to participate and are aware of the need to prevent the harm caused by fat bullying.
- *Changing the knowledge about students.* Promote the idea that health comes in many shapes and sizes. Never focus on body weight; focus instead on wellness and quality of life.
- *Challenging the social dynamics.* Challenge how healthy bodies are portrayed in society. Try to find examples of different body shapes and sizes being active so that all your students can see themselves in role models.
- *Addressing reasons why.* Explore the political, social, and historical contexts of obesity with students (see Campos, 2004; Gard 2011; Gard & Wright, 2005) to help them better understand the many different perspectives about the complex relationship between health and weight. Identify the ways in which we give meaning and make associations about health and bodies, and explore ways to think differently (Cameron, Norman & Petherick, 2016).

Summary

This chapter provides you with a base from which to start thinking about how to address diversity in health and physical education. Though it only scratches the surface, I hope that it provides helpful points of reflection and practical ideas for you to use in your own teaching. I hope that you come away with the following key learnings: deeper understanding of some key diversity issues in health and physical education; deeper understanding of how to address diversity through inclusive teaching practices; and appreciation of the value of examining your own privilege as a teacher so that you can become aware of your attitudes, beliefs, and behaviours in regard to health and physical education. As educator and author Parker Palmer writes in *The Courage to Teach* (2010), "Good teaching cannot be reduced to technique; good teaching comes from the identity and integrity of the teacher" (p. 10). The more we can be aware of who we are as teachers, the better and more reflective teachers we can become.

DISCUSSION QUESTIONS

1. What is the meaning of diversity?
2. What are the benefits of addressing diversity in health and physical education?
3. What are the major issues related to diversity in health and physical education?
4. What is the difference between diversity and inclusion?
5. How can inclusion help address diversity in health and physical education?
6. How can inclusive environments be created in health and physical education?
7. What are some inclusive activities that can be used in health and physical education?

 Visit the web resource for ready-to-use activities that help raise awareness of social justice issues.

Voices From the Field

Kristen Downey

Teacher education candidate, Newfoundland and Labrador

I am a preservice teacher majoring in physical education in St. John's, Newfoundland and Labrador. To date my teaching experience is limited to course placements. During my placement in a local school, there was certainly a diverse group in most classes in terms of race, gender, culture, and many other domains. I was amazed how collaborative they were in physical education classes. It was heartwarming to see young students who are oblivious to personal differences.

In many classes while I was teaching, there would be students struggling in certain activities while others mastered it quickly. Throughout my placement, I had to make adjustments in how I designed and delivered activities to the students so that they would be meaningful to their individual learning. This kind of environment benefits a wide range of diverse learners in that it provided a safe and fun environment for them to be themselves outside a typical classroom setting. Students tried harder and enjoyed the experience of physical education class much more when proper adjustments were embedded in the lessons. It was not easy to adapt to the great diversity of this school as a beginning teacher with minimal practical teaching experience, but when I did adjust my teaching strategies it was clearly worth it for the students.

One activity that I included in a basketball unit during my teaching experience was a directions activity. In an athletic stance, students followed the teacher's motions to know which way to move or what action to do. This activity is excellent for progressions in any unit, and it allows the students to participate at their own pace and skill level. One new student in the class who spoke very little English thoroughly enjoyed this activity, and it enabled him to succeed in an activity where he integrated perfectly with his peers. For the personal development and overall cooperation of the class, activities like this allow for a diverse group of students to participate equally and have fun with their own levels of success. Activities in which differences between students are irrelevant worked well during my teaching experience in the school.

Learning about student diversity in today's schools is one thing, but experiencing and adapting to the needs of students in our schools is another. It was very important for me, as a beginning teacher, to adapt my teaching so that the lessons and activities I create would be more effective in achieving the curriculum outcomes. Many of us new teachers initially think that simply being aware of the diversity is enough to be an effective physical education teacher. As I've learned through my studies, however, we need much more than that. Practical experience and advice from experienced teachers are invaluable for us to be fully aware and supportive to the diversity in physical education classes.

CHAPTER 6

Infusing Indigenous Games and Perspectives Within HPE

Mary Courchene ■ **Blair Robillard**
Amy Carpenter ■ **Joannie Halas**

After studying this chapter, you will be able to

- articulate how Indigenous perspectives can enhance teaching and learning in health and physical education;

- identify ethical and respectful ways to engage with Indigenous students, colleagues, parents, families, and communities in your area;

- incorporate Indigenous knowledge in ways that respect local culture, protocol, and customs;

- describe how holistic approaches to health and well-being can be used in learning activities in the gymnasium, classroom, and outdoors;

- create learning opportunities that include the games and activities described in this chapter; and

- play Indigenous cultural games that allow your body, heart, mind, and spirit to flourish.

Medicine Wheel teachings tell us that we all work toward *Mino' Pimatisiwin* (living a good life). *Mino' Pimatisiwin* is also known as *mino-bimaadiziwin* (using Roman orthography) for the Anishinaabe (Ojibwe), the Innenew (Cree), and the Anishinino (Ojibwe Cree); as *honso ayinnai* for the Dene people; and as *tokatakiya wichoni washte* for the Dakota people (Manitoba First Nations Education Resource Centre, 2008, p. v). Living *Mino' Pimatisiwin* includes the balance of a physical, emotional, mental, and spiritual self. When we live *Mino' Pimatisiwin*, we experience a good life because of balance in all quadrants of Medicine Wheel symbolism and teachings. Recognizing the interconnectedness of all things, we strive for a good life not only for ourselves but also to benefit our families and all peoples (Manitoba First Nations Education Resource Centre, 2008, p. 111). Foundational to achieving *Mino' Pimatisiwin* are the values of sharing and respect (Hart, 2002).

In this chapter, we illustrate how Indigenous teachings related to *Mino' Pimatisiwin* can be used to enrich the experience of health and physical education for learners of all ages, and especially for children. The holistic philosophies of Indigenous peoples—in which the physical, emotional, mental, and spiritual aspects of our human nature are embraced (Lane, Bopp, Bopp, & Brown, 2003)—resonates very well in physical education curricula (Halas, 2014; Kalyn, Cameron, Arcand, & Baker, 2013). The term *Indigenous* refers to the original peoples of a territory. Canada's Indigenous peoples, often referred to as Aboriginal, include First Nations, Inuit, and Métis peoples. There are 617 First Nations communities across Canada, and First Nations peoples often identify themselves by the nation to which they belong.

Given Canada's colonial history, care must be taken to ensure that this knowledge is infused respectfully and ethically. Working with and led by Indigenous teachers, students, Elders, cultural advisors, and colleagues, non-Indigenous teacher educator Brenda Kalyn has shown us how Indigenous knowledges can be introduced ethically into the mainstream (health) and physical education curriculum in ways that value and affirm local knowledges, protocols, and customs, thus ensuring that the teachings are not culturally misappropriated. To put it another way, educators are encouraged to create opportunities for students "to engage in learning experiences *through* Indigenous knowledge, which should be done *through* local Indigenous peoples" (Battiste, as cited in Kalyn et al., 2013, p. 159). We have added

the italics in this citation to emphasize the need to respect local Indigenous knowledge, customs, and protocols in our teaching and learning.

In adherence to this advice, a key purpose of this chapter is to show how the teachings of *Mino' Pimatisiwin* are understood and expressed by Anishinaabe Elder Mary Courchene and translated through the pedagogical practices of a teacher of traditional Indigenous games and culture, Blair Robillard; Métis educator Amy Carpenter; and non-Indigenous health and physical education scholar Joannie Halas. Our collaborative work is a product of years of relationship building and trust that we hope will serve as a helpful example for you in your own teaching practice and school. Whatever your cultural origins, this chapter invites you to join a renewal process that honours and affirms the rich Indigenous cultures, teachings, and world views originating on Turtle Island (known as North America in Western terms).

When infusing Indigenous perspectives into your teaching and learning, always respect local Indigenous knowledge, customs, and protocols.

Creating a New Narrative for Turtle Island

Children want to be active. And young people crave a sense of identity; therefore, it is essential that they see themselves reflected in their schools, classrooms, curricula, and health and physical education settings. Situated as we are on Turtle Island, where Indigenous peoples have lived since time immemorial, our school spaces and all aspects of society should be infused with Indigenous knowledge, culture, and ways of being in the world. For the most part, however, this is not the case, and many Indigenous students do not see their cultural heritage affirmed in their school curriculum or their school experiences. Canada's long and damaging story of colonization—which includes attempted cultural genocide, wherein generations of Indigenous children were removed from their families and communities in order to attend Indian Residential Schools—distorts our current context and the intercultural relationships we build as Indigenous and non-Indigenous peoples. As Thomas King (2012) so eloquently explains, present day realities are shaped by our historical past.

As Indigenous and non-Indigenous educators, we believe that the peoples of Turtle Island have an opportunity to co-create a new narrative that reflects an emerging collective story, including the significant role that First Nations, Métis, and Inuit peoples and communities have played and continue to play in our complex and interconnected spaces. As a preface to the information we share here, we begin with a statement that acknowledges the Indigenous peoples of the territories where we live and work, and we encourage you to adopt similar statements in your own teaching. We have borrowed the wording for this statement from the University of Manitoba (n.d., n.p.), which defines its mission and commitment to reconciliation through its Indigenous achievement strategic priorities. For our purposes, we have made small modifications to the statement you read here:

> [We acknowledge that the work we do is] located on the original lands of Anishinaabeg, Cree, Oji-Cree, Dakota, and Dene peoples, and on the homeland of the Métis Nation. . . . [We are committed to a renewed relationship and dialogue with First Nations, Métis, and Inuit peoples based on the principles of mutual trust, respect, and reciprocity]. We respect the Treaties that were made on these territories, we acknowledge the harms and mistakes of the past, and we dedicate ourselves to move forward in partnership with Indigenous communities [and the community as a whole] in a spirit of reconciliation and collaboration.

When working in the context of an enduring colonial mind-set that denigrates the cultural identities of Indigenous peoples, it is an ethical imperative for us to acknowledge the original peoples of the lands we currently occupy, as well as our commitment to respect and reconciliation. In the remainder of this chapter, we share our personal interpretations of the teachings we have learned and how we use them.

Mino' Pimatisiwin: Living a Balanced Life

In Indigenous communities, knowledge has been and continues to be passed on from one generation to the next in the form of stories. Traditional teachings that share Indigenous knowledge and wisdom have been informed by empirical observations and revelations; these stories are personal and holistic and often use narrative or metaphorical language (Battiste & Youngblood Henderson,

2000; Brant Castellano, 2000; Thomas, 2005). For Indigenous peoples, oral traditions offer an explanation of who we are and how we have come to be; thus they provide a means to connect to and understand our interconnected worlds. Many Indigenous beliefs are based on traditional oral teachings.

One example of storied First Nations' knowledge that has been communicated from one generation to the next can be found in Medicine Wheel teachings. Symbolically, the Medicine Wheel is a circle with four interconnected quadrants, each of which represents one of the four directions—east, south, west, and north—and has teachings that apply to that direction (see figure 6.1). Although many aspects of the Medicine Wheel have shared concepts, such as wholeness, balance, connectedness (relationships), harmony, growth, and healing (Hart, 2002), people may carry different knowledge and teachings associated with each of the four directions. In addition, these teachings may be applied in different ways.

The teachings of *Mino' Pimatisiwin* provide an example of traditional knowledge that has been shared intergenerationally across diverse First Nations peoples. In this chapter, Elder Mary Courchene shares the traditional teachings of *Mino' Pimatisiwin* that have been entrusted to her. Mary is a retired teacher, administrator, community leader, parent, grandparent, and Indian Residential School survivor who was the inaugural principal at the first Indigenous-focused high

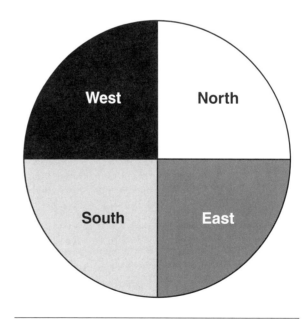

Figure 6.1 The Medicine Wheel.

school in Winnipeg, Manitoba. She is frequently an invited guest in university classes, public schools, and community gatherings. Here, she shares with us the teachings of *Mino' Pimatisiwin* as she has come to know them.

Teaching Active Life and Learning

Elder Mary Courchene

Early in my teaching career, many years ago, I sat down with an Elder who explained to me what *Mino' Pimatisiwin* has always meant to our people, the peoples of Turtle Island. And it made perfect sense to me. *Mino' Pimatisiwin* is about balance; it is about living a good life. It is knowing all parts of one's self and finding solace in that knowing. As I listened to the Elder and reflected on all he had to share, it was like the completion of a jigsaw puzzle from the stories that my dad used to tell me before my residential school years. I really understood *Mino' Pimatisiwin* and recognized that the symbolism of the Medicine Wheel teachings provided guidance for how people could intrinsically and communally live a good life. Unfortunately, I was locked into a system that I felt powerless to challenge at that time. It is different now! Indigenous ways and being are now legitimate in our school system and will be included as part of true inclusiveness.

> *Mino' Pimatisiwin is about balance; it is about living a good life. It is knowing all parts of one's self and finding solace in that knowing.*

For me, *Mino-Pimatisiwin* means "balance" in all aspects of the body and spirit. As you move through life, you are born and begin in the east, which is *physical*. When you are a little baby, this begins the good life, generally speaking. As you progress, by the time you are a teenager, you are in the south direction, which is *emotional*. In the south direction, the emotional and social are together; they are not apart. It is a time when social interactions are important. Emotions are overflowing as young people enter this important phase of life. Adolescence is a time for illumination, friendship, exploration, and extremism; where we might see a teenager, for adolescents, it is another world for them. They are not yet fully developed cognitively, and it is a period of real growth and development.

The west direction is *intellectual*, also known as mental or cognitive; the west represents adult

life. And the north is *spiritual*; it is a time for elders to reflect on their lives, allowing wisdom to manifest. It is a time for sharing, a time for spiritual wisdom to emerge. As one Elder taught me, "Spirituality is your core being." It is always there through the ages. It is your core, and when you reach the north, it should flourish in a time for sharing.

As we move through the Medicine Wheel of life, sometimes we become stuck. If we are hurt by a traumatic occurrence while we are in a certain direction, we can get stuck there even though physically we have progressed. For example, we may still think as a teenager, adopt a narrow perspective, as though our brain has stopped developing, until we do some healing. As Michael Hart (2002) explains, "When individuals are not balanced within, [when they are] disconnected in their relationships, or in disharmony with their environment, change is required. . . . [W]hen an individual attempts to remain in a 'stuck' balanced state, their growth is hindered because the world around them continues to change" (p. 102). Indigenous ways tell us that the issues that hold us back need to be explored, dealt with, and healed. Explore them in depth and you move on quickly.

As we move forward on our reconciliation path, active life and learning are what our teachings are all about; to experience life is medicine along our Medicine Wheel of life. Strive for balance across all directions and you will live the good life.

Playing It Forward With Games and Activities: The Original Intent of Play

Blair Robillard

My name is Blair Robillard; the name that carries me is "North Star Man." My work is inspired by students and colleagues who share and practice the value of traditional Indigenous teachings such as *Mino' Pimatisiwin*. Through many interactions with Elders and traditional knowledge keepers, I have come to understand that the teachings I have acquired through story, research, experience, and creativity are meant to be shared. They are not right or wrong, but valid from my understanding and

> *If it is not kind and gentle, it is wrong. Just be clear about your thoughts, feelings, values, and beliefs; these are not right or wrong, but valid from one's own life and experiences.*

experiences related to the Medicine Wheel teachings that have been shared with me.

The four directions or components of the Medicine Wheel are related to the four components of games and activities. As with the Medicine Wheel teachings shared by Mary, each game and activity has components related to the four directions. Within a play perspective, I teach these components under the names of social and emotional, physical, observational, and strategic. One or two of these directions or components are emphasized in each play activity. As educators, instructors, and coaches, we can highlight specific components to identify the players' strengths and challenges. From this assessment, we can identify areas in which our players are successful, respectfully appreciate them, and introduce developmental activities to increase their abilities or capacities while accepting where they are challenged.

The games and activities shared with you in the web resource for this chapter originate from the Ojibwe, Cree, Oji-Cree, Plains Cree, Rock Cree, Dakota, Assiniboine, Dene, and Métis peoples. Traditional games incorporated purpose with principle; many Dene games, for example, were used to develop both physical skills and cooperation in support of land-based ways of life (Heine, 2013). Games also reinforced the social, political, economic, and spiritual aspects of life; for instance, they included ceremonies and emphasized harmony with the natural world (Hall, 2013). They are as influential and sacred as dance, songs, drumming, music, storytelling, rituals, and practices of traditional ceremonial values and beliefs. When you play these games, keep in mind the rich traditions of the peoples who played them years ago. The games included in the web resource—Four Directions Circle, Gentle Always Wins, Foxtail Toss, Screaming Eagle, Métis Wheel Tag, and Balancing the Four Directions—speak to both traditional Indigenous and contemporary cultural games that are popular among children of all ages.

The Circle We All Share as a Way of Being

Amy Carpenter

I entered the field of education because I saw a need for children and youth to feel loved, cherished, and recognized for all of the gifts they have to offer. As Elders often say, our young people are full of gifts, strengths, promise, and capacity. Particularly for Indigenous children and youth,

I believe it is our job to tap into these capacities rather than make continual attempts to assimilate them into a perceived norm of dominant culture. As a Métis woman from the Red River settlement, a family and community member, an educator, and a vice principal in an urban Winnipeg elementary school, I enter the world with a circular perspective. Similar to a wheel, this circular world view is made of many interrelated pieces that each support and rely on the others (Coalition for the Advancement of Aboriginal Studies, 2002; Lane et al., 2003). The wheel is circular, with no definitive starting or end point. Many of the teachings from nature follow a circular path—for example, seasonal patterns, animal life cycles, and the cycle of day and night. These are some of the teachings that inform circular world views. In an interconnected circular world view, there is a space and place for all peoples, all animals, all spirits, all perspectives.

Part of how I live and teach *Mino' Pimatisiwin* lies in the way I interact nonhierarchically with peoples of all ages. In my day-to-day interactions, I often incorporate talking circles, wherein each individual in the circle has an opportunity to speak while everyone else listens. People know that they can pass if they choose. Whatever one chooses, the circle reinforces that everyone in it shares power; everyone's opinions and perspectives are valued and inform our understanding of the questions at hand. I often incorporate talking circles as a place for everyone to share their thoughts, feelings, opinions, and questions.

The use of talking circles offers a place for us to connect, affirm our sense of belonging, and see that each other's successes rely on our multiple perspectives and abilities. As Hampton (1995) noted, "reflective thinking" (p. 13) offers participants as well as the initiator of the conversation the opportunity to build thoughts together. Not everyone speaks each time, but everyone knows that the opportunity is there. The use of talking circles over many years and with different groups of learners has illustrated for me how this Indigenous practice is always welcomed as creating a good space for discussion. It is also helpful to be reminded that Creator gave us two ears and one

> *The talking circle reinforces that everyone within it shares power; everyone's opinions and perspectives are valued and inform our understanding of the questions at hand. Thus it provides a place for everyone to share their thoughts, feelings, opinions, and questions.*

mouth; therefore, we should listen twice as much as we talk. We live *Mino' Pimatisiwin* through the time and attention we give to each other.

Affirming Indigenous Pathways to Health and Wellness

Joannie Halas

I first became aware of the notion of body, mind, and spirit as key components of healthy development when I was moving through adolescence as a leader-in-training at the YMCA. Years later, as a middle-years physical educator, I often observed how students experienced my pedagogy using a holistic lens. In addition to students' physical movements, I paid attention to their facial expressions and how they interacted with each other. I noticed the child who hid behind the bleachers, afraid to participate, as well as the child who became larger than life in a physical activity environment. And I worked purposefully to encourage students to treat each other better in the gym and to promote the values of caring and respect that resonate in the learning climate. Today, as a university educator with a heritage rooted in North End Winnipeg and East European settlers, I am learning from and embracing Indigenous ways of knowing as strategic pathways to promoting health and wellness.

I begin my first-year games courses by explicitly introducing students to the Medicine Wheel teachings that Elder Mary, Amy, and others have shared with me, as well as the holistic games and activities that Blair has taught me. As part of my intercultural pedagogy, I incorporate the Indigenous values of interdependence and reciprocity. In each introductory class, we engage in a variety of mixer games. These activities are designed to be both physically engaging and socially interactive in ways that quickly transform first-year university students' awkward silence into shared laughter. Once the students are up and moving and getting to know each other through simple activities that are easy to do, I call them over to the whiteboard, where I have drawn a circle with the body, mind, heart, and spirit each located in one of the four directions. Here, I begin the term by acknowledging the territories and traditions of the First Nations, Métis, and Dene peoples who have always lived on the lands now known as Manitoba. I emphasize how we can be proud of Indigenous cultural traditions that have much to contribute to health and physical education.

To illustrate the interconnectedness of the four directions, I ask students to reflect on the activities in which we have just engaged, and we use our senses to describe the learning climate. *What did you hear, see, and feel during the game?* (Laughter, movement, lots of smiling faces . . .) *What was your body doing? What were you feeling and how were you interacting? What were you thinking?* Then I ask questions about spiritual engagement, which Elder Mary describes as "the core of who we are." *As individuals, has your sense of identity been affirmed in the class?*

Thinking back to my work with younger children and youths in the public school system, I recall how important it was for me to ask, *How affirmed do my students feel in my class?* Pedagogically, I reached out to build relationships with my students in ways that communicated to them that I was completely supportive of who they were as individuals in my class, no matter their background or socialized identity. If they were shy and reluctant to participate, I accepted that and encouraged them to try their best, whatever their best might be. If they were fully engaged and outgoing, I welcomed and encouraged their enthusiasm. If they were sometimes disrespectful, I challenged them to think about how their actions affected others, including me.

No matter what, I always tried to engage in ways that respected who they were and, when necessary, I carefully distinguished between behaviour and the individual performing the action. Thinking about issues of gender, race, class, body size, ability, and other socially constructed hierarchies, I did my best to affirm how students saw themselves within the intercultural social world around them and paid particular attention to those who were vulnerable to marginalization and exclusion. I was determined that the core of being of the students in my class would be respected and affirmed. Today, I strive to always have students leave the gym feeling that their sense of identity is intact, and I pay attention to how my students' bodies, minds, hearts, and spirits are experiencing the learning activities I have set up. Interpreted within the concepts of *Mino' Pimatisiwin*, I am hoping to model the importance of balance in all four directions, with the spiritual as a guidepost for testing the effectiveness of my pedagogies.

> Indigenous perspectives remind us to always affirm the personal and cultural identities of our students and to teach in ways that uplift the spirit of every student in every class.

Balancing the Four Directions: *Mino' Pimatisiwin* as Formative Assessment

In this final section, we conclude with a simple activity that illustrates how the concept of *Mino' Pimatisiwin* can be used to assess student progress, both individually and collectively, in our health and physical education classes (see activity 6 in the web resource). As students prepare to exit the class, ask them to identify how balanced they are in terms of the four directions. Using your circle with the four directions on the whiteboard, place a 0 at the centre and draw a line to the outside of the circle for each direction (body, mind, heart, spirit), where you will place the number 10. Invite students, individually or in groups, to leave a mark along the line between 0 and 10 in each quadrant of the Medicine Wheel to represent how their bodies, hearts, minds, and spirits are experiencing the activities just performed, with 10 indicating strengths and 0 indicating challenges. Are all components in balance? As individuals, are they stuck in some areas? If so, what can they do to address any imbalances? In smaller groups or as a class, can we collectively assess how balanced we are in terms of our active engagement, our social interactions, and our mastery of strategies and skills, as well as how affirmed our spirits are in the learning activities? By closing out the day's activities with this simple check-in, we are reminded that living *Mino' Pimatisiwin* calls us to strive for the good life, not only for ourselves but also for each other.

Summary

In Canada, we are living in an exciting time. By recognizing Indigenous knowledges and infusing them into our pedagogies, we give health and physical education an important role to play in the process of reconciliation and renewal (Halas, 2014). As with other Indigenous approaches to health and physical education (Kalyn et al., 2013; Robinson, Barrett, & Robinson, 2016), the teachings and games we have introduced here reinforce the value of Indigenous approaches in mainstream education. It is important for us to tap into Indigenous knowledges, cultures, and experiences—traditional, historical, and contemporary—because our collective history predicates and defines who we are.

The holistic awareness of *Mino' Pimatisiwin* is what we have learned, as well as the way we learn, behave, teach, and share as mentors, parents, educators, leaders, and role models. Our connection with our past teaches us how significant relationships are within the scope of our seven generations: the three generations before us, our own life, and the three generations ahead of us. When health and physical education is informed and infused with Indigenous teachings and world views that respect local customs and protocols, it has much to offer to our personal and collective desires for health, wellness, and a strong identity as a diverse nation with deep Indigenous roots.

DISCUSSION QUESTIONS

1. Who are the First Nations, Inuit, and Métis peoples in the territories where you live, study, and work? What is your familial cultural heritage? How might you acknowledge the contributions of Indigenous peoples in a statement that affirms your own commitment to reconciliation and renewal?

2. How do teachings that emphasize *Mino' Pimatisiwin* and "holism" compare with Western models of teaching and learning? With Eastern models? With other Indigenous teachings?

3. Why do holistic models and teachings resonate well in health and physical education? How might you describe your own physical activity experience in holistic ways?

4. How might you feel when playing the traditional and contemporary Indigenous games and activities shared in this chapter? How might your interconnected body, heart, mind, and spirit experience the activities?

5. Do you know a traditional Indigenous teaching or game to share with your peers or students? What are the ethical considerations when sharing such knowledge?

6. What can you do, through health and physical education, to contribute to the process of reconciliation and renewal?

 Visit the web resource for ready-to-use activities that introduce and reinforce Indigenous values.

Voices From the Field

Blair Robillard

Teacher of traditional Indigenous cultural and historic games and teachings, Manitoba

I have taught at the University of Manitoba, University College of the North, Red River College, and K-12 schools and community agencies throughout Manitoba. I have also taught at camps and festivals and nature-based organizations. Each year, I share my gifts as "*Scabee*" (a working warrior) at Sundances and various Indigenous ceremonies across Manitoba. Over the past decade, I have been a cultural and games educator for the Rec and Read Aboriginal Youth Mentorship Program for All Nations.

I teach diverse populations of students across all levels, from elementary school through postsecondary education, particularly in physical education, social work, native studies, and sociology. My cultural workshops have included students with disabilities, children and youths with emotional and behavioural difficulties, adults, Elders, and olders (people who are older adults). Basically, I teach "kids" of all ages. I have been collecting and creating games based on Indigenous cultural practices and perspectives since I was 18. That makes for 40 years of paying attention to games and how valuable they are to society.

As you have learned in this chapter, I follow a holistic teaching and learning approach that identifies and uses a strengths-based, capacity-building component in health and physical education environments. My goal in being a holistic educator is to provide a service as a guide to the participants, or students, with whom I work. I am there to provide the opportunity for them to learn however is best for them. I'm not the boss! They are the instruments of their own learning. These guiding principles include the notion that play is symbolic of intrinsic motivation without externally imposed rules. I create a space where "what if" and "as if" can be explored and where rules and regulations are established in collaboration with the players. I know I am successful as soon as laughter is shared among the participants, which usually occurs within the first 30 seconds and throughout the day. Through laughter we are united in a safe environment and learning space in which we can discover who we are as both individual and collective holistic beings.

I love to teach the Screaming Eagle game to children, youths, adults, and even members of our oldest populations. Here is why: Screaming Eagle includes all four components of game play—the physical component of breath, speed, and endurance; the emotional context of challenging oneself to move outside of the box and be creative in one's expression; the mental aspect of the strategy of screaming while running (e.g., *how long can you hold your breath?*); and the spiritual component or social context, in which explosive laughter ensues with each runner's attempt to run as far as possible with one breath. The laughter unites our spirits.

For the Ojibwe, Screaming Eagle was an endurance test to see who could run the farthest in one breath; screaming indicated the distance run because you must stop running as soon as you can no longer scream. The Araphora tribe in what is now the southern United States (near the Apache) did a similar activity called *Whoo yee*; instead of screaming, they yelled "whoo yee" as they ran. The Ojibwe game was played between individuals, whereas the Araphora ran in groups. Note: The preference is to do this activity outdoors; it is loud, and when played inside can create a noxious auditory environment.

How do you know you've achieved your learning outcomes with Screaming Eagle? Thinking holistically, the bonding that occurs between the players is evident in their support of each other's attempts and their challenging of both themselves and others to see who can go the farthest or make the most creative scream last the longest!

PART II

Teaching
Health Education

Recommendations for Quality Health Education Teaching

Joe Barrett ■ **Chunlei Lu** ■ **Jillian Janzen**

LEARNING OUTCOMES

After studying this chapter, you will be able to

- describe why health education is taught in K-12 schools in Canada,
- define health literacy as an achievable outcome of quality health education,
- explain the importance of improving health literacy through the provision of health education opportunities, and
- incorporate seven key recommendations into health education teaching practice.

Imagine a town hall meeting where Canadian parents and family members have gathered to discuss what they want most for their children and youth. Imagine further that the participants have set aside any thoughts of material needs or desires. What is it, then, that they will want for their children—through elementary school, high school, and beyond? If we could listen in on these conversations, we would likely hear many hopeful anecdotes, as well as some fears. We would also hear a lot about people wanting what's best for their children and hoping that they will find ways to do and be better than prior generations. More analytically, if we consider what patterns a researcher might find in these conversations, we quickly think of themes such as living healthily, feeling happy, and finding fulfillment in both career and personal life.

On a larger scale, as a country, we want what's best for our Canadian children and youth, and we understand that Canadian schools play an important role in preparing our young people for the future. Canadian teachers help equip young people with the knowledge, skills, and understandings to make decisions that will help them succeed both personally and professionally. As part of this work, Canadian teachers exert a large influence on students' health-related choices. This influence is sometimes forgotten as people get caught up in career goals and pathways and lose sight of those who have helped them maintain or improve their health and happiness.

With that context in mind, this chapter focuses on four key considerations: (a) the rationale for health education and its prominent place in K-12 curricula across Canada, (b) the relationship between health education and health literacy, (c) the fact that health literacy is both important and achievable, and (d) recommendations to support elementary teachers of health education. We begin by reminding teachers and prospective teachers of health education that our children and youth spend a disproportionate amount of time in school between the ages of 4 and 17 years. Given that students spend so many of their hours in school, it makes sense from a public health standpoint for our schools to provide students with consistent opportunities for targeted health-promoting interventions that are driven primarily through health education.

Canadian teachers help equip young people with the knowledge, skills, and understandings to make decisions that will help them succeed both personally and professionally. As part of this work, Canadian teachers exert a large influence on students' health-related choices.

Why Do We Teach Health Education in Our Schools?

Thus far in the 21st century, the lives of Canadian K-12 students have been marked by drastic change and daunting challenges. More specifically, "school-age children and youth may face an array of health challenges, such as violence, poverty, food insecurity, sexually transmitted infections, smoking, substance misuse, and physical inactivity" (Rootman & Gordon-El-Bihbety, 2008, p. 25). Moreover, increasing numbers of our Canadian children and youth face challenges associated with mental health, such as depression, anxiety, and difficulty coping with stressors (Canadian Mental Health Association, 2011). In addition, elementary students are often targeted through emerging user-driven technologies that have changed the ways in which they communicate, access, interpret, and use information.

These health-related challenges and communication changes underpin a variety of emerging predicaments faced by Canadian families. Therefore, parents, caregivers, and society as a whole need schools—and specifically teachers of health education—to provide learning opportunities that help students develop the necessary knowledge and skills to accomplish the following key tasks:

- Understanding themselves and others
- Thinking critically
- Making and promoting healthy choices
- Developing and maintaining healthy relationships
- Being safe, both physically and emotionally
- Being physically active for life and thriving (Ontario Ministry of Education, 2014, p. 1)

In response to this need, 21st-century teachers are challenged to continually reevaluate the following crucial factors in their work: (a) emerging and entrenched teaching philosophies, (b) teaching methods and approaches, (c) tools and resources for teaching, and (d) understandings of provincial and territorial curricular requirements. This reevaluation raises an important question: What exactly are the stated aims that underpin health education curricula across Canada? To address that question, table 7.1 provides a cross-Canada overview of publicly stated goals and visions for

Sample of Provincial and Territorial
Goal and Vision Statements for Health Education

Province or territory	Goal or vision statement	Curriculum document resource
Alberta	"The aim of the Health and Life Skills Kindergarten to Grade 9 Program of Studies is to enable students to make well-informed, healthy choices and to develop behaviours that contribute to the well-being of self and others. To achieve this aim, students require an understanding of self as the basis for healthy interactions with others and for career development and lifelong learning. Students also require a safe and caring school and community environment in which to explore ideas and issues surrounding personal choice, to seek accurate information, and to practise healthy behaviours" (Alberta Education, 2002, n.p.).	Health & Life Skills K–Grade 9 (2002) www.learnalberta.ca/ProgramOfStudy.aspx?lang=en&ProgramId=317413#355116
British Columbia	"The BC Physical and Health Education curriculum contributes to students' development as educated citizens through the achievement of the following goals. Students are expected to • develop an understanding of the many aspects of well-being, including physical, mental, and social; • develop the movement knowledge, skills, and understandings needed for lifelong participation in a range of physical activities; • develop knowledge, skills, and strategies for building respectful relationships, positive self-identity, self-determination, and mental well-being; [and] • demonstrate the knowledge, skills, and strategies needed to make informed decisions that support personal and community health and safety." (British Columbia Ministry of Education, 2016, n.p.)	Physical and Health Education: British Columbia (2016) https://curriculum.gov.bc.ca/curriculum/physical-health-education
Manitoba	"The aim of the [combined Physical Education/Health Education] curriculum is to provide students with planned and balanced programming to develop the knowledge, skills, and attitudes for physically active and healthy lifestyles" (Manitoba Education and Training, n.d., n.p.)."The aim of the [combined Physical Education/Health Education] curriculum is to provide students with planned and balanced programming to develop the knowledge, skills, and attitudes for physically active and healthy lifestyles" (Manitoba Education and Training, n.d., n.p.).	Manitoba Education and Training: Physical Education/Health Education www.edu.gov.mb.ca/k12/cur/physhlth/c_overview.html
New Brunswick	"Today's health education curriculum should teach essential knowledge; shape personal values and beliefs that support healthy behaviours; [and] develop essential health skills necessary to adopt, practice, and maintain health-enhancing behaviours. It has clear goals and behavioural outcomes, as well as instructional strategies and learning experiences that are related to the behavioural outcomes" (Department of Education and Early Childhood Development of New Brunswick, 2016, p. 13).	Education and Early Childhood Development http://www2.gnb.ca/content/gnb/en/departments/education/k12/content/anglophone_sector/curriculum_anglophone.html
Newfoundland	"As teachers, our role is to impress upon students the relevance of the health curriculum to becoming health literate. . . . It is the goal of this curriculum to provide students with the knowledge and skills to make decisions that promote optimum health. Through a variety of teaching and learning strategies, students will examine aspects of their own growth and development in relation to overall health. Equally important to bodily health is mental health. Family and friends play a significant role in the healthy development of our being. Students will reflect on the impact they have on others and develop strategies to deal with others in a positive way. Finally, the health of the environment is examined as a mechanism that sustains life. From the microcosm of our own homes to the community at large, individuals have a role to play in protecting the environment in which we live" (Newfoundland and Labrador Department of Education and Early Childhood Development, 2015, p. 20).	Education and Early Childhood Development: Health www.ed.gov.nl.ca/edu/k12/curriculum/guides/health/index.html

(continued)

TABLE 7.1 *(continued)*

Province or territory	Goal or vision statement	Curriculum document resource
Northwest Territories	"Health is a state of complete physical, mental, and social well-being. It is the result of a dynamic interdependence of these elements, as well as cultural and spiritual elements. . . . The major goals of the Northwest Territories School Health Program are • to provide factual information on the human body; • to enable students to develop skills that, along with the factual information, will allow them to make informed choices related to health; • to enhance students' self-esteem through self-understanding; • to enable students to develop attitudes which lead to positive lifestyle behaviours; and, • to promote positive lifestyle practices which are conducive to lifelong health" (Northwest Territories Department of Education, Culture and Employment and Department of Health and Social Services, 1995, pp. 4, 9).	Curriculum and School List: Health Studies https://www.ece.gov.nt.ca/en/services/nwt-curriculum-and-school-list/health-studies
Nova Scotia	"The purpose of health education in schools is to provide students with opportunities to practice and reinforce life skills in culturally and developmentally appropriate ways, while exploring a range of protective factors in an integrative manner that promotes health and prosocial behaviour. The understanding that the concept of health includes physical, mental, emotional, social and spiritual dimensions, is central to the effective delivery and capacity for students to achieve the general curriculum outcomes for health education. Health education contributes to the promotion of personal and social development, the prevention of health and social problems, and the protection of human rights" (Nova Scotia Department of Education and Early Childhood Development, 2013, p. 121).	Nova Scotia Curriculum Documents https://sapps.ednet.ns.ca/Cart/index.php?UID=MjIKdWwyMDE3MTYxNTAzMTQyLjExExMi4xNjIuMTky
Nunavut	*Note: Nunavut schools follow and adapt the Northwest Territories School Health Program (1995, 1996) to meet the needs of their students (Nunavut Department of Education, 2016, p. 3).* "Health is a state of complete physical, mental and social well-being. It is the result of a dynamic interdependence of these elements, as well as cultural and spiritual elements. . . . The major goals of the Northwest Territories School Health Program are • to provide factual information on the human body; • to enable students to develop skills that, along with the factual information, will allow them to make informed choices related to health; • to enhance students' self-esteem through self-understanding; • to enable students to develop attitudes which lead to positive lifestyle behaviours; and, to promote positive lifestyle practices which are conducive to lifelong health" (Northwest Territories Department of Education, Culture and Employment and Department of Health and Social Services, 1995, pp. 4, 9).	Curriculum and Learning Resources www.gov.nu.ca/education/information/curriculum-learning-resources-0
Ontario	"The revised health and physical education curriculum is based on the vision that the knowledge and skills students acquire in the program will benefit them throughout their lives and enable them to thrive in an ever-changing world by helping them develop health and physical literacy as well as the comprehension, capacity, and commitment they will need to lead healthy, active lives and promote healthy, active living" (Ontario Ministry of Education, 2015, p. 6).	The Ontario Curriculum: Grades 1-8: Health and Physical Education http://edu.gov.on.ca/eng/curriculum/elementary/health1to8.pdf
Prince Edward Island	"Health education involves learning about the habits, behaviours, interactions, and decisions related to healthy daily living and planning for the future. The home, school, and community play important roles in contributing to the healthy personal development of students by providing an opportunity for them to consider information and acquire, practise, and demonstrate strategies for dealing with the challenges of life and living. The aim of the health curriculum is to enable students to make well-informed, healthy choices and to develop behaviours that contribute to the well-being of self and others" (Prince Edward Island Department of Education, 2007, p. 5).	Health Curriculum: Grades 1 to 6 https://www.princeedwardisland.ca/en/information/education-early-learning-and-culture/health-curriculum

Province or territory	Goal or vision statement	Curriculum document resource
Saskatchewan	"The K-12 aim of the Saskatchewan health education curricula is to develop confident and competent students who understand, appreciate, and apply health knowledge, skills, and strategies throughout life. . . . The three K-12 goals of health education are [to] • develop the understanding, skills, and confidences necessary to take action to improve health; • make informed decisions based on health-related knowledge; and • apply decisions that will improve personal health and/or the health of others" (Saskatchewan Ministry of Education, n.d., n.p.).	Saskatchewan Curriculum—Education: The Future Within Us https://www.curriculum.gov.sk.ca/webapps/moe-curriculum-BBLEARN/index.jsp?view=goals&lang=en&subj=health_education&level=1
Yukon	*Note: Yukon schools use British Columbia's newly revised curriculum (2017-2018) to provide a basic framework while adapting it to "include Yukon context and Yukon First Nations' ways of knowing and doing in all grades" (Yukon Education, 2017, n.p.).* "The BC Physical and Health Education curriculum contributes to students' development as educated citizens through the achievement of the following goals. Students are expected to • develop an understanding of the many aspects of well-being, including physical, mental, and social; • develop the movement knowledge, skills, and understandings needed for lifelong participation in a range of physical activities; • develop knowledge, skills, and strategies for building respectful relationships, positive self-identity, self-determination, and mental well-being; [and] • demonstrate the knowledge, skills, and strategies needed to make informed decisions that support personal and community health and safety." (British Columbia Ministry of Education, 2016, n.p.)	Curriculum www.education.gov.yk.ca/curriculum.html

provincial and territorial health-education curricula.

As you can see, the scope of provincial and territorial health education goals and visions moves us far beyond simple retention of health-related knowledge. Rather, emphasis is directed toward helping Canadian students succeed in the following ways: (a) developing and practicing health-promoting skills; (b) making healthy decisions; (c) evaluating their current health-promoting attitudes, values, beliefs, habits, and behaviours; and (d) applying relevant health-related knowledge in their own lives based on both personal and external factors.

Speaking more broadly, health education is often viewed as pursuing the fundamental goal of health literacy. This concept, which is accepted and understood in Canada, addresses "the ability to access, comprehend, evaluate, and communicate information as a way to promote, maintain, and improve health in a variety of settings across the life-course" (Public Health Agency of Canada, n.d.). As distinct from medical and public health perspectives, health literacy in schools can be defined as the developmental competence and knowledge essential for healthy living (Lu & McLean, 2011).

Relationship Between Health Literacy and School Health Education

To fully understand the relationship between health literacy and health education, we can begin by exploring how traditional conceptions of literacy and health literacy relate to health outcomes. For instance, experts point to a strong relationship between literacy, educational level attained, and health:

"Six in 10 Canadian adults do not have the skills needed to adequately manage their health and health-care needs. The fact that there are more people with low levels of health literacy (60%) than there are with low levels of literacy (48%) suggests a difference between the two. In order to master health-literacy tasks, adults are usually required to use their prose literacy, document literacy, and numeracy skills simultaneously. In other words, health literacy involves more than the ability to read or understand numbers. Context matters, as does the ability to find, understand, evaluate, and communicate health-related information."

Canadian Council on Learning (2008, p. 2)

Because the childhood and adolescent years are foundational in determining future health, schools are viewed as key settings for the development of health literacy (Kilgour, Matthews, Christian, & Shire, 2015; Rootman & Gordon-El-Bihbety, 2008). Indeed, given the amount of time spent in school by Canadian public elementary students—roughly 3.3 million of them (Statistics Canada, 2017)—improvements in health literacy are likely to be achieved in part through school health education, which is an important component of a comprehensive school approach (see chapter 9).

The potential benefits of student learning related to health education outcomes may stretch beyond the classroom and into the home, thus positively influencing health literacy among family members.

For some teachers of health education, improving students' health literacy may require rethinking their own approaches to health education curricula and related outcomes. They may also find it useful to consider the effects of health education on health literacy. Though not easily measured, the potential benefits of student learning related to health education outcomes may stretch beyond the classroom and into the home, thus positively influencing health literacy among family members (e.g., parents, caregivers, siblings, extended family). This transfer effect may result from students making conscious choices to lead healthier lives and helping others to do the same (Ontario Physical and Health Education Association, 2010).

Improving Health Literacy

Teachers of health education across Canada are part of a broader, multisectoral effort that comprises various levels of government across Canada, as well as health professionals, educators, community organizations, and other sectors. Thus teachers of health education can rest assured that they are not alone in their efforts to help Canadian students improve their health literacy. In addition to this general assurance, the following list provides examples of action items specific to K-12 education, which, as noted by Mitic and Rootman (2012, pp. 42-43), could be implemented to support teachers in their work to improve health literacy:

- Enhance the knowledge and skill base of early childhood educators in relation to health literacy.
- Increase the treatment of health education in early childhood education programs.
- Mandate coursework in health education for all postsecondary students preparing for a career in early childhood education.
- Require coursework in health education for all future teachers currently enrolled in teacher education.
- Provide professional development for all teachers on health education teaching strategies, topics, and skills.
- Mandate health education classes in all schools from kindergarten through grade 12 and ensure that the curriculum includes topics related to health literacy.
- Incorporate health education into existing K-12 science, math, English, French, social studies, computer instruction, and other subjects or courses by embedding health-related information and skills into lesson plans (i.e., through curriculum infusion).

Though many of these action items have yet to be fully achieved, broad-based multisectoral reforms will continue to emerge as the concept of health literacy becomes increasingly familiar in various sectors, including education. On a promising note for K-12 educators, Canadian efforts to improve health literacy have recognized the importance of health education and issued calls for more health education opportunities (Mitic & Rootman, 2012; People for Education, 2011). Thus, even as we work toward congruence in health literacy efforts across sectors, teachers of health education can continue their efforts to help students develop the health-related comprehension, commitment, and capacity required to make informed healthy choices, promote the myriad of benefits associated with healthy living, and lead a healthy lifestyle.

Recommendations to Support Quality Health Education

With the following recommendations, resources, and examples, we seek to refine and support teachers' health education practices. The recommendations are derived from a combined 50-plus years of experience in K-16 education sectors with specific responsibilities for health education in K-12 settings and health and physical education teacher education in Canadian faculties of education.

1. Consult reliable Canadian sources of health-related information.

Trusted Canadian sources of health-related information and research help us all better understand our health-related needs and identify ways in which we can maintain or improve our health. In addition, local, provincial, territorial, and national organizations and governments have crafted programs and policies geared to Canadian children and youth (in many instances, based on Canadian-derived evidence) that have helped us better understand the unique needs of Canadian school children and youth. To gather health-related information from trusted Canadian sources, you may follow these tips:

- Start with Health Canada and the Public Health Agency of Canada. These two government organizations offer Canadian health-related information on a wide range of topics (e.g., mental health, nutrition education, healthy living) that teachers are responsible for addressing in health education.
- Next, look to your provincial or territorial government agency for health information (e.g., British Columbia Ministry of Health). Such agencies offer health-related information and research that accords with broader federal focuses while specifically addressing the unique needs of your provincial or territorial population.
- Think local. Specifically, look for local sources, such as public health offices and health service organizations. Many of these resources maintain well-developed websites and contact listings. Local public health organizations help assess, promote, and protect the health and well-being of Canadian residents by providing relevant, localized services and information that can enhance your health education teaching efforts.
- Subject-related associations often develop evidenced-based programs, supports, and teaching materials that are aligned with pro-

vincial or territorial health-related outcomes. Many of these organizations ask Canadian teachers and researchers to vet potential programs, health-related information, and resource supports before publicly posting, promoting, or endorsing them.

- Some external organizations, whether governmental or nongovernmental, offer health-related resources that can capably inform Canadian health education teaching. Examples include the World Health Organization and the United States Centers for Disease Control and Prevention.

2. Think critically about sources of health-related information.

With so much information readily available via the Internet, teachers of health education need to think critically—that is, identify, analyze, and evaluate potential sources of health information and consider how they might be interpreted by students. As a starting place, we recommend that you consider the ABCs of evaluating health education information: accuracy, authority, bias, currency, and comprehension.

- Is the information *accurate*? Can you see clearly that it is rooted in scientific evidence?
- What *authority* does the information source possess? To ensure that it is credible, dig a little deeper. Check the site and its information thoroughly. If you are unsure, explore the source further or move on to other potential sources of information.
- Consider the possibility of *bias*. Does the source present one point of view more strongly than another? Does it attempt to sell something to the reader? In any case, consider the possibility that what you are reading is a form of advertising.
- How *current* is the information? It is crucial for you to use information that is evidence based and up to date. Indeed, a body of evidence built on current research often changes the way we think about and approach health education topics. Therefore, whenever possible, use information produced within the past five years.
- Is the information easy to *comprehend*? The trusted sources that we use to inform our health education teaching are not mysteri-

ous or difficult to manage. To the contrary, they present information in a manner that is simple to read yet provides sufficient depth, thus enabling clear understanding.

3. Engage parents as partners.

As noted earlier, children and youth spend a disproportionate amount of time in schools. Even so, parents and other caring adults play a vital role in supporting efforts to help students make informed healthy choices, both at home and at school. Therefore, we encourage you to be proactive in your approach to parent engagement. Specifically, build partnerships with parents based on open communication and use the following strategies to work with parents in supporting students' health education and healthy decision making:

- *No surprises.* Parents usually appreciate it when teachers reach out to share or highlight planned learning. You can do so by sending a letter home, noting information in an agenda, or sending a brief note through a parent engagement app such as Remind. You will find more parent partners in learning when you proactively engage them in their students' education.
- *Guiding questions and conversation cues.* Provide parents with guiding questions that they can use at home to extend students' learning. Offer key points that parents and students can use to cue or prompt health education conversations that may mitigate misinformation and help ensure that students' health-related decisions are guided by accurate understandings.
- *Recognizing and listening.* For a variety of reasons, not all parents are comfortable with topics presented in health education, and some parents may need your help. Listen to parents and try to understand where they are coming from. Initiating conversations with parents may provide occasions for them to ask questions and share concerns. Listen first, and do not feel compelled to have all the answers in a given conversation. It is reasonable for you to seek to understand parents' concerns and indicate when you need time to digest information, explore possibilities, or solicit additional sup-

Parents and other caring adults play a vital role in supporting efforts to help students make informed healthy choices, both at home and at school.

port or information in order to address their questions. Take the time you need, then come back to the parents with an informed and thoughtful response. Parents will appreciate your time, attention, and thoughtful approach to helping them address their concerns.
- *School and board resources and supports.* You are never alone. You have many resources and colleagues, both within your school community and beyond (e.g., school district, community partners), who are there to support your health education teaching efforts. Examples include police, public health workers, and school and community health nurses.

4. Know and manage your biases and beliefs.

Self-awareness is essential to effective health education teaching. Your personal biography—that is, your background, beliefs, and values—will affect the decisions you make in your health education teaching. Therefore, in preparing to teach health education topics, you must consider your beliefs, values, and cultural norms. Moreover, in our education systems, teachers' personal values and beliefs are not to be imposed on students. Rather, our role is to provide students with learning opportunities grounded in factual and trusted sources of health information that help students develop the necessary skills and abilities to make informed and healthy decisions in their own lives. You can use the following steps to address biases, values, and inclinations that may affect your health education teaching.

- Begin by recognizing that all people have biases.
- Review your grade-level health education outcomes and identify any personal biases related to them.
- Consider the potential effect of any biases on your students. Might your bias limit or marginalize students' understandings related to the relevant outcome?
- Decide on a strategy to use in your planning and teaching in order to address each of your identified biases.
- Remember that student-centred teaching begins and ends with consideration of your students' feelings and perspectives (e.g., cultural, religious, socioeconomic, personal

interest). Therefore, in your health education planning and teaching, think specifically about your students' needs in order to mitigate potential disparities in your teaching.

5. Use a mindfulness approach.

Mindfulness is the state of being fully engaged in the present moment and manifesting a here-and-now oneness rather than indulging in contemplation of the past or future (Kabat-Zinn, 2003; Lu, Tito, & Kentel, 2009). The characteristics of mindfulness include mirror-thought (instant thoughts presented as they are, like seeing anything in a mirror), nonjudgmentalism, non-egoism, and impartial watchfulness. Although the practice of mindfulness was developed for thousands of years in the East (in Buddhism), it has been booming around the world in the past 40 years due to its numerous health benefits (Maynard, Solis, Miller, & Brendel, 2017; Tucci & Moukaddam, 2017). Moreover, though mindfulness has been recognized as an ancient wisdom, philosophy, and skill for well-being, it has been missing from Western health education (Lu & McLean, 2011). The integration of mindfulness into schooling can help students rediscover the inner or true self; manage stress; develop patience and openness; accept self, others, and surroundings; attain a balanced life for body–mind unity and holistic nature–human oneness; and enhance happiness (Maynard et al., 2017; Lu, 2012). Due to the nature of mindfulness, assessment of students' mindfulness should be conducted primarily by students themselves.

There are numerous ways to integrate mindfulness into school health education programming (Lu, 2012):

- Having teachers or invited guests teach mindfulness exercises (e.g., Eastern martial arts, yoga, qigong)
- "Mindfulizing" activities (e.g., focusing on doing each task with no rush)
- Avoiding multitasking
- Appreciating subjective feelings and experiences (e.g., joy, dislike)
- Accepting self (e.g., body shape) and others (e.g., of different races)
- Impartially appreciating both the inanimate environment (e.g., classroom, playing field) and the animate environment (e.g., flowers, trees)
- Focusing on process rather than only on product
- Integrating mindfulness (e.g., awareness of breathing, appreciation of the here and now) into daily life and promoting it at home, at school, and in the community

A student self-assessment tool for mindfulness practice is included in the web resource for this chapter. Your students can use this tool at regular intervals throughout their health education to assess and manage their stress, level of engagement, and happiness in the moment. Both you and your students can use it to develop mindfulness strategies that support students' efforts to find balance in their day-to-day lives.

6. Manage student groupings.

Interpersonal interactions are often central to how we organize or structure health education learning experiences (Barrett, Robinson, & Ecclestone, 2016). Increasingly, health education teachers craft student-centred learning experiences that are social and collaborative. In these interpersonal working arrangements, students may learn to explore and better understand differing perspectives, as well as health-related concepts and skills. The make-up and management of these groupings can profoundly affect your efforts to create a safe and respectful learning environment that maximizes well-being and learning for all. Therefore, we recommend that grouping decisions always be made by you. Here are three considerations to help you enable group learning experiences that give your students meaningful opportunities to develop life-sustaining interpersonal skills:

- *Establishment of norms.* At the start of the school year, and routinely throughout the year, HPE [health and physical education] teachers are encouraged to establish and reinforce selection norms together with their students—norms that get at the heart of how and why pairings, groupings, and team selection decisions will be made. Student selection, and more specifically peer selection, affects students' well-being and academic performance. Establishing group selection norms in HPE settings may help teachers set aside intuitive tendencies and tacit understandings related to peer selection in favour of a more systematic approach that aims to ensure [that] students are grouped with quality HPE pedagogy and student well-being in mind (Barrett, 2015).

- *Diagnostic assessments and student groupings.* In HPE settings, diagnostic assessments could be expanded to include an assessment of the impacts of student pairings, groups, and teams on student learning. Across a wide variety of activities, students will have different concerns or needs in pairings, groups, and teams. Teachers, with their students, are encouraged to address students' particular needs using a variety of diagnostic assessments; these may include the use of exit cards, questioning, self-assessments, and large- and small-group conferencing. Understandings gained could lead to more carefully designed HPE group experiences.
- *Selection "cheat sheet."* HPE teachers may also consider putting together a cheat sheet of pairings, groupings, and teams that put students in the best possible situation to be successful. As with all planning and teaching in HPE, reflection will inevitably lead to grouping changes being made to support students' emotional, social, and academic success in HPE settings. As the HPE teacher learns more about her/his students, this cheat sheet can be further tailored to particular types of activities. This type of resource can also be left for supply/occasional teachers to help mitigate potential issues that might arise as a result of student groupings.

Student selection, and more specifically peer selection, affects students' well-being and academic performance.

Barrett et al. (2016, pp. 5-6)

7. Help students take learning beyond the classroom.

For this particular recommendation, we went out to the field to discuss the idea of moving health education beyond the classroom and making connections with broader focuses, whether schoolwide, as in comprehensive school health, or systemwide, as is the case with Ontario's well-being strategy (Ontario Ministry of Education, n.d.). In support of this recommendation, Deb Shackell, an Ontario provincial educator and advocate for student well-being, offers the following considerations (personal communication, November 9, 2017).

Taking health education beyond the classroom is the collective responsibility of students, educators, administrators, school staff members, and the entire school community. Together, we can participate in a narrative that educates students about making informed healthy choices and promotes overall student well-being. Regardless of the level of implementation—classroom, schoolwide, or systemwide—the promotion of well-being intersects with health edu-

cation in a variety of ways. Successful integration of health education into a broader well-being approach includes the following aspects:

- *Equitable policies, structures, and resources.* One fundamental starting point is for all stakeholders to make conscious efforts to remove systemic barriers in schools and classrooms that may unintentionally put certain populations at a disadvantage. Equity is essential for well-being.
- *Relationships.* All members of the school community (e.g., educators, custodians, administrative staff) can do their part to build strong, trusting relationships in order to help ensure that students and staff alike feel valued, safe, important, and *seen* in their school community.
- *Comprehensive and community-driven approach.* It takes a village! Educators can connect with and leverage community partners, and this approach can serve a dual beneficial purpose. First, educators and students can tap into the wealth of community-based knowledge and resources related to health; second, community connections can lead to an increased sense of belonging for students and enhanced relationships with stakeholders.
- *Transformed and culturally responsive pedagogy that is inclusive and places students at the centre.* With the transformation of pedagogy and a student-centred approach to learning, we no longer rely on traditional "sit and get methods," in which educators serve as the main source of information to help students make healthy choices. Instead, students become co-facilitators of their learning. When educators use knowledge-building practices and inquiry-based learning opportunities, they provide opportunities for students to develop soft skills (e.g., critical thinking, collaboration) that may contribute to overall well-being that is sustainable. This kind of empowering and engaging pedagogy contributes not only to an improved sense of self for students but also to the culture of well-being in a school. Students become leaders and change agents and own their learning and their environment.

Summary

Teachers of health education play a vital role in helping students develop healthy habits, make informed healthy choices, and achieve greater levels of health literacy. Learning about health can be a key equalizer in helping all of our 21st-century Canadian students find success in life. We hope this chapter helps you develop understanding of the rationale for including health education in K-12 Canadian schools, develop understanding of the concept of health literacy and its relationship to health education, value the broad-based recommendations offered for infusing quality and care into health education teaching, and use the case examples provided in the web resource to extend your learning beyond these pages in order to interrogate and confront potential disconnects in your health education teaching.

DISCUSSION QUESTIONS

1. What are the implications for Canadian society of *not* updating our health education curricula?

2. What are some ways to ensure that you are teaching from an evidence-based point of view?

3. What challenges might you face in your grade-level health education teaching? For each challenge, provide two solutions.

4. What personal biases do you think you will need to address or consider as you prepare to teach health education curricula?

5. Why is mindfulness important in health education?

6. What challenges might you face in teaching mindfulness? For each challenge, provide two solutions.

 Visit the web resource for case studies and questions, as well as a mindfulness self-assessment.

Voices From the Field

Danielle Coulson
K-2 Teacher, Ontario

I am a 0.8 teacher who teaches four days a week in a one-and-two combination grade. I teach language, mathematics, social studies, drama and dance, health, and daily physical education at Esker Lake Public School in Brampton, Ontario. My diverse students come with various abilities and levels and range from five to seven years old.

Healthy living is a huge part of my life, so I try to lead by example. My students see me making healthy choices on a daily basis, such as snacking on fruits and vegetables, drinking water, and prioritizing my physical health by participating in activities alongside them. In my health education teaching, I try to help students explore what we eat and what various foods do to our bodies. We also incorporate mathematics by graphing food quantities eaten and we have fun through activities in the classroom. These activities include small, measurable, and personal goal tracking tied to student nutrition education (e.g., water consumption, healthy food choices based on personal circumstances). We also bring these activities schoolwide—for example, initiating a healthy-eating "apple a day program" in which all school students eat an apple at the same time each day! In these ways, our health-promoting classroom works to set an example for all students across the school.

During open house, I talk with parents about the effects of healthy eating on my students while being mindful to recognize and acknowledge that student circumstances vary. I try to help my students make the healthiest choices they can in their own lives, and I want parents to leave these meetings knowing that I will be a supportive resource and ally.

One of my favourite activities is to have my students create a grocery list using the flyers from several food stores in our community; the list includes pictures and prices for all of the foods. My students often feel empowered to share what they have learned with their family. Thus they are teaching their parents and are becoming healthy advocates for the family. Many of my students come back to class sharing stories of visits to the food store and feeling excited that they were part of the experience. This is a fun way to incorporate a cross-curricular math focus with our health education teaching.

I believe that students learn more about their own health by doing—by moving and using their bodies to deepen their understanding of various health-related concepts; by actively engaging in science experiments; by creating a fun grocery store in the classroom when learning about how to use money and counting. I include little games and activities throughout the day to get students excited about learning through movement. I use physical activity cue words that I will whisper to students while they are working. The cues are often tied to particular physical activity stations and activities that I have set up for the students about the classroom. When the cues are shared, students will, at their own pace, move to various locations in the classroom to take part, independently, in daily physical activity (DPA) that often relates directly to our curricular teaching foci under exploration. I also created "DPA eggs," which are plastic eggs covered with images that relate to a particular sport or physical activity. In each egg, I have printed various movement activities. Once the students have completed one egg, they can move on to another one. They know they can go to these eggs throughout the day if they need a short break. I want them to see the relationship between healthy living and daily physical activity participation. I have found that these small activities also encourage positive self-regulation. In classroom settings, I know my children need a controlled and responsible way to expend their energy throughout the day.

I also know that the health and wellness of my students at school stretches beyond my health education teaching into our whole school community. Thus I am a passionate advocate of schoolwide health promotion. I try to teach my students that making informed healthy choices can influence not only their own health but also the lives of their fellow students. One of my favourite ways to reach students is by incorporating drama and dance into my health-focused schoolwide initiatives. For example, I hosted an assembly based on the theme of happiness. As a class, we created a dance for the song "Happy" by Pharrell Williams; my students created each step from start to finish. I then worked with the physical education teacher, who allowed five rotating students from my class to come and teach the dance to the various PE classes for the first 10 minutes of each scheduled class. At the end of the assembly, the entire school did the dance to the song that my class had created, and it was so powerful and rewarding to see my class be responsible for the happy feeling that filled the school for weeks after! We also placed happiness posters throughout the school and created happiness class cheers. It was a happiness movement and a very proud moment for me to see my students exert such a positive influence on the social, physical, and emotional well-being of our school population.

In addition, I want parents and students to know that our class recognizes and celebrates the diversity in our classroom. It adds a richness to all that we do. From this recognition, I work to learn about students' and families' understandings associated with making informed healthy choices. I am a strong advocate for the use of technology to enhance both learning and parental engagement. To foster parent engagement, I use an app called Seesaw, which allows me to take pictures of my students and text parents directly. In this way, I can regularly capture students making healthy choices while at school. I work to create and nurture an open dialogue with parents and students, and I believe this dialogue is foundational to my efforts to help my students make informed healthy choices.

I conduct my major assessments in the middle of the week. I try to understand all of the factors that might influence my students' success in learning. For example, I take sleep and restfulness into consideration. On Mondays, I often notice that my students are tired after the weekend; as we approach Fridays, I sometimes see their energy levels wane as we head toward the weekend. I also try to be mindful of their eating habits and patterns. It is important to understand the effects of these factors before expecting children to be fully present in learning. If students are hungry and tired, then getting them to move or engage in health education is difficult for obvious reasons. I strongly believe in considering the totality of what is affecting a student. Once I have considered potential factors, I am able to figure out a plan that makes sense for individual students. Also, recognizing that some students may not be ready to engage with my health education teaching, I try to find alternative teaching strategies that are fair, engaging, and fun. I try to consider and respect all abilities and levels of interest. My ultimate goal is to foster a love of learning that helps students make healthy choices in their own lives.

CHAPTER 8

Promoting Positive Mental Health

Susan Rodger

After studying this chapter, you will be able to

- explain how understanding mental health, mental health promotion, and healthy emotional development is relevant to all students and all health and physical education classrooms;

- take effective steps if you are concerned about a student's well-being;

- focus on students in the classroom and during activities, notice and listen to them, and speak with them when you are concerned about their well-being;

- adopt an inclusive mind-set and consider students' behaviours as reflecting their development, context, level of well-being, and mental health;

- help students—and yourself—recognize and cope with stress;

- describe how adverse experiences can affect well-being;

- reflect on your confidence and readiness to promote healthy emotional development of your students; and

- engage in conversations about mental health and well-being with students, families, and colleagues.

Every year, in every school, many students arrive ready to engage in learning; to form lasting and healthy relationships with peers and teachers; and to build the social, cognitive, behavioural, and emotional capacities that promote a lifetime of success. Some students, however, need more support in order to achieve these same goals. In our work as teachers, we have the opportunity to make a critical difference for these students by creating classrooms that promote learning, safety, inclusion, and engagement for all. An estimated 14 percent of Canadian children and young people struggle with mental illness (Waddell et al., 2005) and even more arrive at school with heavy burdens related to the context in which they live, including poverty, exposure to violence, maltreatment, unstable or unsafe housing, and caregivers who struggle with mental illness or addiction.

This chapter introduces you to the building blocks you need in order to create a mentally healthy classroom and support students in their journey to mental well-being. These building blocks include the following:

- Developing mental health literacy
- Understanding mental health and resilience
- Noticing student mental health and behaviour
- Helping students manage stress
- Thinking critically about the necessary conditions for mental well-being
- Understanding activities, strategies, and tips for bringing mental health into the classroom

Developing Mental Health Literacy

Although teachers are not expected to be mental health experts, they *are* expected to be present as caring adults in students' lives and to support all students, including those who struggle with mental illness or poor mental health. In order to provide this support, one of the building blocks you need is mental health literacy, which has been defined as "knowledge and skills that enable people to access, understand, and apply information for mental health" (Canadian Alliance for Mental Illness and Mental Health, 2008, p. 8). You can develop mental health literacy over time through opportunities to learn and apply knowledge and strategies that help create mentally healthy classrooms in alignment with whole-child approaches to education. Developing mental health literacy includes the following elements:

- Normalizing the need to attend to mental health as part of overall wellness
- Being culturally aware and responsive
- Taking a holistic approach to wellness
- Focusing on social determinants of health and mental health literacy in order to address inequities and build capacity
- Taking a collaborative and relational approach

For teachers, mental health literacy is dynamic; that is, you will learn, develop, and apply strategies, knowledge, and awareness throughout your career. Today may be the first time you have thought about mental health in your classroom, or you may be farther along in your journey. Mental health literacy among teachers is demonstrated in the following ways:

- Knowing how to speak with children and families about mental health
- Understanding what mental health looks like in the classroom and recognizing children who may be experiencing difficulty
- Being willing and prepared to connect students with pathways to mental health care and support in schools

Possessing and demonstrating mental health literacy does *not* mean that you will identify, diagnose, or treat students with mental illness. Your role as both a teacher and a caring adult in the life of a child includes the following aspects:

- Noticing a student who is struggling, which may be manifested in changes in the student or in ways that look like problems with behaviour, discipline, or attendance
- Responding to what you notice by doing something—for example, speaking with the student, the student's caregiver, and support people in your school and, if you suspect a child is at risk for maltreatment, making the necessary report to child welfare authorities
- Communicating that you care and are there to help

Although teachers are not expected to be mental health experts, they are expected to be present as caring adults in students' lives and to support all students, including those who struggle with mental illness or poor mental health.

Understanding Mental Health and Resilience

As you may have noticed, mental health, or lack thereof, is referred to by a variety of names, such as emotional health, emotional well-being, resilience, and mental illness. Let us consider a few definitions that will help us think about a teacher's role in supporting mental health as part of healthy living. Mental health is defined by the World Health Organization (2014) as "a state of well-being in which . . . [an] individual realizes his or her own potential, can cope with the normal stresses of life, can work productively and fruitfully, and is able to make a contribution to her or his community" (n.p.). Thinking about mental health as not just the absence of illness but *the presence of wellness* can provide important insight into how to engage and include students in the classroom. To help us understand the illness and wellness parts of mental health, we can turn to the dual continuum model offered by Keyes (2002), which is represented in figure 8.1.

As the figure shows, one can have a mental illness yet flourish—that is, experience positive mental well-being—if one is engaged in effective treatment and surrounded by a circle of support. On the other hand, one who does not have mental illness can languish—that is, experience negative or low levels of mental well-being—if one is engaged in risky behaviours, not taking care of oneself, not making good decisions about one's body and relationships, or isolating oneself. Look around you for examples and invite your students to do the same. For instance, many successful athletes and other celebrities are open about their mental illness diagnoses and treatments, whereas we also see many others (especially young pop stars) who struggle with what look like unwise life choices, publicly documented struggles, and negative judgment of them by the press and on social media.

When we combine the ideas of illness and wellness, we create a valuable framework for including children and youth and supporting their healthy development. Well-being includes both emotional components (e.g., happiness, life satisfaction) and psychological components (e.g., self-acceptance, sense of purpose, need for relationships, need for autonomy). Fortunately, there are things we can do in the classroom to help students develop self-awareness, healthy coping skills, good relationships, and independence—all of which are part of mental health and resilience.

Understanding Resilience

Resilience is a normal, adaptive process in response to adversity. Resilient people are generally able to withstand the difficult things that come their way and to keep functioning in ways that are healthy. Our understanding of resilience has been aided greatly by leading Canadian scholar Michael Ungar, who views resilience as

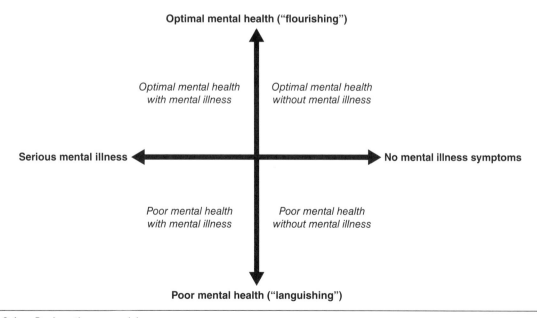

Figure 8.1 Dual continuum model.

Canadian Mental Health Association, Ontario, based on the conceptual work of Corey Keyes.

"both the capacity of individuals to navigate their way to the psychological, social, cultural, and physical resources that sustain their well-being, and their capacity individually and collectively to negotiate for these resources to be provided in culturally meaningful ways" (Ungar, 2011, p. 10).

In order to fully understand resilience, we must consider the role played by privilege. For children who grow up with stable access to food, safe housing, and health care—and in the presence of caring adults—resilience in the face of challenging experiences (such as exposure to violence) is supported because they begin their journey through the difficulty from a place of strength. In contrast, when children lack such privileges—and let us recall that children have no control over whether they live in a safe and secure home—they may start their challenging journey from a far different, and distant, starting point.

Knowing your students and their experiences, as well as those of their families and communities, can inform your development of strategies to help them build the necessary skills and knowledge to become resilient.

We must also recognize that resilience is not only an individual strength; it is also held and supported—or compromised—by the community. For instance, if a child or youth comes from a community that has experienced historical violence, poverty, or other long-term challenges, then the community may not possess the necessary social, cultural, psychological, or physical resources to share with the individual in need. For these reasons, knowing your students and their experiences, as well as those of their families and communities, can inform your development of strategies to help them build the necessary skills and knowledge to become resilient.

If you are working with a number of students from a particular community, learn about their culture and their cultural practices related to health and well-being. For example, elements such as connection with nature, community elders, language of origin, and customs help individuals build a sense of self and confidence that can make a difference when facing adversity. If you don't know anything about your students' cultural practices, ask adults from the community and seek out cultural organizations, community centres, and other resources.

Here are three guidelines to follow when seeking information about cultures with which you are unfamiliar:

1. Don't ask students to bring in materials or explain it all to you. It is your responsibility to learn about their culture; do *not* try to make it their responsibility. Seek out credible sources of information and conduct some research.

2. Adopt an attitude of "awareness but not knowing." It can be daunting to think you need to know about many cultures. In fact, you don't need to be an expert. Simply recognizing that culture is important and being open to cultural differences will help you create a safe and inclusive classroom.

3. Make it a lifelong goal to learn about various cultures, your own cultural assumptions and cultural beliefs, and the ways in which culture can influence learning and participation in class.

Noticing Student Mental Health and Behaviour

A diagnosis of mental illness is not a catastrophe; in fact, it is the opposite. Early identification and proper treatment, combined with acceptance and support, give affected children and youth what they need in order to participate, be part of their community, and live full and productive lives. Despite what biases and stigmas may tell us, children will not "grow out of," "get over," or "learn to deal" with a mental illness on their own. We wouldn't expect this to happen if a child were diagnosed with any other serious (and potentially life threatening) illness—why would we expect mental illness to be different?

According to Polanczyk, Salum, Sugaya, Caye, and Rohde (2015), one in five children and young people worldwide will develop a diagnosable mental illness. Moreover, many mental illnesses emerge between the ages of 4 and 24—in other words, the years when most children and young people are in school. You might hear people talking, or find yourself thinking, about a sudden rise in mental illness among children, youth, and young adults. Certainly, there has been an increase in awareness, which is partially responsible for the sense of a rise, but consider also the following facts:

■ More children, and more children with exceptionalities, are attending community schools, for longer.

■ We have developed schools and classrooms to respond to the needs of the majority of students; those who have exceptionalities (including mental illness) often struggle with trying to fit in and become visible in their struggle.

■ Many children come from homes marked by stressors, including discrimination, poverty, forced migration, hunger, substance abuse, and violence, as well as involvement with child welfare authorities, the justice system, and social services. These stressors put children at risk for mental distress, mental illness, and poor outcomes.

■ Of the children and youths who will develop a mental illness, only one in four will ever get help for it through our health care system. As Senator Michael Kirby (2013) writes, we must change this harsh reality and ask ourselves if we would allow a child or youth with any other disease—for example, cancer or diabetes—to live with the disease in silence or, worse, give the individual the message that he or she must simply be stronger, try harder, and get over it. That we do so in the context of mental illness is both unacceptable and a call to action for change.

Teachers are in the best position to notice and attend to students' mental health in at least three ways:

1. As teachers gain more experience, they understand what constitutes typical versus atypical development among students of a particular age group. Do you notice a child who is unable to function in the environment even as others are thriving? You can also look for attendance patterns, including late arrivals and early departures—missing part or all of the school day can be connected with mental health problems such as anxiety. Try letting children who experience anxiety come into the classroom five minutes early. This practice lets them get ready and settled in before the rest of the group arrives; as a result, they can begin the class with calmness instead of heightened anxiety.

2. Teachers observe children in environments that place high demands on their concentration, emotional regulation, ability to cope with stress (e.g., assessments, sport events), and ability in both play and social situations (e.g., recess, team or group work). Do you see differences in how children cope with structured and unstructured time? With peers and on their own? Think about the child who always seems to be on the outside of things, perhaps looking unmotivated or disengaged. When children cannot cope with stress or demands, they often act out or, on the opposite end of the spectrum, withdraw from activities. When children are struggling, they most often tell us so not with words but with behaviour. Thus we need to develop our ability to look beyond behaviour and toward the struggles that a child is having. You can help reduce your students' stress levels and increase their sense of capacity by establishing and following routines that enable them to know what to expect—and what is expected of them. With practice and support, they can be ready for anything!

3. Teachers build relationships with children in many ways. As a caring adult in your students' lives, you have the opportunity to welcome them into your classroom, get to know them and appreciate them for who they are, and make your class a fun and safe place to be. When students come into your class, greet them by name and say, "[Name], I'm so glad to see you today!" If you have a new student, pair him or her with a buddy who can act as a guide to the class and the school. If you know that a student is dealing with something difficult—even if you do not know what it is—make space for the student and ask how he or she is doing. Such students may choose not to share, or may not respond as you expect, but they will know that you noticed, and that is a powerful experience for a young person who may feel very alone and isolated.

When children are struggling, they most often tell us so not with words but with behaviour.

Helping Students Manage Stress

Stress is a normal response to environmental demands or pressures that threaten our well-being or overwhelm our coping strategies. It is experienced physically (e.g., increased heart rate and respiration), cognitively (e.g., worry), and emotionally (e.g., anxiety and trepidation). These responses are linked to survival in the most basic sense—if we perceive danger, our built-in alarm system activates to protect us. This system often creates particular behaviours referred to in the common phrase "fight, flight, or freeze."

The stress response (which we often refer to simply as stress) occurs whenever we are faced with a challenge or change in our environment that demands our adaptation. The challenge, or stressor, may be a school or social situation, a sport competition, a touch, a threat, or anything that pressures us to adapt. The specifics of how we interpret danger—and feel stress—vary from person to person; overall, however, the stress response is simply the brain's signal to the body, and to itself, that adaptation is needed. Everyone experiences the stress response every single day. In the vast majority of situations, it is low in intensity, transient, and helpful.

Children are observant, and they learn how to interpret their own stress response by watching others. If they are told that what they are feeling is helpful—that the body signals they are experiencing are helping them prepare to perform well—then they tend to do well. In such cases, they focus on learning or on applying the skills necessary to succeed in the given situation. When they are successful, the stress response dissipates. Moreover, they remember what they did to adapt, and now they have embedded a skill and thus become more resilient. Because they remember what they did to solve the problem, they can apply that strategy in the future.

> Instead of saying to a student, "You look depressed," you might say, "I'm noticing that your energy is really low today. What's going on?"

Instead of saying to a student, "You look depressed," you might say, "I'm noticing that your energy is really low today. What's going on?"

If, on the other hand, children are told that what they are feeling is harmful and negative, then they may spend much of their time trying to shut down the stress response or avoid the situation eliciting it. Both of these outcomes lead to poor adaptation and decreased resilience. Thus we must realize that we have a key role to play in helping students learn to handle stress constructively.

In order to do so, we must avoid confusing the daily stress that helps us grow, develop, and adapt with the type of stress that can lead to problems and be difficult to overcome independently. Not all stress is the same, yet people often forget the huge differences between various kinds of stress. As a result, they often confuse normal and helpful everyday stress with toxic stress—that is, the acute stress that protects us from danger. This confusion may help explain why many educators view stress as bad, when in fact most stress is healthy and even necessary for human growth and development. The following descriptions summarize three types of stress response: positive, tolerable, and toxic (Harvard Center for the Developing Child, n.d.).

- *Positive stress response* is a normal and essential part of healthy development. It is characterized by brief increases in heart rate and mild elevations in hormone levels. A positive stress response might be triggered, for example, by the following situations.
  - In childhood: receiving an immunization shot, meeting a new caregiver
  - In adolescence: writing examinations, going to a new school, failing a grade, not making the team, giving a public lecture, performing on stage, asking someone for a date, going to a party with unfamiliar people
  - For new teachers: meeting students' parents, writing report cards, getting to know colleagues
- *Tolerable stress response* activates the body's alert systems to a greater degree than positive stress response as a result of more severe, longer-lasting difficulties—for example, a natural disaster, a frightening injury, or the loss of a loved one. If the activation is time limited and buffered by relationships with adults who help the child adapt, then the brain and other organs recover from what might otherwise be damaging effects. Here are some examples.
  - For students: moving to a new home and school, being diagnosed with a chronic disease (e.g., diabetes, asthma), losing a grandparent or parent
  - For teachers: ending an intimate relationship, moving to an unfamiliar place to begin a career, being reassigned at the last minute and needing to rebuild lesson plans and resources
- *Toxic stress response* can occur when a child experiences strong, frequent, or prolonged adversity—such as unsafe housing, hunger, physical or emotional abuse, chronic neglect, substance abuse or mental illness in a caregiver, exposure to violence, or economic hardship—without adequate adult support. This kind of prolonged activation of the stress response systems can disrupt the development of brain architecture and other organ systems. It can also increase the risk for stress-related disease and cognitive impairment well into the adult years.

You may have heard the saying, "Be kind; everyone is fighting a hard battle." Being kind means really looking at our students, seeing what might underlie their behaviour, considering how their personal wellness or context might influence how they react in a particular situation, and—as the caring adult—creating a safe space in which they can develop their sense of self.

This perspective is particularly important when reflecting on how we think children and youth (and we and our peers) "should" handle stress. Do you have a student who is very anxious about "getting into trouble"? Perhaps the student has experienced maltreatment at the hands of caregivers in response to transgressions. Depending on the child's age and coping style, this anxiety may manifest in the form of noncompliance ("defiance"), being anxious to please ("goody-two-shoes"), or being withdrawn ("bored" or "not motivated"). Do you have a student who is focused on getting high marks and other positive evaluations? Again, depending on age and history, such students may present as being overly focused on meeting your criteria ("needy" or "demanding"), helpless ("lacking confidence"), or distracted ("needing to focus" or "apply themselves").

How does this overview of stress fit with what you have been taught? How does it challenge common beliefs suggesting that normal and everyday stress is bad, that we should protect children from it, or that there may be things over which we have no control that influence how a person copes with stress?

Instead of being silent when a student says, "That guy is crazy" or "She is nuts," respond to what you are hearing: "I am hearing some language that worries me. Let's take a minute and talk about this."

Here are some strategies to keep in mind when helping students develop the necessary skills to cope with stress:

- When possible, give students choices regarding assessments. A student who experiences performance-related anxiety is likely to be negatively influenced by the anxiety (which does not mean that he or she doesn't know or can't do it).
- Consider different ways in which students can contribute to others' learning. Are they too nervous to demonstrate the skill in front of the class? Then have them record others doing so. Are they overwhelmed by the expectation? Then talk with them about it and guide them to reasonable alternatives for demonstrating their learning. This is not about giving students a way out; it is about giving them a way in.
- Start small and focus on building their capacity. We all benefit from opportunities to learn, practice, and receive constructive feedback.
- Explore simple ways to build a sense of mastery in your classroom—for example, using jigsaw or cooperative learning.

And here are some individual factors to consider:

- Does the student possess the necessary skills to complete the task? Some students may need coaching or extra practice.
- Is the person naturally more open or more resistant to new experiences? Some students may need encouragement and time to explore new experiences.
- Is the person generally more anxious or less anxious? For students who tend to be more anxious about life in general, being reminded of times when they coped effectively with anxiety can help them generalize the relevant skills to new situations.
- Is the task simple, clearly explained, and well resourced (e.g., in terms of time, materials, and support)? It can be helpful to break a large task into smaller steps, provide tools (e.g., an outline) and reminders (e.g., posters or instruction sheets), and check in frequently.

Remember also that children often mirror an important adult's response to an unexpected or unpleasant situation. If, upon seeing a child fall down and bang a knee, we swoop in to help, then we transmit the message that the fall was a catastrophe and the child or youth is incapable of handling it. Instead, we can make eye contact and check in: "Hey [Name], you took quite a tumble. Are you ready to go back in [to the game or class activity], or do you need to sit out for a few minutes?" In this way, we send the message that we noticed the event and are letting the student choose the next step because he or she *can*.

Adverse Effects on Well-Being

Research and practice tell us a great deal about the ways in which the well-being of children and youth are affected by social determinants of

(sidebar)

Instead of being silent when a student says, "That guy is crazy" or "She is nuts," respond to what you are hearing: "I am hearing some language that worries me. Let's take a minute and talk about this."

health, such as income, health care, education, and safe living conditions. We also know that serious childhood trauma—often referred to as adverse childhood experiences (ACEs; Anda, Butchart, Felitti, & Brown, 2010)—can create toxic stress in a child's brain, which in turn can devastate their ability to engage, learn, and perform at school. Taken together, ACEs and social determinants of health can exert considerable influence on the mental health and well-being of children and youth. In turn, poor mental health is one of the most common reasons for absences, school refusal, compromised academic achievement, dropping out, and low school engagement.

But exactly how do these damaging effects happen? Consider this example: The class returns after recess, flooding the room with noise and movement. You see Janine come in and head right back to the coat racks. After she sinks down onto the bench to change her shoes, her head drops, her shoulders slump, and a shoe dangles from her hand. The other students are taking their seats, chattering loudly, and you need to get on with things. The way to avoid complete chaos is to get busy, so you decide to let Janine take her own time to change her shoes while you get started with the lesson. Eventually, Janine takes her seat, but she does not appear ready to learn.

As noted earlier, children usually tell us how they are feeling not with words but with their behaviour. They exhibit different types of behaviour depending on a combination of factors, including gender, exposure to violence, age, and ability. For example, there are three basic responses to a threatening situation: fight, flight, and freeze. What makes a child aggressive and confrontational rather than "spaced out" or otherwise avoidant? For her part, Janine exhibits what are often referred to as "internalizing behaviours"; that is, she is withdrawn, uncommunicative, avoidant of eye contact, and apparently sad or worried.

Now, let us imagine that Janine did use her words and said, "Teacher, I am feeling really scared and upset right now. I can't think about schoolwork because I am so worried about my mom and me. We are moving because my dad is getting out of jail today and he says he is going to come to our house and make her pay for calling the police the last time he beat her up. Mom said she will pick me up from school today and we are going to our new house—but it is a secret and I can't tell anyone. What happens if he finds us? What if he comes to our old house and she is still there? What if he tries to kill me? I'm scared."

Janine is unlikely to say any of that, and the reasons have everything to do with her and little to do with you. Seeing her mother treated violently constitutes one of those ACEs mentioned earlier; other examples include homelessness, emotional neglect, substance abuse by a parent, and marital separation or divorce. Children and youth who experience four or more of the ten ACEs are seven times more likely to not finish school, to end up in the criminal justice system, and to end up with addiction problems.

But back to Janine. What is likely to happen if, as in the example, you say nothing to her? In terms of the class, the rest of your students will notice Janine sitting in the back (even if they don't show it) and will learn that it is okay to not acknowledge or pay attention to someone who is alone and struggling. Children engage in this kind of social learning all the time. For Janine, she learns that she *is* alone, that she *is* somewhat invisible, and that this fact is noticed and ignored by her teacher. In other words, this scenario serves as an example of how silence is *not neutral* but rather sends a clear message of accepting, without questioning, two realities: that a vulnerable person is struggling and that he or she does not deserve our help.

So, if silence is not an option for you, what do you say? Imagine that when you notice Janine's demeanor, you ask the rest of the students to take out their books and read quietly while you go to Janine. You sit beside her, close enough for her to feel your nearness but not crowding her. You are beside her, which reduces any potential feelings of being challenged or threatening. You don't insist on eye contact; you just want Janine to know that you are there. You say, "Janine, I noticed that you are sitting here and looking lost. What are you thinking about? Can you tell me what is going on inside you right now?"

This approach gives Janine two important gifts. First, she is not invisible—you noticed her! Second, you are giving her the opportunity to share her state of mind and emotion. She may decline to say anything, and that is fine. She may have reasons not to: Perhaps she promised her mom not to tell. Or maybe the last time she talked to a teacher about how she was feeling, the teacher called child protective services and a lot of bad things happened. Or perhaps she doesn't have the words to describe how she is feeling. All of that, however, comes in a distant second to the first gift: You noticed. A trusted, caring adult has taken a moment to just sit beside her and ask how she is doing. Having one stable, trusted, caring adult has been demonstrated (Resnick et al., 1997) to be pivotal in helping vulnerable children and youth be resilient in the face of great adversity, whether it comes from exposure to ACEs or from insufficient access to the social determinants of health. Even if you don't know it, *you* will be that stable and trusted adult for many students in your classes.

Imagine further that you call Janine's mother that evening or arrange to spend a few minutes with her when she comes to pick Janine up from school. Imagine that you say to her, "Today I noticed that Janine seemed to be very sad or worried. Have you noticed this at home, too? Yes? Can you share with me how you help her at home when she is feeling like this? Do you have any ideas that I could use here at school?" Or, "Once I noticed her at the back of the class, I went and sat beside her and spoke quietly. She seemed to respond really well to that." In this way, we open the conversation and create partnerships with parents.

So, you've given Janine an important relationship, and it is now crucial to use it wisely and give yourself over to "bearing witness"—letting someone know that you notice and being willing to engage fully and listen. This is the most important skill in any helping relationship. The helping comes not from doing and problem-solving but from listening and attending.

Normalizing Mental Health Discussion

Bringing up the topic of mental health can be a challenge, and it is natural to feel apprehensive about doing so. It's not just new teachers who report feeling unprepared or nervous when talking with students about mental health; even experienced teachers report feeling that they don't have enough information or skill to bring mental health into the classroom. Yet talking about mental health normalizes it, sending messages to students that it is a welcome topic, that the classroom is a safe place, and that they are part of a caring community.

The key to teaching about mental health is to make it part of everyday experience. One way to do so is to recognize the natural and well-established connections between mental and physical health; in this way, you can help students understand that learning how to cope with stress and distress is an essential part of healthy living. Check your language and help students develop the vocabulary to describe mental health in ways that avoid mocking, minimizing, and excluding.

Talk about stereotypes, stigmas, and being part of a community in which people support and care for one another. Remember that silence is not neutral and that if you say nothing, you are signaling your approval of your students' language.

Summary

This chapter addresses the importance of developing mental health literacy, which is a process of building knowledge, capacity, and understanding for both teachers and students. The chapter presents case examples of what happens (or doesn't happen) based on how we respond to students in need of a caring adult. It also explores how conditions in their lives, such as adverse childhood experiences and lack of access to the social determinants of health, can pose challenges for both mental well-being and learning. The chapter also presents tips and strategies for breaking the silence with students and their families. This effort is crucial because silence is not neutral. As the caring adult in the classroom, you are well positioned to make a real and important difference in the lives of children who struggle with mental health.

DISCUSSION QUESTIONS

1. Think back to your own experiences in elementary or secondary school. Do you remember a favourite teacher, one who was liked by all students and whose class everyone enjoyed? What did that teacher do, say, or share to create that feeling of being in a safe and welcoming environment?

2. What is important for you to notice about how students are doing in your class with respect to mental health and wellness? What behaviours or emotional responses will get your attention, and how will you respond?

3. Thinking about the ACEs study and the effects of adverse childhood experiences on children and youth, what do you predict that students will carry with them into your classroom? How might their experiences affect their ability to be engaged and successful learners?

4. What can you do to promote mental health and wellness in your classroom?

 Visit the web resource for ideas and resources for fostering a mentally healthy classroom.

Voices From the Field

©Carolyn Lewis

Carolyn Lewis
Teacher (grade 1), Ontario

I teach grade 1 at Stuart Baker Elementary School in Haliburton, Ontario. For my health units, resources such as *Spark* by John Ratey and *Calm, Alert, and Learning* by Stuart Shanker have inspired me. Through them I have come to recognize the value and importance of involving the whole body in learning and to facilitate the empowerment of students to self-regulate through physical activity. Learning opportunities are enriched with the integration of movement and physical activity. There are times when the movement is a transition between lessons or a separate body break. This might look like a math song playing on YouTube (e.g., *I Can Count to 100* by Mark D. Pencil) while facilitating a follow the leader dance around the room that develops spatial awareness. We are practicing our counting, burning some energy, and having fun! There are also times when the movement is an integral part of the lesson. For example, when first introducing coding, I have students code each other on a large carpet grid with obstacles. One student prepares the code that the other then follows to navigate the "field."

My students and I enjoy using Phonic Dance, a program created by Ginny Dowd, daily. It is a program that uses rhyme, movement, and chant to teach phonics and develop the decoding skills of young readers.

For me, before using Phonic Dance, reading and writing was less physical; it was mostly sitting with oral and written practice. Now, if a student needs a reminder of the letter sounds or the sounds a group of letters, called Hunks and Chunks, we can move our bodies and gesture to help us. This increase in physical activity promotes attention and retention.

I know my students are learning and enjoying the physical activity of Phonic Dance when they can:

- point out Hunks and Chunks in a piece of shared writing
- choose to sing the Hunks and Chunks when reading independently
- use the phonics we have practiced to successfully decode words
- be excited to learn a new Hunk and Chunk and somewhat disappointed when there are none left to do
- willingly and independently practice the dance as a class at the beginning of each day

CHAPTER 9

Comprehensive School Health

Rebecca Lloyd ■

Joanne G. de Montigny ■ **Jessica Whitley**

LEARNING OUTCOMES

After studying this chapter, you will be able to

- describe and compare various school health models;
- explain the complexity involved in forming partnerships between schools, health units, and the community;
- locate and apply health-promoting curriculum and support documents to further develop your teaching practice;
- access and gain inspiration from real-life examples of pre-service and in-service teachers who champion health; and
- discover and formulate practical strategies to promote comprehensive health.

If you are interested in becoming a champion of health in your university, college, or school, the following prompts will help you determine your readiness, motivation, and interest in regard to creating capacity. For each, indicate your answer in the form of a number from 1 (least) to 10 (most).

- How motivated are you to promote health? _____

- If you were asked to lead a health-promoting initiative today for your peers (i.e., pre- and in-service teachers), how motivated would you be to do so? _____

- If you were invited to attend a health-promoting workshop offered by a peer, how motivated would you be to do so? _____

- How important is it to you to promote health in a relational, community-forming way? _____

These prompts are designed to orient you to the relational dimensions of comprehensive school health (CSH). As you learn about CSH in this chapter, you will see that you cannot experience and promote it by acting as a "lone ranger." Your energy for leading initiatives is important, but the key to long-term success lies in your ability to work with others and create a team of health-promoting champions in your institution.

Becoming aware of your own readiness to champion health, as well as that of your peers, will also help you determine appropriate roles in a health-promoting team. A good leader requires supportive followers. Moreover, similar to the way a flock of Canada geese fly—by taking turns in the demanding spot at the front of the V formation—it is essential to share the responsibility of leadership. If such dynamics are not acknowledged, tensions can arise, as we ourselves discovered when we formed a group of pre-service teachers to champion health on campus, at local schools, and in the community (University of Ottawa Faculty of Education, n.d.; Lloyd, Whitley, & Olsen, 2013). For example, the following excerpt from an end-of-year interview indicates frustration on the part of someone who felt an imbalance in leadership:

> People are always gonna find a reason why they can't go to something or do something outside of class. And I think the expectation should be set that, you know, by being part of this group, you know, you're expected to go a little bit above and beyond for the, for the group. . . . And it seems like they're in two separate camps. People who are always puttin' into the pot, and people who are always takin' out.

In order to experience and promote authentic CSH, the health-promoting team must have a sense of agency. The process of working together to create a vision and a CSH action plan departs from the typical hierarchical relationships that professors and teachers have with their students. When we first created a CSH team, we asked our students to share their ideas. As indicated in the following excerpt from an end-of-year interview, this approach was not expected, and it posed a challenge for some students who were accustomed to being told what to do:

> The big question mark at the beginning was what is expected of us. I think a lot of people thought, coming to that first day, "Okay, well, you're gonna tell us how to roll with this," and instead it was, "Okay, what do you want it to be?"

These interview excerpts speak of the tensions that can arise when pre-service teachers are invited to become involved in health-promoting initiatives above and beyond their coursework. When our participants realized that they were being invited to champion health and become part of the process of setting goals, planning, and promoting health, they reacted in various ways. Some became leaders, others became supportive followers, and a few chose to opt out of the CSH activities and focus on their coursework since completing a teacher education program constitutes a challenge in and of itself.

We began this chapter by giving you an opportunity to assess your readiness to champion health. Now we have shared some of our personal experiences with promoting CSH in our institution. In the next sections, we provide definitions, models, and resources to help you champion CSH. We also include a section that addresses the benefits and challenges of forming sustainable CSH teams.

What Is Comprehensive School Health?

Comprehensive school health is an integrative and holistic approach to promoting health and well-being (Stolp, Wilkins, & Raine, 2015). Much more than a school subject or a unit to cover, CSH is a far-reaching, cross-curricular, relational phenomenon that lives in vibrant interconnections formed between students, teachers, parents, policies, and communities. Construing health in this way not only shifts it from being a noun, as in a thing to learn, but also embodies the definition of health put forth by the World Health Organization (WHO) in 1948: "Health is a state of complete physical, mental, and social well-being and not merely the absence of disease or infirmity" (2003, para. 1).

Thinking about health as a state of being affords a verb like conception of health in that it may grow, flourish, or fade. This perspective also invites us to approach health in action-oriented ways. In fact, formulating key actions for health promotion was the main focus of the WHO's first international conference on health promotion, namely The Ottawa Charter for Health Promotion, which was held in 1986. This conference created the foundation for the CSH approach, as those who gathered saw the need to build healthy public policy; create supportive environments for health; strengthen community action for health; develop personal skills; and reorient health services in ways that enable, mediate, and advocate health for all (World Health Organization, 2016).

Much more than a school subject or a unit to cover, CSH is a far-reaching, cross-curricular, relational phenomenon that lives in vibrant inter-connections formed between students, teachers, parents, policies, and communities.

Schools are ideal settings in which to promote health because improvements in well-being may also improve academic performance throughout the school year (Nyaradi, Li, Hickling, Foster, & Oddy, 2013; Nyaradi, Foster, et al., 2014). In turn, succeeding in school contributes to enhanced life management skills and favourable socioeconomic status in adulthood, both of which are associated with better health outcomes (Commission on the Social Determinants of Health, 2008; Furnée, Groot, & Maassen van den Brink, 2008).

Broad, comprehensive conceptions of school health are mobilized by many models and curriculum support documents. Despite the different terminology used throughout the world—namely, "health-promoting school" in Europe and Australia, "coordinated school health" in the United States, and "comprehensive school health" in Canada—there are many commonalities. Although variations exist in the way each framework is put into practice, the underlying dimensions for action remain the same: curriculum integration, enhancement of the social and physical environment (including through policy development), and family and community involvement. This multicomponent approach, also referred to as the "healthy school" approach in North America and Europe, is distinguished in part by its emphasis on simultaneously addressing a broad array of health concerns. These topics include nutrition, physical activity, mental health promotion, sexual health, individualized health services, and prevention of injury and substance misuse.

For you as a developing teacher, it is a good idea to become familiar with various school health models firsthand. The following paragraphs provide an overview of open-access models and resources available to you. As you read about each model, think about how it may inspire you to assess the state of health in your institution and understand the complex, interrelational nature of school health.

World Health Organization

The World Health Organization formulated its Global School Health Initiative in 1995 to strengthen health promotion at the local, national, regional, and global levels. According to the WHO, a health-promoting school (HPS) "constantly strengthens its capacity as a healthy setting for living, learning, and working" (World Health Organization, 2016, n.p.). More specifically, an HPS

- promotes health through all available measures and resources;
- integrates efforts by health officials, teachers, teachers' unions, students, parents, health providers, and community leaders;
- creates a healthy environment through various programs offered to both students and staff that are premised on holistic conceptions of health in areas such as safety, nutrition, physical education, recreation, counseling, and mental health promotion;
- implements health-related policies and adopts health-related practices that offer high rates of acknowledged success; and
- continually strives to improve the health of students, school personnel, families, and community members.

The WHO (n.d.) offers many resources for creating a health-promoting school and for introducing specific lessons and initiatives on topics such as reproductive health, nutrition, physical activity, malaria prevention, prevention of sexually transmitted diseases and related discrimination, violence prevention, and life skills. The organization also offers links to groups dedicated to HPS assessment, as well as networks and partners who have a vested interest in promoting school health.

Joint Consortium for School Health

The Pan-Canadian Joint Consortium for School Health (JCSH) is arguably the most valuable resource for pre-service and in-service teachers situated in Canadian schools. It is premised on a partnership of 25 health and education ministries across Canada who share the same vision—that "Canadian children and youth experience optimal health and learning" (Pan-Canadian Joint Consortium for School Health, 2016, para. 3). The JCSH model is based on four interrelated pillars: social and physical environment, teaching and learning, healthy school policy, and partnerships and services (Pan-Canadian Joint Consortium for School Health, n.d.).

To put the JCSH model into context, imagine how you might approach a health-related fundraising initiative in a grade 3 classroom. For years, let us imagine, the school in which you are situated has celebrated a cakewalk, in which cakes donated by parents are raffled off. As the teacher now in charge of this classroom, you wish to involve your students in healthy eating. However, before you act on your instinct to simply cancel or replace the event, you decide to assess the tradition through a relational lens mediated by the JCSH pillars:

- *Social and physical environment.* How meaningful is this event to the students, parents, and school community? How many people usually participate? Where in the school does the event usually take place? How much money does it typically raise? Are other fundraising events equally popular?

- *Teaching and learning.* What curriculum links to healthy eating and nutrition might be assessed in order to support an inquiry approach to learning about cakes? Are some cakes healthier than others? What resources might be accessed to promote healthier cake recipes or other foods to sell?

- *Partnerships and services.* Have community members typically been involved in the annual fundraiser? Might they be receptive to discussing healthier food options for fundraising events?

- *Policy.* One of the best ways to advocate for change is to become familiar with existing health-promoting policies—for example, Ontario's Policy/Program Memorandum No. 150, which addresses school food and beverage policy (Ontario Ministry of Education, 2010)—and offer support for aligning fundraising initiatives more closely with such policies.

In addition to information about the conceptual pillars of comprehensive school health, the JCSH website also offers many resources to help you with health promotion, such as the Healthy School Planner, the Positive Mental Health Toolkit, and the Youth Engagement Toolkit. It also offers resources addressing policy, as well as resources on substance use, that are geared to youth, families, classrooms, and communities. In addition, JCSH offers opportunities for partnership, connection, and membership.

Physical and Health Education Canada

Physical and Health Education (PHE) Canada has advocated for quality health and physical education in Canadian schools for more than 75 years. It provides health and physical education teachers with resources such as lesson and unit plans, ideas for recreation, and opportunities for professional development through its annual conference and quarterly journal. Specific to the comprehensive school health movement, PHE Canada has developed a model for cultivating healthy school communities premised on five core components: teaching and learning, physical and social environment, evidence, policy, and community partnerships and services. The healthy school communities section of its website (www.phecanada.ca/programs/hsc) offers lesson plans; links to health curricula across Canada; and other resources, such as Ontario's Foundations for a Healthy School document and health promotion materials specific to parents, students, and teachers.

PHE Canada also works to acknowledge associations, health professionals, parents, and students who make exceptional contributions to promoting school health. The organization's Health Promoting Schools Champion Award formally recognizes those who make a difference. For more information, visit the web page for the award program (www.phecanada.ca/awards/health-promoting-school-champion) and consider acknowledging the efforts of someone you know who is committed to promoting school health. In addition, PHE Canada supports the development of healthy school communities through conferences and forums. Membership in this vibrant, health-promoting organization is open to students, teachers, and schools.

Whole School, Whole Community, Whole Child

In the United States, the Centers for Disease Control and Prevention's coordinated school health model, initiated in 1987, has recently been combined with the whole child approach promoted by the Association for Supervision and Curriculum Development to create a new model addressing the physical and emotional needs of students from a unified health and education perspective. The result is the Whole School, Whole Community, Whole Child (WSCC) model (Lewallen, Hunt, Potts-Datema, Zaza, & Giles, 2015), which includes 10 key components:

1. health education
2. physical education and physical activity
3. nutrition environment and services
4. health services
5. counseling, psychological, and social services
6. social and emotional climate
7. physical environment
8. employee wellness
9. family engagement
10. community involvement

The WSCC model reflects the need for "greater emphasis on both the psychosocial and physical environments as well as the ever-expanding roles that community agencies and families must play" (Association for Supervision and Curriculum Development, 2014, p. 6). Furthermore, the model positions students as active participants in their learning and health and posits that improvements in both areas also require integration of policy, process, and practice. An in-depth description of the model is provided on the CDC website (www.cdc.gov/healthyyouth/wscc), which also includes online tools for assessing and improving school health.

Becoming a Champion of CSH: Forming a Community of Practice

Implementing a CSH approach can be overwhelming, particularly for those who are accustomed to more formal modes of teaching and learning associated with the banking model of education, in which information is delivered to students as if it were a commodity (see Freire, 1990). Such modes present a challenge for those who wish to implement a CSH approach, because they are based on a hierarchical conception in which teachers act as experts on subject matter that is inputted into students' minds. In contrast, given that CSH is based on a broad conception of health, it is highly unlikely that any teacher—and particularly a generalist elementary teacher who is responsible for teaching every subject across the curriculum—will become an expert in every dimension of health (e.g., physical, social, emotional, political). Instead, becoming a champion of school health requires a conceptual shift from teaching as a process of inputting information to teaching as a relational phenomenon (Lloyd, Garcia Bengoechea, & Smith, 2010).

Thus, for those who wish to champion school health, a sociocultural approach to teaching and learning is highly recommended because it is premised on the notion of learning in community. For example, the situated learning perspective put forth by Jean Lave and Etienne Wenger (1991) describes the learning process in relation to legitimate participation in a community. Such a conception shifts the localization of thought from the individual mind and acknowledges that learning may be understood as a relational, participatory phenomenon that takes into account "the whole person acting in the world" (Lave & Wenger, p. 49). The learning that occurs in such relationships—which Wenger (1998) later termed "communities of practice"—hinges on the fact that all members are engaged in the practice of something, in our case the promotion of health.

Therefore, in order to become champions of health, we must form meaningful relationships with others who share a health-promoting vision and participate in health promotion through various means, such as supporting others who are engaged in

In order to become champions of health, we must form meaningful relationships with others who share a health-promoting vision and participate in health promotion.

health promotion and leading health-promoting initiatives that take into account what is needed in a school or university community. Such an approach may help new teachers better understand the complexity of CSH because participation in a learning community helps people comprehend what is learned in a community of practice (Cuddapah & Clayton, 2011). To learn more about communities of practice (COP) and resources that facilitate such an understanding of learning, see the COP website (http://wenger-trayner.com).

Creating Partnerships Between Schools and Communities

As a champion of CSH who is ready to venture into health promotion in the school context, you need to find guidance, inspiration, and assistance in the broader community. Schools provide an ideal setting to anchor the valuable contributions made by various external stakeholders in school health. Through relationship building, these external stakeholders can play a vital role in the development and implementation of initiatives (e.g., policies, programs, projects) to encourage healthy living and well-being in the student population.

CSH is rewarding work, but it does have its challenges. Fortunately, as an emerging champion of school health, you are not alone. Indeed, much support exists all around your school, and this support can be especially helpful in overcoming resistance. Not all school administrators are

prepared to prioritize the link between students' health and well-being and their academic performance (Maras, Weston, Blacksmith, & Brophy, 2015). This reluctance may relate to competing demands due to limited capacity and, in certain cases, to crisis situations that overshadow opportunities for health promotion across the whole school (Firth et al., 2008; Flaschberger, Nitsch, & Waldherr, 2012). Even so, amid the educational pressures and community issues, some school administrators and fellow teachers remain willing to engage in health promotion initiatives. Buy-in comes about when school personnel believe that such efforts could possibly meet a perceived school need or enhance their students' school experiences.

Although your school's buy-in is necessary to the CSH approach, it is not sufficient. Additional challenges usually arise during implementation, and you can receive help in meeting these challenges by joining forces with community partners. Indeed, we are more likely to improve student well-being when we engage and motivate each other and build capacity together with the aim of sustaining health promotion initiatives. Table 9.1 presents the fundamentals of school health partnerships. The first three partnership components were derived from Emerson and colleagues' theoretical framework for collaborative arrangements (Emerson, Nabatchi, & Balogh, 2012); the elements that make up each component refer specifically to partnerships for the promotion of comprehensive school health.

■ TABLE 9.1

Overcoming Comprehensive School Health Challenges With Community Partners

Partnership components	Partnership elements			
Engagement	Diverse partners	School buy-in	Common understanding	Stepwise approach
Motivation	Ongoing communication to cultivate trust	Mutual support	Commitment and school ownership	Passion
Capacity building	Interorganizational structures	Adequate resources	Operational knowledge	Leadership at all levels
Sustainability	Cost-effective initiatives, including progress monitoring and professional development	Notions of a healthy way of life embedded in school culture	Alignment of organizational priorities among partners	Whole-school participation with strong focus on student engagement

©Joe Barrett

Engaging With External Stakeholders

More can be done to engage with external stakeholders from various sectors in order to promote health in a school setting (Ahmed, 2005; Stewart, 2008). Working directly with a variety of community partners can ensure that initiatives complement one another and provide greater benefits to students (Christian et al., 2015). Diverse partners may be found in your broader community, such as your public health unit, community health centres, police department, social service agencies, not-for-profit organizations, clubs for children and youths, recreation and sport groups, local businesses, the media, and, most important, parents. Public health units, for example, offer their specialized skill set in relationship building across the broader community and in facilitating team work. Furthermore, public health personnel can help secure buy-in for health promotion at the school level. Strategies to secure buy-in include raising awareness of research showing that student well-being benefits both academic performance and classroom behaviour; seeking and valuing students' input on ways for them to take action on their own behalf; and supporting opportunities in schools, school boards, and parent councils to discuss students' well-being and develop a sense of shared responsibility (Stolp et al., 2015).

Partnerships with the school community flourish when we use open dialogue to foster a common understanding of what we and our partners wish to achieve together and how to do so. Engaging openly with one another creates opportunities to share information, examine concerns, and explore possible ways to address them. Meaningful engagement occurs naturally when we talk about shared visions and goals, begin to speak the same language, and clarify roles and procedures for common understanding (Corbin & Mittelmark, 2008; Thomas, Rowe, & Harris, 2010). As you engage with partners, keep in mind what your school considers to be feasible in order to maintain its buy-in. Comprehensive school health initiatives may need to be implemented in a stepwise manner while continuously engaging with partners (Firth et al., 2008); it may be advantageous to build gradually on what is already happening in the school to avoid overwhelming the participants.

As you engage with partners, keep in mind what your school considers to be feasible in order to maintain its buy-in.

Motivating Partners Through Committed Relationships

The CSH approach depends on cultivating positive, reciprocal, and committed relationships among partners; in turn, the development and strength of these relationships depend on the role played by school health champions (Rothwell et al., 2010). Relationships are usually strengthened through ongoing communication, especially face-to-face gatherings in which participants engage openly with each other. Regular communication maintains the connection between partners and enables them to appreciate what each partner has to offer. This appreciation enables partners to develop the mutual trust necessary to sustain interdisciplinary relationships (Aston, Shi, Bullot, Galway, & Crisp, 2005; Coulter & Coulter, 2003).

Motivation also emerges through helping each other, or providing mutual support. Teachers value their community partners when these partners readily respond to their requests for assistance; similarly, community partners appreciate teachers who take care of organizational tasks in support of the partnership. Such connections carry the relationship forward and enrich the partnership experience (Thomas et al., 2010).

Mutual support between your school and the broader community goes hand in hand with committed engagement, which is a critical aspect of school health partnerships. Commitment and school ownership develop when partners demonstrate their responsiveness to the school community's perceived needs and adapt their offerings to meet the school's identified priorities and existing capacity (Christian et al., 2015; Firth et al., 2008; Senior, 2012). The partnership is more likely to succeed when schools have a say about how to get started and how to build on what has been done so far. This voice gives them more control, and thus greater appreciation, of the direction they are taking for positive change. When teachers, other school staff, and students are invited to work on goals that directly cater to their interests and level of readiness, they are more willing to fully engage.

Engagement is also motivated by the passion shared among like-minded partners who are acting as change agents for the health and well-being of students. The passion shared by teachers and community partners fortifies their relationships and increases the effectiveness of their shared work (Jack, 2005; Thomas et al., 2010).

Building Capacity for School Health Promotion

Building the capacity to engage in a partnership involves establishing the interorganizational structures, resources, knowledge, and leadership that are required in order to achieve a shared goal (Emerson et al., 2012). Various forms of interorganizational structure may be encountered in school health promotion—for instance, a steering committee managing a local network of various community organizations at a district level; a consortium coordinating services for a specific group of students with similar needs; and a school-based group composed of the principal (when available), the school health champion, fellow teachers, other school staff, students, a health professional, and other community representatives who all work together to plan and implement whole-school initiatives (Davidson, Schwartz, & Noam, 2008; Flaschberger et al., 2012; Rothwell et al., 2010; Thomas et al., 2010). This latter type—the school-based group—is often referred to as a health action team or, more generically, a school council. By any name, such a group is charged with preparing action plans based on needs assessments, and it is a key component of the CSH approach. In cases where all team members come from the school community, the group can still seek input from community partners as needed (Ahmed, 2005).

As for financial capacity, schools often lack district-level mechanisms to seek grant funding, and additional school resources for promoting students' health and well-being may not be readily available. As a result, in order to make up for workforce shortages and lack of teacher release time, teachers often volunteer their services. Funding limitations may also force schools to choose only those activities that involve minimal costs. Therefore, the main benefit of working in a partnership is that it allows participants to pool valuable community resources in order to expand the realm of possibilities for greater impact (Butterfoss, Goodman, & Wandersman, 1993; Stewart, 2008).

Another major challenge of health promotion in schools is posed by personnel changes, whether in the school community or in partner organizations. When people move to other positions, relationships must be rebuilt, which can result in loss of momentum and even changes in direction. To maximize stability, then, it is important for participation in school health teams to last at least three years (Firth et al., 2008). Still, turnover is often inevitable; fortunately, the effects can be lessened by sharing action plans with teachers, school board representatives, and parents, thus helping to ensure that school health initiatives remain at the forefront of school administrators' thinking and retain their ongoing support (Staten et al., 2005).

Time is an equally valuable partnership asset. It takes much time to cultivate relationships, set up school health teams or committees, conduct needs assessments, and prepare collaborative action plans. Feeling that there is not enough time to get everything done is a frequently cited challenge that can leave participants feeling overburdened (DeWitt, Lohrmann, O'Neill, & Clark, 2011). For this reason, it is crucial for partners to establish mutual support, commitment, and passion.

In order to implement health promotion initiatives comprehensively, participants must acquire knowledge in the form of CSH expertise and professional skills on an ongoing basis. Since teacher release time is likely limited for professional development, some of the knowledge gap can be filled through external organizations. For example, government departments and other community partners may help meet knowledge requirements by providing training opportunities (Ahmed, 2005). Furthermore, local public health units can provide information about best and promising practices, thus minimizing the time required for school staff to find creative ideas for engaging the school community. Involvement in networks, or other partnership meetings, offers another practical way of learning what has worked well in schools and how to overcome obstacles along the way.

Even with sufficient knowledge, resources, and interorganizational structures, CSH depends heavily on effective leadership. Leaders, who can be found at various levels in schools and school boards, drive initiatives forward. In fact, the departure of a leader has been shown to delay progress until the replacement can fully assume his or her new responsibilities (Rothwell et al., 2010). Leadership by school administrators may take various forms—for instance, serving as the formal point of contact with external partners, seeking available resources, and supporting teacher release time for planning activities (Firth et al., 2008; Viig & Wold, 2005). Another type of leader is the school health champion, who may fulfill a number of roles, such as steering a school team or committee engaged in action planning and encouraging participation in school health promotion activities. If you are a CSH champion, your vision and passion for creating a healthy school will inspire and attract engagement and support both within and beyond your school.

Aiming for Sustainable Implementation

One major challenge in CSH is that of sustaining the initial enthusiasm by means of continued support and resources. Health promotion initiatives with start-up funding must be cost effective in the long run if the school is to cover ongoing expenses (above and beyond what can be expected from community partners). These initiatives also need to establish effective ways to monitor their progress in order to keep interest high, make course corrections as required, provide appropriate professional development opportunities, and maintain activities after the intervention period concludes (Christian et al., 2015).

If you are a CSH champion, your vision and passion for creating a healthy school will inspire and attract engagement and support both within and beyond your school.

Sustainability can also be ensured by taking steps to embed notions of a healthy way of life in school culture. Such steps might include making the school's ethos, or social environment, more conducive to healthy living; pursuing goals identified by the school for a sense of ownership; and integrating healthy school concepts into the curriculum and into daily school practices (Firth et al., 2008; Flaschberger et al., 2012; Stewart, 2008). Historically, teachers and school staff have viewed health promotion as an add-on—that is, something to be done on a voluntary basis outside of routine tasks at school. But times are changing, and new ways of thinking are emerging. Now, school personnel are beginning to view health promotion activities as an "add-in"—in other words, as part of their day-to-day jobs (Flaschberger et al., 2012; Viig & Wold, 2005).

In order to achieve lasting change, health-promotion efforts require school health partnerships in which all partners align their organizational priorities. Such partners help ensure sustainability through shared goals, complementary resources, and contributions to school staff development (Inchley, Muldoon, & Currie, 2006; Warwick et al., 2005). Sharing goals not only means "being on the same page" but also signifies that community partners are meeting their respective

organizational priorities and are therefore well positioned to continue their engagement.

Special attention must also be given to engaging the whole school community as much as possible. When only a few teachers get involved, they may feel overloaded with additional responsibilities. This outcome can be avoided by distributing the work more evenly among teachers and staff members, as well as reaching out to community partners for support. Furthermore, responding to ideas and preferences expressed by students—who are key internal partners—can produce remarkable health outcomes because students generally listen attentively to what their peers have to say. Thus school champions and fellow teachers serve not only as essential role models of healthy behaviour but also as significant mentors to bring out the leadership potential in schoolchildren and sustain their engagement (Stolp et al., 2015).

Becoming a Champion of CSH: A Mindfulness Example

Based on our personal experiences, we began this chapter by speaking to the tensions involved in forming a CSH team in an institution. We wish to conclude by sharing a success story—an example that highlights what can be accomplished through positive synergy. Along with CSH professor Jessica Whitley, a small group of students opted to develop and lead an eight-week mindfulness-based program in a nearby elementary school. As a team, the students learned about mindfulness, which has been defined by Kabat-Zinn (2003) as "the awareness that emerges through paying attention on purpose, in the present moment, and nonjudgmentally, to the unfolding of experience moment by moment" (p. 145). This program appealed to preservice teachers as an extracurricular activity that might enable them to help students with a range of learning profiles, including those with anxiety, ADHD, and learning disabilities (Flook et al., 2010; Haydicki, Wiener, Badali, Milligan, & Ducharme, 2012). Research shows that practicing mindfulness can also help educators improve their well-being, reduce stress and burnout, and prepare to create environments that reflect mindfulness principles (Jennings, Snowberg, Coccia, & Greenberg, 2011; Poulin, Mackenzie, Soloway, & Karayolas, 2008).

The activities that made up the mindfulness program were collected from a number of resources, including the key work of Susan Kaiser

Greenland (2010). Our goal for the program was to help students become really aware of experiences, both inside and outside of themselves. To this end, we focused quite a bit on breathing deeply and purposefully. Other activities focused on helping students develop awareness while sitting, eating, walking, listening, and observing. To help students make connections to abstract concepts, we used child-friendly books, concrete objects, and simple discussion questions. We are hopeful that students will continue to practice the skills they learned with us when they are outside of the classroom.

In preparing to engage with students through the program, the CSH cohort members met once per week throughout the fall semester in order to explore mindfulness principles and either begin or deepen their own mindfulness practice. This preparation time was crucial to understanding and modelling elements of mindfulness in their classrooms. During the winter semester, this group of CSH champions visited a classroom once per week for about 40 minutes. In addition, a letter was sent home to parents describing the program and inviting questions, and a brief overview of mindfulness concepts and activities was provided to parents and school staff (figure 9.1).

Practicing mindfulness can help you develop strategies for building relationships with students, parents, and colleagues; it can also help you recognize and respond effectively to student difficulties. Even without a specific program, bringing elements of mindfulness into the classroom can help you with everyday management and class climate. For example, many teachers integrate mindfulness practice into the classroom by inviting students to take part in a few minutes of silent, focused breathing during transition times and other times when they need to focus or regroup.

Many relevant resources are available on this topic, and a few of them are noted in the following list. Many boards offer training opportunities, and some have purchased packaged programs—for example, MindUP (Hawn Foundation, 2011a, 2011b)—for teachers to use with their students. Some boards also include social workers, resource teachers, or psychologists with expertise in mindfulness who can work with schools, teachers, and

Exploring Mindfulness With Children for Parents and Educators

The Importance of Mindfulness

Being mindful means using your breath, your open and curious mind, and your senses to experience what is happening right now. Mindfulness encourages you to develop awareness of your body, your mind, and the world around you. This practice builds concentration, emotional awareness, and healthy coping skills in children and adults alike.

Making Mindfulness a Part of Each Day

Here you'll find three daily activities that offer an opportunity to practice mindfulness. The simple act of noticing details that you may take for granted promotes self-awareness and a sense of calm. Thus it reminds you to enjoy the present!

Mindful Breathing

The simplest way to anchor yourself in the present moment is to be aware of your breathing. Mindful breathing can calm your body and mind at any time of day. With your hands on your belly, feel your breath fill your belly as you inhale and relax as you exhale. Notice the length of each breath. Notice how your body feels from head to toe.

Mindful Walking

Practice paying attention to the present moment by using your senses and an open mind while taking a mindful walk. Notice your deep breaths, the way your body moves, and the thoughts in your mind. Enjoy the world around you! What sounds, sights, and smells are you taking in?

Figure 9.1 Mindfulness handout for parents and educators.

Mindful Eating

Choose a food to eat mindfully, perhaps a raisin. Explore the look, touch, smell, and, finally, the taste of this food. What does it feel like in your hand? What does it smell like? What does it feel like on your tongue? How would you describe the taste of it?

Mindful Activities

Sound in Space and the Sparkle Jar introduce the concepts of breath awareness, mindful listening, and letting go of our thoughts and emotions (that is, practicing "beginner's mind"). These exercises can become daily or weekly rituals that leave us calm, present, and ready to focus.

Sound in Space

Begin with a mindfulness bell. (A resonant instrument can be used instead.)

1. Getting ready

   Prepare to be mindful by sitting in a comfortable position (legs crossed). Imagine there is a zipper from your belly button to your nose. Zip it up as you sit up tall and strong.

2. Mindful breathing

   Notice your breathing. Let each breath become longer and deeper. Put your hands on your belly. Let your belly expand with air as you breathe in, and relax as you breathe out.

3. Listening to the bell

   Play one note on your bell or chime. Close your eyes or focus your eyes on your hands in your lap. Listen mindfully to the full sound of the bell and follow the sound with your ears until it is silent. When you think the sound has completely disappeared, put up your pinky finger. (Repeat this activity up to three times.)

Sparkle Jar

Begin with a jar full of water and a bag of sparkles or a box of baking soda.

1. What happened today?

   Remember the events of your day and the thoughts and emotions you had.

2. A pinch of sparkles

   Name each thought or feeling and release it into the jar with a pinch of sparkles.

3. Shake it up!

   Once your jar is full of today's sparkles, cap the jar and shake it vigorously.

4. Ahhh . . .

   Watch as the sparkles slowly settle to the bottom of the jar, leaving the water still and clear. Breathe deeply. As you breathe, the thoughts in your mind are settling down, just like a tiny sparkle. A still and clear mind that is free from thoughts and emotions of the past is called "beginner's mind."

Resources

You can use these resources to discover ways in which parents and educators empower children through mindfulness and how to create a mindful practice of your own.

Websites

- Mindful hub: www.mindfulhub.com
- The Hawn Foundation: https://mindup.org/thehawnfoundation/
- Susan Kaiser Greenland: www.susankaisergreenland.com
- Mindful Schools: mindfulschools.org

Books

- *The Mindful Child* by Susan Kaiser Greenland
- *Planting Seeds: Practicing Mindfulness With Children* by Thich Nhat Hanh
- *The MindUP Curriculum* by the Hawn Foundation
- *Mindful Teaching and Teaching Mindfulness: A Guide for Anyone Who Teaches Anything* by Deborah Schoeberlein David with Suki Sheth

Figure 9.1 *(continued)*
©Jessica Whitley

students. Even in the absence of such structural supports, many of our CSH cohort students and graduates find ways to integrate mindfulness into their lives and their teaching.

If you are interested in bringing mindfulness approaches into your own classroom or school, here are a few tips that we have learned along the way:

- *Develop expertise.* It is crucial to develop a mindfulness practice of your own before trying to teach students about it. You must be able to model mindfulness and share personal experiences of it.

- *Reach out.* As discussed earlier, taking a team approach is the most effective way to bring CSH practices into a school. You can likely find practitioners at local community-based organizations or universities who are trained in coaching mindfulness and would be willing to work with you to bring these approaches to children and staff.

- *Don't reinvent the wheel.* Many books, websites, videos, and apps have been developed to bring mindfulness-based approaches to children and others in educational settings. Some of these resources may be a perfect fit for your particular context. Explore the resources available to you!

- *Start small.* Many teachers with whom we have worked were initially nervous about implementing mindfulness-based approaches with their students. As with any CSH innovation, it can be helpful to begin on a small scale and build confidence and acceptance. For example, as described earlier, some teachers begin by creating "sparkle jars" with students to serve as mindfulness tools for focusing and feeling calm. Others work with students during snack time to learn about eating mindfully. Many focus on mindful games or activities to help with transition times.

> *It is crucial to develop a mindfulness practice of your own before trying to teach students about it.*

- *Open dialogue.* It's important to have open discussions with parents, staff, and students who may not have a thorough understanding of mindfulness or what it looks like in a school context. You can also send a letter home (as we did) to invite parents to reach out and ask questions or express concerns, which you can then address.

- *Be flexible.* Many activities or approaches that we thought would work well with students turned out to be disasters. They also served as great learning experiences for us and allowed us to make necessary changes. We learned that we needed different approaches for certain ages, grades, and times of day. Flexibility is key!

Creating Ongoing Opportunities to Promote CSH

This chapter was written with the intention of providing information and examples in order to inspire more people, such as *you*, to champion health. Not every university or college has a team dedicated to CSH, and not every school has a health-promoting committee in place. Great journeys in life begin with small steps, and those who have experienced CSH realize that every step matters.

Many resources are available to help you establish a health-promoting school and community. For instance, the *School Health Guidance Document* created by the Ontario Ministry of Health Promotion (2010) provides a user-friendly summary of CSH-related resources, as well as a checklist to follow when you engage in the planning process. For each recommendation, the document provides information about how comprehensive health is promoted in schools in various countries, along with clear steps and supporting references. We suggest that you review this document, as well as the many relevant resources provided by the World Health Organization; the Joint Consortium for School Health; Physical and Health Education Canada; and the Whole School, Whole Community, Whole Child model of coordinated school health—all introduced earlier in this chapter.

Concluding Exercise

Form a group of four or five individuals who share a passion for promoting health, either on your campus or in local schools. Engage in a needs assessment for the community you wish to address, then determine how you will work together to plan, promote, track, and improve your health-promoting initiative. Consider the degree to which your program depends on your presence in order to continue for the long term. Is it sustainable? Could it eventually run on its own if a structure is put into place?

Please share your efforts and experiences in promoting CSH and consider writing an article that details your success. A number of magazines and journals are interested in how CSH is being promoted, including the *Physical and Health Education Journal*. You can also share your story on the website for the University of Ottawa's comprehensive school health program (http://uottawa-comprehensive-school-health.ca/)—we want to expand our health-promoting community! We wish you the best in your health-promoting journey, and we look forward to learning about your CSH success stories.

Summary

We hope you will come away with several big ideas after reading this chapter and consider your developing role as a champion of health. CSH is an active, dynamic approach to promoting well-being that can be reflected in all elements of school practice and policy. CSH is addressed through many terms and models worldwide, but all agree on the following:

- CSH must be integrated throughout the curriculum—not just limited to physical education and health.
- CSH must include enhancement of the social and physical environment.
- Families and communities need to be involved.
- The effort must address multiple components of health (e.g. nutrition, physical activity, mental health, sexual health).

Multiple organizations have developed models, resources, and tools and made them freely available to educators and school communities. Examples include the World Health Organization, the Pan-Canadian Joint Consortium for School Health, Physical and Health Education Canada, the U.S. Centers for Disease Control and Prevention, and the Association for Supervision and Curriculum Development.

Any successful and sustainable approach to promoting health in schools must be supported by a strong team. In order to create such a team, you must examine your own beliefs and strengths, seek out others who bring energy to the work at hand, and share the responsibility for championing health. The team can then decide on a shared vision and set concrete goals within the framework of a CSH action plan.

To help with the shift toward a CSH focus, consider the following strategies:

- *Form a community of practice.* Such a community enables members to learn with and from one another.
- *Create partnerships with the broader community.* Health services have typically been located in the community rather than in schools, and health-related needs can often be addressed by external stakeholders. Many community members possess expertise, experience, and resources and are happy to share them. Examples include parents, religious leaders, public health nurses, social service agencies, and local businesses.
- *Stay motivated!* Motivation depends on ongoing communication, mutual support, and sustained connection to your passion to work as a change agent for student health.
- *Build capacity for CSH promotion.* Effective CSH requires infrastructure, physical and human resources, dedicated time for planning and sharing, sustained leadership, and ongoing professional learning.
- *Aim to be sustainable.* Initiatives come and go in schools every year. In order to have staying power, CSH needs to be embedded in all aspects of school culture and promoted across the school community.

DISCUSSION QUESTIONS

1. What underlying conceptual threads are shared by the comprehensive school health models described in the chapter?
2. How does the subject-specific understanding of health (which is often paired with physical education) differ from a CSH conception?
3. What components of the CSH approach resonate with you and your teaching or leadership experiences to date? Describe a health-promoting experience in which you were successful.
4. When you consider the various models of comprehensive school health, which components present the greatest challenge in terms of implementing a program and developing the necessary skills and expertise? Now, work with a peer to develop three strategies for managing these challenges.

5. How might you gather a CSH team of like-minded individuals (e.g., teaching staff, administrators, students, community members) to promote health in your school?

6. What are the administrative steps required by your institution for proposing a new program, event, or initiative?

7. How might you create opportunities for teachers, support staff, students, and members of the community to get involved in promoting health at your school?

8. What activities might you plan to help build synergy within your CSH team?

9. Where might you find relevant resources for implementing and assessing CSH interventions?

10. Determine what each person on your CSH team might offer in terms of supporting the various dimensions of health.

 Visit the web resource for ready-to-use activities that develop mindfulness.

Voices From the Field

Patrick McKinnon
Health and Physical Education Teacher (Grades 7 and 8),
St. Patrick's Intermediate School, Ottawa

When I'm asked about the approach we take to health and physical education (HPE) at our school, I often begin by talking about—believe it or not—video games. The video gaming industry is continuously becoming more creative in finding ways to get kids hooked on its products. In this process, it has created games for just about any genre, topic, or theme that can engage the wide range of personalities and learning styles found in our children. Imagine if our HPE programs were that effective at promoting physical and mental well-being!

At St. Patrick's Intermediate, we understand that we have to broaden our approach in order to inspire and motivate more students to become active. With video games and television programs, if you don't like the show, you can simply change the game or the channel instead of turning the device off. Similarly, at St. Patrick's Intermediate, our program offers a wide range of independent and group activities, which range from the traditional sports of basketball, volleyball, track and field, and badminton to less traditional ones such as rock climbing, orienteering, geocaching, spinning, KIN-BALL, and snowshoeing. We also bring in groups from the community to promote these sports and activities to our children. If you don't like the activity of the day, we'll change the channel: Don't go away—we'll be right back! Our goal is to promote health and wellness as a lifestyle rather than a school subject.

Let's look at two examples: the spinning class we offer and the circuit training that is available in our fitness room. In both cases, students write their own fitness goals and choose activities to help them reach those goals. To make the spinning workout more appealing to my students, I have installed a high-definition, ceiling-mounted projector that allows them to spin amid scenes from various parts of the world. Another important element is music. I have noticed that when students can listen to their own music, they are generally more focused on their workout and less distracted by other people. I also provide each student with a heart rate monitor to track heart rate during the activity and evaluate it in reference to figures provided on wall-mounted charts. In the fitness room, everyone can train at their own pace regardless of ability level. There is *no* focus in these classes on winning, losing, or competing against anyone other than oneself. Instead, we focus on improving our mental and physical wellness. After class, most students leave with a good sweat and a smile.

We hope that what we teach here, because it has personal relevance, will be carried through into students' community living. In these efforts, I work in conjunction with the school principal to ensure that health and physical education is scheduled daily so that students can experience the Ontario government's daily physical activity policy in an educational, supportive, and positive environment. My approach to teaching and planning HPE over the school year offers many opportunities for students to experience success and form a positive relationship with physical activity.

PART III

Teaching Physical Education

CHAPTER 10

Teaching Team Building Activities

Carol Scaini ■ Catherine Casey

LEARNING OUTCOMES

After studying this chapter, you will be able to

- describe the role that team-building activities play in developing a positive classroom environment;
- explain the various roles that students can play in completing a team task;
- describe the importance of using various methods to select teams and groups;
- challenge students to work together both collaboratively and cooperatively to achieve a specific activity task; and
- challenge students to think critically, communicate clearly, and include all group members in solving tasks.

Team building is the cooperative process that a group of individuals uses to solve both physical and mental challenges. While using this process and solving the challenges, the group learns how to share ideas, how to praise and encourage one another, how to support one another physically and emotionally, and how to start becoming a team.

Midura & Glover (2005, p. 1)

Team-building activities give you an excellent way to build a classroom community and encourage positive student interaction. These activities involve group challenges that require critical thinking, problem solving, leadership, communication, and of course teamwork. Whether in the gymnasium or the classroom, these skills help students be more prepared to learn because they contribute to a safe and supportive learning environment. Team building provides a positive way to start the school year by giving students a chance to get to know each other and learn to trust, respect, and value each other's thoughts and ideas. They are also useful throughout the year for helping your students strengthen their group interaction. Thus team building involves more than just participating in cooperative games; it teaches kids how to be good teammates (Midura & Glover, 2005, p. 1).

> *Team building involves more than just participating in cooperative games; it teaches kids how to be good teammates (Midura & Glover, 2005, p. 1).*

When participating in team-building activities, students are required to work in groups to solve problems, which can either be posed by the teacher or created by the students. Either way, the activities give students an opportunity to work through a project together by setting goals and achieving them through fun interactions. Along the way, the activities build students' confidence as they persevere to complete each activity. The activities can be used at any point during a lesson to give students a chance to get up and move, talk with peers, and think differently. They can also be used in the gymnasium, either as a separate unit or as part of every health and physical education class meeting. Begin with simple team-building games and progress to more complex activities as students become more familiar with and proficient in meeting the challenge.

To illustrate how team-building activities can be used, let's consider an example. Let's say that students are organized into teams of eight using an app that electronically chooses teams for you, such as the Team Shake app. The teams are asked to move to the sideline of the gym, and each group is given seven poly spots (each with a diameter of 30 centimeters). The teacher informs the students that the gym is now a lake and that they need to get across it by using their seven lily pads (poly spots) so that no one gets wet! Each team then works collaboratively to decide how to stay dry while moving across the lake. If anyone on the team gets wet anywhere along the way, the team must go back and start again.

You can approach such activities in several ways. One approach is to assign specific roles for students to play as the team completes the activity. Such roles might include organizer, motivator, supporter, summarizer, and recorder. The organizer helps ensure that group members work together to clarify the task and helps direct the group's efforts to meet the challenge; the organizer also contacts the teacher if struggles arise (e.g., disagreements, arguments that can't be resolved, questions the group has that they can't solve, team is stuck). The motivator provides encouragement by using positive words to inspire team members while they work through the challenge, whereas the supporter praises students who provide good suggestions or help each other. After the activity has been completed, the summarizer recounts how the team solved the challenge, including any struggles, highlights, and instances of group members helping each other. Finally, the recorder writes down encouraging words and phrases that were used during the activity so that group members will recognize the importance of supporting each other with positive words (Midura & Glover, 2005, pp. 13-14). In selecting roles, you might consider students' levels of self-confidence, leadership skill, and ability to work collaboratively with others. This approach is most likely the best way to approach the activity with younger students.

Another approach is to introduce the activity, give very little in the way of direction, and then observe each group to see what happens:

- Which students take on leadership roles?
- What do those leadership roles look like?
- What other roles do students take on?
- What do the students value during the activity?
- How do the students resolve conflict?

> *Team-building activities are also designed to encourage students to take risks.*

Team-building activities are also designed to encourage students to take risks—not the kinds of risks that can result in physical injury but the risks involved in offering the group an idea to address the challenge at hand. When the team is functioning well, team members can offer their ideas without fear of being ridiculed or put down. This openness is a crucial aspect of team building, and you may need to facilitate positive and respectful feedback when team members disagree with a suggestion. Students should learn to provide valuable and productive feedback to their peers that will help the team meet the challenge. Through this positive talk, students learn how important their feedback can be in the overall success of a team.

Team-building activities also provide an interesting way to level the playing field for students because many of the activities do not require significant athletic ability. In addition, the cognitive component of team-building activities requires students to think in creative ways. Encourage students to think "outside the box" when problem-solving. In addition, in many of the activities, there is no single "right" way to solve the problem. Although it may be tempting for you to offer support for teams that run into road blocks or experience failure, allow them to work it through and learn to function together. In other words, allow teams to fail, but be there to recognize their good ideas and provide encouragement. When groups face challenges and failure, students may be quick to criticize each other or lose their focus on the task. In such cases, your role as a teacher is to reinforce the importance of using encouragement, both in words (e.g., "We can do it," "Let's try again") and in gestures and actions (e.g., pat on the back, high five). It is fun to see how students approach and solve the problem and to listen to their rationale for how they solved it.

It is fun to see how students approach and solve the problem and to listen to their rationale for how they solved it.

The benefits of this approach are worth the work: "As group members work together, they become characterized by a sense of profound respect, appreciation, and joy. Practicing team building in schools gives students concrete, practical experience for community building within society later in life" (Midura & Glover, 2005, p. 4).

Organizing Teams

Choosing teams is an aspect of game playing that receives very little attention but can have far-reaching effects. You may have had the experience of standing in a line against the wall of a gymnasium while your peers stare back at you and decide who to pick. In our experiences of working with teachers and teacher candidates, this is one of the first issues they raise when asked about their elementary school experience in physical education. The detail in which they describe their experiences is quite thought provoking. This finding has helped us realize the importance of providing pedagogically sound ways of choosing teams that do not marginalize or humiliate any student. To put it plainly, the fear of standing in that line waiting to be picked is very real, and this practice needs to stop *now*. This way of choosing teams is unacceptable, and this chapter provides you with various ways to choose teams in a respectfully dignified manner. Teachers are the biggest factors in a child's education; therefore, it is essential that you help your students develop respect for all.

Teachers are the biggest factors in a child's education; therefore, it is essential that you help your students develop respect for all.

In addition, consider the size of the groups you are creating. Members of smaller groups may experience less struggle in working through the task, because all members can be engaged. Larger groups, in contrast, may run into roadblocks if too many voices provide input or a few strong voices take over. Use your knowledge of your students to determine what group size will work best for them.

Here are some constructive methods for organizing teams:

- Numbers Game
  - Have students sit or stand in groups with the number of members you call out.
  - Start with the total number of students in the class.
  - Call out other numbers, each time having students move into groups of the indicated size (do this fairly quickly, and have any extra students stand with you).
  - End with the number of students you would like in each group. Make sure that the math works out so that everyone can be included in a group; if necessary offer two numbers (e.g., four and five) so that all students will be included.
- Barnyard Madness
  - Have the class choose four or more types of animals.

- Provide each student with a picture card depicting one of those animals.
- Have all students meet in the middle of the gym or playing area with their eyes closed (or open, depending on their comfort level).
- Students then make the sound or action—or show the picture card—of their animal and try to find the other members of their animal group.

■ Playing Cards

- Provide each student with a playing card.
- Students then each raise their card in the air while calling out its suit—heart, diamond, club, spade—and find the rest of their group members.

■ Beanbags

- Gather a set of beanbags based on colour and geared to the number and size of student groups you require. For example, if you want four groups with six members each, then prepare six red bean bags, six blue, six yellow, and six green.
- Provide each student with a beanbag.
- Students each raise their beanbag in the air to find the rest of their group members based on colour.

■ Bucket Drawing

- This approach mirrors that of beanbags but uses letters of the alphabet instead. For example, if you want four groups with six members each, then prepare six letter A's, six letter B's, six letter C's, and six letter D's.
- As students enter the playing area, have each student draw one card from the bucket.
- Students each raise their letter in the air while calling it out in order to find the rest of their group members.

■ Birthday Month

- Place students in groups based on birth month.
- Depending on how the math works out, each group can be based on one month or more than one—for example, January, February, and March in group 1; April, May, and June in group 2; and so on.

■ Clothing Characteristics

- Place students in groups based on shirt colour.

- Alternative: Place students in groups based on type of clothing (e.g., shorts, capris, track pants).

■ Name Game

- Have students get into groups based on the first letter of their first or last name.
- Groups with the letters A, B, C, D, X, Y, and Z
- Groups with the letters E, F, G, H, U, V, and W
- Groups with the letters I, J, K, L, S, and T
- Groups with the letters M, N, O, P, Q, and R
- Change the letter combinations. Place cards with one letter on each one in a bucket. Randomly pull out the cards to make new groups.

■ Counting

- Have students each count the number of letters in their first or last name.
- Then ask them to each find and partner up with someone in the class who has the same number of letters. If there is no match, the teacher can match the students.
- Next, connect pairs to form groups.
- Alternative: Have students each find a partner whose first or last name starts with the same letter. Any extra students go to you, and you can either assign them to a group or to a neighbouring letter's group (e.g., if your name starts with C, you can pair up with a student whose first name starts with the letter B or D).

■ Teacher's Choice

- Determine group membership in advance.
- Note students' names and groups on a card or list posted on the wall before class.

Now, with your teams chosen, you are ready to begin! To help you get started, the web resource for this chapter includes many fun and respectful team-building activities. Begin with the simple activities, then move to more challenging ones. You may wish to set up a few challenges to avoid having all student groups performing the same task at the same time. You can also set up an extra challenge so that if one group finishes a challenge earlier than the other groups, it can still move to a new one. Another option is to use an app such as GooseChase to set up a scavenger hunt of challenges using electronic devices.

Remember to remind students to be respectful, which is not only the right thing to do but will also help them succeed in meeting the challenges. To facilitate this reminder, here is a sample team pact (Glover & Anderson, 2003, pp. 39-40):

> For our team to be successful, all members will adhere to the following guidelines. (Be specific. If you say that everyone needs to respect each other, what does that mean? What behaviours show respect?)

- Don't use put-downs.
- Encourage teammates when they make a mistake, when they are down about something, and when they are doing something that is difficult.
- Praise teammates when they do something well.
- Listen to whoever is talking and don't interrupt.
- Don't always just sit by friends in huddle activities.
- Include everyone on the team and be nice to all.
- Always high-five each other after class.
- Don't always be the one who has to go first.
- Find a fair way to make decisions.
- Help teammates solve problems.

Summary

When you are introducing these activities, your presentation will make the difference in your students' attitudes. The more excited you are, the more excited your students will be! Then, during the activity, take the time to really cheer them on and motivate them to continue, even when they think the challenge cannot be achieved. Celebrate the successes of each group. If a group cannot achieve a given task, celebrate the fact that the group members tried their best, worked together, and communicated effectively. Also note that they can try the activity again. These activities are not mainly about winning or losing but about working together as a team—a whole team. Thus they give students opportunities to learn about inclusion and how it contributes to building a positive classroom and school community. In addition, leadership development begins at an early age, and we can guide our students to become respectful, responsible, and insightful leaders.

DISCUSSION QUESTIONS

1. Describe how the principles of inclusive education are reflected in the activities presented here for choosing teams.
2. Discuss the potential effects of team-building activities in other curricular areas.
3. Discuss how team-building activities contribute to a child's emotional, social, and physical development through the use of effective communication, collaboration, and cooperation.

 Visit the web resource for ready-to-use team-building activities.

Voices From the Field

©Andrew Chin

Andrew Chin

*K-8 Teacher of Health, Science, Library, Physical Education,
and Physical Education for the Complex Needs Class*

Aurora Heights Public School

Making physical education fun is much like making classroom education interesting—it all starts with your own love and enthusiasm. If you can create a sense of excitement and be an active participant rather than just an observer, then students really get engaged. At the same time, I also find it important to listen to students' interests. Some students, and even some classes, have a particular interest in certain activities. Although I believe that students should participate and try everything presented to them, we can also tailor certain activities to their specific interests.

One activity I like to use in my classes is called Reverse Leader. It requires planning four stations with activities for partners or groups. Students begin by playing follow-the-leader to any of the four stations. The trick is that the leader must have his or her eyes closed (in older grades, the leader can be blindfolded) and must be led by the follower, who is not allowed to touch the leader but walks closely behind while giving verbal directions. Once the students arrive at the station, the leader can open her or his eyes, and the students can complete the partner-based challenges. After completing a challenge, students switch roles so that the leader is now a follower and vice versa.

Despite the apparent simplicity of this activity, I like it very much because there are so many adaptations to be made in it. The activity will look completely different at the end of the year than at the beginning because students will have forged a much better relationship throughout the year; they will also be able to communicate with and direct each other more effectively. Adaptations are key to what keeps this activity great and interesting for all grades and skill levels. Here are some examples of possible adjustments:

- With primary grades, one can start by assigning each pair a specific station to start from and then explain to them that they must rotate in a certain way. For intermediate students, all the students can start at the centre of the gym and choose where to go from there.
- The stations you set up can be different each time you use this activity, depending on what skills you are working on.
- Students can work with different partners to develop relationships, or you can use a different number of partners each time.
- The way in which followers direct leaders can also vary. For example, they might use not only words but also hand gestures or slight taps on the shoulder. This interaction builds trust between students!
- If any students are uncomfortable with closing their eyes, they can walk backward while the follower walks forward.
- This activity is not a race, nor is there any pressure to complete all of the activities; partners should simply do their best to complete as many activities as possible.

How do you assess students to measure success, and what are the look-for learning points? Because this activity focuses on team building, I stress to my students that it does not matter how quickly a task is completed or how well it is performed; instead, the focus is on the effort they put into participating in the activity. Are the students following instructions for each task in order to ensure safe play? Are they cooperating in a positive manner with their partner(s) to travel safely to each station and complete the challenge? Thus this activity connects to overall curriculum expectations of demonstrating participation and cooperation between students, as well as demonstrating behaviours that maximize safety. Expectations based on movement competence can also be assessed at each station if you so choose.

CHAPTER 11

Teaching Movement Skills and Concepts

Helena Baert ■ **Matthew Madden**

LEARNING OUTCOMES

After studying this chapter, you will be able to

- summarize the theories that form the framework for teaching fundamental movement skills and concepts;
- identify fundamental movement skills and concepts;
- apply your knowledge of fundamental skills and concepts when observing, analyzing, and assessing student performance;
- explain the importance of implementing developmentally appropriate progressions for students at different stages of motor development; and
- identify common errors and provide constructive feedback by using teaching cues.

Teaching the whole child involves teaching cognitive, emotional, social, and physical skills in a variety of environments. For example, consider a typical beginning of a kindergarten class. On a signal, all students walk to and sit on their designated square or spot on the carpet to begin their morning activities. The teacher calls on the assigned student for the day to stand and walk slowly, while maneuvering around his or her peers to the front of the carpet, for calendar time. Cognitively, students are learning about day, time, and weather. Emotionally, they are demonstrating their ability to follow directions. Socially, they are performing in front of and with their peers. And physically, they are moving safely through the general space while staying in their own personal space. They choose different pathways, levels (e.g., sitting, standing), and paces (e.g., slower, faster) while using a movement skill (walking). This example shows how movement skills and concepts are used in everyday experiences.

In general terms, elementary teachers have typically focused on the foundation of science, technology, language, and mathematics while preparing students to engage with the more specialized knowledge they will gain in upper grades (Clark, 2007, as cited in SHAPE America, 2013). Similarly, health and physical education (HPE) in elementary school should provide students with basic knowledge and practice of movement concepts and fundamental movement skills by focusing on skill acquisition in the early years (SHAPE America, 2013). Mastering a variety of movement skills and concepts allows students to transition into applying movement in more complex or combined motor patterns, as in games, fitness activities, dance, and gymnastics in upper grade levels. Skill acquisition, then, is essential for continued participation in physical activity beyond school (Barnett, van Beurden, Morgan, Brooks, & Beard, 2010; Gallahue, Ozmun, & Goodway, 2012; Stodden, Langendorfer, & Roberton, 2009).

With that context established, this chapter provides you with a practical approach to incorporating movement skills and concepts into your curriculum. The discussion begins with a brief overview of the theories of movement education and motor development that are necessary for understanding movement skills and concepts. Next, it offers practical strategies in the form of user-friendly instructional materials (movement skill posters) that include performance indica-tors, teaching cues, stages of motor development, assessment examples, developmentally appropriate progressions for each motor stage, and suggestions for identifying common errors.

Movement Education

Dance theorist Rudolf Laban (1948), identified as a pioneer of movement education, believed that the body and its movement serve a purpose in everyday life. Laban, a choreographer and dancer, studied the language of human movement and created a system for observing, analyzing, prescribing, and performing movement. Laban's vision was expanded by Stanley (1977) and Logsdon and colleagues (1984), who brought movement education into elementary health and physical education. Specifically, they identified four major movement concepts—body, space, effort, and relationship—and added categories and subcategories to create the movement education framework (see table 11.1). Whereas these movement *concepts* describe how individuals move (e.g., fast, strong), movement *skills* consist of the body actions that individuals perform (e.g., running, kicking) (Graham, Holt/Hale, & Parker, 2013).

Movement Concepts

Movement is the language of the body. Through the understanding of Laban's (1948) principles, the movement education framework was introduced to elementary teachers as a means of helping students master motor skills. With every movement, the four main concepts are defined as follows:

- *Body.* Movement is observed by taking note of what the body does. The body is *what* moves; consequently, one must be aware of the body and its parts.
- *Effort.* Movement is observed in relation to the quality of *how* the body moves.
- *Space.* Movement is observed in space; it involves direction and spatial awareness that describes *where* the body moves.
- *Relationship.* Movement is done in relation to something or someone; it *relates* to the environment that encompasses people and objects.

As an analogy, let's review our kindergarten classroom example from the introduction. On

Movement Education Framework

Movement concepts	Categories and movement elements				
Body	**Body parts** Head Neck Shoulders And so on	**Body shapes** Straight Round Narrow Wide Twisted Symmetrical Asymmetrical	**Body actions** Locomotor (e.g., running, jumping, hopping) Manipulative (e.g., catching, throwing, kicking) Stability and balance (e.g., static, dynamic)		
Effort	**Time** Fast Slow	**Force** Strong Light	**Flow** Free Bound		
Space	**Location** General Personal	**Directions** Forward Backward Sideways Up Down Clockwise Counterclockwise	**Levels** High Medium Low	**Pathways** Straight Zigzag Curved	**Extensions** Far Near Large Small
Relationship	**Of body parts** Near each other (e.g., curled) Far from each other (e.g., stretched) One part rotating	**With objects and people** In front of Behind Alongside Far from Near Above Below Meeting Parting Over Under	**Organization** Alone (solo) With a partner In a group Between groups In unison In contrast Matching Mirroring Leading Following		

the signal, all students walk to (body: action of walking) and sit on (space: from high to low) their designated square or spot on the carpet (space: general and personal) to begin their morning activities. The teacher calls on the assigned student for the day to stand up and walk (body: walking) slowly (effort: slow) forward (space: direction) and around the peers to the front of the carpet (relationship: around, in front of) for calendar time. In every movement we make, we apply these four general movement concepts: body, effort, relationship, and space.

HPE teachers are concerned with using these four movement concepts to meet student learning outcomes (Langston, 2007). Here are some sample outcomes:

- *Body.* Students understand and apply locomotor skills (e.g., jumping), stability skills (e.g., balancing), and manipulative skills (e.g., underhand rolling) while emphasizing a particular body part or segment.
- *Effort.* Students demonstrate and understand force, flow, and time to improve quality of movement.
- *Space.* Students recognize and use personal space, general space, levels, pathways, and extensions to perform high-quality movement in a particular context or environment.
- *Relationship.* Students understand and use skill as it relates to other individuals, groups, equipment, and additional apparatus.

Each movement concept must be applied to an action. The actions are often categorized as fundamental movement skills, and each skill contributes to building the foundation necessary for a variety of physical activities.

Fundamental Movement Skills

Teaching fundamental skills using the movement education framework provides students with the building blocks for a lifetime of physical activity. For example, teaching underhand rolling, dynamic balance, and jumping in isolation eventually allows students to combine these skills in more complex contexts in games, gymnastics, and dance (Rovegno & Bandhauer, 2013). Fundamental movement skills are common in many physical activities; therefore, a child who masters them is more able than a child who does not to participate in a diverse set of physical activities (see figure 11.1).

The many fundamental movement skills are often grouped into three categories: locomotor, manipulative, and stability.

- *Locomotor skills* involve movements that are responsible for transporting the body from one place to another. They include walking, running, sliding, galloping, hopping, jumping, leaping, and skipping.

- *Manipulative skills* involve movements that are responsible for either sending away, receiving, or traveling with an object, such as a ball, puck, or disc. They include underhand rolling, catching, underhand throwing, overhand throwing, kicking, dribbling, striking with a long implement, and striking with a short implement.

- *Stability* is the ability to sense a shift in the relationship of the body parts that alters one's balance, as well as the ability to adjust

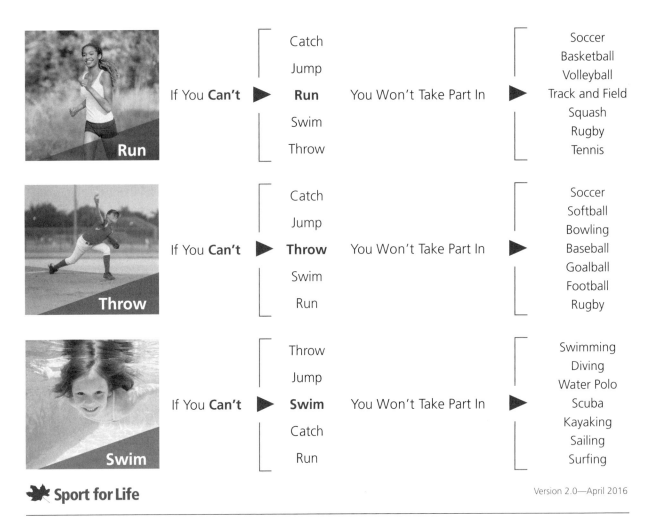

Figure 11.1 Consequences of missing a fundamental skill.
Reprinted by permission from Sport for Life Society. www.sportforlife.ca, www.sportpourlavie.ca

rapidly and accurately for such changes with the appropriate compensating movements (Cleland Donnelly, Mueller, & Gallahue, 2017, p. 57). Stability skills include static balance, dynamic balance, rolling, turning, twisting, and curling.

In a developmental sequence, stability skills are typically taught first, followed by locomotor skills and then manipulative skills. Understanding how students learn and develop movement skills over time is critical to your ability to help young learners become efficient movers. This understanding will help you improve your students' movement performance by analyzing their movement and providing activities that are appropriate for their development.

Motor Development and Learning

In order to teach to your students' developmental level, you must understand some basic principles of children's motor development and learning. According to Wickstrom (1983), motor development is defined as "changes over time in motor behaviour that reflect the interaction of the human organism with its environment" (p. 3). All children have the ability to become competent movers in a variety of movement skills and environments, but the pace and sequence varies from student to student according to principles of motor development and learning (Haywood & Getchell, 2011).

- Children develop at different rates, and development is age related but not age dependent. Thus some children develop earlier than others, and we must recognize that every child learns a skill in his or her own time.

- Skill development is sequential, and we must guide students through developmentally appropriate progressions that meet their personal needs. The sequence of development is predictable. For example, children learn first to crawl, then to walk, and then to run. They also mature within each skill—for example, from running with a wide base due to their lower centre of gravity when young to running with a narrower pattern as they grow taller.

- Children bring with them different experiences, which are affected by both nature and nurture. In terms of nurture, development is strongly related to opportunities for practice. For instance, toddlers who grow up in an environment enriched with move-

ment experiences often enter school more developed than those who did not (Rovengo & Bandhauer, 2013). In addition, Gallahue, Ozmun, and Goodway (2012) suggest that children progress through the various stages of skill development at different rates due to dynamic or environmental factors, biological readiness, and movement experiences.

- According to motor learning theory, teaching the whole child involves learning in three domains: cognitive (thinking and understanding), affective (emotion and feeling), and psychomotor (physical and kinesthetic). For example, when learning how to jump and land (psychomotor), students need to understand (cognitive) how to do so; they also need to take responsibility for jumping and landing in their own personal space (affective).

Phases and Stages of Motor Development

From birth through approximately age 14, children progress through four phases of motor development: reflexive movement (ages 4 months to 1 year), rudimentary movement (ages 1 to 2), fundamental movement (ages 2 to 7), and specialized movement (ages 7 to 14) (Gallahue, Ozmun, and Goodway, 2012). In this chapter, we focus on the fundamental movement phase, which is generally experienced at ages 2 through 7. The fundamental movement phase includes three stages: initial, elementary, and mature.

- In the initial stage, children often show limited coordination and flow, exaggerated movements, and improper or missing sequencing of movement parts. For example, when children learn to balance on a beam, they often lose their balance and need support (see figure 11.2); they may also have their eyes on their feet and use a sliding motion.

- During the elementary stage, children gain greater motor control and rhythmical coordination of movement skills. They are often highly focused and concentrate on keeping control of the movement. For example, in the elementary stage of dynamic balance, children are often able to walk along the balance beam with an alternating step motion while keeping their eyes on the beam, but they may lose their balance. Consequently, they often need to slow down to keep control of their movement.

Stages of motor development		
Stage 1	Stage 2	Stage 3
Initial stage	**Elementary stage**	**Mature stage**
Balances with support, eyes on feet, uses follow step with dominant foot lead	Eyes focused on beam, loses balance easily, uses alternate stepping action	Eyes focused beyond beam, movements are fluid, relaxed, and in control, may lose balance rarely

Figure 11.2 Stages of motor development for dynamic balance.

Adapted by permission from D. Gallahue, F. Cleland Donnelly, *Developmental Physical Education for All Children,* 4th ed. (Champaign, IL: Human Kinetics, 2003), 423.

■ In the mature stage, children's movement becomes mechanically efficient, coordinated, and controlled. For example, children in the mature stage of dynamic balance are able to walk the balance beam with flow and control while keeping their eyes forward and only rarely losing their balance.

Movement Skill Posters

To teach movement skills and concepts, you must provide children with a sequence of progressions that are task oriented and promote the whole child while also giving positive and corrective feedback to help students learn. We advocate a method that includes the following steps:

■ Identify performance indicators and teaching cues for the selected skill.

■ Observe student performance of a movement task that demonstrates the selected skill.

■ Assess student performance according to performance indicators and identify stage of development.

■ Use developmentally appropriate progressions to identify tasks suited to students' stage of development.

■ Provide constructive feedback using teaching cues.

For an instructional tool to guide you through this method, see the sample poster shown in figure 11.3; several more posters are available in the web resource. These posters include the following sections relevant to a given skill (in this example, dynamic balance):

■ Performance indicators and teaching cues

■ Videos (which can be accessed via QR code), illustrations, and descriptions of the three stages of motor development

■ Literacy terms

■ Assessment of each student's ability to demonstrate the performance indicators and identify their stage of development

■ Developmentally appropriate skill progressions for each of the three stages

■ Common errors and ways to address them

Now, let's look more closely at this method.

Performance Indicators and Teaching Cues

Performance indicators are the elements necessary for a skill to be performed effectively and

Dynamic Balance

Performance Indicators/Teaching cues[1]	Instructional Video QR[5]	Literacy		
• Maintains balance while using alternate stepping action – "alternate" • Maintains and upright posture – "good posture" • Maintains balance by using arms as needed – "control" • Focuses eyes forward – "looking forward"	[QR code]	balance	beam	dynamic
		forward	control	eyes
		stability	focus	alternate

Stages of Motor Development[3]

Stage 1	Stage 2	Stage 3
Initial Stage	**Elementary Stage**	**Mature Stage**
Support or Side step	*Focused, Eyes, on beam*	*Relaxed, Eyes forward*
Balances with support, Eyes on feet, Uses follow step with dominate foot lead	Eyes focused on beam, Loses balance easily, Uses alternate stepping action	Eyes focused beyond beam, Movements are fluid, Relaxed, and in control, May lose balance rarely

Pre or Post Assessment

Directions[2]: Walk across a balance beam forward for 10 steps

Students (example n=20)

Performance Indicators[1]	1	2	3	4	5	6	7	8	9	10	11	12	13	14	15	16	17	18	19	20
Maintains balance while using alternate stepping action																				
Maintains and upright posture																				
Maintains balance by using arms as needed																				
Focuses eyes forward																				
Total # of Performance indicators met																				

Developmentally Appropriate Progressions[3,4]
I: Initial / Emerging: Limited indicators visible in any context
E: Elementary / Able: Some indicators in closed contexts
M: Mature / Competent: All indicators in closed contexts

Developmentally Appropriate Progressions

Initial Stage / Emerging	Elementary Stage / Able	Mature Stage / Competent
1. Walk in a straight pathway 2. Walk in a straight pathway on a line 3. Walk in straight line heel to toe 4. Walk in different pathways (straight, zigzag, curved) 5. Walk at different levels (low, medium, high) 6. Walk at different levels on lines (low, medium, high) 7. Walk while changing directions (forward, backward, sideway) 8. Walk while changing directions on lines (forward, backward, sideway) 9. Walk while changing speed (slow, fast) 10. Walk while changing speed on lines (slow, fast) 11. Walk on numbers or abc poly spots that are somewhat far away so they have to stretch their bodies to get there. At times they may lose their balance – talk about what to do with your body when they become unstable (far, near) 12. Walk across wide gymnastic equipment (wide beam, bench) and repeat tasks # 3-10 13. Side step on wide beam (4"/ 10 cm) with and then without support 14. Side step on narrow beam (2.5"/ 6 cm) with and then without support 15. Alternate stepping on narrow beam while supported by teacher straddling the beam while walking backwards	16. Alternate stepping on narrow beam while slowly removing the level of support by teacher 17. Walk across narrow beam with low level support using extended arms for support 18. Walk across narrow beam with extended arms without support 19. Walk across the narrow beam while balancing a bean bag on shoulders (posture) 20. Walk across narrow beam at different levels (low, medium, high) 21. Walk across the narrow beam stepping over beanbags (levels) 22. Walk across the narrow beam and pick up an object without losing balance (levels) 23. Looking at the narrow beam, walk across as smoothly as you can. 24. Walk across wide balance beam with support (teach them how to scoop – looking forward, moving foot downwards next to beam when moving) 25. Walk across wide balance beam while scooping without support	26. With eyes forward walking across narrow beam while scooping with support (eyes) 27. With eyes forward walking across narrow beam while scooping without support (eyes) 28. With eyes forward walking across wide beam while scooping and balancing a beanbag on their head (eyes, posture) 29. With eyes forward walking across narrow beam while scooping and balancing a beanbag on their head (eyes, posture) 30. With eyes forward walking across narrow beam at different levels (low, medium, high) 31. With eyes forward walking across the narrow beam stepping over beanbags (levels) 32. With eyes forward walking across the narrow beam and pick up an object without losing balance (levels) 33. With eyes forward walking across the narrow beam while identifying numbers or letters held up by the teacher (eyes) 34. Looking forward, walk across a narrow beam as smoothly/relaxed as you can. (control) 35. Combine various movement concepts while walking on lines or across low beams. 36. Combine various locomotor skills and movement concepts with on lines or across low beams.

Difficulties to watch for[1]

If...	Then...
They are not able to keep their balance using their arms	Allow them to perform the skill while balancing light objects on shoulders
They have difficulty alternating steps	Allow for external support (wall or bar)
Children are visually checking their feet or beam	Encourage children to keep their head up by looking at something on the wall
Children have difficulty maintaining balance	Start with short distance and gradually increase length

References:
1. PHE Canada (2011). *Fundamental movement skills: An educator's guide to teaching fundamental movement skills.*
2. Ulrich, D. (2000). *Test of Gross Motor Development, 2nd ed. (TGMD-2) Assessment protocol*
3. Gallahue, D., Ozmun, J., & Goodway, J. (2007). *Understanding motor development: Infant, children, adolescents, adults (7th ed.).* McGraw Hill: New York, NY.

References Continued:
4. Baumgarten, S. & Langton, T. (2006). *Elementary Physical Education: Building a Solid Movement Foundation.* Stipes Publishing L.L.C.: Champaign, IL.
5. Poster created by Drs. Helena Baert & Matthew Madden, SUNY Cortland, 2016

Figure 11.3 Dynamic balance poster.

© Helena Baert and Matthew Madden

efficiently, whereas teaching cues help students understand and remember the indicators (see table 11.2). When teaching elementary students in health and physical education, you must keep your explanations brief and focused. When explaining how children can enhance their movement skills, use brief, child-friendly phrases that they will remember. For example, for students who are just starting to learn how to jump and land, teaching cues might include "bend, swing, spring, and squish" to help children remember to bend their knees before jumping, swing their arms forward, extend their body in flight, and land softly on two feet.

Providing students with appropriate teaching cues also makes it easier for you to focus on and observe critical elements of the movement and provide individual feedback. Teaching cues take time to develop and should be specific to both you and your learners. Thus, even though HPE teachers may share the same performance indicators for jumping, their cues may vary depending on their unique contexts and cultures. The poster shown in figure 11.3 provides examples of performance indicators and commonly used teaching cues at the top left.

QR Codes

Each poster includes links to videos by means of QR codes. The codes can be accessed using a QR reader on your mobile phone or other smart device (free apps are available). Essentially, scanning the QR codes will provide you with access to the instructional videos. The videos outline and demonstrate performance indicators, teaching cues, and stages of motor development.

Literacy Terms

In order for students to be efficient movers, they must not only practice skills physically but also understand them cognitively. The literacy terms for each movement are the most common terms you use when teaching the skills. You can use these words to help students acquire the academic language for each movement skill. In addition, creative planning of academic language may help students understand interdisciplinary knowledge. Literacy tasks could include matching, grouping, spelling, defining, and demonstrating words. For example, students could pick up the word *control* on a laminated card and discuss with the teacher its meaning in relation to the movement—in this case, dynamic balance. Next, they walk across the balance beam showing control of their movement. Finally, they match the card to the exact word on the poster outlined in the literacy table. This task provides a cognitive link between the academic language and the movement.

Stages of Motor Development

Each stage of motor development is depicted on the poster in the form of a picture and a short description. In addition, the videos available via the QR codes provide visual demonstrations of movers in each stage of motor development. When analyzing movement, you can use these instructional materials as references to inform your planning.

Once you have gained an understanding of the various movement skills, their performance indicators, and the motor development stages, you can observe students, assess their ability to use the performance indicators, and identify where they are in their development.

Assessment

Health and physical education teachers use assessment as a form of accountability; more specifically, they use performance indicators as

■ TABLE 11.2

Performance Indicators and Teaching Cues for Three Movement Skills

Movement skill	Performance indicators	Teaching cues
Balance	Maintains balance by using arms as needed. Focuses eyes forward.	Airplane. Look ahead.
Jumping	Bends knees and body at waist in preparation for jump. Extends body in flight.	Squish the grape. Reach for the stars.
Underhand rolling	Rolls ball with backward and forward arm swing. Follows through toward target.	Ticktock like a clock. Point.

benchmarks for gauging a student's skill level. Your ability to design effective learning tasks depends heavily on your ability to observe, analyze, and assess movement. To observe the performance indicators, create an assessment task in which students demonstrate their performance ability (each poster includes one assessment task). Here are some options:

- Locomotor skills can be observed within low-organized games such as tag.
- Stability skills can be observed within a gymnastics circuit.
- Manipulative skills can be observed in station work.

The assessment tools included in the posters provide you with two measures (see table 11.3). First, you can assess individual performance indicators by writing a 0 or 1 depending on whether the student shows the performance indicator. Next, you can identify the motor development stage demonstrated by the student. Both measures are crucial to recognizing where the student needs to improve. In addition, you will use the information gathered from the assessment to help you plan appropriate tasks. In the example shown in table 11.3, the student is using an alternating stepping motion and using his arms as needed, but he is not walking along the beam with control or looking forward. Developmentally, then, he is in the elementary stage for dynamic balance and needs to work on control. Based on this recognition, you can provide him with appropriate tasks by looking at the elementary stage progressions.

Developmentally Appropriate Progressions

Continuing with our example from table 11.3, the student was identified as performing in the elementary stage of dynamic balance. Next, you would move down the poster and locate the progressions appropriate for the elementary stage (see table 11.4).

Note that the progressions focus on gaining control over posture. Once the student is able to walk with an upright, controlled posture, the focus turns toward looking ahead.

As we observe the different progressions across the stages, common characteristics for each stage become apparent with each skill; for example, the initial stage of jumping has characteristics similar to those in the initial stage of rolling. Therefore, you must understand the commonalities among the stages rather than merely adding the number of performance indicators observed. Characteristics for each stage include the following:

Initial

- Tasks are focused on exploration and self-discovery.
- Practice in isolation and individual practice are highly encouraged.
- The task focuses on the general idea of the skill.
- Only one cue is addressed per task.
- The focus is on how the student performs the skill (i.e., process).
- Tasks are simple, focused, and performed in closed environments.

■ TABLE 11.3

Sample Assessment Tool

Directions: Walk forward along a balance beam for 10 steps.	Student									
Performance indicators	**1**	**2**	**3**	**4**	**5**	**6**	**7**	**8**	**9**	**10**
Maintains balance while using alternating stepping action.	1									
Maintains an upright posture.	0									
Maintains balance by using arms as needed.	1									
Focuses eyes forward.	0									
Total # of performance indicators met	2									
Developmentally appropriate progressions I = initial/emerging: few indicators visible in any context E = elementary/able: some indicators visible in closed contexts M = mature/competent: all indicators visible in closed contexts	E									

■ TABLE 11.4

Developmentally Appropriate Progressions for Dynamic Balance

Initial	Elementary	Mature
1. Walk in a straight pathway.	1. Walk with alternating steps on narrow beam while slowly reducing level of support provided by teacher.	1. With eyes forward, walk along narrow beam while scooping with support (eyes).
2. Walk in a straight pathway on a line.		
3. Walk in a straight line heel to toe.	2. Walk along narrow beam with low-level support while using extended arms for support.	2. With eyes forward, walk along narrow beam while scooping without support (eyes).
4. Walk in different pathways (straight, zigzag, curved).		
5. Walk at different levels (low, medium, high).	3. Walk along narrow beam with arms extended and without support.	3. With eyes forward, walk along wide beam while scooping a beanbag and balancing it on the head (eyes, posture).
6. Walk at different levels on lines (low, medium, high).	4. Walk along narrow beam while balancing a beanbag on shoulder (posture).	
7. Walk while changing direction (forward, backward, sideways).	5. Walk along narrow beam at different levels (low, medium, high).	4. With eyes forward, walk along narrow beam while scooping a beanbag and balancing it on the head (eyes, posture).
8. Walk while changing direction on lines (forward, backward, sideways).	6. Walk along narrow beam while stepping over beanbags (levels).	5. With eyes forward, walk along narrow beam at different levels (low, medium, high).
9. Walk while changing speed (slow, fast).	7. Walk along narrow beam and pick up an object without losing balance (levels).	
10. Walk while changing speed on lines (slow, fast).	8. Walk along narrow beam as smoothly as possible while looking at the beam.	6. With eyes forward, walk along narrow beam while stepping over beanbags (levels).
11. Walk on numbers or poly spots that are somewhat far away and thus require stretching the body to get there (far, near). At times, student may lose balance; if so, talk about what to do.	9. Walk along wide beam while "scooping" with support (teach students how to "scoop"—looking forward and moving foot downward next to beam when moving).	7. With eyes forward, walk along narrow beam and pick up an object without losing balance (levels).
	10. Walk along wide beam while scooping without support.	8. With eyes forward, walk along narrow beam while identifying numbers or letters held up by the teacher (eyes).
12. Walk along gymnastics equipment (e.g., bench, wide beam) and repeat tasks 3-10.		9. While looking forward, walk along narrow beam as smoothly as possible (control).
13. Sidestep on wide beam (10 cm) with and then without support.		10. Combine various movement concepts while walking on lines or along low beams.
14. Sidestep on narrow beam (6 cm) with and then without support.		11. Combine various locomotor skills and movement concepts on lines or along low beams.
15. Walk with alternating steps on narrow beam while supported by teacher (who straddles the beam while walking backward).		

- Tasks include minimal movement concepts (isolated concepts, such as jumping and landing lightly).
- Movement concepts addressed are intentionally related to focused cues. For example, when teaching how to jump and land, you may want to use the word *softly* to encourage bending the knees on landing.
- Provide learners with lots of variations and time to explore different movement concepts.

Elementary

- Tasks are more specific and practice oriented.
- More than one cue is addressed.
- The focus is on correct form and control of the movement.

- Quality of movement increases (e.g., faster, more accurate).
- Learners may begin to combine two movement concepts (e.g., picking up a beanbag at a low level while balancing).
- Focus on reinforcing the cues in a positive and constructive environment.
- Tasks may become more complex but are still performed in a closed environment.

Mature

- By now, the learner should be competent in the skill.
- Practice focuses on presenting students with challenges and a variety of closed and open environments so that they learn to adapt their movement.

- Students gain more independence and perform tasks both alone and with partners or small groups.
- Learners are often encouraged to come up with new ways to move, thus inspiring creative thinking.
- Students can combine multiple fundamental skills.
- Locomotor skill practice may be used in different forms in dance or gymnastics.
- For manipulative skills, small-sided games can be incorporated, and learners will begin to explore tactical components of game play.

Identifying Common Errors

Each poster includes a table identifying common errors and suggesting ways to help learners who experience them (PHE Canada, 2011). For example, if students have difficulty alternating feet while walking along a balance beam, you can provide them with outside support from your hands or from a wall, beam, or hockey stick (see table 11.5).

Summary

You can use instructional materials such as the posters presented in this chapter to understand your students' abilities and plan for their needs. Here are five keys to help you facilitate the learning process effectively:

1. Develop your foundational knowledge of movement and of movement theory.

2. Practice identifying movement skills and concepts.
3. Practice observing, analyzing, and assessing student performance.
4. Implement developmentally appropriate progressions for students at different stages of motor development.
5. Identify common errors and provide constructive feedback using the teaching cues.

By keeping this process in mind, you can help your students become more efficient movers. Specifically, you can use the strategies and instructional materials provided in this chapter to help your students acquire gross motor skills and learn movement concepts.

DISCUSSION QUESTIONS

1. Explain why the movement education framework is used in elementary physical education.
2. Describe the four main categories of movement concepts.
3. List the three main categories of movement skills and provide examples of each.
4. Explain how movement concepts relate to movement skills.
5. Describe how motor development theory informs the planning of developmentally appropriate progressions.
6. Describe how you could use posters effectively in your classroom.

■ TABLE 11.5

Common Errors and Solutions in Dynamic Balance

If . . .	Then . . .
They are not able to keep their balance using their arms.	Allow them to perform the skill while balancing light objects on the shoulders.
They have difficulty with alternating steps.	Allow for external support (e.g., wall, bar).
They visually check their feet or the beam.	Encourage them to keep the head up by looking at something on the wall.
They have difficulty maintaining balance.	Start with a short distance and gradually increase the length.

Visit the web resource for printable movement skills posters for locomotor, stability, and manipulative skills.

Voices From the Field

Joey Feith

Physical education teacher (K-6), Quebec

To make physical education fun and educational for all, I use many small-team activities. Doing so allows for more students to experience success. By having only 3 to 4 students per team, each student has more opportunity to actively engage in the activity and it prevents students with greater athletic ability from dominating the activity.

We also use peer assessments in many of the class activities. Part of our class culture involves having students provide feedback that is both positive and constructive to their peers on a regular basis. It's great to see students as young as 6 years old help their classmates improve their skills through observation and feedback!

Because I teach some of our younger students (i.e., grades 1-3), the early development of fundamental movement skills is one of the main aspects of my physical education curriculum. Skills are broken down into critical elements and then built back up one element at a time. Students are given time to explore each skill before I start introducing the mature pattern of the skill. Discussions around what makes for a great runner, hopper, slider, or galloper help students build an understanding of how to move effectively when using the various movement patterns we see in class. Our peer assessment system has students observing each other's performance and noting whether critical elements are being displayed in their performance.

Over the years, I have developed a variety of games that put emphasis on each fundamental movement skill. The games are broken down to their simplest versions and then built back in in a process I call layering. In the early layers, students have an opportunity to practice the fundamental movement skills in a personal space where they can move in directions and at speeds that are not affected by the movement of other students. As students grow more comfortable with the movement skills, I add layers to the game, which will have students perform the skills in a general space in relation to various objects or areas or at different speeds and rhythms.

I love to use the fundamental movement skills posters (included on the web resource). For me, the most important benefit of the posters is how they provide physical educators with a clear picture of what they should be looking for in their students' performances. In my own teaching, I have found it difficult at times to envision what a fully mature pattern looks like at different age levels or what to do if you see repeating difficulties that students display in the different fundamental movement skills. The posters provide educators with a guide on how to help each child fully develop these skills, which serve as the foundation of physical literacy.

When using these posters to help children develop skills, I look for the following:

- *Shared vision of what a mature pattern looks like for each fundamental movement skill.* Remember to use examples of the skill being performed with a mature pattern by a student of similar age of those you are teaching. I've developed a video-based anchor portfolio that serves this purpose.

- *Use of critical elements (teaching cues).* Provide students with one critical element at a time in order to allow them to focus on displaying that element in their performance. Overloading students with too much information about the skill all at once will only lead to students not focusing on developing a mature pattern.

- *Student-friendly language.* Younger students may not always understand more complex terms such as "opposition" or "mid-line," but they can understand "busy hand, busy knee" and "bellybutton." Although you want to teach them the appropriate language over time, make sure you are not overwhelming them with technical terms early on.

If you are new to using the posters, I suggest the following tips:

- *Use the posters to fully understand each skill prior to teaching.* Teaching physical education requires a lot of thinking on your feet. Having a clear understanding of where you are trying to get your students prior to jumping into the lesson will help you identify areas that need improvement and make necessary changes on the fly.

- *Use the posters to help you with ongoing assessment.* Do not wait until the end of a lesson or unit to assess your students' skill level. The posters provide you with an assessment tool that you can use throughout your teaching in order to track where students are in their learning and what changes they need to make to their performance in order to improve and grow.

- *Use the provided progressions as extension and refinement tasks for each student.* Allow students to learn as fast as they can or as slow as they need to by individualizing your instruction using the provided progressions. There is nothing wrong with different students working on the same skill in different ways. In fact, such differentiation will allow all of your students to master the fundamental movement skills in their own way and at their own pace.

CHAPTER 12

Teaching Games Using a TGfU Approach

Nathan Hall ■ **Brian Lewis**

After studying this chapter, you will be able to

- explain what games are and how they fit into physical education (PE) in elementary school,
- describe different types of games and what they offer as educational tools,
- explain what is required to make a game successful,
- use tactics and strategies to select and design games that help students achieve desired outcomes through proper progressions,
- understand Teaching Games for Understanding (TGfU) and how it works,
- explain what a TGfU-based lesson might look like and how TGfU can be used in PE as a strategy to help teach games, and
- describe strategies for implementing and managing games as part of your PE program.

If you wanted to encourage a child to complete an activity, chore, or learning task—or if you wanted to make these tasks more fun and engaging for children—what would you do? If your first thought is to make them into a game, then you are not alone. In fact, you may remember a time from your own childhood when someone helped you make a game of cleaning up, or when you used simple mathematics as part of a game you were playing. In education circles, the idea of using games to promote student participation and learning has received a great deal of attention in recent years. This educational practice is often referred to as "game-based learning" or (when it involves computers) "digital game-based learning," and it is now the subject of international conferences (e.g., European Conference on Games Based Learning) and full-length textbooks (e.g., Muzurura, 2012; Whitton & Moseley, 2012). Physical education is no exception to this trend; in fact, in many schools, physical education is the subject in which games are most commonly used.

There are several possible reasons for the prevalence of games in many physical education programs. One obvious reason is that many children perceive games as fun. Furthermore, research has found that games can help engage students and aid their learning of course material (Allison & Thorpe, 1997; Bright, Harvey, & Wheeler, 1979; Ellington, Gordon, & Fowlie, 1998; Sleet, 1985; Yolageldili & Arikan, 2011). It has also been argued that games contribute to students' development of social skills, as well as noncognitive skills such as patience, creativity, and discipline (Mackay, 2013). Another conceivable reason lies in the tradition of using sport as a means of teaching physical education and the fact that many sports, especially team sports, are considered games. In fact, we often refer to them explicitly as such—for instance, "a game of basketball" or "a game of ultimate"—and teachers often invoke the prospect of "full games" (i.e., scrimmages) at the end of a class as an incentive for students to complete prior tasks. Another reason for the ubiquity of games in today's physical education programs is the development of teaching methodologies dedicated to using games to teach physical skills—most notably, the Teaching Games for Understanding approach developed by Bunker and Thorpe (1982).

All of these reasons provide acceptable justification for including games in your physical education program. However, including games in your program does not guarantee enjoy-ment, skill development, or learning. With that reality in mind, this chapter has been designed to help you appreciate where games can fit into your physical education program and understand how to use games to achieve your desired outcomes. We begin by discussing key strategies for selecting and designing games that are educational and engaging for all students. Next, we introduce the concept of Teaching Games for Understanding as one potential foundation for game-based learning in physical education. With these building blocks established, we then consider the potential for transferring ideas and skills from existing games to new games in order to diversify your physical education program. We also offer insights into strategies for managing games and modifying them on the fly to enhance their effectiveness. We conclude the chapter by addressing issues of assessment that you may encounter when teaching physical education through a game-based strategy.

> *Including games in your program does not guarantee enjoyment, skill development, or learning.*

Defining Games in Physical Education

The word *game* elicits different thoughts from different people. Some think immediately of a card or board game such as cribbage or Monopoly. Others may think of playing video or computer games, and still others may recall common childhood activities such as hide-and-seek and freeze tag. All of these activities, and many others, could be considered games, depending on one's definition of the word. For the purposes of this chapter, we define *game* as an individual or group-based activity defined by a specific set of rules and resulting in a quantifiable outcome. In the realm of physical education, this definition can accommodate a large number of the activities and sports regularly included in elementary school programs. These games can be categorized in many ways, but their success is influenced by a few key elements.

Competitive, Cooperative, and Individualistic Games

All games in physical education can be classified as either competitive, cooperative, or individualistic. At the elementary school level, common competitive games include traditional sports such as soccer and badminton, as well as activities such as duck-duck-goose, dodgeball, and most forms of tag. These activities are characterized by the pursuit of conflicting goals and desired outcomes by participants. Specifically, if one individual or team attains the goal or desired outcome, such as scoring more points than the opponent, then it guarantees that the opponent does not achieve the same goal. To put it simply, a competitive game always results in one side being considered successful (the "winners") while the defeated side is considered unsuccessful (the "losers") (Deutsch, 1949).

You may be less familiar with a large number of cooperative games that are played in physical education classes at the elementary level. Examples include "the human knot," "hoop pass," and many of the games played with a parachute (e.g., making it into a giant mushroom). A game is considered cooperative when the participants can achieve their own individual goals only by working cooperatively with other students who are simultaneously achieving their goals (Deutsch, 1949; Johnson, Maruyama, Johnson, Nelson, & Skon, 1981). Such games can include a competitive component in the form of intergroup competition, in which students in a group work together cooperatively on a task while other groups do the same, all the while competing to see who can perform the chosen task better (e.g., faster or with fewer mistakes) (Marsh & Peart, 1988). More information on cooperative games can be found in chapter 14.

In the third category, individualistic games, students play by themselves and do not compete directly with anyone else. In addition, Johnson and Johnson (2013) suggest that in these types of games students work by themselves to accomplish learning goals unrelated to those of other students. In physical education, this approach can include individual keep-it-up games such as footbag, as well as other games such as

Commonly used competitive games always result in one individual or team being classified as successful (i.e., "winners") while defeated opponents are considered unsuccessful (i.e., "losers"). Therefore, although competitive games can be essential for motivating certain types of students, limiting your program to only this type of game can be extremely demotivating to other students.

golf if the focus is placed on individual performance rather than comparing one's outcome with those of others.

All three game types can play a role in elementary school physical education thanks to the diversity among students. Some students are competitive by nature and thrive in competitive situations, or at least need some form of competition as motivation to fully participate in a game. Other students dislike competition and may be turned off by a constant stream of competitive games; these students are more likely to thrive in cooperative situations. Finally, some students may just prefer to work on their own, in isolation from the rest of the class; of course, these students may enjoy individualistic games the most. At the same time, all students can benefit from each type of game, and physical education programs that are one dimensional are not catering effectively to the differences that exist among students.

Small-Sided Games

Another way to understand games in physical education is to categorize them as either full-sided (large-sided) or small-sided, although this terminology can be a bit misleading. The easiest way to think of this division is to consider small-sided games (whether created games or modified versions of existing games) as those that use a relatively small number of players and a smaller playing area (Whelan, 2011). Such games are also sometimes called "minigames." Typically, small-sided games involve teams of fewer than five players each (although, depending on the sport or activity, it could be more), and they often use modified rules or equipment. Common examples include three-on-three basketball and a version of tennis played with a foam ball on a smaller court. In contrast, large-sided or full-sided games are the traditional versions of games (typically sports) that follow the traditional rules, playing structure, and space dimensions, such as five-on-five basketball played on a full-size court.

The use of small-sided games in physical education has often been advocated at the elementary level. Two key benefits noted by researchers are that small-sided games increase the number of learning opportunities provided to children (Tallir, Philippaerts, Valcke, Musch, & Lenoir, 2012) and help children improve their motor skills by getting them more involved (Mandigo & Holt, 2000). It has also been suggested that small-sided games provide students with the following benefits (Griffin, Mitchell, & Oslin, 1997):

- Increased amounts and intensity of physical activity
- Opportunity to take on various roles (e.g., catcher, fielder)
- Reduced game complexity and subsequent increases in student success
- More fun and authentic skill practice and development than is provided by contrived skill drills
- More even groupings based on ability

In addition, small-sided games require simpler decision making, which means that they are easier for students to analyze (Hubball, Lambert, & Hayes, 2007). Finally, these games may be particularly useful for developing students' understanding of the principles of play related to basic offensive and defensive tactics (Launder, 2001; Pill, 2012).

Here are a few other factors to consider when deciding whether to use small-sided or large-sided games. It is often easier to manage and provide instruction to students, especially those in the elementary grades, when they work in smaller groups. Furthermore, it is well understood that younger children often struggle to fully comprehend or function in large-sided activities and that adjustments must be made in order to increase individual success (consider, for instance, the format of most early-years youth sport leagues, such as Timbits hockey and soccer, where the numbers of players competing is reduced and the playing surfaces and nets are smaller). This is not to say that playing full- or large-sided games cannot be a viable option in elementary school physical education, but the benefits of small-sided games make them quite worthy of consideration. At a minimum, physical education teachers who work with elementary school students should think twice about playing full- or large-sided games until they are confident that students' skill levels are sufficient to make a full-sided game enjoyable, educational, and engaging for all class members.

Younger children often struggle to fully comprehend or function in large-sided activities, in which case adjustments must be made to increase individual success. Therefore, we endorse the use of smaller groups when using games to teach elementary school physical education.

Student-Created Games

When considering games as part of your physical education program, give some thought to student-created games, also known as "inventive games," which are created with teacher supervision. This type of game maximizes students' engagement in and ownership of their learning and development. Your level of influence on the game design is completely up to you. At one end of the spectrum, you might be constantly engaged throughout the process of game creation and be responsible for assessing the process and its outcomes. In this approach, students would need to seek your approval of various aspects of their game and then make modifications or refinements based on your input. At the other end of the spectrum, you might allow students to exercise nearly complete control over the development process and determine how the process and the game that is produced will be assessed. In deciding your level of involvement, consider the goals of the game creation activity, the ages and abilities of the students, and the time available for the activity.

You can also take various approaches to leading student-created games. On the broadest level, you might simply say "design a physically active game" and leave it at that. More commonly, however, teachers impose a degree of limitation—for example, using certain kinds of equipment, such as hoops, rugby balls, pylons, and scooters. You might also ask students to create a game focused on developing a certain motor skill or set of skills, such as eye–hand coordination and jumping. Students can also create games geared toward certain curricular outcomes, such as improving social or communication skills or developing or improving their understanding of common game strategies or tactics.

Teachers incorporate such games into physical education programs for a number of reasons. For one thing, many elementary school teachers are trained not as physical education specialists but as generalists; therefore, they may lack confidence in their subject knowledge or skill level in certain sports or activities: "I can't teach this because I don't know the rules" or "I myself am not good at this game." In such cases, a traditional approach—that is, skill drills and full-sided games—can seem daunting, and one solution is to use small-sided games created by students and based on traditional sports and activities. This approach allows students to discover and develop for themselves

Incorporating student-created games into your physical education program helps students learn game structure and game play, as well as the importance of rules and how they relate to a game's playability.

the knowledge and skills that are needed to succeed in the chosen activity or sport. It also helps students learn game structure and game play, as well as the importance of rules and how they relate to a game's playability (Casey & Hastie, 2011). Finally, it helps students gain insight into the transferability of skills and strategies between many physical games. For example, the strategy of using short passes rather than long ones to increase the success rate of passing typically works in any game that requires passing between teammates.

Identifying Successful Games

At this point, you may be wondering, "Are some games better than others"? The simple answer is yes, but there is a lot more to it than that. The success of a game depends on a great many factors, ranging from students' moods to curricular outcomes. There are, however, a few essential considerations that must be satisfied in order for a game to be considered successful as part of a physical education lesson. These essentials hold true for all games—competitive and cooperative, small sided and large sided, teacher driven and student created.

The first essential is that the game must be educational; more specifically, it must help all students develop knowledge or skills related to a specific curricular outcome. Merely getting students physically active is not enough. Many physical educators believe that a class is successful if the students are "happy and busy" (i.e., having fun and being active) and being "good" (i.e., behaving well) (Placek, 1983; Henninger & Coleman, 2008). Certainly, these things are desirable, but if a game is not educational—that is, if students are not learning anything—then we would suggest that it cannot in good conscience be considered successful by a teacher who believes in delivering a physical *education* program.

The second essential is for the game to have clearly defined rules that are not too hard for students to follow and that help create equal opportunity for all players. If students are unsure

how a game should be played, this uncertainty immediately undercuts its potential for success. Specifically, game flow may be disrupted by frequent stops due to rule infractions, and students may be less engaged in the activity because they don't fully understand what they are—and are not—allowed to do. As a result, games with demanding rules are often problematic at the elementary school level. For example, it would nearly impossible to play a full game of either Canadian or American football with elementary school students; there are simply far too many rules for students to remember and understand. Even at the secondary school level, teachers typically use a modified version (e.g., flag football) or a small-sided version with simplified rules. Of course, problems can also arise if a game has too few rules. For example, safety issues could be problematic for a modified game of floor hockey where the only rule provided is that a goal will be counted when the ball enters the opposing team's net. Keeping sticks down and body contact, for example, should also be addressed.

The final essential is that the game should be enjoyable and high in "playability" (Casey & Hastie, 2011). Although the need for fun is unsurprising, students' perceptions of it can be affected by a variety of factors, many of which are hard for a teacher to control. That said, one factor that is sure to influence a game's level of fun is playability. Students typically want games to feature a balance between offense and defense; even more important, they prefer games that allow for success. For example, in elementary school, volleyball typically lacks playability because it requires very specific skills that are too advanced for most of the students. Therefore, in order to make the game successful with these students, teachers need to find ways to improve its playability—for example, using a beach ball instead of a traditional volleyball. This simple modification gives students more time to set up and make contact with the ball, thus increasing the average length of rallies and increasing students' ability to succeed in playing the game. Essentially, then, this modification makes the game playable!

For a game to be deemed successful in physical education, it should be fun, but enjoyment and physical activity are not enough—the game must also develop students' knowledge or skills, or both.

Strategies for Selecting and Designing Games in Physical Education

It is one thing to know what a game is and appreciate the different forms that games can take. It is something entirely different to implement games in a way that helps students increase their knowledge and develop their movement skills. Yet it is essential for us to ensure that students not only participate in games but also learn from doing so. To help us fulfill this responsibility, the World Wide Web makes finding resources easier than ever; indeed, countless games and physical education lessons are a mere click away. The question is how to select or design games to ensure that they are educational, clearly defined, and playable by our students. Let us begin by considering a story told by an elementary student in what many would view as a traditional physical education experience:

> Our teacher blows the whistle to signal the start of class. We put away the basketballs we were playing with and circle up to listen to the teacher tell us what will happen today. When she says today we're continuing with our basketball unit, lots of kids cheer and get excited. But I feel my stomach sink—I'm not good at basketball. We start by working on what the teacher calls "skill development"—activities that will help us get better at basketball. I think I am getting better but I still sometimes have to chase down the basketball or I mess up the activity for others.

> "Now it is time to put our skills to work," says our teacher. The class is divided into four teams, and all of them have very good players and players like me. While we play, I try to get involved, but I have no idea where to go. I see my teammates passing the ball around me, not to me, even though I'm open and waving my hands. Why won't they pass it to me? If they do pass it to me, what do I do with it? What if I miss the pass? I don't want to let my teammates down. I guess I will just keep running up and down the floor, following everyone until our teacher tells us we are done for the day.

Perhaps you can remember similar instances from your own experiences in physical education. Reflecting on the story, we wonder if knowledge and skills are being developed while "running up and down the floor, following everyone until our teacher tells us we are done for the day." What games could be selected or designed to support greater understanding? How do we plan to ensure that all students can succeed and develop the knowledge and skills required to play basketball, or any other sport or game? Traditionally, the starting point for planning physical education lessons revolved around seasonal sports (e.g., basketball) or popular games that many students found enjoyable (e.g., capture the flag). From this perspective, the game is the focal point of the lesson, and working through activities "will help us get better at basketball."

What if the starting point for planning was not the game itself? Stephen Covey (1998) talks about the importance of beginning with the end in mind. This notion of starting with a clear idea of the destination is echoed in McTighe and Wiggins' (1999) Understanding By Design framework, also known as backward design, which is commonly used by educators today. When using backward design, the teacher begins with the following question: What is the goal or *big idea*? The answer guides the teacher in creating or planning assessments and then in developing the lesson plan (McTighe & Wiggins, 1999). If we apply this approach to the student's question—"Why won't they pass it to me?"—we have a new starting point for planning. One goal or big idea in games such as basketball is that of getting open to receive a pass. If we plan with this goal as our starting point, then the selection or design of games becomes more specific and intentional: The games in the lesson should help students understand what it looks like to be "open." With this approach, perhaps fewer students will have to wonder why they never receive a pass.

Thus, as teachers, we must ask, "What is the goal or big idea we are looking to support?" This essential question needs to drive our game selection and design. We must also consider various secondary questions that address other important factors. Thinking again of playability (Casey & Hastie, 2011), we offer the following questions to ask when incorporating games into a lesson:

- *Is the game safe?* All movement activities carry some inherent risk; therefore, we must think about safety when implementing games and keep it at the forefront of our planning.

- *Will the game work in the space available?* To ensure a safe and enjoyable experience, some games are better suited to larger spaces; thus our planning must consider both class size and available space.

- *What equipment is needed?* We must not only have enough equipment but also ensure that it is in good condition. We must also consider the developmental level of our students and use oversized, lighter, or softer equipment when appropriate.

- *Can the game be modified to support multiple skill levels?* Some games are just too complex or require more skill than elementary students can handle. Planning a lesson that can be adapted to multiple skill levels goes a long way toward ensuring that students will be engaged.

When taking this approach, planning is no longer centred on the game itself. Instead, beginning with the end in mind (Covey, 1998; McTighe & Wiggins, 1999) ensures that students are not simply playing games but are learning from them. This focus on selecting or designing games with the end in mind is an essential attribute of the teaching model known as Teaching Games for Understanding, which was first developed by Bunker and Thorpe (1982) and later enhanced by Griffin and Butler (2005). We now take a closer look at that model.

> *We must ensure that students not only participate in games but also learn from them. Therefore, quality physical education depends on selecting or designing games with the end (i.e., learning outcomes) in mind.*

Teaching Games for Understanding

The Teaching Games for Understanding approach offers many potential applications for physical education in elementary schools. TGfU promotes using games to teach games through a learner-centred focus. The approach helps students develop understanding of and ability to perform the technical and tactical skills that are essential for success in a vast array of games (Mandigo, Butler, & Hopper, 2007). Learners start by participating in modified games as a way to promote decision making while developing game knowledge and tactical proficiency. In contrast, a more traditional or technique-based approach encourages students to develop and improve specific skills in order to build toward playing specific games or sports.

The TGfU approach was developed by David Bunker and Rod Thorpe (1982) at Loughborough University in the United Kingdom. They created it on the premise that humans have an inherent desire to play. They also based their approach on research findings suggesting that, due to an emphasis on performance, students in British PE programs at that time (the early 1980s) often experienced minimal success in games, developed very little knowledge of the games they played, exhibited inflexible techniques and poor decision-making capacity for games, and often relied on a coach or teacher to make decisions during games. Since the inception of TGfU, research findings have suggested that it can improve students' overall learning and enjoyment as compared with traditional lessons about games (Mitchell & Oslin, 1999) and that it enhances students' understanding of tactical knowledge (Rink, French, & Tjeerdsma, 1996). It has also been argued that TGfU may serve as one of the most effective teaching approaches for developing physical literacy (Mandigo & Holt, 2004).

At the same time, some academics have recently advocated caution when interpreting these findings because the overall study of TGfU has not proven it to be superior to other teaching approaches for all teachers and students (Stolz & Pill, 2014). Be that as it may, TGfU is undeniably a useful approach for elementary school physical educators, and we believe that all teachers of physical education should consider using it in some form during their careers.

Understanding the Basics

The easiest way to understand how TGfU can be implemented is to consider the model put forth by its creators (Bunker & Thorpe, 1982). In this model, shown in figure 12.1, the learner is placed at the centre, and the learning process involves six steps.

As mentioned earlier, the TGfU approach begins with game play—specifically, with the introduction of modified or simplified games. During this step, success depends on ensuring that the modifications allow all students to participate fully and engage actively in the game. The second step involves developing students' appreciation for the game, and the main focus here is to provide opportunities for students to understand the importance of rules in a game. This understanding can be facilitated by inviting students not only to help create or refine rules but also to implement and apply them through officiating (Griffin & Butler, 2005). The third step focuses on helping students develop tactical awareness. This learning occurs during game play as students are required to solve problems related to the offensive and defensive strategies that are possible within the scope of the game's rules. You can promote tactical problem solving

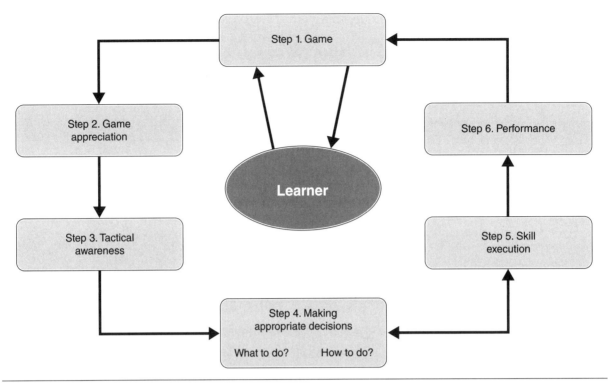

Figure 12.1 The TGfU learning process.

Reprinted by permission from D. Bunker and R. Thorpe, "A Model for the Teaching of Games in Secondary School," *Bulletin of Physical Education* 18, no 1 (1982): 5-8.

by asking questions related to potential actions that students might take to improve their odds of success or limit the opponent's ability to succeed. The fourth step addresses decision making. Because games are dynamic, students are required to think on their feet and decide what course of action provides the best option in a given situation and what skills they will use to carry out that course of action; the answers often depend on what they think an opponent is going to do or how an opponent is likely to react.

All of the preceding steps in the TGfU model work together to lead to the fifth step: skill execution. Griffin and Butler (2005) suggested that at this point in the process, students will be motivated to learn and improve on the skills required for a game because they can understand the context within which the skills are needed. In other words, students understand the game and the tactics best suited to successfully perform; as a result, they recognize the value of developing proficiency in certain skills. The sixth and final step consists of the observed outcome that results from following the other steps. Ideally, student performance has improved, and the cycle can now begin again with another game that requires new rules, tactics, and skills.

The TGfU model can be useful for teaching any game, but in order to reap the full benefits, you must think carefully about what games to teach, and in what sequence. The developers of TGfU have suggested that it is intended to help learners understand that tactics and skills for one game can be transferred to many other similar games (Bunker & Thorpe, 1982). Thus, when using a TGfU approach, games are typically selected based on some form of categorization that groups games with similar overall objectives, required skills, player roles, playing areas, and strategies (Griffin & Butler, 2005). Games are most often grouped according to the following four categories:

- *Target games.* Participants propel an object at a defined target; examples include bowling, golf, and curling.
- *Striking-and-fielding games.* Participants strike an object in an attempt to direct it to a space that is free of defenders; examples include baseball, cricket, and kickball.
- *Net and wall games.* Participants try to direct an object into a space where the opponent is unable to return it; typically, these games involve directing the object over a net or off

of a wall. Examples include badminton, volleyball, and Spikeball.

- *Territory games.* Participants invade an opponent's territory in order to score points; examples include basketball, football, and hockey.

The use of such categories allows us to expose students to a range of activities while still helping them develop their cognitive and physical abilities. Therefore, it is important to select games that fit into a category and thus enable students to build on the tactics and skills learned in previous games.

Implementing TGfU

The TGfU approach does require some work. As mentioned in the previous section, the choice of games requires careful consideration, as does the sequencing. For instance, many territory games require participants to possess some of the skills and tactical understandings that are common in target games and striking-and-fielding games. As a result, Griffin and Butler (2005) have suggested that teachers consider starting with target games, followed by striking-and-fielding games, before progressing to net and wall games and territory games.

As for specific lessons using the TGfU approach, you must attend to many factors. One of the leading Canadian advocates for the TGfU approach, Joy Butler (2014), has provided the following guidelines for starting and continuing with a TGfU lesson.

Starting a Lesson

- Observe students playing small-sided games.
- Start with modified games, traditional games, and invented games.
- Keep explanations and rules to a minimum.
- Emphasize play.
- Check for safety and engagement.
- Provide fun mental warm-ups.
- Use Q&A to connect this lesson with the preceding one.
- Use short video clips of play.

Continuing a Lesson

- Play games that provide new challenges while reinforcing students' learning.
- Have students work in small groups.
- Ask learners to suggest next stages.

- Highlight good practice by individuals and teams.
- Conclude with competition between evenly matched players or teams.

A TGfU lesson will certainly look different from traditional approaches. For insight into the differences, let's consider once again the student who asked, "Why won't they pass it to me?" If that lesson had been delivered through a TGfU approach, how might it have looked different? If it had followed many of the guidelines (Butler, 2014) just listed, would the experience have been a more positive one for all students? To help you envision the answer, the sample lesson plan presented in the web resource focuses not on a specific sport but on a thematic approach. Thus, instead of engaging in drills and then being launched into a game of basketball—in which the student was resigned to "following everyone until the teacher tells us we are done for the day"—the lesson conceptually teaches tactics that will help students understand not only basketball but also other games that fit into the theme or category of territory games.

Specifically, this lesson helps students understand what it means to support teammates and maintain possession. For instance, beginning with bridge tag, it challenges students to touch as many floor spots as possible, thus helping them begin to understand the importance of moving to open space. Of course, this understanding comes from being immersed in games (e.g., touch 'em all), beginning with very simple activities and slowly building through additional rules and challenges. Along the way, students begin to recognize what it looks like to support their teammates. These "look-fors," or criteria, can be provided by students themselves through discussion, and they become the focus moving forward in the lesson. By the time they are ready to engage in stack 'em all, students have developed a clear understanding of what you are assessing. The result is that students pass to each other rather than merely waving their hands to no avail.

> *If you wish to use a TGfU approach, consider starting with target games, followed by striking-and-fielding games, and then progressing to net and wall games and territory games.*

Teaching for Transfer

When teaching any activity in PE, especially a game, we should not overlook the concept of transfer—that is, the idea that each game involves skills, tactics, and sometimes even rules that are similar to those used in other games. As mentioned, the sample lesson presented in the web resource is designed to help students understand the tactics involved in maintaining possession. By engaging in multiple games throughout the lesson, students recognize the tactics needed to support their teammates. That is, they come to understand that common tactics apply in basketball and other territorial games, such as soccer and floor hockey, and they develop the ability to transfer these tactics between games. In this way, the games played in the sample lesson help students develop the ability to succeed in any territorial game in which they choose to participate. The transfer process also applies in helping students develop understanding of rules that are similar across games. For example, the rule in tennis that a ball landing on a line is considered in play also applies to volleyball, badminton, and baseball. Thus, when teaching games, you can remind students of other games they have learned that use similar skills, tactics, and rules as a means of speeding up the learning process.

At the same time, you must also be aware of the potential for negative transfer. In this phenomenon, skills, tactics, or rules from one game cause confusion or make things difficult when learning a similar game. For instance, the rule declaring a ball on the line to be in play can be very hard to accept for a student who has played a great deal of squash or racquetball, in both of which a ball on the line is considered *out* of play. Therefore, you must consider both similarities and contrasts between games and remember that skills, tactics, and rules can transfer either positively or negatively—which means that they can make it either easier or harder for students to learn a new game.

Management

When using games as part of your PE program, you may encounter many potential issues, which we refer to as "what-ifs." Games are typically dynamic and therefore unpredictable, and students' behaviour while playing them can also be unpredictable. For this reason, you must take steps ahead of time to reduce the potential for unwanted student behaviours and other activity-related issues, such as injuries. One of the most effective ways to minimize what-ifs is to carefully consider game rules and communicate them clearly. Use only the essential rules so as to minimize constant disruption to game flow and

avoid overloading students' ability to remember or follow the rules. The easiest way to determine rules is to ask the following two questions:

- What rules *must* students know in order to minimize the likelihood of injury?
- What rules *must* students know in order to allow the game to achieve its desired outcomes?

Once the rules are set, use the following simple strategies to communicate them effectively:

- Keep the expression of rules simple in the beginning and add more complicated rules only as students improve their understanding and ability to play the game.
- Demonstrate acceptable and unacceptable actions according to the rules; for example, physically demonstrate to students that when playing soccer the ball can touch the feet, legs, body, and head but not the arms or hands.
- Inform students of consequences for breaking the rules.

Another way to minimize what-ifs is to establish overall behavioural protocols for playing games; in other words, make a list of behavioural expectations that apply throughout the school year for any game. The list can include both behaviours that students should avoid (e.g., arguing over team selection or rule applications; engaging in verbal or physical aggression; using negative language) and behaviours that students should exhibit (e.g., giving full effort, being open minded about new games, always putting safety first). Such protocols not only help minimize "what-ifs" but also save you considerable time by reducing the need to provide certain behavioural reminders for each class or for each new activity.

You can also reduce what-ifs by ensuring that the activities you choose maximize student participation. An engaged student is less likely to be a disruptive student! Maximizing participation depends in part on game selection and in part on game modification. For instance, to maximize participation in hockey, you might institute a rule that everyone must touch the puck once before anyone on the team can shoot; in soccer, you might put multiple balls in play, thus increasing the number of opportunities for engaged participation by all students. You can also increase participation by reducing or increasing the number of players or the size of the playing area—for example, in basketball, playing half-court three-on-three instead of full-court five-on-five.

Summary

This chapter helps you appreciate the important and diverse roles that games can play in an elementary school physical education program. Using games effectively to drive students' learning requires you to engage in detailed thinking and planning. Specifically, games serve students best when they are selected or designed with the end goal or outcome in mind. When approached in this manner, all types of games—competitive, cooperative, and individualistic; small sided and large sided; and traditional and student created—can be equally important depending on what you want to achieve. In addition to making the final decision about game rules, you also need to consider the skill levels of your students, the space available, the equipment that will best serve the purpose, and of course safety. Teachers who are new to outcome-oriented game selection can find a great source of help in educational models such as Teaching Games for Understanding.

Including games in your PE program offers many benefits. In the end, however, the true value of any game that you decide to use lies in its potential to function as an effective tool for student learning.

DISCUSSION QUESTIONS

1. Why is it essential to take a multifaceted approach to game play in physical education?

2. How can small-sided games benefit learners in elementary physical education?

3. What makes a game successful for all involved? Consider how the three criteria for success (educational value, clear rules, and playability) can affect what game play looks like.

4. When planning a physical education lesson, the starting point should not be a game per se but rather a "big idea." How is this approach to planning complemented by the TGfU model?

5. The sample lesson provided in the web resource for this chapter is designed to teach for transfer. In what ways can the idea of transfer support success for all students in game play?

 Visit the web resource for a sample games-based PE lesson.

Voices From the Field

Graham Hayes

K-12 Health and Physical Education Teacher, Saskatchewan

I have done a number of things to help make physical education engaging and educational for all. Through experience, I have learned that each group of students is different and may require different approaches to help them engage in certain movement activities. Knowing my learners and building relationships with them is critical in helping me plan meaningful and engaging learning experiences for all. It is also important to be passionate and knowledgeable about what I am teaching. Passionate teachers create an atmosphere in which their enthusiasm is contagious and students develop the desire to engage in learning experiences. As teachers and students become engaged and enthusiastic, the teacher–student relationship flourishes and creates limitless opportunities for learning.

I have to admit that early on in my teaching career, I tended to follow a sport model as my primary approach to teaching physical education. I taught in the way that I had been taught. Typically, my lesson content involved the "sport of the season," for which I would teach the basic skills in an attempt to prepare students for the "real game." In fact, I took great pride in teaching students the fundamental skills and rules associated with a variety of sports. They seemed to develop more confidence and greater ability to participate in each of these sports as they progressed throughout the lessons. There was a real sense of self-satisfaction and accomplishment when they were able to incorporate all of their knowledge and skills into actual game play. The game play was always the highlight and the target that I promoted as our end goal.

Though I still believe there is merit in that model, one of the challenges I continually encountered was ensuring that students were provided with enough active learning time. For example, many of the sports and games required students to rotate on and off the court in shifts. I experimented with a variety of adaptations to maximize the amount of time for which each student was moving during each class, but I still found myself looking for a better solution.

The most significant transformation in my teaching practice occurred when I began to incorporate small-sided games into learning experiences. This simple approach allowed me to introduce more equipment, provide more individual learning experiences, and differentiate more appropriately for varying ability levels while also providing additional opportunities for students to learn games by playing games. Perhaps the greatest success I have experienced with small-sided games is that it creates a safe learning space in which students who are less skilled or less experienced in traditional sports became more willing to engage as part of the class. Due to the increased opportunities to contribute and be involved in the game—as well as modifications of the games themselves—students experience greater improvement through active participation.

In conjunction with small-sided games, I began to adopt a Teaching Games for Understanding (TGfU) model more regularly. In fact, it became the predominant model in my program, especially at the middle-years level. This model put much more focus on tactics and strategies as they relate to various sports and games. As a result, I was able to encourage the transfer of learning more easily from one sport to another, and I began teaching concepts within categories rather than specific sports. For example, in the category of territory games, the focus might be placed on maintaining possession or defending one's own goal, and this focus can be accomplished in basketball, soccer, hockey, or a combination of them all. I also invented my own games using the tactics and strategies I wanted to highlight for students. Using small-sided games to structure learning experiences with a tactical or strategic focus allowed students to understand the similarities between a variety of games and transfer their learning skills from one game to another. Thus the content shifted daily, and I discovered that student engagement was greater than with my previous sport model, in which we might spend weeks focusing on a particular sport in which some students were not interested.

As a physical education consultant, I promote the concept of purposeful planning and the backward design model. As teachers, we need to know what "big ideas" or end goals we want our students to achieve. Once you have a good grasp of what your students are to accomplish, you can incorporate games or activities that support those learning goals. Too often, teachers spend time looking for games or activities that get students moving but aren't sure what they want students to accomplish by engaging in the activities. Students should be able to understand the objective of every lesson and articulate it clearly. Doing so allows them to engage actively in the learning process, make sense of formative feedback, and internalize their own progress toward the learning goal they are trying to achieve.

CHAPTER 13

Incorporating Activities for Functional Fitness

Brian Justin

After studying this chapter, you will be able to

- explain why physical fitness activities are integral to every student's education;
- identify the components of physical fitness;
- implement physical fitness activities in your classes;
- explain the link between fundamental movement skill development, Laban's movement framework, and fitness activities; and
- begin implementing functional fitness in your classes.

In the past, fitness activities have sometimes been used by health and physical education (HPE) teachers as punishment for "poor listening" or failing to follow instructions. This is not a way to help children (and the adults they become) learn to revere the benefits of physical fitness. Fitness activities should be exhilarating experiences, during which students meet the challenge of increasing their physical capacity, improving their movement competence, and building their self-esteem because they know they can handle the physical opportunities that life presents to them.

Starting With Why

Fitness activities constitute an important component of HPE curricula. Research indicates that the human brain is not hardwired but is constantly being rewired; moreover, it is significantly affected by physical activity (Ratey & Hagerman, 2008). This influence means that as physical education teachers we have the means to rewire our students. When children exercise, they set the brain up for improved learning. Specifically, physical activity causes an increase in blood flow, which in turn unleashes a number of proteins that fuel tissue growth and synaptogenesis in the brain. The more complex the movement is, the more complex the synaptic connections are. Although these connections were made through movement, they are also available for use in thinking and learning. In fact, research shows that engaging in aerobic exercise (at 60 percent to 70 percent of maximum heart rate) alongside complex activity and a social atmosphere (in which the participant must react to another person) provides a stimulating environment that readies the brain to perform and learn (Ratey & Hagerman, 2008). In a review by Howie and Pate (2012), physical activity was found to exert a positive effect on constructs related to academic achievement, such as working memory, inhibition (self-control), and fluid intelligence (problem-solving ability).

Of course, fitness activities also affect a person's overall health. For instance, they play a crucial role in avoiding or resolving both overweight and obesity, which together affect one-third of Canadian children from age 5 to age 17 (Statistics Canada, 2012). Yet only 4 percent of girls and 9 percent of boys meet the Canadian Physical Activity

When children exercise, they set the brain up for improved learning.

guidelines (for ages 5 to 17) of 60 minutes per day of moderate to vigorous activity (Tremblay, 2012), including vigorous activity and muscle- and bone-strengthening activities on at least three days per week to support healthy growth and development. Sadly, modern school environments often add to the overall problem of sedentary living by requiring students to sit for long periods of the day. Accumulated sedentary behaviour can lead to metabolic disease (such as type 2 diabetes) and orthopedic problems (such as neck and back pain). In contrast, fitness activities can help not only with these conditions but also with strengthening ligaments and tendons, increasing stamina, improving mobility and joint stability, relieving stress, boosting mood (which can aid student interactions), and help manage psychological disorders such as anxiety and depression. When taught in an encouraging environment, fitness activities can also help children increase their self-confidence.

In addition, fitness activities provide children with the movement skills to pursue enjoyable activities and the capacity to engage in those activities for sustained periods of time. They also enable children to interact physically with our wonderful planet when, for instance, they build body awareness or kinesthesia, learn to handle gravity by jumping and hopping, and traverse terrain through force production and reduction in activities such as running.

Thus we know that fitness activity primes the brain for learning, helps combat childhood obesity, reduces the risk of metabolic and orthopedic illness, supports growth and development, and provides the movement skills and capacity to pursue enjoyable physical activities. Now it is time to shift our focus from why to what.

Components of Physical Fitness

Physical fitness is the ability to meet life's physical demands and still have enough energy to respond to unplanned events. It provides us with the foundation to pursue activities of physical, mental, social, and emotional origin. Within this broad framework, the key components of physical fitness can be categorized into two domains: health related and skill related. Health-related components enhance health and reduce disease risk, whereas skill-related components enable sport performance. Of course, one could argue that many skill-related components are also important for health enhancement—for example, balance. Here are some of the components in each category:

Health-Related Components

- Cardiorespiratory endurance—ability to perform prolonged, large-muscle, dynamic exercise at moderate to high levels of intensity
- Muscular strength—amount of force that a muscle can produce with a single maximum effort
- Muscular endurance—ability of a muscle or group of muscles to remain contracted or contract repeatedly
- Flexibility—ability to move joints through their full range of motion
- Body composition—proportion of fat mass and fat-free mass (i.e., muscle, bone, and water)

Skill-Related Components

- Agility—ability to change body position quickly and accurately
- Balance—ability to maintain equilibrium while moving or stationary
- Coordination—ability to perform motor tasks accurately and smoothly by using body movements and the senses
- Speed—ability to perform a movement in a short period of time
- Power—ability to exert force rapidly (i.e., strength plus speed)
- Reaction time—ability to respond or react quickly to a stimulus

These components need to be reflected in the activities that students perform in class. Some activities isolate one component, whereas others integrate two or more components.

Now that you know the why and the what of fitness activities in physical education, we can turn our attention to the how.

Implementing Physical Fitness Activities

When designing physical activities for your class, it may be useful to ask yourself the following questions:

1. What physical fitness components and fundamental movement skill categories am I addressing with this lesson?

2. What movement skills should my students possess in order to perform the activity safely and effectively?

3. What equipment do I have?

4. What are the risks? Have I checked my provincial or territorial safety guidelines?

5. What modifications should be made for students with varying levels of skill?

6. What am I doing for each part of the lesson—warm-up, lead-up (to practice skills before doing main stations), activity stations, cool-down, and reflection.

Exercise provides students with opportunities to build movement skills that they may need in future sport endeavours or physical activities of daily living. Skill also tends to be in the forefront of children's minds: "Kids care very little about fitness. They care a great deal about gaining skill" (Johnston, 2013, p. 4). Therefore, when you design stations, remember to emphasize the skills that students are developing and let fitness be characterized as a by-product in their minds—even if it is a primary goal in your lesson plan!

A hierarchy for implementing fitness activities is presented in figure 13.1. The bottom layer of the pyramid is the most important one because it addresses the fundamental movement skills needed for all activities, including fitness activities. Children who do not develop these skills tend to experience higher risk of injury and lower ability to participate proficiently in various activities. A fitness unit that supports the fundamental movement skills addresses movement patterns known as the primal patterns. The middle layer of the pyramid is concerned with developing the physical fitness domains mentioned earlier: health related and skill related. The top layer shows the result of the two layers below it. Specifically, it combines the movement *competence* (ability to move well) from the bottom layer with the movement *capacity* (ability to sustain good movement) from the middle layer, thus enabling successful participation in sport and recreation for life. The top layer is not addressed further in this discussion because it lies beyond the scope of this chapter.

Exercise provides students with opportunities to build movement skills that they may need in future sport endeavours or physical activities of daily living.

Fundamental Movement Skills

Fundamental movement skills serve as the building blocks for human movement, thus enabling development of more complex or sport-specific skills (Physical and Health Education Canada, 2011). They are grouped into three categories—stability, locomotion, and manipulation—which are summarized in table 13.1.

The fundamental movement skills represent one domain of physical literacy, which has been concisely defined by Margaret Whitehead (2010, pp. 11-12): "As appropriate to each individual's endowment, physical literacy can be described as the motivation, confidence, physical competence, knowledge, and understanding to maintain physical activity throughout the life course." The four domains of physical literacy are as follows: physical fitness (cardiorespiratory capacity, muscular strength, flexibility), motor behaviour (fundamental motor skill proficiency), physical activity behaviours (objectively measurable daily activity), and psychosocial and cognitive factors (awareness, knowledge, understanding). Physical literacy is not a destination but a journey, and physical education class helps set each student on his or her path.

How can we use fitness activities to help students develop fundamental movement skills? One approach is provided by the primal pattern system, developed by neuromuscular therapist Paul Chek (2000) and focused on fundamental

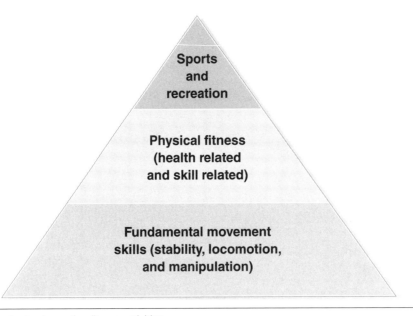

Figure 13.1 Hierarchy for implementing fitness activities.

■ TABLE 13.1

Fundamental Movement Skills

Stability	Locomotion	Manipulation
Creating equilibrium and balance	Traveling across an area	Controlling an object
Stork stand Log roll	Walk Run Skip Gallop Dodge Sprint Jump Hop Leap	Underhand roll Overhand throw Underarm throw Kick Pass Strike (sideways, overhand, underhand) Catch Trap Dribble

Based on PHE Canada (2011).

movement patterns necessary for survival in our Paleolithic past. The patterns are as follows:

- Squat: Use maximal knee bend and hip bend to lower the body.
- Lunge: Use knee and hip bend in a split-stance position to lower the body.
- Bend: Use maximal hip bend and minimal knee bend to "hinge" at the hips.
- Push: Use the upper body to drive a load away from the body.
- Pull: Use the upper body to move a load toward the body.
- Twist: Turn or rotate through the transverse plane.
- Gait: Walk, march, run, or sprint in various directions or gradients.

Primal pattern sequences make up all sport and occupational skills. For example, throwing a ball requires the thrower to combine a push, a twist, and a lunge; therefore, by fortifying these patterns in your fitness unit, you help students build a foundation of movement competence that they can apply in learning to throw a ball in a future class unit. As indicated in table 13.2, certain primal pattern movements are associated

with certain performance characteristics of the fundamental movement skills. As a result, when students improve their mobility and stability in a variety of primal movement patterns, they grow their physiological capacity or potential to learn movement skills. Therefore, when you emphasize primal patterns in your activities, you set the foundation for students to learn sport skills, participate in various PE experiences (e.g., weight training in high school), and engage in fitness and wellness activities as adults.

Before incorporating any particular movement into a fitness activity, make sure that the student can maintain adequate technique while performing the associated primal pattern with body-weight resistance. This point is crucial because if a child repeatedly performs a pattern that is not technically proficient, then that quality of performance may get programmed in—becoming the child's default pattern.

Physical Fitness

Physical fitness activities are designed to change the student's physical capacity. For example, repeated performance of running improves cardiorespiratory endurance, and repeated performance of push-ups increases muscular endurance.

■ TABLE 13.2

Primal Pattern Movements and Associated Fundamental Movement Skills

Fundamental movement skill category	Specific fundamental movement skills	Primal pattern movements
Stability	Static—holding a shape in stillness Dynamic—holding a shape while traveling	All
Locomotion	Running Dodging Sprinting Jumping (2 to 2, 1 to 2, 2 to 1) (Leaping, hopping, jumping for distance or height)	Lunge Squat Twist Gait Bend
Manipulation	Projecting skills * Underhand roll * Overhand throw * Kick * Pass * Strike (sideways, underhand, overhand) Recovery skills * Catch * Trap Retaining skill * Dribble	Push Pull Bend Twist Lunge

Physical fitness activities are designed to change the student's physical capacity.

When such activities are laid down on a platform of well-developed fundamental movement patterns, they build the student's physical resilience.

When thinking about such activities, we can benefit from applying the movement framework established by Rudolf Laban (1879-1958), a pioneer in the study of human movement. Laban viewed the body as an instrument of expression and viewed movement as either expressive (as in dance) or utilitarian (as in functional movement for sport, games, or general life). Laban's movement framework highlights four aspects of movement: body (something to move), space (a place in which to move), effort (energy with which to move), and relationship (movement in connection to things, ideas, pieces of apparatus, or other people) (Physical and Health Education Canada, 2011; Abels & Bridges, 2010). You can consider activities that encompass the elements of Laban's movement framework when planning fitness activities for a class. To help you with this work, table 13.3 indicates fitness connections for Laban's four aspects of movement. You can use this approach to modify and advance activities in order to produce a variety of fitness activity opportunities.

Fitness Skill Acquisition

Students develop fitness skills in the following stages, which were identified in 1967 by Paul Fitts and Michael Posner (Johnston, 2013):

- Cognitive
- Associative
- Autonomous

The cognitive stage is characterized by excessive thinking in an effort to form a mental picture of the particular skill. Therefore, when observing students in this stage, you are likely to see poorly timed movements and a large number of errors; moreover, the student typically recognizes the poor quality of the performance. The teaching of skills in this stage may need to be divided into parts in order to focus in on a limiting component. In the next stage, the associative stage, the student has learned the skill and executes it much more smoothly and consistently; the student can also detect and correct errors. In this stage, you can add challenges, such as changes in environment, tempo, and direction. Finally, after much practice,

the student enters the autonomous stage, wherein he or she can execute the skills habitually, automatically, and consistently and perform variations in speed and direction. Some students do not reach this level in a given year but may reach it over several years of PE.

Fitness Variables

When designing a fitness class, consider how you will challenge your students to develop greater capacity as they progress, both through the unit and through their years of PE. To create challenge, you can manipulate the following design variables:

- *Load.* This is the easiest variable to adjust because it simply involves using a heavier load, thus requiring the performer to exert more effort.

- *Amplitude.* This variable involves making the movement larger in order to challenge fitness capacity. For example, in the case of medicine ball throws against a wall, you might move the student back to increase the distance or magnitude of the throw; of course, doing so also increases the space needed for the activity.

- *Tempo.* This variable involves increasing exercise speed, thus requiring more reactivity and more force reduction and production, which in turn requires the performer to exert more effort.

- *Complexity.* This variable involves changing the amount of movement in a particular exercise. For example, in the case of a standing chest press performed with rubber tubing, you might make it more complex by adding a squat before the press. Doing so changes the relationship of the performer to the equipment because the performer must now handle the loads using two compounded movements.

- *Repetitions.* Adding more repetitions increases muscle endurance. (In contrast, adding more load decreases the number of repetitions but provides more strength gains; in other words, the amount of load and the number of repetitions have an inverse relationship.)

- *Timed sets.* This variable involves doing an exercise or series of exercises for a prescribed amount of time.

Laban's Movement Framework in Relation to Fitness Activities

Aspect of framework	Categories and subcategories	Movement element examples	Fitness connection
Body What do we move?	Body parts	Trunk Upper extremities Lower extremities Total body integration	Isolated body-part exercise Movement pattern exercise
	Body shapes	Narrow (pin) and wide (wall) Round (ball) Twisted (corkscrew) Symmetrical (same) Asymmetrical (different)	Stance chosen Changes in body position Rotary exercises Reciprocal and nonreciprocal movement
	Body-part actions	Weight bearing Force reduction and production Weight transfer Action led by body part	Load Deceleration to acceleration Body shifts Parts that move an implement
	Whole-body actions: • Stability • Locomotor • Manipulation	Balance, static shape holds Walk, run, crawl, jump, skip, roll Throw, roll, strike, kick, carry	Balance activities Gait training activities Medicine ball and dumbbell activities
Space Where do we move?	Location	Self-space (kinosphere) or general space (gymnasium or court boundaries)	Activities performed in stances or over a distance
	Direction	Forward, backward, sideways, up, down, clockwise, counterclockwise	Where the body part is moving to
	Level	Low (below knees), medium (trunk height), high (above shoulders)	Movement of resistances to varying heights
	Pathway	Straight, curved, diagonal (zigzag)	Exercise path of motion
	Plane of motion	Sagittal (up and down motions), frontal (sideways motions), transverse (rotation motions)	Exercises that challenge one plane while stabilized in the other two
	Extension	Small (near the body) or large (far from the body)	Exercises close to the body or involving a fully outstretched limb
Effort How do we move?	Time	Fast, slow, accelerating, decelerating	Exercise tempo
	Force	Hard (strong) or soft (light)	Exercise intensity
	Flow	Bound (stoppable) or free (ongoing)	Exercise amplitude or sequence
	Focus	Direct (straight) or indirect (wavy)	Exercises with targets
Relationship What or whom do we move in connection with?	People	Solo, pair, group	Individual, partner, or group activities
	Position	Above, below, beside, around, supported, lifted	Exercise activities in relation to partner orientation
	Timing	Mirror, contrast, movement sequence, action–reaction, leading–following	Partner activity variations
	Goal	Cooperative, competitive, collaborative	Activity or exercise outcome completed efficiently and effectively using the examples to the left
	Environment	Static (fixed apparatus) or dynamic (ball or other apparatus in motion)	Activity performed on fixed equipment or with moving piece of equipment or partner

- *Miscellaneous variables.* A performer's development of capacity can also be modified by changing grip width, grip thickness, or grip orientation (e.g., one hand pronated and the other supinated) or by using unstable surfaces, changing from double leg to single leg, or adding manual resistance provided by a partner.

Focused Fitness Qualities by Age

This last section discusses a progression of movement and fitness capacities to focus on at different ages in order to support students' movement and athletic development. This progression, known as long-term athlete development (LTAD), helps students not only improve their athleticism but also embrace active living for the life span. LTAD is a seven-stage model that provides a general framework for athlete development, as well as guidelines for selecting activities and exercises that are appropriate for a child's developmental age, thus maximizing the child's learning and performance. Using this model in sport and physical education also maximizes the student's chance of leading an active life after he or she graduates or stops participating in competitive sport.

The following LTAD stages are relevant to children in grades K through 8 (i.e., ages 4 to 13 years old):

- Active Start (up to age 6)
- FUNdamentals (ages 6 to 9 for boys and 6 to 8 for girls)
- Learn to Train (ages 9 to 12 for boys and 8 to 11 for girls, or until onset of the growth spurt)

Table 13.4 presents each of these stages along with associated physical activity outcomes and possible PE class activities to augment development.

Guide to Using Activities

The web resource for this chapter includes appropriate fitness activities for you to use. When setting up your fitness activities, try any of the following types:

1. *Circuits.* This activity type sets up various activities in a set rotation. Students do each activity for a prescribed amount of time, then rotate to the next one. Depending on the equipment available, consider setting up obstacle courses with stations that have different fitness components.
2. *Bubbles.* These outdoor activities involve students moving to catch bubbles in different positions and are great for teaching the primal patterns.
3. *Animals.* Activities that mimic animal movements, such as bear walks or crab soccer, ignite children's imaginations and allow for learning about animals while performing stretching and strengthening movements.
4. *Games.* Fitness activities can be set up as games to help students develop various aspects of physical fitness (e.g., tag for cardiorespiratory endurance).
5. *Modified sport games.* These games provide endless options depending on your focus.

Your lesson plan should include the following elements:

- *Warm-up.* This element gets the tissues warm and mobile. It can be accomplished through a game and some focused, active, targeted exercises for the whole body. (5-10 minutes)
- *Instructions.* To promote accurate execution, make sure that students know what to do at stations and in activities. In addition, if you are energetic in your description, that energy will flow into your students and motivate them to engage. (10 minutes)
- *Main activity.* Plan your theme and set your activities to develop the skills of the theme. For example, if your theme was core stability, you may program an animal movement class developing core stability in different crawling patterns. (15-40 minutes)
- *Cool-down.* This element can be handled through games or an activity (e.g., the animal movement activity mentioned earlier); you can also lead students in some stretching. (5-10 minutes)

The suggested times can be altered as appropriate for each individual teaching situation.

Movement Competence Activities

The first set of activities provided in the web resource for this chapter is designed to help you assess whether students are moving correctly. In order to avoid building fitness on top of movement *dysfunction*, you must ascertain that students are

■ TABLE 13.4

LTAD Stages, Activity Outcomes, and PE Activity Possibilities

LTAD stage	Physical activity outcomes	PE activities
Active Start (up to age 6)	Brain development* Coordination Social skills Gross motor skills* Positive self-esteem Bone building Sleep improvement Healthy weight promotion Stress reduction Fitness improvements Skillful movement Enjoyment of activity Emphasis on fun	Learning through child-led play ABCs (agility, balance, coordination, and speed) 60 minutes of activity per day Running Throwing, catching, and kicking
FUNdamentals (ages 6 to 9 for boys and 6 to 8 for girls)	Fundamental movement skills ABCs (agility, balance, coordination, speed) Locomotor skills in varied environments Games that develop strength, endurance, and flexibility Strength development through body-weight activities Multilateral development Emphasis on fun	Swimming levels Skating Jumping and landing Body-weight calisthenics Mobility exercises Running activities Aerobic activities of low intensity (high-intensity lactic acid accumulation *not* appropriate at this age) Variety of fitness activities to promote multilateral development
Learn to Train (ages 9 to 12 for boys and 8 to 11 for girls, or until onset of the growth spurt)	Stamina Strength Speed Skill Flexibility Fundamental movement skills Overall sport skills Movement-to-music activities Land-, water-, snow-, or ice-based activities	All items from the previous two stages, as well as Swiss ball and medicine ball exercises

*The period from birth to age 5 is a sensitive one, both for brain development and for development of gross motor skills (e.g., running, walking, jumping, catching, throwing, kicking). For students in this period, provide as much opportunity as possible for whole-body movement and wide-ranging skill development.

doing the movements with sufficient competence as pointed out in the instructions and teacher points within the activities. These fundamental activities will help you assess each student's movement competence in the push, pull, squat, twist, bend, and lunge (running mechanics are addressed later, in the section on physical fitness activities) movements.

The web resource also shows where these activities belong in the realm of the fundamental movement skills, as well as how to categorize your activities using the Laban movement framework. Each activity is followed by a reflection question (where applicable) to solidify students' learning of the activity and its application. You can imple-

ment these activities in the form of a circuit or set up as a movement challenge to see who has "skillz" (as the kids like to say!).

Following this section in the web resource, activity templates provide examples of different types of fitness activities, along with instructions that encompass the following components of physical fitness:

- Cardiorespiratory fitness
- Muscular fitness
- Agility
- Balance
- Speed

I hope that you see how the system works and how you can use Laban's framework to change any activity in its four key aspects to create and modify various activities. This approach allows you to generate countless ideas!

Physical Fitness Activities

The physical fitness activities provided in the web resource provide challenges for the cardiorespiratory and musculoskeletal systems. The cardiorespiratory system involves the heart, lungs, blood, and blood vessels, whereas the muscular system involves the muscles, tendons, ligaments, fasciae (the shrink wrap of the body), and bones. In order to promote positive attitudes toward such activities, take care to help students have fun with them (Lancaster & Teodorescu, 2008). For example, highlight the relevance of what they are doing to their lives both now (e.g., sport participation, household chores) and in the future (e.g., working as part of a team in a job). Moreover, it is crucial for students to build stamina and muscular strength because we live in a society characterized not by fitness but by gaming and sedentary behaviour; therefore, activities that develop fitness give them a much-needed opportunity to develop the capacity to participate in activities they enjoy while also minimizing their risk of injury.

Here are some options for fitness activities:

- Circuits
- Obstacle courses (a form of circuit training)
- Animal exercises
- Games
- Use of outdoor running trails with fitness stations

As you implement your activities, please consider the following key questions:

- What primal pattern or fundamental movement skill are you addressing?
- What other fitness components does the activity develop?
- How can you modify the activity by using Laban's movement framework?

Remember that every activity helps program the child's nervous system, and each exercise involves a skill. With this in mind, table 13.5 provides a checklist of running mechanics to look for in mature runners during the activities (Physical and Health Education Canada, 2011).

Summary

As a physical education teacher, you can set the stage for your students' lifelong adoption of physical activity. More specifically, you can help them build the foundation for enjoying any activity by teaching them how to move well and then how to develop their physical capacity in order to move at higher speeds, against greater resistances, and for longer periods of time. Physical literacy is a lifelong journey that is just as important as reading, writing, and arithmetic. In fact, it sets the brain up to learn all subjects more efficiently. Enjoy the experience!

■ TABLE 13.5

Running Mechanics and Developmental Changes in a Mature Runner

Mature run	Cue words	Developmental changes to observe
In slow running, foot contact is made with the heel under the body.	Heel to toe	• Increasing length of stride • Greater hip, knee, and ankle extension at push-off • Longer flight time • Increase in distance above ground of heel as knee drives forward • Increase in height of knee drive • Narrowing in base of support and decrease in vertical movement
As speed increases, foot contact is made with the ball of the foot under the body.	Balls of feet	
Swing leg is raised high.	High knees	
Support leg moves from slight bend to complete extension.	Extend your leg	
Elbows are bent at right angles (and stay there) and move in opposition to the legs.	Hands brush hips in back swing	
Upper arm drives forward and back.	Drive arms—elbows in	

DISCUSSION QUESTIONS

1. Describe how you would explain physical fitness to the following student groups in a way that helps them see its relevance to their lives: K-3, grades 4-6, and grades 7-8.

2. Pick any exercise you like and describe 10 modifications of it using Laban's movement framework.

3. Why is it important to attain movement competence before building fitness capacity?

4. What primal patterns set the foundation when a student throws a ball? What fitness activities could be used to support its development?

5. Design a fitness circuit for a grade 6 class that uses all of the primal patterns.

6. How does physical activity provide a foundation on which learning can occur?

 Visit the web resource for ready-to-use activities that help students develop movement competence and practice key components of fitness.

Voices From the Field

Celine Charbonneau
Teacher (Grades 1-7), Surrey School District, British Columbia

As a generalist elementary teacher, I have worked in an assortment of teaching positions, including grade 1, grades 2 and 3, grades 5-7 (learning support), and French. This year, I have a grade 4-5 class. Physical education has been one of my favourite subjects since I was a student. In order to make PE fun for all, I use a variety of strategies to change up the class dynamics and encourage all students to participate. The focus in my class is never on how well students perform a skill but on how much effort they put into trying and improving. I also focus on how well students work in teams and exhibit leadership skills and sportspersonship.

To help guide my units, I often use the Teaching Games for Understanding model. I find this model effective for teaching students the various skills used in physical activity, how those skills transfer between activities, and how students can develop these skills by playing invented games. Students love creating their own games and are always excited to share, learn, and play each other's games. Another strategy I use is creating theme-based units, such as cricket and Paralympic sports. These units excite students because they bring something new to the whole class, thus putting all students at the same level as they explore the topic together.

When it comes to fitness, I tend to think about things I enjoy in my own fitness routine, such as variety, music, and choice. In our classroom, fitness is not limited to our PE block; instead, we incorporate it more broadly into our daily schedule. At the beginning of the year, for example, we started a kilometer club, which allows students to set their own goals and work toward improving their cardiorespiratory fitness; we also set class goals so that we can celebrate together as a community. In addition, we use our daily physical activity (DPA) time to play cooperative games and work on balance, flexibility, and strength. Students decide on a schedule for the week based on what they feel like developing. Students also create and lead our fitness routines; they do so by deciding the type of fitness they want to focus on and designing an activity based on that decision. We also work on a class playlist that we listen to during our fitness activities. Students love having a say in how the class is organized!

When it comes to assessment, I view participation as a major look-for. If a student is not participating, it is typically because his or her needs have not been met. Perhaps the student does not understand, or feels that his or her voice or idea was not heard, or does not feel safe enough to try. In addition, I present a rubric to the students at the beginning of the year to indicate what I am looking for and what they should be looking for in themselves. I use this rubric as part of a teacher–student check-in to see where we agree and do not agree on performance. I also love having students write journal reflections, which provide me with great insight into students' perspectives—what each student is working on, finding difficult or easy, likes or dislikes, and feels about physical activity. Their answers always surprise me.

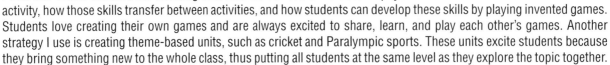
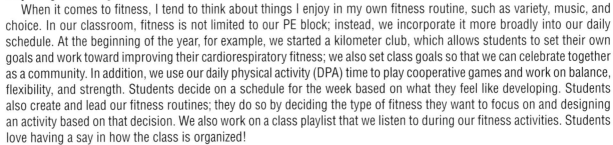

Designing Games

Carol Scaini ■ Catherine Casey

After studying this chapter, you will be able to

- create your own games and activities;
- use a template, guiding criteria, and questions to help create games and activities;
- inspire students to develop their own games and activities;
- help students build confidence and empower them to be creative in developing activities and games; and
- create fun interactive classes centred on student creativity through collaboration.

Now that you have learned the basics of teaching health and physical education, we want you to feel inspired to create your own games and encourage your students to do the same! We also want you to feel confident in creating effective rules and establishing the level of competition or cooperation that your students need. Creating games gives us the opportunity to differentiate instruction in order to better meet the needs of individual students or specific groups of students. It also offers us a way to emphasize skills and strategic play and break them down into a simpler form so that students can better understand the game and the strategy involved. In this way, students learn key concepts while playing a game that is interactive, fun, and challenging—both cognitively and physically. The importance of the cognitive aspect is highlighted by the Teaching Games for Understanding (TGfU) model, which teaches us that simplifying the rules and demands of a game helps students grasp the intent of game-specific skills and strategies, as well as the rules associated with the full version of the game.

When introducing game creation, start by simply changing the object used to play a game. For example, instead of teaching passing and catching with a basketball, why not start with a rubber chicken?

When introducing game creation, start by simply changing the object used to play a game. For example, instead of teaching passing and catching with a basketball, why not start with a rubber chicken? This approach provides multiple benefits: The chicken is easier to catch and throw, students don't worry about injury, and the focus is on fun and movement. Of course, there is no dribbling with a rubber chicken, but students do learn how important it is to move in order to receive a pass from a teammate. More generally, this type of game highlights the simplicity of game playing with little equipment, simple instructions, and few rules. At the end of such a class, you can ask the students what they liked or didn't like about the activity and what a game of basketball might look like if they played it with a rubber chicken. What rule changes would they make? What rules would they need? What would scoring look like? Thus, with this activity and the follow-up questions, you have introduced the notion of creating a game. You could incorporate this approach at

the end of a cooperative games unit or treat it as a unit of its own.

From this example, it may seem simple enough to develop a game, but there are some misconceptions that elementary teachers and generalist teachers may have when allowing their students to design games. Table 14.1 shows potential outcomes of these misconceptions, as well as suggested alternatives to help ensure successful game design.

Across all curricular areas, we want our students to develop as critical thinkers and problem solvers; we also want them to learn to take responsibility for their own learning. To meet these goals, we need to allow our students to engage in the creative process, and that includes the process of creating games: "An inventing-games learning context results in a better understanding not only of game structures, game play, and situated skills but also of self and others, as well as issues of social justice and what makes democracy work (e.g., collaboration, negotiation, inclusiveness, and fairness) (Butler, 2016, p. xv).

In addition, due to various social and environmental factors, today's children are not playing outside as much as they used to. However, when left on their own to play, children being to create their own games and engage in free play. That is why this chapter is so important: We need to reintroduce our students to the creative aspects of game play. We hope you

When left on their own to play, children being to create their own games and engage in free play.

embrace this opportunity to gain confidence in your own teaching and develop your ability to guide your students through the process of game creation.

The next section of this chapter provides you with examples to help you design your own games. Each example includes guiding questions to help you develop your understanding of the requirements of designing a game. Once you feel confident in designing games, you can challenge your students to create their own games and present them to the class. The first example presented here includes a list of questions to help you develop a basic cooperative game. Cooperative games are fun, increase heart rates, and allow students to develop strategies while working with teammates to achieve a task. The second example allows you to consider how you would create a

■ TABLE 14.1

Misconceptions About Student-Designed Games

Misconception	Potential outcome	Suggested alternative
All you need to do is explain the skill, give students some equipment, and say, "Make up a game."	Students will focus on the skill itself rather than on a component of game play.	Focus on a smaller component of a game (i.e., one TGfU category or one component of a TGfU category) and build from there.
Children understand why games have rules, regulations, and penalties.	Children think that rules are something to follow (or break), and they often argue about rules when they don't understand them. They are less likely to consider rules as tools to make a game better.	During the game design process, ask questions about game elements. Help students understand that changing the rules changes the game. With older students, begin with a game and have them change it.
Children will learn strategy on their own.	Many children won't develop strategic understanding simply through game play.	Determine the focal strategic concept for the lesson and monitor the children to ensure that they remain on task. Design games that enable them to learn the concept
You cannot tell students what to do. They have to come up with it by themselves.	Left unchecked, students may design games that are unsafe or treat each other without respect.	Always intervene when games are not safe. Intervene also if students are being disrespectful to one another or if a conflict is getting out of hand.
You should not interrupt the planning process.	Students rarely stop and reflect about their games unless prompted to do so.	Stop the design process at certain points during the lesson to invite critique and modifications.

Reprinted by permission from P. Hastie, *Student-Designed Games* (Champaign, IL: Human Kinetics, 2010), 7.

cooperative game with limited equipment available.

Designing Cooperative Games

Your task is to create a cooperative game that is unique. Your responsibility is to introduce the game, establish the requirements, provide all needed equipment, and address any safety issues. The following questions will help you get going:

- What is your game called?
- How is it played?
- How many players are required? What are their roles?
- What is the primary challenge (i.e., the problem to be solved)?
- Are there any additional challenges or variations to the game?
- What are the rules and restrictions?
- What equipment is required?

- What is the game design—that is, the playing area and setup?
- What is the game's duration?
- What are the safety concerns related to game play? Related to equipment?
- Where did the game originate (e.g., resources used, previous experience)?

As you consider your ideas, remember that your game must exhibit the following characteristics:

- Active participation by all students
- Fair play
- Cooperation
- Good sporting behaviour
- Safe play

Some school settings lack the necessary equipment for a particular game. Such instances give you a great opportunity to design your own game using a variety of equipment. Creating games with minimal equipment allows you to be innovative and often makes the game easier to learn and play. Your task in this case is to select a few different pieces of equipment from the storage room that are not connected to any particular game. For example, you might choose a skipping rope, a scoop, a rubber chicken, and two poly spots. Using the same questions just listed, think about how you might use these pieces of equipment to build a game. Then try it out and, if needed, alter it so that your students can be successful with it.

Designing Tag Games

Tag games provide one of the easiest and most popular ways to get students moving. They are fun, require little or no equipment, increase heart rates, and allow students to learn how to defend themselves (and sometimes how to work together as a team). Table 14.2 offers questions to help you create your own tag games, and table 14.3 shows an example of a tag game using the questions as a guide.

■ TABLE 14.2

Template for Designing Tag Games

Design consideration	Options
What is the game's format?	• Is it a continuous game of chasing, dodging, and fleeing? Or is it more of a player-versus-player format?
What is the game's goal?	• Is the challenge to get to a specific target (e.g., other side of playing area) without being tagged (e.g., on a certain part of the body?) Or is the goal to accrue a certain number of tags in a specific time, or to be the last player tagged?
What are the limits of play?	• What sort of space is used (e.g., shape, size, out of bounds area)? • What rules govern penalties for moving out of bounds?
Are there safety zones?	• Is the safe spot a designated area (e.g., marked by spots, pylons, lines, or hoops)? • How long is a player allowed to remain in the safety zone?
How are players involved?	• Do the teams have even numbers? • What is the total number of taggers? • Do tagging players have special privileges or restrictions? • Are there specialized tagging roles?
How do players move?	• Do players run? Walk fast? Use scooters? • Using other types of locomotion (e.g., skipping, hopping) is a good idea, but usually students go back to the norm of running or fast walking.
How are players tagged?	• Do they tag with one hand? Two hands? An object (e.g., pool noodle, scarf, beanbag, stolen belt flag)?
How are players unfrozen?	• Are they unfrozen by a teammate (e.g., high five, shoulder tap)? • Do those who are caught exchange places with the taggers? Become part of the taggers' team? Return to their end zone? Go to a jail from which they can be released by a teammate? • Can players get a flag from another player? Grab a flag from a player running by?

Reprinted by permission from P. Hastie, *Student-Designed Games* (Champaign, IL: Human Kinetics, 2010), 58.

■ TABLE 14.3

Sample Tag Game: ABC Tag

Design consideration	Options
What is the game's format?	• Continuous game of chasing and dodging
What is the game's goal?	• Tagger chases other players in an attempt to tag or touch them using his or her hands
What are the limits of play?	• Gymnasium or outdoor space with pylons to identify the playing area
Are there safety zones?	• No safety zones
How are players involved?	• Select two students to be the taggers.
How do players move?	• Running
How are players tagged?	• With one hand
How are players unfrozen?	• Two students are selected as ABC Rescuers, who help unfreeze tagged students by giving them each a letter of the alphabet. If the tagged student says three words beginning with that letter, then he or she can unfreeze and reenter the game. If not, the tagged student trades places with the ABC Rescuer.
Look-fors	• Students are breathing heavily. • Students are demonstrating spatial awareness by effectively moving away from objects and other players. • Students are working together to unfreeze players who have been caught.

Designing Games Through TGfU

This part of the chapter narrows the focus to highlight the process of creating games based on the Teaching Games for Understanding philosophy, which is explored in greater detail in chapter 12. The guiding questions posed here will help you develop a deeper understanding of the four TGfU game categories and enable you to create games that are engaging and tactically challenging. TGfU highly values both the role of the teacher as facilitator and the role of the learner as active participant in the learning process (Griffin & Butler, 2005, p. 1). As your students begin to create their own games, your role as a teacher is to ask skillful questions that prompt students to "analyze the constraints of their games and change their rules to make them more flowing, challenging, and fun" (Butler, 2016, p. 1). Enabling your students to experiment and solve problems while designing games helps them acquire meaningful, in-depth knowledge of game structures and tactics. It also encourages them to "develop thinking and social skills through group work", which requires them to "learn how to cooperate and make decisions, how to explain and justify their ideas, and how to consider the needs and opinions of others" (Butler & Griffin, 2010, p. 224).

TGfU considers game types to fall into one of four categories: target, striking-and-fielding, net and wall, and territory. For a snapshot of the four categories and their primary goals, see table 14.4. This chapter includes templates that will help you create your own TGfU games for each of the four categories, as well as sample games we created using the same questions as a guide. Table 14.5 is a template for designing target games and table 14.6 is a sample target game; tables 14.7 and 14.8 cover striking-and-fielding games; tables 14.9 and 14.10 cover net and wall games; and tables 14.11 and 14.12 cover territory games. Once you answer the questions provided for the particular TGfU category you plan to use, describe how the game is played, indicate the equipment required, and make a simple drawing of the layout of the game. Point form is fine as long as you provide enough information for all players to understand. All of the templates are also available on the web resource so you can easily download and edit an electronic version.

▪ TABLE 14.4

TGfU Categories and Primary Goals

TGfU category	Primary goal (intent)
Target (e.g., archery, bowling, curling, golf, pool)	To send an object and make contact with a stationary target in fewer attempts than the opponent requires
Striking-and-fielding (e.g., baseball, cricket, Danish longball, rounders, softball)	To send the ball away from fielders in order to run the bases and score more runs than the opponent
Net and wall (e.g., badminton, pickleball, tennis, volleyball; handball, racquetball, squash)	To send a ball in such a way that the opponent is unable to return it or is forced to make an error (ball held only when serving)
Territory games (basketball, football, hockey, lacrosse, soccer, team handball, water polo, ultimate)	To invade the opponent's defending area and shoot or take the object of play into a defined goal area while simultaneously protecting one's own goal

Reprinted by permission from J. Butler, *Playing Fair* (Champaign, IL: Human Kinetics, 2016), 5.

Template for Designing Target Games

Design consideration	Options
Target information	• What is the target? • What is the distance to the target? • What is the size of the target? • Where is the target placed?
Player and target movement	• Is the target moving or still? • Is the player moving or still?
How object is sent to target	• Roll? • Overhand toss? • Underhand throw? • Kick? • Push? • Striking with an object?
Goal of the game	• Get the most points by hitting the target with the highest value? • Hit the most targets? • Be closest to the target? • Be first to remove, knock down, or progress through all targets? • Take the fewest turns to hit all targets?
Hindering of opponent allowed?	• Can players move or block an opponent's ball (e.g., bocce, pool)?

Reprinted by permission from P. Hastie, *Student-Designed Games* (Champaign, IL: Human Kinetics, 2010), 73.

■ TABLE 14.6

Sample Target Game: Tic-Tac-Toe

Design consideration	Options
Target information	• Tic-tac-toe grid measuring 3 m by 3 m (or smaller to increase the challenge) and located 2 m from the player (or farther away to increase the challenge)
Player and target movement	No movement
How object is sent to target	• Underhand throw of beanbags: 6 bags with X written on one side and a physical action on the other; 6 bags with O written on one side and a physical action on the other 1. Student 1 picks up an X beanbag, performs the activity indicated on the other side of the bag, and then tosses the bag onto the grid. 2. Student 2 picks up an O beanbag, performs the activity indicated on the other side, and then tosses the bag onto the grid. 3. Repeat this sequence until one player lands three markers in a horizontal, vertical, or diagonal row. • A beanbag that lands outside the grid is considered a miss and may not be thrown again. • If neither player lands three bags in a row, a tie is called and the game is started again.
Goal of the game	Two players compete, tossing one at a time, and the first one who lands three bags in a row (horizontal, vertical, or diagonal) wins the game.
Hindering of opponent allowed?	No
Look-fors	• Students use proper underhand throwing technique to hit the target. • Students use strategies to improve their game play.

Template for Designing Striking-and-Fielding Games

Design consideration	Options	
How many people play?	• Even numbers against each other?	• Uneven numbers against each other?
How do players score?	• Hit over a boundary? • Run to or past a point?	• Run a particular pathway?
How do players get out?	• Ball caught in air? • Throw to base? • Certain number of missed swings?	• Tagged? • Running out of the playing area? • Batting out of the playing area?
What implements or body parts are used?	• Hand or foot? • Whole body?	• Bat, paddle, or racquet? • Chicken?
How does the striker receive the ball?	• Pitch from own team? • Pitch from opposing team? • Pitch from a machine?	• Toss to self? • Off a tee? • Tossing out the object?
Where do strikers hit?	• From an end line? • From two end lines? • From the middle of the playing area to anywhere?	• From a corner? • From home plate?
What is the shape of the playing area? What are the boundaries?	• Rectangle, fan, or oval? • No boundaries?	• Walls or ceiling?
When do teams change from batting to fielding?	• After a certain number of outs? • After a certain amount of time at bat?	• After a certain number of scores? • After everyone bats? • After a specific number of batters?

Reprinted by permission from P. Hastie, *Student-Designed Games* (Champaign, IL: Human Kinetics, 2010), 115.

Sample Striking-and-Fielding Game: Chicken Baseball

Design consideration	Options
How many people play?	• Half of the group on one team, other half on the opposing team
How do players score?	• Run the bases as in baseball.
How do players get out?	• Tossed rubber chicken caught in the air • Runner tagged with rubber chicken before reaching base
What implements are used?	• Rubber chicken
How does the striker receive the ball?	• Not applicable (Striker tosses chicken into fielding area.)
Where do strikers hit?	• From home plate
What is the shape of the playing area? What are the boundaries?	• Baseball field; foul area behind first and third base lines.
When do teams change from batting to fielding?	• After three outs or after an entire team bats (i.e., throws out the chicken)
Look-fors	• Students breathe heavily. • Students engage in moderate to vigorous physical activity. • Students pass the implement using an overhand pass, underhand pass, or both hands. • Strikers throw the implement to an open space, away from defenders. • Fielders make appropriate decisions: moving to catch the implement and passing it to get runners out. • Students revise strategies based on success or failure in game play.

Template for Designing Net and Wall Games

Design consideration	Options
How many people play?	• Singles? • Doubles? • Teams on each side?
How do players score?	• Opponent misses the ball? • Ball is hit out of bounds? • Hit is not retrieved? • Rally scoring is used? • Score only when serving?
Where does the ball travel?	• Over a net? • Over a line? • Across a space? • Above a line on a wall? • Within a boundary?
How many touches or bounces are allowed?	• One? • Limited number? • Unlimited?
What body part or implement is used for striking?	• Paddle? • Racquet? • Hand? • Foot? • Arm?
What type of object is used?	• Ball (size, inflation level, density)? • Shuttle? • Disc? • Ring? • Other?
How does a game or rally start?	• Ball toss? • Bounce and hit? • Throw? • Kick? • Serve?
What are the court dimensions?	• Length and width? • Sides or ends? • Net height?
After a rally, what happens?	• Winner gets to serve? • Loser gets to serve? • Ball is tossed in? • One side serves for a set number of times?
What faults or penalties are included?	• Foot fault? • Serving to wrong area? • Illegal serve action? • Hitting the net?

Reprinted by permission from P. Hastie, *Student-Designed Games* (Champaign, IL: Human Kinetics, 2010), 131-132.

Sample Net and Wall Game: Handball Tennis

Design consideration	Options
How many people play?	• Singles or doubles
How do players score?	• Opponent misses the ball or hits the ball out of bounds.
Where does the ball travel?	• Over a line? • Over a low net?
How many touches or bounces are allowed?	• One touch, one bounce
What body part or implement is used for striking?	• Hand (palm) or handmade cardboard racquet
What type of object is used?	• Foam tennis-size ball of low density
How does a game or rally start?	• Ball bounced and hit underhand into the diagonally opposite square
What are the court dimensions?	• Foursquare court (larger dimensions for more challenge)
After a rally, what happens?	• Winner gets to serve.
What faults or penalties are included?	• Serving to the wrong area • Hitting the net (if a net is used) • Point awarded to other player
Look-fors	• Students breathe heavily. • Students engage in moderate to vigorous physical activity. • Students work independently or together in a group to develop offensive and defensive strategies. • Students revise strategies based on success or failure in game play.

Template for Designing Territory Games

Design consideration	Options
How many people play?	• Even numbers against each other? • Uneven numbers against each other?
What is the playing area, and what are its boundaries?	• None? • Sidelines only? • Walled in? • Scoring line?
What are the goals?	• Goal size and shape? • Number of goals?
How do players score?	• Making a goal? • Ball moved to a person in a certain place? • Gaining possession? • Moving ball past a line?
How can players progress toward the goal?	• Dribbling? • Running with the ball? • Passing? • Throwing? • Pushing? • Striking? • Kicking?
What object is used?	• Ball or puck? • Flag? • Beanbag? • None?
What implement or body part is used to move the object?	• Scoop to carry the ball? • Stick to hit the ball? • Hand or foot?
How do players get possession?	• After a score? • After a fumble or interception? • After being tagged? • By rebounding? • If the ball goes out of play?
How do players start the game or begin a new period?	• Tip-off or face-off? • Designated receiver? • Coin toss?
How does play resume after a score?	• Simple continuation of play? • Possession by opponent? • Jump ball? • Face-off? • Throw-in by referee? • Alternating possessions?
What faults or penalties are used? How physical should play be?	• Loss of possession? • Throw-in? • What is a foul? • What happens if the foul is accidental? Deliberate? • If a student is pushed, does his or her team gain possession of the ball?

Reprinted by permission from P. Hastie, *Student-Designed Games* (Champaign, IL: Human Kinetics, 2010), 95.

Sample Territory Game: Keep the Chicken

Design consideration	Options
How many people play?	• Even numbers against each other (or uneven numbers against each other for an added challenge)
What is the playing area, and what are its boundaries?	• Half of a volleyball court
What are the goals?	• Goal (hoop) on each end of the playing area
How do players score?	• Pass the rubber chicken to a teammate standing in the goal area (hoop).
How can players progress toward the goal?	• Passing the rubber chicken
What object is used?	• Rubber chicken
What implement or body part is used to move the object?	• Hands
How do players get possession?	• After a score • After the chicken is intercepted • If the chicken is fumbled • If the chicken or a player goes out of bounds
How do players start the game or begin a new period?	• Rock-paper-scissors for possession
How does play resume after a score?	• Possession goes to the opponent.
What faults or penalties are used? How physical should play be?	• Dropping the chicken • Player with the chicken goes out of bounds or throws it out of bounds • Faults or penalties are resolved with a loss of possession • Players guard at arm's length
Look-fors	• Students breathe heavily. • Students engage in moderate to vigorous physical activity. • Students pass the implement using an overhand pass, underhand pass, or both hands. • Students react to the following: defensive player's position; teammate's position; position of the implement. • Using awareness of positioning, students move into open spaces to evade defenders, get open to receive the implement, and create space for teammates. • Students revise strategies based on success or failure in game play.

Summary

Creating a game is an empowering activity, and students enjoy the creative process. In doing so, they work collaboratively to establish rules and formulate how to play the game. When they try out their idea, they realize what works and what doesn't and make appropriate adjustments before presenting their game to the class. After receiving feedback from the class, they make more modifications to make the game better and, of course, more fun!

DISCUSSION QUESTIONS

1. What effect does involving students in the creation of a game have on developing their own games?
2. What elementary teacher or generalist teacher learning occurs when students create their own games?
3. How do students develop higher-level thinking skills when they collaborate by building on each other's ideas?
4. How do students build a positive classroom community when designing games?

 Visit the web resource for templates to guide the design of various game types (tag, target, net and wall, territory, and striking and fielding).

Voices From the Field

Courtesy of Edge Imaging.

Adele Chester

Teacher, Grade 6 Core (Language, Math, Social Studies) and Grades 6, 7, and 8 Physical Education, Cummer Valley Middle School, Toronto District School Board

In order to make physical education fun and educational for students, I make a point to consider students' interests and peer interactions, as well as my own outlook on fitness. Inviting students to provide input often increases their motivation, and the class is more fun when students have an opportunity to make suggestions for skills or games and see how their ideas improve their learning. Supporting their peers helps students learn from one another and further develop their skills in a safe learning environment; they also develop their ability to provide and accept positive feedback. Finally, one's own enthusiasm for physical education should be evident and motivational, thus helping students to recognize that fitness is a lifelong process that is essential to our overall mental health and well-being.

One of the favourite games in my PE classes is kingpin, which I learned from a colleague and which students always ask for. Here's how it works:

Object of the Game

Knock down all pins on the opponent's team.

Number of Players

Any number can play

Equipment

Hoop and pin for each pair or trio and approximately 10 coated foam balls

Game Play

1. Divide the class into two teams and then into pairs (or trios, if the number of students is uneven).
2. Each pair sets up a hoop and a pin set inside the hoop somewhere in its half of the gym.
3. Line up the balls along the centre line of the gym and have each pair of players place their heels on their hoop.
4. On your signal, one student from each pair can repeatedly obtain a ball from the center of the gym and try to throw it to knock down another pair's pin. The other student guards the pair's own pin and may use any part of the body to do so.
5. If a pin goes down, that pair of students is "out" and must ensure that their pin is on its side in the hoop to indicate that it is down and to keep it safely out of other students' way. Then they go to the opposite end of the gym (behind the opponent's baseline) and attempt to knock down opponents' pins from there. Thus students who are still in the heart of the playing area now face the added challenge of defending their pins from two sides.
6. When a team knocks down all of the opposing team's pins, it scores a point. The game is then reset and begins again.

When I asked my students to identify the elements that make this game fun, their responses were very interesting. For one thing, they noted the element of risk and reward. Specifically, players might succeed by venturing away from their hoop to go on the offensive, but doing so could also place their own pin in a vulnerable position. Students also enjoy the fact that no one is ever truly out of the game; rather, a knocked-down pin just moves the affected pair to another location, from which they continue to play. In addition, students appreciate that the game involves both an individual and a team component: As individuals, they can choose when and where to throw the ball, defend, and even place their hoops; however, they are still part of their team and need to help their teammates by gathering and sharing available balls and helping on defense.

(continued)

(continued)

Students also noted that the game involves a good bit of strategy and that the more they play it, the more ways they think of to be successful. For instance, in some cases, they sacrifice a pin in order to go to the opposite side of the playing area so that their team can attack from both sides. Also, because the game involves continuous play, students need to be alert or aware all the time in order to retrieve balls, pass them over the entire playing field, and defend their pin from all sides. Finally, the game requires minimal equipment, and game play can be easily monitored for safety concerns.

After performing this analysis, I challenged students to develop their own games that had the same elements of success they identified for kingpin. The results were intriguing, and many new games were developed. Students had to be reminded about safety issues (e.g., linking hands, wrists, or arms in a tag game; kicking balls in a confined space; throwing balls at one another) and had to modify their rules as the process continued. It was a fun process to go through with the class, and I encourage you to try it. If you do, take some time to get to know your students and their abilities and temperaments. This knowledge will give you the opportunity to establish routines and general expectations so that the game creation process will be creative, inspiring, and rewarding for all.

This activity includes various elements that can be used to assess students' learning. Look-fors include full participation; offensive and defensive game strategy; basic movement skills, such as throwing at a moving or stationary target; defending an object; playing fairly and safely; and cooperating, both with a partner and with the team as a whole, to achieve a common goal. As the year progresses, so do the skills used in this activity, and you can adapt it to suit the varying needs of both students and yourself.

CHAPTER 15

A Wellness Approach to Teaching Physical Education

Michelle Kilborn ■ **Kim Hertlein**

LEARNING OUTCOMES

After studying this chapter, you will be able to

- summarize a different way of thinking about curriculum and apply it to physical education,
- explain the meaning of wellness and describe a wellness approach to teaching physical education,
- create different ways to plan for and practice mindfulness in physical education,
- articulate the role of interconnectedness in promoting wellness among children and youth, and
- apply the concept of balance when planning a wellness approach to physical education.

It is hard to focus and do things sometimes and it's very stressful and overwhelming. This class [a wellness-oriented PE class] allows and helps me to stop for a bit and reconnect and, of course, focus. I've already noticed that my attitude is getting better and I'm starting to think better like I used to. I may be quite shy and a bit uncomfortable for a bit, especially 'cause I don't really like doing these sorts of things in front of people. . . . But by the end of the class I am more comfortable with everything. I feel like this class will help me find myself again and I'm really glad and excited for that, 'cause since the accident it's been hard to do things and cope with things on my own.

16-year-old student, Edmonton, Alberta

It is becoming increasingly difficult for our young people to be healthy and well. Children are experiencing stress, depression, and anxiety at school and in their daily lives that is often overwhelming at a very young age (Canadian Mental Health Association, 2011). In addition, although physical education has the potential to help children be well, physical education programs often follow a sport-technique model (Kirk, 2010) focused primarily on skills and objective measurements. This approach emphasizes only one part of a child (the physical dimension), often to the detriment of other parts (the social, emotional, and mental dimensions) (Hart, 2008). Therefore, we want to expand our understanding of what it means to educate children about their physical well-being and its connection to other parts of the self, as well as other people. That is, we want to encourage educators, including both teachers and school leaders, to reconsider how we think about physical education and to move toward a wellness approach to physical education.

When planning for physical education, we need to consider the whole child— body, mind and spirit. This approach requires us to expand our understanding of what it means to educate children about their physical well-being and its connection with other parts of the self, as well as other people.

The purpose of this chapter, then, is to introduce you to a way of understanding physical education that helps students learn how to live healthy, active lives in a more holistic and wellness-oriented way. The word *health* derives from an Old English root meaning "whole," and here we explore the concept of the whole person— body, mind, and spirit—in the context of physical education. Key concepts in this chapter include a rethinking of physical education; a wellness way of being a teacher; and the concepts of mindfulness, balance, and interconnectedness.

Rethinking Physical Education

We often see primary school children exhibit energetic behaviours and excitement when experiencing physical education in school. The mere mention of "gym" or going outside to play can create a buzz in the classroom. However, as children move through the school system and experience more structured lives in our communities, it seems that their enthusiasm for physical education begins to wane. Indeed, it is not uncommon to hear young people describe negative experiences in physical education (Dyson, 2006; Gibbons, Wharf-Higgins, Gaul, & VanGyn, 1999; Humbert, 2006; MacDonald & Hunter, 2005). Perhaps you are one of those who did not have pleasant experiences in school physical education. Today, the problem does not seem to lie in what we teach children in physical education in Canadian schools; in fact, quality physical education curricula are found across the nation (Kilborn, Lorusso, & Francis, 2016). Instead, what may need reconsidering is *how* we bring this curriculum to life in a way that nurtures wellness and the whole child—in a way that helps students feel and remember how good it feels to play and be healthy.

Traditional understandings of physical education have been based primarily on sport-technique models (Kirk, 2010; Devis-Devis & Sparkes, 1999; Hardman & Marshall, 2000). Moreover, throughout history, the dominant teaching practices in physical education have been based on performance, objective measurement, and a mechanistic view of the body (Tinning, 2010). Although many pedagogical models and programs have been suggested in order to better meet the needs of contemporary children and youth—for instance, play practice, sport education, health-based physical education, and Teaching Games for Understanding (Kirk, 2013)—these programs all lack a holistic way of teaching physical education that respects children's innate awareness of how to be healthy and live well (Kilborn, 2016).

Yet the central aim of all physical education curricula across Canada is for children to learn how to be healthy and active for life (Kilborn

We need to reconsider how we (as teachers and schools) bring the physical education curriculum to life. Physical education needs to nurture wellness in the whole child in a way that helps students remember how good it feels to play and be healthy.

et al., 2016). If we recall that the original meaning of *health* is "wholeness, a being whole, sound or well" ("Health," n.d., n.p.), then we are reminded that the whole person—body, mind, and spirit—is paramount to a wellness approach in physical education. Such a holistic, wellness-oriented way of teaching physical education begins with us, as teachers, and our understanding of children as individual whole beings with physical, mental, emotional, and spiritual dimensions, as well as connections to others and to the community. This approach requires us to bring conscious awareness, mindfulness, compassion, and acknowledgment of interconnectedness among all living things.

Rethinking physical education also involves understanding curriculum as more than a document that outlines learning outcomes to "cover." The Latin root of *curriculum* is *currere*, which means "running the course of life" or "journey of life"; thus it encourages us to think of curriculum as active, dynamic, and social (Grumet, 1980; Kilborn, 2016; Pinar, 2012). In essence, curriculum involves dialogue between teachers, students, and the community about life and how to live it (Kilborn, 2016). For us as teachers, this understanding means that a wellness-oriented physical education curriculum focuses on our way of being with and relating to our students. As we strive to help them learn how to live well, we must recognize how our own manner of living connects with students and with the greater community. If curriculum is viewed as a journey, teaching is not only about *what* we teach but also about *how* we teach; moreover, it is not something we apply *to* students but an ongoing dialogical journey *with* them.

Planning and teaching in a wellness-oriented way involves not only choosing specific activities for physical education class but also doing various other things on an ongoing basis. To help you practice a wellness-oriented approach to teaching both in and out of the physical education classroom, some suggestions and examples are provided in the web resource for this chapter.

A Wellness Way of Being a Teacher

Definitions of wellness share a common thread in the notion that wellness is intrinsic to us. In this view, the source of wellness is present awareness, and this mindfulness connects the individual—body, mind, and spirit—to the collective well-being of society (Kilborn, 2014; Welwood, 1992). Bill Hettler, co-founder of the National Wellness Institute, describes wellness as a conscious and evolving process of achieving full potential; moreover, this process is multidimensional and holistic, encompassing emotional and spiritual well-being as well as lifestyle and the environment (Hettler, 2015). In a similar definition, world-renowned researchers Sweeney and Myers (2006) describe wellness as "a means of living which is oriented toward optimal health and well-being; involves the integration of mind, body, and spirit; requires conscious choices to engage in healthful behaviors; and has a goal of helping you live your life more fully in all areas" (Shannonhouse et al., 2014, p. 5).

Narrowing the focus to teaching per se, Kilborn (2014) explored what it means to teach a wellness-oriented physical education curriculum and focused on "the way a teacher is with her students to help them learn how to live well" (Kilborn, 2016, p. 13). Table 15.1 outlines several characteristics of a wellness approach to teaching physical education.

A wellness approach is about how you teach, not just what you teach. It is not one-size-fits-all, and outcomes are not attached to any specific physical activity. You must get to know your students, work with them, and live the curriculum together with them.

Mindfulness

Mindfulness involves purposefully attending to and being fully aware of what is happening in one's body, mind, and spirit within one's environment. It is nonjudgmental and happens without criticism or competitiveness. Jon Kabat-Zinn (1994) explains mindfulness as the "art of conscious living" and a "practical way to be more in touch with the fullness of your being through a systematic process of self-observation, self-inquiry, and mindful action" (p. 6).

■ TABLE 15.1

A Wellness Approach to Teaching Physical Education

Characteristic	Description
Journey of life	Planning and participating with students in class in an authentic way allows students to continue practicing healthy, active living beyond class and for the rest of their lives.
Not a kit, model, or binder	It is about *how* you teach, not just what you teach. It is not one-size-fits-all, and outcomes are not attached to any specific physical activity. You must get to know your students, work with them, and *live* the curriculum together with them.
Mindfulness	Mindfulness involves paying attention to body–mind–spirit connection in all we do, engaging with students as whole beings, and understanding and respecting their life-worlds.
Confidence	A major goal is for students to feel confident about participating in activities outside of class, even if they are not highly skilled. To this end, we must introduce activities that can be done at home, in the community, or in nature.
Interconnectedness: kindness and connecting beyond the self	Here we help children understand how they are connected to each other, the community, and the planet. Course activities are planned and practiced with kind, compassionate living in mind.
Community building	To build community, we support students in connecting with each other in a safe environment where they feel they belong and are all in it together.
Communication and sharing of stories	We are willing to be vulnerable—to share thoughts and experiences, talk about successes and failures, and show a level of humanness that contributes to an inclusive and positive environment.
Balance	We plan for balance among the dimensions of the whole child—physical, emotional, mental, and spiritual.
Beyond the test—(non)assessment of wellness	Be mindful of how assessment practices can undercut the promotion of overall health and wellness for children. Ensure that assessment is ongoing; includes student input (self or peer assessment); and addresses the mental, physical, emotional, and spiritual dimensions of the whole child.

Data from Kilborn (2016).

In the fast-paced, competitive environment of modern society, students are more at risk of being disconnected both within the self (body, mind, spirit) and from others, as well as from nature. Thus they can benefit from learning how to pay attention to what it feels like to be active and healthy so that they can develop their ability to live well on their own. To help students become more connected, we can begin by offering them ways to practice mindfulness in the physical education environment and in everyday life.

Activity 2 in the web resource, Mindfulness 101, provides a simple series of tasks that promote mindfulness and begin to build a culture of practice in which children can maintain their ability to connect body, mind, and spirit in a variety of situations, both in and out of class. These tasks also promote a sense of interconnectedness, through which students learn to attend to how their way of being is connected with others and with nature.

Interconnectedness: Kindness and Compassion

It is important for us to help students experience their connections to each other and beyond—to the community and to nature. When we provide students with opportunities to experience how small things can be connected to the most significant events (Kornfield, 2000), we extend physical education outcomes beyond the self and classroom and into the community. This practice helps students understand kind and compassionate living, learn how to be serenely present with struggles, and be more accepting of themselves and others without judgment or criticism. For example, a student buddy program might partner older students with younger ones to help teach them games and activities in the physical education setting. In a buddy program, students experience mindfulness, interconnectedness, communication and story-telling, and community-building through the mentor-mentee relationship. Student buddies helping their younger counterparts learn is both an act of kindness and an opportunity for connection with other students in the community. This allows both partners to share their individual stories, skills, and attributes, help build confidence, and feel supported.

The philosophy and practice of interconnectedness teaches young people about relating to others and themselves; specifically, it helps them understand how to "engage with others in holistic and meaningful ways that support health and well-being" (Creative Commons, 2016, n.p.). As teachers, we can emphasize how all people are connected—to the communities in which we live, to our ancestors, to our future descendants, to the land, and to all living things. When children experience these links, they can develop a passion for helping individuals, communities, and all life to thrive and be healthy. One way to illustrate this interconnectedness can be found in activity 3 (Yarn Toss) in the web resource for this chapter; this simple activity can be done in any classroom environment.

One way to promote a wellness approach is to help children understand how they are connected to each other, to the community, and to the planet. To this end, course activities should be planned and practiced with kind, compassionate living in mind.

Balance

To support students in being healthy and active—the aim of physical education—we must help them balance their physical, emotional, mental, and spiritual dimensions. If we focus on only one dimension, we neglect the others to the detriment of the whole self. Therefore, a wellness-oriented

physical education program includes a balance of activities that promote holistic ways of living. This balance requires going beyond merely choosing a variety of physical activities; it also affects *how* we present the activities and how students participate in them. No matter what activities you include in your program, always consider whether and how they encourage balance, both within individual students and among all living things.

Summary

This chapter challenges you to think of physical education differently and to consider teaching with a wellness focus. A wellness approach to physical education is critical to meeting the needs of contemporary children and youth and helping them live in a way that is healthy, connected, and fulfilling both now and in the future. The challenge of physical education lies in shifting perspectives away from the dominant world view—in which teaching practices are grounded in mechanistic ways of thinking about the body and about our children—and toward a wellness-oriented approach that engages all of the dimensions of the whole child.

DISCUSSION QUESTIONS

1. Compare the traditional understanding of curriculum with the "journey of life" perspective.
2. Discuss the benefits of a wellness approach to physical education.
3. What are some activities or ways of thinking that you can adopt in order to teach with a wellness approach?
4. What challenges might you face in beginning to use a wellness approach to physical education?

 Visit the web resource for ready-to-use activities that incorporate wellness principles and practices in the classroom, as well as suggestions for things teachers can do daily to plan and teach in a wellness-oriented way.

Voices From the Field

Mandy Krahn

Teacher (Grade 5), Coronation School, Edmonton Public School District, Alberta

I always try to integrate a variety of activities focused on holistic health and wellness throughout the day for my students. This approach helps maintain their interest; if they find any given activity not so enjoyable, they have others to look forward to. I also like to incorporate all of the dimensions of a child (spiritual, emotional, mental, and physical) and reinforce to the children that maintaining health involves more than physical activity—it requires balance among the dimensions. Here are some activities (Pura, 2002) I have done with students:

- *Listening to your breath.* This exercise helps students relax and focus their energy before a lesson. It is simple to perform: Breathe in for a count of four, hold for one second, release for four counts, hold for one second, and repeat.

- *Shaking it out.* Students shake each limb in turn, then finish by bending forward to shake out their shoulders while allowing the torso to relax and hang. Then they move in various ways (e.g., jumping jacks, shoulder rolls, arm circles) and finish by shaking out their shoulders and relaxing the torso again. Cue students to notice what their body feels like before, during, and after the actions.

- *Atmosphere walks.* Narrate the class through experiences with different kinds of atmospheres—for example, walking through a cornfield, pushing plants aside with every step; walking on the moon with its light gravity; walking through cotton candy, sticky taffy, or marshmallows; swimming through a clear lake while magically breathing underwater; and walking on fluffy clouds. This activity can act as a bit of a physical warm-up while helping students connect with their own bodies and control their movements.

- *Listening to the room.* This activity involves concentration in its simplest form. Ask students to lie on their backs with their eyes closed and listen to whatever sounds they can hear outside of the class. After acknowledging what they heard, they close their eyes again and focus on the inside of the classroom. Repeat again with a focus on what they can hear inside their own bodies.

One way to help students tap into all dimensions of the self is to lead them through guided visualizations. I do this in a variety of ways and integrate it with multiple subject areas. Essentially, I ask students to close their eyes and envision different scenarios connected to wellness. This vision in their mind's eye is then expressed artistically through drawing or through body movement, thus giving students a chance to incorporate their learning physically. This is a favourite approach because it can be applied not only in health and physical education but also in any subject area in order to help students feel a personal connection to their learning.

Following the artistic response to the guided visualization, students are instructed to articulate (in writing, orally, or in another creative technology-based medium) what they have expressed through their bodies or artistically on paper. By seeing them make connections in a variety of modalities, I can assess how well they understand the concepts of health and wellness.

CHAPTER 16

Education for Sustainability and Well-Being

Thomas Falkenberg ■
Michael Link ■ **Catherine Casey**

After studying this chapter, you will be able to

- explain how elements in a system can affect each other and how that dynamic can be illustrated through physical activities;

- describe how our well-being, particularly our physical well-being, depends on the well-being of the ecosystem;

- explain how the parts of our complex ecosystem depend on each other and how this interdependence affects our physical well-being;

- demonstrate appreciation of the complex dynamics between and within life systems and their relevance to human health and well-being; and

- explore and identify local plant and animal life within a larger living system as part of active living.

ustainability is concerned with creating and maintaining living conditions that allow current generations to satisfy their needs while maintaining the opportunity for future generations to do the same. This concern involves our relationship to the natural environment and our understanding of the complex systems in which we humans are embedded. Many of our unsustainable actions can be linked to an unappreciative relationship with the natural environment and a failure to understand how the things we do affect other life in the larger, complex system. Therefore, this chapter focuses on developing an appreciative relationship with the natural environment and on understanding the complexity of the systems of which we are part. It also presents physical activities that you can use to help students develop such appreciation and understanding, both in health and physical education and in regular classrooms.

> *Sustainability is concerned with creating and maintaining living conditions that allow current generations to satisfy their needs while maintaining the opportunity for future generations to do the same.*

Physical Well-Being in Complex Systems

Understanding ourselves as part of a larger, complex system helps us understand how to teach and learn from an interdisciplinary perspective. Of course, healthy, active living is a key concern for teachers of health and physical education. It is also relevant to teachers of other subject areas, because students should experience physically active engagement throughout the school day. Moreover, this engagement should be handled in such a way that it helps students experience, through physical activity, their interconnections with other parts of the complex system in which they live and gain insight into how their actions affect other parts of the system.

Let's take a moment to consider the effects of physical activity and physical well-being on various systems of which students are part—specifically, the socioeconomic, sociocultural, and socioecological systems:

Socioeconomic System

- Students who are active are more likely able to focus, concentrate, stay on task, and sleep than those who are not regularly physically active. These capabilities can lead to greater school success.
- Students who are more successful in school are more likely to get a well-paying job.
- Students who are physically active are more likely to be healthier and to require fewer services from the health care system.
- Requiring fewer services from the health care system saves money that can be used in other ways, including to provide better conditions in schools for students' physical activity and well-being.
- Not all physical activity experiences are equitable for students in terms of factors such as space, equipment, type of programming, access to community resources, and money allocated specifically to physical education. In fact, a school's socioeconomic situation can lead to its students lacking equitable opportunities for physical activity.

Sociocultural System

- From a biochemical perspective, even simple physical activity releases "happy" hormones into the brain, which have a positive effect on students' mood and outlook on life. Happier students, in turn, should positively affect social experiences in school, leading to a more positive school culture.
- Positive experiences with physical activity enculturates in students a deeper sense of the importance of staying physically active.

Socioecological System

- Being physically active in the outdoors provides students with opportunities to explore and better understand the natural environment.
- The ecological context of a school can affect the types of physical activities that are available and of interest to students. For instance, many inner-city schools have playgrounds made of asphalt, which may be generally less inviting of physical activity than are the fields of green grass available to students in many rural and suburban schools.

Appreciation for the Natural Environment

Outdoor physical activities can help students develop agility and endurance, social skills, and the ability to negotiate risks. Being physically active in the outdoors invites open-ended and spontaneous play, adventure, and exploration; along the way, it invites self-directed discovery and connection with the natural world while helping students develop their ability to cope with change and adversity. Linking outdoor physical activity to sustainability fosters respect for nature and provides students with opportunities to become more ecologically literate and engaged citizens with a stronger sense of place in the local landscape.

Linking outdoor physical activity to sustainability fosters respect for nature and provides students with opportunities to become more ecologically literate and engaged citizens with a stronger sense of place in the local landscape.

Students who live in urban settings stand to benefit the most from outdoor physical activity. It is more challenging for people living in cities to experience the connection between their actions and the consequences for living systems, and outdoor physical activity provides opportunities to develop values and perspectives informed by direct experience in the natural world.

Guide to Using Activities

This chapter's activities on the web resource offer an active and fun path to holistic learning for students exploring the concept of complex systems and their relationship with the natural environment. Guiding questions embedded within the activities assist the teacher in making these connections. For example, in the game Fill the Bucket, students line up and pass water by handfuls down the line from one bucket to another, racing against each other in teams. They realize quickly that their system is ineffective and inefficient, and as the teacher guides them through thinking about concepts like waste, limited resources, and cooperation, learning results that transcends the seemingly simple goal of filling their team's bucket faster than other teams fill theirs. Of course, because this is a *physical* activity, there are physical benefits, too! Students must focus on coordination and balance as they pass water, and they keep their heart rate up as they constantly change places in line.

We encourage you to use the provided activities in your classroom not only to provide fun physical activity but to help your students grasp important abstract concepts related to sustainability that are crucial for them to understand as global citizens. We also encourage you to seek out other activities that help students learn concepts associated with sustainability, such as *50 Games for Going Green* (Carol Scaini and Carolyn Evans, Human Kinetics, 2012).

Summary

As a school subject, physical education is usually not viewed as relating to issues of sustainability; instead, when people think of sustainability, they often think of subjects such as social studies and the natural sciences. However, a holistic approach to sustainable living suggests that we should understand it as linked to all aspects of our lives, including our physical activity in both natural and human-made settings. The activities provided on the web resource, together with the discussion questions at the end of the chapter, exemplify how physical engagement can help students develop their understanding of systems thinking and their appreciation of the natural environment. To fit with the overarching approach of this book, the activities are designed for use by general classroom teachers, who have the opportunity to pick up on students' reflections on the activities when they address issues of sustainability in other subject areas.

DISCUSSION QUESTIONS

1. What connections do you see between being physically active and being healthy (or ill)?

2. What connections do you see between a society in which people spend a lot of time outdoors and a society in which people are well?

3. How is a society affected if students in some schools have little opportunity to spend time outside or in a natural environment?

4. How does our well-being depend on the well-being of the ecosystem?

Visit the web resource for ready-to-use activities that help raise awareness of issues related to sustainability.

Voices From the Field

Gavin Winchar

Physical Education Teacher (Grades 3-6), O.V. Jewitt Community School, Winnipeg, Manitoba

I see outdoor education as enhancing both personal and social development while also helping participants forge a deeper relationship with nature. I view outdoor education as experiential learning in, for, and about the outdoors. I give students opportunities to participate in a variety of adventurous challenges and outdoor activities, such as hiking, climbing, canoeing, ropes courses, group games, scavenger hunts, archery, and rock climbing.

As much as possible, I try to make outdoor education fun and educational for all. I find it vitally important for students to experience joy in learning. We need to foster a curriculum of joy and excitement that has the potential to engage students in their lives and the lives of those around them. Developing a curriculum that is responsive to student interests fosters intrinsic motivation and stimulates the passion to learn. I try to provide lessons that engage students and make learning enjoyable. My ultimate goal is to see smiles on all students' faces while they are in my presence! Thus I continuously ask students to reflect on their enjoyment, and I adjust what we are doing in order to make them happy. For example, I figure out ways to teach students specific skills while also having fun by incorporating them into some form of game. If students are doing archery, for instance, we have a competition focused on hitting a balloon; similarly, if students are canoeing, we form a racetrack with a finish line. When students are excited and enjoy what they are doing, they become more motivated to continue their learning.

One strategy I use to foster learning in outdoor education involves listening to students' voices. Not often enough do we allow students to play an active part in their learning, and I find that the more I do so, the more success I have in meeting their needs. Specifically, I provide students with options, and they choose the activities in which they want to participate. This power to choose their own activities in outdoor education helps them remain enthusiastic about what they are doing and keeps participation levels high for a lot longer than when I determine what students will do.

The form of assessment I use to support student learning in outdoor education is a self-assessment rubric. A huge part of being a successful teacher involves being able to properly assess students. Is my assessment a proper measure of a student's ability? Should I use alternate methods of assessing students based on the diverse learners I find in my classroom? Numerous questions can be asked. Whatever the answers, we must ensure that our assessment and evaluation programs are best suited to measure the capabilities of our students so that students can obtain valuable information from assessment and work on the necessary areas to enable their success.

Assessment not only documents what students know and can do but also affects their learning and motivation. As teachers, we carry the primary responsibility for assessing and evaluating student achievement with the intent of supporting student learning. Accordingly, decisions regarding assessment and evaluation should focus on what is valuable—not simply what is measurable. I ask students to assess themselves, thus putting them in charge of their continuous and ongoing evaluation. Students provide themselves with a score that indicates how well they have met the assessment criteria on which we have agreed. The criteria often include how well they have participated, helped other students, demonstrated good sporting behaviour, come prepared for class, exhibited a positive attitude, and followed fair play guidelines.

CHAPTER 17

Curricular Integration

Carol Scaini ■ **Carolyn Evans**

LEARNING OUTCOMES

After studying this chapter, you will be able to

- explain the importance of incorporating movement activities through basic literacy and numeracy concepts and skills;

- describe how a learning environment that is engaging and fun helps students gain confidence;

- describe how working together to achieve a task through physical activity helps students build their social, emotional, mental, and physical skills; and

- implement fun physical activities that address basic literacy and numeracy concepts.

Research has consistently shown that students in integrated programs demonstrate academic performance equal to, or better than, students in discipline-based programs. In addition, students [in integrated programs] are more engaged in school, and less prone to attendance and behaviour problems.

Drake & Reid (2010, p. 1)

When we think back to our own experiences in the classroom and in physical education, most of us remember learning language and math skills at a desk and learning traditional sports in a gymnasium. In comparison, imagine the excitement on students' faces when they have the opportunity to learn math and language skills while being active! With that possibility in mind, this chapter breaks away from traditional learning and explores ways to incorporate a variety of engaging games and activities with a literacy and numeracy twist.

In a traditional class environment, students typically sit for long periods of time, listening and watching as the teacher provides information about a particular subject. Over the years, however, many theorists have posited that children do not all learn in the same way and therefore would benefit from multimodal learning experiences, including the auditory, visual, kinesthetic, and tactile modes. One such theorist is Howard Gardner, whose theory of multiple intelligences (MI) proposes that people learn and show their intelligences in different ways. Specifically, the theory describes eight intelligences: linguistic, musical, logical-mathematical, spatial, bodily-kinesthetic, interpersonal, intrapersonal, and naturalist (Gardner, 1983). By examining how you learn, you can begin to recognize the learning methods that are best for you. One simple way to analyze your own learning is to answer the following question: If you have just purchased a new item that needs to be put together, what do you do first? Do you (a) read the manual before you begin, (b) look at the pictures in the instructions, or (c) just open the box and begin putting the item together?

By examining how you learn, you can begin to recognize the learning methods that are best for you.

If we all have our own ways of learning and doing, then it is vital for us as teachers to open our minds and incorporate a variety of teaching and learning methods in our classrooms. In a way, this approach is more familiar than it may seem: "MI theory essentially encompasses what good teachers have always done in their teaching: reaching beyond the text and the blackboard to awaken students' minds" (Armstrong, 2000, p. 39).

In addition to the various ways in which students may learn, we must also consider the amount of time that students spend in their chairs during a school day. In a study conducted by Mullender-Wijnsma and colleagues (2016), "the findings suggest that physically active academic lessons should be part of the school curriculum because . . . [this approach] is an innovative and effective way for teachers to improve children's academic achievement. Physical activity should specifically be integrated into math and language lessons to optimally improve those important skills" (n.p.).

What Does It Mean to Integrate?

Faced with the multitude of provincial or territorial curriculum expectations, some educators find it easier to meet them by connecting one subject with another—for example, language and health—while others connect more than two subjects when doing so is possible and appropriate for student learning. The process of meaningfully connecting curricular expectations from different subject areas is referred to as *integration*, or *cross-curricular connection*. It involves "coordinating, blending, or fusing individual components into a functioning, unified, and harmonious whole" (Bradford and Schmidt, 2016). According to Alberta Education (2007), making cross-curricular connections offers the following benefits:

- *Promotes flexibility.* Teachers can plan for the development of primary skills and understandings that transcend individual strands and subjects.
- *Builds upon prior knowledge and experiences.* Integration makes learning more meaningful by helping students build on their diverse prior knowledge and experiences.
- *Unifies student learning.* Integration enables students to acquire a unified view of the curriculum to broaden the context of their learning beyond single subjects.
- *Supports how students think.* Integration matches how young students process information (e.g., children take in many things while processing and organizing them at one time).

Potential Benefits of Integration in Health and Physical Education

Physical education takes precedence during physical education periods—integration is a

"At their best, integrative activities highlight the . . . [distinctive] aspects of each subject and fuse them, so that they reveal relationships among subjects that would not have been understood had each subject been taught alone" (Bradford & Schmidt, 2016, n.p.).

bonus! In other words, we are not suggesting that you integrate in every lesson; rather, we encourage you to occasionally activate a piece of another curricular subject through physical activity. The goal is this: "At their best, integrative activities highlight the . . . [distinctive] aspects of each subject and fuse them, so that they reveal relationships among subjects that would not have been understood had each subject been taught alone" (Bradford & Schmidt, 2016, n.p.).

This kind of integration can help us meet a very real need. Many children in Canada today exhibit an inactive lifestyle and poor dietary habits; as a result, they face increased risk of developing health conditions. Much research acknowledges that a healthy, active lifestyle benefits an individual's overall health. For instance, the Heart and Stroke Foundation of Canada (n.d., n.p.) acknowledges that physical activity can

- dramatically lower your risk of heart disease and stroke;
- help prevent and control risk factors such as high blood pressure, high cholesterol, type 2 diabetes, osteoporosis, certain types of cancer, [and] obesity;
- reduce stress levels;
- increase energy;
- improve sleep; and
- improve digestion.

The World Health Organization (2017, n.p.) also states that "insufficient physical activity is one of the leading risk factors for death worldwide" and maintains that

regular and adequate levels of physical activity:
- improve muscular and cardiorespiratory fitness;
- improve bone and functional health;
- reduce the risk of hypertension, coronary heart disease, stroke, diabetes, various types of cancer (including breast cancer and colon cancer), and depression;
- reduce the risk of falls as well as hip or vertebral fractures; and
- are fundamental to energy balance and weight control.

Insufficient physical activity is one of the leading risk factors for global mortality and is on the rise in many countries, adding to the burden of NCDs [noncommunicable diseases] and affecting general health worldwide. People who are insufficiently active have a 20% to 30% increased risk of death compared to people who are sufficiently active.

In addition to the health benefits provided by physical activity, integration benefits the school by enabling classroom and physical education teachers to work together while maximizing their students' learning. Here are some additional benefits of integration:

- Provides an opportunity to expand your physical education programming.
- Supports schoolwide literacy and numeracy initiatives.
- Allows students to review and apply classroom learning in physical education settings.
- Provides learning experiences that are meaningful, enjoyable, and rewarding.
- Engages various learning styles.
- Enables learning to be transferred from one subject to another through movement.
- Increases students' enthusiasm and motivation for learning.
- Helps create a positive learning environment.

Integrating Academic Subjects Into Physical Activities

Integrating math and language skills into games and activities not only makes learning fun, but it is also easier than you think! Challenge yourself to approach each subject with an open mind regarding methods and applications. More specifically, consider introducing a task in the classroom using paper, resources, or manipulatives and then challenging students to incorporate that task into a simple game or activity. For example, in a math lesson focused on recognizing geometric shapes, you might divide the class into small groups and ask them to use their bodies to make various shapes. You might also provide a ball of yarn (or string) and ask students to work together to form the yarn into certain shapes.

Integrating math and language skills into games and activities not only makes learning fun, but it is also easier than you think!

When using this approach, keep in mind its complementary intent:

"Movement experiences are not meant to replace traditional methods [that] a classroom teacher uses to teach. Instead, they should be used in conjunction with these methods to enhance the learning experience. When children use their bodies as . . . learning tool[s], they will better understand a concept and retain the information longer. When academic learning experiences are combined with related physical activity, learning is more likely to occur."

Rink, Hall, & William (2010, p. 100)

For instance, if the class is studying the provinces of Canada, students might research the provinces and create a game or activity based on their learning. Here is an example adapted from the Western Newfoundland and Labrador School District (n.d.):

Tour du Canada

Equipment

Action cards (prior research about Canadian provinces and territories)

Setup

Ask students to stand at their desks (ensure that the area is safe and allows enough space to perform the movements); alternatively, ask students to stand with enough space around them in the gymnasium or another playing area.

How to Play

Lead students on an imaginary tour of Canada by inviting them to move as follows:

- March across the Confederation Bridge to Prince Edward Island.
- Surf in the Atlantic Ocean, off the coast of Nova Scotia.
- Climb up a Douglas fir, one of the tallest and longest-living trees in British Columbia.
- Jog or run (on a spot) like our Canadian hero, Terry Fox.
- Stomp grapes in Niagara, Ontario.
- In-line skate across the prairies in Manitoba.
- Ski downhill in Banff, Alberta.
- Climb Mount Robson, the highest peak in the Canadian Rockies.
- Crawl through the Okanagan Valley in British Columbia.
- Hit a home run for the Blue Jays in Toronto.
- Paddle the Mackenzie River in the Northwest Territories.
- Ice-skate on the Rideau Canal.
- Knee-slap and toe-tap with Bonhomme at the Quebec Winter Carnival.
- Cast a fishing line in Bonavista, Newfoundland.
- Cross-country ski through Manitoba.
- Kayak at the Bay of Fundy.
- Hike through Nunavut's Auyuittuq National Park.

Variation

Use the same concept for a different geographic or subject area.

Here is another example—a simple math activity in which students move around the classroom (or playing area) and solve problems with a classmate.

It can be implemented as a simple warm-up in the gymnasium or at the beginning of a math class.

Math Challenge

Equipment

- Uno cards (or standard numbered playing cards)

Setup

- Ask students to stand at their desks (ensure that the area is safe and allows enough space to perform the movements); alternatively, ask students to stand with enough space around them in the gymnasium or another playing area.

How to Play

- Provide each student with two cards.
- Ask students to walk around the classroom or playing area.
- Every time they meet a classmate, they are to add (or subtract or multiply) the numbers shown on their own cards, then exchange one card with the classmate.
- After the exchange, each partner once again moves around the playing area and finds another classmate to work with, and the activity continues in this manner.

Variation

- Change the mode of movement (e.g., jogging, skipping).
- Use the same concept for a different topic.

In summary, these two activities show how you can integrate physical activity into a core lesson plan simply by having students use a physical component to engage with information they have obtained through research or to warm up while reinforcing simple math skills.

Integrating Physical Activity Into Academic Subjects

This chapter focuses on more than just taking a physical break during the school day; it also provides a way to activate students as part of an academic lesson. Rather than forcing physical activity into every lesson, look for opportunities where it may logically fit. The benefits are worth the effort:

"Integrating physical activity into classroom learning provides another opportunity to infuse meaningful activity during the school day. Physical activity in the classroom helps activate the brain, improve on-task behavior during academic instruction time, and increase daily in-school physical activity levels among children. Classroom teachers have the potential to influence children's healthy behaviors

and lifetime choices by including bouts of physical activity . . . [in] the total learning experience, and in turn, maximize student learning during academic activities that are mostly sedentary."

National Association for Sport and Physical Education (n.d., n.p.)

You can start by adding movement to simple classroom lessons. For instance, you might ask students to count by twos while jumping or perform a certain number of jumping jacks to answer a math question (e.g., 4 + 5 = 9 jumping jacks). You might also teach students how to spell words by asking them to move to letters of the alphabet scattered around your classroom and perform a simple exercise while at each letter. Students could also identify movement words and then use them to create a simple dance routine.

Why not change up your physical education class to include basic literacy or numeracy skills? For example, ask students to participate in a relay to collect the pieces of an oversized puzzle and then work together to put it together. Or, bring math equations to the gymnasium, scatter some numbered beanbags on the floor, and ask your students to work in pairs to solve each equation and find the beanbag bearing the number that is the answer. Take a look at your current lessons and brainstorm ways to activate your students! The possibilities for incorporating physical activity into core subjects are endless.

We hope the activities presented in the web resource will help you develop active minds and active bodies! The games can be tweaked to suit a variety of ages, abilities, and skill levels; they can also be played in a variety of settings, and most require only minimal equipment. Some of the activities involve using numbers, equations, letters, or words, which can easily be created by you and your students or purchased from an educational products catalogue.

Have fun with these games and activities! Encourage your students to build on them, change them, and come up with their own ideas to connect physical activities to academic lessons.

Summary

This chapter helps you see that physical education provides many opportunities to strengthen learning skills and competencies in other subject areas. The games and activities presented here are familiar ones that have been modified to help teach a variety of literacy and numeracy skills in an enjoyable way. They offer starting points and allow for further variations and extensions in order to connect to other areas of interest. We encourage you to try them out and see how easy it is to teach various skills and concepts through physical activity. We also hope you take some time to consider how you can activate other curriculum areas to support learning and meet the needs of all students.

DISCUSSION QUESTIONS

1. Explain the importance of incorporating movement activities into academic lessons.

2. Describe how addressing literacy and numeracy skills in your physical education program can benefit students' learning.

3. Summarize the importance of collaboration and explain how it can enhance a physical education program.

 Visit the web resource for ready-to-use activities that integrate physical activity with academic learning.

Voices From the Field

Nicki Keenliside
Instructional Leader, Toronto District School Board, Ontario

Over my 20-plus years in education, I have taught grades 6 and 7 with core responsibilities including literacy, numeracy, history, and geography, as well as health and physical education for K-8. In my current position as instructional leader for the largest school board in Canada—with nearly 600 schools and approximately 232,000 students—the majority of my time is spent providing support for K-8 health and physical education (HPE) teachers responsible for delivering the Ontario HPE curriculum.

To make learning fun, you need to know your students' interests and concerns both inside and outside of school (e.g., hobbies, perceived strengths and weaknesses). This knowledge goes a long way in helping you support student engagement and participation. For example, if students are video game fans, you could include a reference to their favourite characters in the game instructions; for instance, Harry Potter fans might enjoy the use of "houses" rather than "teams."

Kids also tend to have more fun in class if they know what's expected of them and feel that they can be successful. Since success should not be a secret, you can use gymnasium walls to facilitate learning by posting learning goals and success criteria for elements such as active participation, fair participation, and movement skills.

It is also important to be honest with yourself and with your students. If you try a new game and it's a disaster, stop and debrief by posing the following questions: Is the game working? What can we do to make it better (e.g., make it fairer or more active)? You can also post a list of the class' favourite games and activities.

In addition, learning is not fun without a meaningful context, so it is good to share prerecorded content (e.g., dance videos, professional sport performances) to provoke students' thinking and aid their understanding of effective movement skills, strategies, and concepts.

Students also remember the fun they have had when given opportunities to share their learning in meaningful ways—for example, in Yoga Buddies, Sport Pals, and Technology Friends. In these programs, older students share their learning and work with younger students.

Learning is reinforced in an enjoyable way when students have a chance to display their work and see that their presence is felt. For instance, they can be given the opportunity to use their learning to create authentic messages with content that directly affects their peers (e.g., "Be cyber safe," "Make healthy eating choices"). These messages can be used in schoolwide campaigns featuring materials such as posters and daily announcements.

Students enjoy technology, so consider using it to engage students in learning. For instance, you can use video-recording apps or devices to allow students to see their own participation. This viewing enables them to self-assess their performances and provide feedback to classmates. You can also record debriefings conducted after activities in order to provoke meaningful discussions during the next class meeting. In addition, playing students' favourite music is fun and a great motivator.

One of my favourite activities has always been to provide students with an opportunity to create their own themed movement missions—lists of tasks to be completed by all members of a group at the same time. The mission is not a race; it focuses on having all group members complete all tasks to the best of their ability. Each task is active and includes a fitness skill or movement connected to the overall theme. For example, you might ask students to create a movement mission including 10 tasks related to the theme of the Olympics or of moving underwater. In the follow-up, students explain how each task connects to one of the components of fitness, or how the mission contributes to healthy, active living. Here are some student samples I have seen:

Winter Olympics

- *Ice hockey.* Run to all corners of the activity area, taking five imaginary slap shots in each corner.
- *Figure skating.* Use a skating motion to move to all corners of the activity area, performing 10 tuck jumps in each corner.

(continued)

(continued)

Underwater Mission

- *Crab walk.* Walk like a crab around the edge of a small activity area.
- *Scuba diver.* Jump up and then pretend to dive down by touching the ground with your hand; do this 15 times.

I like the mission activity because it allows students to make connections between HPE and their learning in other subjects. It also facilitates literacy development because it requires students to express each task in the mission in a clear procedural statement. If students are then asked to create task cards that include visuals and a textual description of how to complete the activity, then they are creating a text for the authentic audience of classmates, thus facilitating media literacy. Missions can also be used as warm-ups in future classes, thus reinforcing reading skills.

To use this activity on a regular basis, you might have Mission Mondays, wherein students introduce their missions to their classmates, thus developing their oral communication skills. Students could also create a class collection or book of missions and lead selected missions with classes of younger students at the school, thus developing leadership skills.

Here are a couple of suggestions for consideration when creating and assessing movement missions with students:

- Clearly state the learning goal and success criteria and post them in the learning space.
- Post all assessment rubrics clearly for students to see, including expectations for health and physical education and other areas (e.g., literacy).

As assessment of the learning extends to more than one subject area, ensure that students have the required knowledge. For example, do they know the features of a good media text? Can they identify the components of fitness? If you are assessing oral communication as students teach younger students, what do they need to know about speaking (e.g., using an audible voice, chunking the text)?

CHAPTER 18

Taking Physical Education Outside

Andrew Foran

After studying this chapter, you will be able to

- decide when to take a lesson outdoors (for more than the novelty factor),
- select a location for outdoor learning (by envisioning desired outcomes enacted),
- plan and prepare for the lesson (for due diligence),
- connect student understanding to learning outcomes (for high-quality learning),
- monitor outdoor learning (for safety in concert with learning), and
- implement tips for teaching outdoors (to ensure a high-quality experience).

To address the complexity of youth health, many educators are seeking alternative and innovative instructional approaches to engage youth, and it seems that the outdoors is becoming the go-to fix as teachers take students outside to get their "vitamin N." Therefore, I want to state upfront that going outside is not a simple remedy; nor is it a panacea for sedentary lifestyles, screen domination, and outcome-laden instruction. In short, the outdoors does not provide a dose of nature as a cure-all. Natural environments can, however, support quality learning, and this benefit can be obtained as an extension of an elementary school teacher's practice. Like adults, children and youth need the outdoors as part of their lives, and we can help make that happen by implementing quality outdoor practices—not as another quick prescription or recycled trend but as a meaningful approach to enriching the learning experience.

On the surface, it seems simple enough—go outside, let nature "take its course," learning occurs . . . and there's the plan! In reality, it is not simple; to the contrary, quality outdoor teaching takes careful planning, an eye for detail, and thoughtful consideration of the students you are leading. Sure, going outside to learn is a good thing. It allows for experiential possibilities that are hard to replicate indoors (Foran, 2005; 2008a, 2008b), thus sparking your creativity as a teacher, helping you relate effectively with students, and providing students with health gains (Foran, Stewart Stanec, & Mwebi, 2009; Foran & Smith, 2011a, 2011b; Foran, Redmond, & Loeffler, 2016). Your focus, however, must be on student learning (Redmond, Foran, & Dywer, 2010). Here are the key questions for elementary teachers: When should I take children outside for learning? Why should we go outdoors as part of the learning process? How should I lead students outdoors as part of their learning? With those questions in mind, this chapter provides you with a series of activities that establish a framework for taking learning beyond the walls of the classroom.

As teachers, our aim is to provide an outdoor learning experience that is well planned, properly resourced, and connected to our school curriculum. Teachers who are familiar with making indoor lesson plans can appreciate the fact that bringing children outdoors requires planning and preparation (P&P). This fundamental step ensures due diligence in offering a high-quality learning experience for our students. We need to do more than provide students with an excursion or diversion; we need to reach desired curricular outcomes. At the same time, we must avoid structuring outdoor learning so rigidly on the basis of indoor practices that we negate the outdoor experiential opportunities to explore, discover, wonder, and wander—a full sensory experience (Mannion & Lynch, 2016). Let us also be mindful of the fact that good things also happen inside and that some not-so-good things can happen outside and thus ruin the positive possibilities.

In a nutshell, the decision to teach outdoors should be based on the following perspective from L.B. Sharp: "That which ought and can best be taught inside the school rooms should there be taught, and that which can best be learned through experiences dealing directly with native materials and life situations outside the school should there be learned" (Carlson, 2008, p. 4). Without over simplifying Sharp's wisdom, I use this mantra: *If it's best taught indoors, then do it. If it's best learned outdoors, then take them.* Again, however, we should not expect to just take students outdoors, watch them learn and make numerous health gains, and let nature dissolve the pressures that confront all of us in modern living. In order to be safe and effective, outdoor education requires diligent planning and leadership on your part. The reward is that going outdoors opens learning up to many wonderful experiences.

If it's best taught indoors, then do it. If it's best learned outdoors, then take them.

Three Teachers in the Outdoors

When developing a lesson plan to achieve learning outcomes outdoors, start with the idea that a child's experience can be shaped by the following three teachers:

- *The curriculum.* Instruction is enriched when it is experienced in a natural environment through direct experience.
- *The environment.* Meaningful curricular outcomes can be achieved through concrete examples of key concepts in settings such as the schoolyard, a community park, and camps.
- *The people.* The teacher in charge must be prepared to lead instruction outdoors and guide children in making learning connections in teachable moments. And as we know in education, students can learn from one another; therefore, allow them to share

their discoveries and understanding of the outcome. This level of exchange between children is rich and meaningful, and when a lesson is well prepared for student discovery, this level of engagement is more than possible.

I use these three considerations to help me determine whether the outdoors can enhance what I am teaching indoors, introduce concepts concretely for young people to help solidify learning that will occur later indoors, and provide a means of active exploration that is appropriate for the purpose.

After the foundation is laid by addressing the three-teachers considerations, the next layer is built by asking the following question, which addresses what I refer to as the "seven rights": Am I in the right place, with the right group, at the right time, with the right equipment, using gear in the right way—and have I provided the right resources and supports, along with the right levels of instruction, to ensure high-quality learning? The takeaway here for elementary teachers is to *really* plan for an outdoor learning lesson.

We want our youth to be active, focused for maximum learning, and motivated to reach for lifelong health benefits. Going outdoors can help us achieve these goals with our students. The three teachers and the seven rights provide you with a starting point for planning outdoor lessons in order to avoid the common mistakes made by those who go out unprepared, unskilled, and unaware—and thus produce only hit-or-miss learning. Indeed, a poorly planned experience can ruin the allure of the outdoors for everyone, and, from an educational perspective, it dilutes the learning with sensory novelty (low-level learning); moreover, distracted teachers can miss learning opportunities and leave students open to unnecessary risk.

Scope and Benefits of Outdoor Education

Recently, there has been a surge, even a social movement, to reconnect people with the natural world. In response, teachers at all levels are making a concerted effort to engage students in meaningful outdoor experiences (Foran & Olson, 2012). Outdoor activity can help children unplug, connect to nature and their peers, and once again experience play as a means for learning. Many educators discuss outdoor education using the following terms: environmental education, outdoor pursuits (teaching skills), and outdoor programming that includes outdoor leadership and adventure education activities. Some teachers may view outdoor education as a one-time event (one-lesson or one-unit) or annual field trip. I prefer to approach outdoor learning not as a curricular add-on but as an ongoing educational experience throughout the school year.

The goal of outdoor education is to learn how to transform experience into knowledge and to use this knowledge for our individual and collective development—in short, to make meaning of direct experiences in nature. When students construct knowledge outdoors, both individually and communally with students, it tends to become more concrete if they are guided in reflecting on the experience. Our role as teachers is to help students connect to their understandings—that is, to make meaningful connections to the outcomes of experiential moments. These moments often mark high points in children's self-esteem due to the tangibility of what they accomplish in their hands-on learning. Thus outdoor experience for children produces more than textbook knowledge or something learned by hearing it or watching it on a screen. Instead, it comes from something they *did*, and they take ownership of their learning and find a place in the natural world around them. This kind of learning is grounded in an experience of mind and body with an emphasis on unifying the learning process individually and sometimes as a shared experience in a class community.

The activities included in the web resource for this chapter will help you consider the possibilities for teaching and learning outdoors. By exploring a larger concept of outside learning, and developing a framework that is applicable to school groups in schoolyard settings and local park environments, you position yourself to begin grasping the multiple subjects that students can connect with outdoors, including math, science, language arts, social studies, and health and physical education (HPE). Thus outdoor education can serve as a hub from which children can actively achieve many desirable outcomes. Leading children outdoors as part of an instructional day allows them to appreciate the beauty of their surroundings,

Leading children outdoors as part of an instructional day allows them to appreciate the beauty of their surroundings, see and touch a bit of nature, and attain better physical and mental health.

see and touch a bit of nature, and attain better physical and mental health. My effort here is to share ideas so that you can learn to engage with your teaching environments and see subject possibilities in schoolyards, back fields, urban parks, community trails, and parkland. Each area offers numerous possibilities to explore and play—as long as we get outside!

To illustrate just a few of the possibilities, here is a brief list of cross-curricular activities and the subjects they engage:

- Hiking and sketching (HPE and art)
- Geocaching and an adventure race (HPE and geography)
- Educaching in the community (HPE and social studies)
- Eco-art (math and art)
- Tree (or leaf) identification (science [environmental issues and sustainability] and social studies [forestry, land use, historical settlement])
- Snowshoeing (HPE and social studies [Indigenous history, exploration])
- Cross-country skiing (HPE and science)
- Backpacking (HPE, nutrition and geography)
- Orienteering (math, social studies, and PE)

Though not exhaustive, this list serves as a friendly reminder of the possibilities for having fun while learning in the outdoors. However, on a pragmatic note, I have worked with many teachers who have asked, "How can I lead students *out there* in a way that is comfortable, safe, and beneficial?" Some teachers feel overwhelmed by the amount of planning and preparation involved in simply going for a jaunt when the environment dictates all. Take heart! This type of teaching gets easier with practice. My intention here is to show you how outside teaching, specifically as an active learning experience, is possible in an elementary setting. You and your students can be active, gain confidence in executing skills, have fun, and connect with the natural world.

Any outdoor learning activity for primary level through grade 8 should include a play-based approach that allows students to indulge their natural curiosity in exploring the world. It should also include variety: higher-tempo games for increased activity as well as lower-key activities for students who are more interested in a calm nature experience. In order to be effective, instruc-

tion must keep elementary students interested and engaged, which requires lessons that direct hands-on exploration geared toward the desired outcome in the natural world. Thus there is a synergy of outcome, environment, and action:

- Cross-curricular possibilities—rich learning in multiple ways, allowing for many avenues of representing student learning
- Direct experience in the environment through messy hands-on activities that allow students to be in contact with the world as they connect to the outcome
- Movement not as an add-on but as part of the learning, thus keeping students kinesthetically engaged

Try to keep these three elements central to the outdoor focus of your lesson plan.

Planning and Preparation

Achieving quality instruction outdoors requires more than half measures—just going outside is not good enough to enable learning. Instead, we need to plan to go outside and be prepared to teach outside; that is, we need to engage in P&P. Going outside as part of the school experience can be exciting for students, but we must provide them with more than novelty. We must ensure that the learning benefits are not left to chance. Therefore, we must ask the following question: Will real learning occur when we venture "beyond the walls"? There is a lot to balance between managing students, resources, time, and the environment. If left to chance, the outdoor experience could even be a colossal waste of instructional time. Remember, outdoor education should infuse and complement whatever is being taught indoors! Our children are counting on us to be teachers—not nature guides, camp counselors, or overextended adults trying to pull something together based on a whim. That is inferior teaching.

Fortunately, by creating a planning framework that balances outcomes with fun, skills, conceptual enrichment, and safety, we can prepare students to go outdoors for learning after consistent practice of an established procedure. P&P is about building an outdoor foundation consisting of concrete steps to ensure an experience that is fun, comfortable, and challenging for your students, whether in the schoolyard or at a local park. The key is to maintain consistent, solid practice in P&P. Of course, poor planning is also a problem for an indoor lesson, but there is very little room for half measures when leading young people outdoors. However, if the little things are in place, then you can focus on high-quality learning and on the children.

The stakes are magnified when you consider the potential for environmental challenges, such as winter weather, wind, rain, and heat. The potential for fun remains, but you need to be a bit more on your game by knowing your group, focusing on the desired lesson outcomes, remaining aware of the terrain, and respecting the weather. To teach outside, you are expected to build on your own classroom routines and expectations and extend your classroom practice beyond the walls. Keep in mind that the planning detail required when on-site will not be as extensive if you plan to take the class to off-site locations. The further you are away from typical school supports, the more your plan will need to take into account contingencies.

Planning Phase

The first step is to establish the purpose of the outdoor lesson. Ask such questions as the following:

- Who is in my class, and what are their fitness levels and past learning experiences?

- What types of activities do I want to facilitate? Are there any special interests for the lesson? Do I want a hands-on or student-centred approach rather than just an outdoor lecture?

- How much time do I have with students outdoors (e.g., half hour, whole hour, full morning, whole day)?

- How will I measure student learning? (The activities need to be central to reaching established curricular outcomes, and you need to be clear that a natural setting can help support this learning best. If the answer is yes, begin considering additional learning supports required by your students.)

- Do any special considerations need to be taken into account in order to maintain an inclusive learning environment? (Examples include additional adult supervision [chaperones], parent helpers, and teaching assistants to facilitate activities and meet required school adult-student ratios. I recommend holding a pre-outing meeting with chaperones to define roles and responsibilities and inform them of the lesson's purpose. This meeting allows members of the leadership group to be on the same instructional page once you leave the classroom.)

The next step is to consider setting up activity stations and key transitions to prevent downtime and standing around. To make the stations and activities flow, consider what instructional materials students will need. Be thorough; it is not always possible to run in to the school and grab a needed resource from the shelf.

You also need to begin considering a plan B—important for any indoor lesson plan and mandatory outdoors, especially if you are going off-site. You just never know why or when a different activity will be needed!

Thinking about an activity means thinking about the teaching resources and gear you will need in order to support the activity. What type of gear, equipment, and resources can you provide for each participant? Can you modify equipment to meet the needs of all students? In addition to taking stock of the equipment, take stock of the group's ability to use the equipment. You may need to build in time to familiarize students with the equipment that will be used.

Thinking about an activity means thinking about the teaching resources and gear you will need in order to support the activity.

Site Assessment

As you establish a lesson plan, begin considering the match between activity and location. There are many important issues to consider.

- In deciding whether to stay on school grounds or go off-site, consider whether the location enables students to move toward achieving desired learning outcomes.

- Evaluate the location for potential hazards, such as the following:
  - Trail conditions and technical difficulty (if hiking)
  - Poison ivy or giant hogweed (if allowing for exploration within a designated area)
  - Potential urban park hazards (e.g., glass, garbage, syringes)
  - Wildlife reports (a seasonal concern in some districts)
  - Terrain that is difficult to navigate for young students and those with mobility challenges

- Sun exposure or wind chill (if there is little or no tree coverage)
- Water hazards (e.g., rivers, streams, lake edges)

  ▪ Going off-site, even to a local park, may require gaining permission, both as a courtesy and to determine whether the park is active in other ways that could interfere with the lesson plan.

  ▪ Of course, going off-site also requires a transportation plan.

When all of these points have been addressed, consult with your administration (even if staying on-site). Specifically, share your lesson plan in the form of a trip itinerary (see the at-a-glance checklist provided later in this chapter) and explain your outdoor instructional plans and, if applicable, your travel plans.

When considering location, inventory the natural features and infrastructure of the potential teaching area. Here are some specific factors to consider when selecting outdoor locations, whether on-site or away from school grounds:

▪ Terrain conducive to student performance of the learning activity

▪ Few if any obstacles

▪ Varying types of terrain to allow for a range of activities

▪ Wooded and open grassy areas that will support groups engaged in active learning

▪ Easy access to streams and ponds (in parkland)

▪ Marked trails (in a park)

▪ On-site warming shelter

▪ Access to drinking water within the boundary

You will need to be able to flex with seasonal realities. If some desired conditions do not exist in your area, that does not mean you must abandon the idea of heading outdoors to learn. It just means that you need to adjust your plan to draw on the available features for optimum learning. You can still get outside but may need to change your planned activities in order to enable desired outcomes.

In addition, be aware that even the school site requires risk assessment. For example, will you have mobile access to 911, and what will the response time be? Do you have basic first aid training (emergency first aid, standard first aid) to support students' health? Such training is strongly recommended, especially if you are going off-site to a local green space. Has the first aid kit been checked, stocked, and made field ready (for on-site or off-site use)? Do you know the medical conditions of your students and of any adult chaperones? Health should not be taken for granted when being active outdoors.

Whether staying on-site or heading off-site, I also examine the location ahead of time to clean up any distractions (e.g., dog waste in grassy areas) and look for potential hazards. Take care to note areas that could lead to injuries (e.g., holes in the ground in activity areas, wasp nests in break areas). During the examination, I try to rule out or assess potential risks noted during my planning.

Preparing Students

After reviewing the curricular outcomes I am trying to reach with students, I begin gathering the resources, extra supplies, and gear that will be needed to ensure a positive and comfortable outdoor learning experience. For some lessons, especially if going off-site, I issue a student preparation list that goes home to parents and guardians specifying needed clothing, footwear, hydration, food, and any special considerations to match the environment and season. I also send a permission slip if required for an off-site excursion. Even if I am on-site, I may send a note home to explain the outdoor lesson, which both reminds parents and caregivers to help prepare their child and helps establish strong home–school relations.

Along the way, I challenge the outdoor lesson plan by asking whether I have provided enough indoor instruction to support the outdoor plan. In addition, have I reviewed expected behaviours with my class? Have I identified what I can do during regular class instruction to enhance what is being taught or about to be taught? Have I clearly shared the purpose for going outside to learn with my students as we work together to prepare?

It is particularly important to prepare for the effect of outdoor conditions on students' comfort and learning. Though I cannot control the weather, I want to know what is coming my way; therefore, I check days before and on the day of the outing for alerts and warnings regarding rain, snow, heat, and sun intensity (i.e., UV index). Regardless of such pre-

It is particularly important to prepare for the effect of outdoor conditions on students' comfort and learning.

dictions, I always consider bringing a shelter to support the lesson—specifically, a tarp to provide shelter from rain or a break from sun or wind. If going off-site, I also determine whether the site has an outbuilding that we can access (with any needed permissions) and a washroom. In addition, in case things become unworkable outdoors, I am always aware of how close we are to the school.

If going off-site, I like to have a park or trail map. If walking is required, I discuss the planned route with chaperones and determine an evacuation route at the location for use in case of emergency. Once we reach the site, I review a few key etiquette practices that teach respect for the environment (a "leave no trace" approach). Then I make a final check to ensure that all learning resources are ready. Whether going outside on-site or off-site, the last thing I want is to realize that I left something behind! When we stay on school grounds, I often use a wagon to help me cart the resources and supplies. When off-site, I still use a wagon if possible; if not, I share supplies with students and chaperones (more on this a bit later).

I realize that many teachers may want to just get outside. However, if the outing is away from school grounds, then the logistics automatically become more complex. In any case, the P&P process by no means replaces your school district's planning policies for school outings. Make sure to complete any paperwork required by your school administration.

Beyond supplies and logistics, I identify individuals who may need additional support outdoors and share this information with any teaching assistants, parent helpers, and chaperones. I also isolate expected student behaviours and note the group dynamics of the class. In addition, I spend time developing class cohesiveness by inviting students to participate in team-building activities, which help them come to know one another on respectful terms and give me insight into their behaviour (I also share this information with teaching assistants and chaperones). I even group students by colour designation for group work in the field and for easy in-field organization. I will then assign an adult supervisor to monitor students within their colour grouping.

At-a-Glance Checklist

Teaching a lesson in the schoolyard does not require the same level of P&P as an off-site excursion, but many of the discussion points just addressed are still relevant in the development of the lesson plan. Still, in most instances, an off-site excursion requires more detailed planning and preparation, beginning with paperwork required by the school district. There is really no standard "at minimum" level of P&P, and the at-a-glance checklist presented in table 18.1 can be modified to meet your teaching needs and school requirements. Making a plan on paper is very different from implementing the plan in the field, and a solid P&P procedure can make the difference in whether the experience enables high-quality learning.

The at-a-glance form gives you a quick overview of your planning and preparation, and each chaperone should receive a copy in case there is a need to split the class into groups for different activities. As the form indicates, each student team is assigned a colour, which allows for quick monitoring through group check-ins by the assigned chaperone, whether on school grounds or at a local park. You can easily adapt the at-a-glance form to accommodate any other information required by the school administration. You can also leave a copy of the completed form with the administration team so they know where to look for you if for any reason you are overdue for return or if a parent comes looking for a child. The form also helps you organize the other key pieces discussed next; it should never stand alone as the only completed paperwork supporting the lesson plan.

Student Medical Form

Your school district likely has a standard student medical form, which provides a starting point for discussions with chaperones, parents and caregivers, and students about any important health issues that need to be considered when going outdoors. As part of standard practice, I check and, if necessary, update these forms at least every three months. Why? Our health changes over time, and having accurate snapshots of my students' health helps me plan activities that are respectful of their capabilities. In addition, a dated form is no good if a student health concern arises in the field. Moreover, up-to-date forms alert me to any pressing medical conditions that require vigilance, such as asthma and severe allergies. This is important, especially if a child needs an accessible rescue inhaler or epinephrine autoinjector (e.g., EpiPen); running back to the school for such an item is not an option if a student is experiencing an anaphylactic reaction.

■ TABLE 18.1

At-a-Glance Checklist

Lesson topic	Chaperones 1. 2. Pre-outing meeting dates 1. 2.	First aid kit checked Date: Carrier: Med forms checked Date: First-aiders:
Outcomes 1. 2. 3.	Students Red group 1. 2. 3.	Park maps: Travel arrangements and permits Date:
Outing information sent home Date: Departure information Date: Time: Arrival information Date: Time: Signed permission forms Off-site: Date:	Green group 4. 5. 6. Blue group 7. 8. 9. Purple group 10. 11. 12.	Student daypack checked Date: Teacher leader pack checked Date: Instructional resources checked Date: Specialized equipment checked Date: Site check Date: Comments:
Safety plan updated Date: Designated emergency contact: Phone number:	General student comments for chaperones:	Weather report checked Morning: Afternoon:
Activity list 1. Name, description, setup, considerations, resources, boundaries 2. Name, description, setup, considerations, resources, boundaries 3. Name, description, setup, considerations, resources, boundaries		

Assessing and Managing Risk

Teaching in the outdoors presents physical and emotional risks to students. Although no risk factor is completely avoidable, solid preparation helps you lead effectively. Thus your risk management plan must outline ways to recognize and reduce both physical and emotional risks. Before carrying out the lesson, visit the site (with chaperones, if possible) to do a risk assessment. Walk around, look for problems, and go through your plans and activities step by step.

Your risk management plan must outline ways to recognize and reduce both physical and emotional risks.

- Visualize each step in the lesson, including transitions from activity to activity.
- Identify potential hazards that need to be reported to chaperones and students.
- Assess the age-appropriateness of the activities, the environment and terrain, and the people participating. Then ask, "What could happen?"
- Determine how you will explain to students what to do if something does happen. Will you give an emergency signal? Establish an

emergency gathering point? What constitutes a minor concern, and what is considered a major concern? How should incidents be reported? In order to understand what to do, children need examples.

- Begin preparing a written plan outlining response actions for participants to take if something happens—for example, if thunder is heard when they are in an open space.

- Evaluate and reassess the safety plan and review it with students and chaperones, both before and during the lesson.

Unique considerations will arise with every location, lesson, class, and activity. And again, any outdoor activity entails some risk, whether the cause is weather, participants' abilities, equipment failure, or simply students' limited ability to focus. Anticipate all potential risks you can think of and form a good plan for dealing with them. In handling an incident of any size, you and your chaperones must know how to respond according to the safety plan. You are responsible for ensuring that your students have a safe and positive learning experience.

Be sure to review travel and play guidelines with students and reinforce expectations of community standards for outdoor lessons. Positive group dynamics are foundational to leading outdoor learning experiences that are positive, cooperative, and safe. Try to keep the guidelines simple by using statements such as the following: Avoid negative comments or name-calling; lend a hand if someone needs a boost; stick to the boundaries established by the teacher; if you're not sure about something, ask; and practice fair play. The goal is to build a safe learning community for all students. Keeping communication respectful and open is just one of the trust dynamics needed for outdoor lessons. If a group is functioning well, then more possibilities open up: activity choice, type and duration of excursion, and personal growth for all participants.

The general aspects of managing risk are the environment, the people involved, students' skill levels, your leadership ability, the equipment used (and how it is used), and the class' ability to stay within set parameters. To maintain focus outdoors, I recommend conducting an ongoing review of the seven "rights" discussed earlier. Remember, the goal is for you to be familiar with the expectations for the outing—the purpose, learning outcomes, and boundaries. This preparation should be reviewed before heading out,

along with safety expectations (which must also be communicated with administrators, parents, and caregivers).

Equipment and Instructional Resource Checks

No outdoor lesson, whether on school grounds or off-site, should proceed without a few equipment checks:

- *First aid kit.* Check contents, restock as necessary, and seal with a zip tie so that you know it has not been used (particularly crucial when sharing a kit with others at school). Also bring current student medical forms.

- *Group gear and learning resources.* This gear should include assorted sizes to fit the age group and be clean and in good repair (i.e., field ready). Bring ample instructional supplies.

- *Leader gear.* As needed, bring a portable shelter, GPS device, means of water purification, extra clothes (according to season) big enough to fit the largest person in the class, and resources and class supplies required for the intended activities.

- *Student gear.* Check for all items required by each person participating (a list was most likely sent home in advance, along with the parent and caregiver permission form). Some common pieces of gear should accompany any type of outdoor lesson, and any specialized pieces should be included as needed for students to participate fully and safely in the planned activities.

Leader Pack

One nonnegotiable practice for an outdoor educator is that of maintaining a "leader pack" for both on-site and off-site outings. This pack includes an assortment of items that you consider essential for leading groups in the field. One thing to consider here is transferability from one activity to another. For instance, what I carry for a hiking and geocaching event can be adjusted and broken down to support a "ditch kit"—the essentials appropriate for snowshoeing, half-day canoeing, or full-day environmental activities in the local park. The pack can also be adapted for seasonal realities depending on the type of activity I am leading with my students. In short, the leader pack needs to be flexible to fit the activity, group, location, and season.

My leader pack contains a personal collection of gear that I trust and have used consistently. Over the years, I have also made various changes and upgrades based on field experience. I take this pack with me no matter where I am going outside, on my own or with students, including outings on school grounds; again, the pack can be modified to fit the location, as well as the purpose and season. In short, the leader pack should contain what you need in order to support the group in doing the planned activity in the selected environment. The list below has as an asterisk by items that are essentials, no matter where I am teaching outside. The other items are selected based on the extent of my outing with students, the season, and the activity.

- Daypack with 30- to 50-litre capacity and water resistance or a pack rain cover (Remember, this is not just for you! You will need to carry backup gear to take care of students, supplies needed for teaching in the field, and the essentials included in this list.)*
- First aid kit appropriate for the size of group you are leading (Basic kit contents will need to be supplemented with various items to meet your needs, such as moleskin if hiking and hot packs for cold hands if snowshoeing.)*
- Map case or waterproof bag large enough for the needed maps and paperwork*
- Compass and GPS device
- Emergency signaling system (e.g., SPOT, InReach) if going to an area with spotty cell service (Tracking features also allow administrators and parents to follow the outing's progress.)
- Foam pad for sitting (or resting a tired student)*
- Plastic or nylon tarp measuring 3 meters by 3.5 meters for shelter (For extended programs in the field, I use a nylon tarp measuring 5 meters square, which gives students a place to do assigned fieldwork.)*
- Bag of rope (assorted lengths) to rig the tarp*
- Bothy shelter (instant shelter made of nylon for use in emergency)*
- Head lamp
- Repair kit (extra batteries, tools, parts to fix gear)

- Pot, stove, fuel, and food (e.g., dehydrated soup for a hot, healthy drink in the field)
- Waterproof matches or fire-starters
- Water filtration system and a backup, or water purification tablets
- Change of clothes (large enough to fit the largest person) in a waterproof sack*
- Rain gear*
- Water bottle and snacks*
- Seasonal hat, sunscreen, lip balm, and sunglasses*
- Folding saw
- Knife
- Resources and supplies to teach the lesson*

Student Equipment

A key outcome for outdoor education is student independence. I require all my students to begin developing self-resiliency by taking responsibility for their daypack. I expect, and hope, parents and caregivers will be involved in helping them prepare. The list below is a general guide to help students prepare:

- Daypack with 15- to 20-litre capacity (e.g., book bag type of pack)
- Personal first aid kit—"ouch pouch" with any required medications
- Foam pad big enough to sit on (I sign out "bum spots" for my class made from a full-length pad cut into squares large enough to sit on.)
- Change of clothes (to meet seasonal requirements) in a waterproof sack
- Rain gear
- Water bottle and snacks
- Seasonal hat, sunscreen, lip balm, and sunglasses
- Waterproof envelope to carry field journal or activity sheets
- Portion of shared supplies and resources needed to teach the lesson (if appropriate)

Managing Groups Outside

During your time outside with your students, it is your responsibility to monitor their health, energy levels, lesson focus, and temperature—in short, their comfort and learning. Do an on-site

During your time outside with your students, it is your responsibility to monitor their health, energy levels, lesson focus, and temperature—in short, their comfort and learning.

final check to ensure that students have their daypacks for the field lesson, including all the needed items such as hat, water bottle, sunscreen, lip balm, sunglasses, and so on. The following list of considerations can help you maximize positive energy for your class. Cold and wet, or thirsty and hot, can be a lethal mix!

- A cold person requires more motivation to participate, stay moving, stay warm, and make sure the outing is fun. More generally, if people are standing around too long in any season, their focus fades, gear-fitting issues emerge, and instructions fail to sink in—any of which delays active involvement.

- The same is true for heat. When students get too hot, sweaty, or thirsty, they have a hard time focusing, and their learning potential plummets. Build in hydration breaks and stop for rest periods in the shade (don't forget your tarp!).

- If possible, all gear checks and fittings should be done where it is warm and dry. This way, participants can comfortably practice putting on gear, make needed adjustments, and determine what needs to be done in order to be field ready! You will still have to make adjustments outdoors. Smile, make a joke, and lend a helping hand. Making adjustments for two students is not an issue, but making adjustments for 28 means downtime and boredom! Remember, students are learning how to use the resources provided, sometimes for the first time.

- Use meaningful activities that are fun and serve an educational purpose. I plan for a number of possible activities that are quick and field friendly and get students moving. Consider a range of possibilities, from low- or no-prop games that are fun and energetic to more complex team-building games that nurture community. Include these activities as part of your lesson plan (and your plan B). The point is to plan for your students to be moving, not standing.

- Outdoor teachers know that "making the plan" means "working the plan" because the outdoors has its own agenda. Again, know

the flow—activity, transition, activity—and be clear about learning station setup and the time required to get students started. Whether at the school or on the trail, be prepared to adjust as needed. Consider transitions from activity station to station to prevent the dreaded downtime from disrupting the flow of learning.

Teaching outside involves more than just covering a given subject outdoors. Outdoor educators need to develop situational awareness and be alert to the potential of outside learning experiences. This attunement is based on your ability to stay connected to the four areas listed in the matrix shown in figure 18.1: group mood, environment, people, and activity.

Group mood	Environment
general feel	temperature
the atmosphere	the weather
attitude	terrain
People	**Activity**
energy levels	skills and abilities
engagement	participation
attitudes	challenge
goals	fun

Figure 18.1 Situational awareness matrix.

I use these quadrants as the basis for in-field assessment (scoring 1 for poor, 2 for below average, 3 for average, and 4 for exceptional) to evaluate how well the plan is working. To help generate these scores, I ask questions associated with the four areas of attunement: Is the class interested? Are students focused? Do students seem bored? Is it too hot? Is the task too difficult to complete in the field? Are students enjoying the outdoor setting? Are they functioning well in small groups, or in large-group activities? Do I need to shift to plan B? In most cases, I can step in and help move things along as needed to motivate or refocus students, but if scores are low across the board (1s and 2s), then plan B may very well be the logical step.

Locations

Well, after all of the P&P, you've arrived at the site—now what?! Let's explore some examples that include both schoolyard learning (Broda, 2007) and community-based lessons in a local park or camp setting. When we open our teaching practices to the outdoors, we are afforded many more cross-curricular opportunities for activities, games, initiatives, and explorations. In setting up these experiences, we can use instructional methodologies such as free play, guided instruction, learning stations, and learning through games.

I have found it quite easy to lead a number of activities in both urban and rural schools. Not all locations provide for everything, but many of our schoolyards and local parks offer more than we think. When assessing a location's usability, make a point to be creative, flexible, and willing to modify or adapt an activity. Of course, each activity must be both age appropriate and developmentally appropriate, but it does not take much to shift an activity to fit what the schoolyard or green space enables.

Not all locations provide for everything, but many of our schoolyards and local parks offer more than we think. When assessing a location's usability, make a point to be creative, flexible, and willing to modify or adapt an activity.

Whether on-site or off-site, your planning helps frame how to select a location and what activities can be implemented there. You cannot force a program. The location can give you only what is there—if you need trees, you can't just imagine a forest and think that the activity will work. The location is what it is. Planning activities also requires you to know your group, how it will function in a particular location, and how to modify an activity to meet the group's unique needs in a given location.

I have learned that activities can be adapted to address certain learning goals, and careful modifications make it possible to enjoy positive group experiences even if a location is somewhat lacking. Ingenuity can compensate! However, if your natural wooded area does not boast a lake and you were really hoping to build an end-of-school unit based on canoeing, then you may need to think about alternatives. Not all schools are located within walking distance of a pond or lake—it is that simple. The alternative is to transport students to a facility that offers access to water and canoes, which typically means an established camp. This type of trip requires more detailed planning, especially if it involves an overnight stay; for instance, you will need to secure canoeing instructors (unless you are certified as such) and

plan for other activities. No matter where you are teaching outdoors—the schoolyard, a local park, or a camp—each location has its advantages and limits.

School Sites

The biggest benefit of conducting your lesson right outside your school's front door is the ability to return immediately. When introducing a variety of outdoor activities to a class, it is advantageous to have a structured support base nearby. In the event that someone gets cold or wet, needs a washroom break, or forgets an item, it is relatively simple to go back inside the school building. Another advantage is the ability to draw on stored props and materials for lessons—you don't have to haul it all with you! In addition, the school building allows you and the group to get set up in a controlled environment before venturing outside. In contrast, it is unlikely that a park or other green space will be located within a "stone's throw" of school, especially for schools in urban areas. Sure, some schools have the best of both worlds, but when your location lacks natural features, it is nearly impossible to replicate them. Granted, there are always things that can be done outdoors, but having a wooded trail or other terrain to explore at school allows for a relatively convenient outdoor learning experience.

Parks and Natural Settings

When you select a natural location to host an outdoor lesson, it is of course desirable that it provide ease of access. Little pockets of trees, scrub bush, or high grasses allow the magic of nature to be enjoyed with minimal effort, and that micro-wilderness feel is available in many community parks and school boundary areas. Convenient access helps keep our focus where we want it to be—on the group, not on logistics. Being immersed in nature often brings the experience to a different level. Exploring a wooded patch, even if it is only as remote as an urban or municipal park, can give us that deeper appreciation for outdoor explorations. For instance, being among the trees can provide opportunities to track wildlife, experience natural diversity, and identify types of trees. Natural settings also provide students with a solitude that is hard to find in a city core.

The ideal park location is a local one with an available shelter, gazebos, or roofed picnic areas that can be used as a base camp. These little buildings can make all the difference in the world. They allow for the possibility to store supplies for different activities; provide a retreat from cold, rain, wind, or sun; and serve as a designated space for taking care of individual needs such as changing wet clothing or having a snack. More often than not, such settings do not offer much open space for games and activities, as would be found in a schoolyard setting. Therefore, you must select games that can work with the given terrain, and you may want to bring a wagon for hauling supplies. If the setting does not have a shelter to use as a base, you can set one up in the form of a tarp or bothy.

Camps

Going to an established camp for most schools will most likely offer an extensive range of possible outdoor pursuits and nature-based activities. Many camps offer buildings: a cookhouse, sleeping quarters, and activity rooms for programming, all surrounded by a natural setting. The drawback will be the travel and scheduling logistics, along with funding required to bring a class to these established outdoor centers.

Activities

The web resource includes many activities for different settings. Here is a brief overview.

Schoolyard Ideas

I like schoolyard lessons because they allow me to use various activities with minimal logistics. Of course, I still have my leader pack, notify my administration that I will be outside, and check with other teachers to see if other classes will be outside. In short, with a bit of planning, I can implement a quick outing for outdoor learning to help make a concept concrete for students or set up a new concept. It is rare, however, for a school setting to provide everything that you are looking for. Therefore, you will sometimes have to be innovative and creative in order to enable desired outcomes. The web resource offers a couple of examples of activities for the school setting.

Community Setting: Geocaching or Educaching

The geocaching activities included in the web resource follow a progression that allows for schoolyard learning to expand into the community with a number of lesson configurations. As a reminder, when you feel that the class is ready for off-site outdoor experiences, logistics grow

more complex and planning and preparation come more into play. Geocaching is a wonderful way to activate children's learning through screen technology, and handheld GPS devices are now accessible at many schools. This type of activity is ripe for cross-curricular learning that can take you to rich environments in your school community.

Park Setting or School Site: Snowshoeing

Sometimes a trip away from school serves as a mini-adventure. Snowshoeing, for instance, gives you a way to build seasonal learning into your school program; examples are included in the web resource. Winter should not be a reason for people to retreat and disconnect from the world! For a full physical education program, connecting to nature should occur all year long, in all weather. Students enjoy snowshoeing because it is simple yet requires a little skill and allows for play and exploration.

For a full physical education program, connecting to nature should occur all year long, in all weather.

Camp Setting

For most schools, going to an established camp greatly opens up the range of possible outdoor experiences. Not many schools have their own canoes or kayaks! When camps are built into a school's outdoor education program, canoes are the most accessible option since many established camps have their own fleet of canoes for water-based programing. The canoeing activity included in the web resource demonstrates that canoeing for children is not about learning the J-stroke—that will come in time—but about learning how the boat responds and how their bodies can move to become part of the boat. I have found that after teaching just the basics, canoe games allow students to understand paddle awareness in an experiential way. When building the plan to provide a camp experience, consult with the camp leadership team to make sure that they value play over skill instruction for children.

Summary

Meaningful education is not something that can be easily packaged. Teachers that are capable of leading and allowing students to engage in outdoor learning will, hopefully, allow students to grow and connect not only to themselves and one another, but also to the natural world. A positive experience plants the seeds for more activity and outside adventure. Outdoor education promotes concrete, practical problem solving, insofar as participants encounter tangible challenges that holistically connect them to learning, and allows students to experience naturalistic teaching methods, an active form of learning that promotes healthy lifestyles. Connecting children to the outdoors can be integrated into a lifelong pursuit of outside activities.

DISCUSSION QUESTIONS

1. What reasons can you identify as a teacher that would motivate you to plan a lesson, or series of lessons, outdoors?

2. List three to five essential features that you want in a site when teaching lessons outdoors, and explain why these are a "must-have" part of your outdoor learning plan. Can you think of alternatives if one of these features were not available?

3. Discuss the conditions and reasons that would prompt you to move to an alternative plan.

4. When leading children outdoors, what priorities will be monitored to ensure safety and quality learning?

5. List two tips for teaching outdoors that you want to make sure are a part of your outdoor teaching practice. Why is it important for you to build these tips into your teaching?

 Visit the web resource for ready-to-use activities that take physical education outside in a variety of settings.

Voices From the Field

Courtesy of Scott MacKay.

Janice Howlett-MacKay

Physical Education Teacher (P-2), Beechville Lakeside Timberlea Jr. Elementary School, Halifax Regional School Board, Nova Scotia

I have the pleasure of teaching students who are just beginning their educational journey. My goal is for every student to have a positive experience in physical education so that they can lead a healthy, active lifestyle in the future. My young students love to go outside for physical education! I teach and promote outdoor games and activities that students can transfer from physical education to the school playground to the home and community. Examples include hopscotch, foursquare, kick the can, rope skipping, scavenger hunts, snowshoeing, and igloo making.

In Nova Scotia, when the snow is perfect, I change my lesson plans for the day and go outside for winter fun, because the conditions could change the next day or even in the next few hours. Therefore, I always have a sled packed and ready to go with equipment such as snowshoes, igloo-making supplies, shovels, and buckets. It's like a day at the beach but in the snow! I do this because I have discovered that our students are not getting outside to play in the snow as much as I did when I was young. When I ask students, "Who played outside in the snow on the weekend?" or "Who made a snowman or igloo?" the responses are few.

When outside, I look for and assess the following physical education outcomes developed by the Department of Education and Early Childhood Development (2015):

- When students are building igloos or other structures, I look for them to "plan, with others, and participate in an outdoor movement activity (e.g., walk, hike, cross-country ski, snowshoe) in a park or appropriate natural setting, both in cold and warm weather."

- When students are doing activities such as snowshoeing: I look for them to "use effective movement skills and strategies to participate in winter activities for enjoyment that happen in an outdoor environment or a community facility (e.g., cross-country skiing, skating, snowshoeing, making snow angels, building snow figures)."

- Through conversation, I look for students to "demonstrate the ability to co-operate in a group activity (share ideas, listen to others, try completing a task using a different solution)."

CHAPTER 19

Teaching Dance and Movement Education

Michelle Hillier

LEARNING OUTCOMES

After studying this chapter, you will be able to

- outline the benefits of including dance education in your health and physical education programming;
- describe what dance education is in schools, and what it is not;
- apply a three-step process—move it, learn it, and live it—in your programming;
- describe the foundational elements of dance and how they are demonstrated;
- experiment with the Groove teaching strategy to engage students in dance; and
- develop success criteria to help students create dances.

Many people have memories—and opinions—of their own dance experiences in school, whether positive or negative. Whatever your own experiences may have been, I encourage you to bring an open mind to your reading of this chapter about the benefits of including dance education in your health and physical education (HPE) program. Children love to dance! And regardless of whether you have little, lots, or *no* dance experience, you can use the content presented here to enable meaningful dance experiences for your students. The distinct approach described here presents dance to students with a focus not on the aesthetic but on the intrinsic. By learning three key steps—move it, learn it, and live it—you will be prepared and supported to make dance education happen in your HPE program.

Why Teach Dance?

Teachers often think that in order for children to move their bodies and be physically active they have to participate in some form of sport, game, or traditional fitness activity. But dance education offers endless possibilities for meeting the goals of health and physical education: "Dance education is a crucial component of a comprehensive education for all students. It is a movement art form that promotes learning to communicate and express ideas, feelings, perspectives, and concepts through kinesthetic modes of learning" (Cone & Cone, 2011, p. 28). When we incorporate dance and movement (really, that's all dance is—movement, with or without music!) as part of a quality HPE program, we enable a multitude of benefits for the total health and well-being of our students, both in and out of the classroom.

Despite the fact that dance offers a fun and highly effective way to gets kids moving, many teachers feel reluctant to include it in their programming because they don't know where to begin in terms of planning, instruction, execution, or assessment. This chapter addresses these concerns and provides help both for teachers with dance experience and for those without such experience. It gives you what you need to be confident, prepared, and excited about implementing dance education with your students!

Physical Literacy and Physical Activity

We can all recognize that dancing allows the body to be active, whether students are doing creative movement, line dancing, hip-hop, African dance, Bollywood, or other culturally specific dances. The physical benefits include increased heart rate, muscular strength, endurance, agility, flexibility, and balance, as well as improved cardio-respiratory function, coordination, and spatial awareness. Dance can also be used to explore and develop fundamental movement skills such as running, hopping, skipping, galloping, balancing, rolling, and crawling. All of these movements can be done in creative and expressive ways; indeed, that *is* dance! In addition, dance is an excellent way to create the building blocks for physical literacy: confidence, competence, and creativity for lifelong movement.

Dancing also provides children with benefits in the cognitive, social, and emotional domains. In these regards, the way in which you teach dance, and the strategies you implement in the classroom, are integral to creating meaningful dance experiences. The goal is for children to feel successful so that they create positive cognitive, social, and emotional connections to dance. You can exert a lasting influence on children's perceptions of dance well into their adolescence and adult life. If children have negative or unpleasant experiences with dance in early elementary school, such experiences can influence their feelings about dance for life. Don't forget that even adults feel uncomfortable with dancing in front of others, or feel that they just "can't dance." Where did that idea come from? More often than not, it can be traced back to an experience they had as a child in school during a dance lesson or event. So let's work to recognize the effect that dance education can have on our children. Let's empower ourselves as teachers to create (and experience for ourselves!) the benefits of dance.

Kids Love to Dance!

Have you watched children move when you put music on? They move without judgment or inhibition, with smiles on their faces, and allow their bodies to move organically. As soon as they can stand, they can dance. In fact, in their mother's womb, they hear the heartbeat as their first rhythm or beat. We are born to move, and we can see this innate ability when we watch a group of preschool children move to music; there is pure joy in their faces! We need to maintain that natural joy and intuitive aspect of fun in dance as kids move into our classrooms.

Cultural Connections

Dance is the oldest form of celebration in most cultures around the world. It brings together people of all ages and allows people to move their bodies. In Canada, one of every five people is foreign born (Statistics Canada, 2015). As a result, our classrooms across the country are rich with diverse cultures, and dance is celebrated in many forms in students' homes and communities. Many parents of your students will feel strong connections to their culture, and these connections can serve as a valuable resource for your program! When we as teachers make cultural connections with our students, they feel respected as part of the classroom community.

When we as teachers make cultural connections with our students, they feel respected as part of the classroom community.

Teamwork and Social Skills

Dance has a way of bringing people together, whether for cultural events, celebrations, performances, or just moving to music together as a team or unit. There is something powerful about a group of people of any age moving together to music. Since we all move our bodies differently (and we want to encourage that in our students!), we also need to respect others in our dance experiences and allow them to express themselves in their own way. This respect creates a sense of trust and acceptance while advancing social skills through positive interaction.

It's in Your Curriculum

Dance-related movement expectations are included in arts and HPE curricula across Canada. Dance allows students in health and physical education classrooms to express themselves physically and creatively while exploring rhythm, timing, and connections to music.

Who Can Teach Dance?

The answer is everyone! However, this is not something that all teachers realize. When teachers across Canada are asked, "Are you including dance in your HPE program?" and the answer is "not really," why is that the case? Teachers agree that children love dance, need to dance, and would benefit from dance. Thus the barrier usually resides with the teacher. For instance, many teachers believe that they must know how to dance in order to teach dance. This is not the case. Many also believe that they must have a dance background, know all the current moves and songs, and be able to demonstrate a choreographed dance in order to teach their students. This is also not the case.

Of course, teaching dance with little or no experience would naturally create some anxiety for teachers, as they envision themselves being "on stage" in front of their students and feel responsible for memorizing a dance and modelling the movements for students to copy. But what do students learn from that? The ability to copy and follow the leader? Are they being creative? Not necessarily. However, if the teacher uses music and movement to lead children in exploring a theme or subject and encourages their self-expression in performing movements, then not only are the students being creative and inspired but also the teacher can feel confident that there is no wrong way to lead.

What Does Dance Look Like in HPE?

The goal of a quality HPE program is to create happy, healthy children who have the ability to move and express themselves physically. Dance is an ideal vehicle for realizing this goal. If we take a trip down our own memory lane and think of how dance was taught in our HPE classes as children, many visions may include learning a social dance, line dance, or ballroom dance. Or perhaps you explored creative movement (which may have seemed a bit obscure) or followed a video-game dance. Or maybe a peer taught everyone else in the class a choreographed routine. Even more common, perhaps the reality was something like, "Dance? Oh, we didn't do any dance in school."

The goal of a quality HPE program is to create happy, healthy children who have the ability to move and express themselves physically.

I am not saying that there is anything wrong with learning a choreographed dance or a style of dance with set steps and conventions, but let's consider why we do that. Dance in education is different from dance in the media, in private training, in a studio, or in the performance world. When students learn choreographed movements, learning moves away from being student centred. We must then wonder whether students are learning simply to copy and memorize movements and rhythms, which may not allow all of them to feel successful or to have a positive experience. Yes, they may be moving, but let's get them creating and growing as well! Let's also take the responsibility off of the teacher and allow kids to express themselves in the ways that feel best to them.

You may now be wondering, "How do I do that?" To answer that question, I would like to share a detailed and integrated approach for helping your students explore and create movement using dance. The approach involves those three basic steps mentioned earlier: move it, learn it, and live it.

1. Move It

In this first step, you introduce students to dance in a way that ensures success, builds their confidence, and allows them to move their bodies in a variety of ways. With this approach, students see possibilities as they explore movements from a range of dance styles, genres, and decades. As the teacher, you know your students, and of course your own interests and experiences, which means that you have a lot of choices available for exposing students to various kinds of dance. You can expose them to *any* form of dance—including but not limited to line dances, social dances, culturally specific dances, and traditional folk dances—as long as the students are moving confidently, without inhibition, and building their movement vocabulary. It's fine to choose dances that you feel more confident with as a teacher, but don't get caught up in the technical aspects or choreography.

Here, I introduce you to an innovative and creative approach to teaching dance and movement called the Groove. The method was created by Misty Tripoli of the World Groove Movement, and its application in education is affiliated with and inspired by that work. Both the definition of Groove and the words that teachers use to describe it usually refer to music, movement, rhythm, enjoyment, zone, flow, and "getting into the groove." Thus, for most people, the term carries a positive connotation.

The Groove uses a simple combination of being united as a group while also allowing students to show their unique styles and personalities. To implement this approach, the teacher unites students in a simple movement (e.g., hop, skip, run, roll, shimmy, wave, walk, point) in order to create a sense of togetherness, then adds a creative exploration of that movement (e.g., using directions, pathways, levels, rhythms, speeds, and range of motion). We all move our bodies differently, and the Groove allows students to express that individuality. When students are in the Groove, they are first united in a simple movement (as simple as a walk) and then coached and encouraged to make their walk unique in their own way. Hold in your own mind, and help your students remember, that when they Groove they cannot get their creative choices wrong! Prompt your students to say it before you start the Groove: "You can't get it wrong!" They can say it to each other and to themselves!

Prompt your students to say it before you start the Groove: "You can't get it wrong!" They can say it to each other and to themselves!

The Groove addresses both body and mind, thus helping to equip children for their journey into physical literacy. It involves not only movement form but also confidence and motivation to perform. It requires only minimal preparation and does not require extensive knowledge to implement in the classroom or in a recreational setting (Dean Kriellaars, Ph.D. Department of Physical Therapy, University of Manitoba, personal communication).

To help you get started with using the Groove method, table 19.1 shows 10 sample songs and moves that are appropriate for K-6 students. Remember, you also "can't get it wrong" when interpreting the movements and deciding when in the song to do them. Once you have explored a variety of songs, you can begin to create a "word wall" noting all the moves your students have done. Post a piece of chart paper and let students list all the moves they can remember. If they call a move something different from what you did, that is not a big deal! We want to reinforce the idea that they "can't get it wrong," so if you called something "lightbulb arms" and they call it "twist the lightbulbs," it doesn't matter. In this *move it* step, you are building students' movement vocabulary and their confidence in being creative and interacting with others.

■ TABLE 19.1

Sample Groove Songs and Teaching Notes

Song name	Artist	Dance style or genre	Groove moves
Tribal Funk	Benjamin Bidlack	African	Heavy stomp Drumming Jump and move
We Will Rock You	Queen	Rock 'n' roll	Stomp, stomp, clap Air guitar Pump, pump, throw
Wipe Out	Surfaris	1960s pop	Swimming Surfboard tricks Deep-sea dive
Beware of the Boys	Panjabi MC	Bhangra	Lightbulbs Driving the car Windshield wipers
Hernando's Hideaway	Alfred Hause's Tango Orchestra	Tango	Dramatic walks Picking roses Dramatic poses
Everybody Gonfi Gon	Two Cowboys	Country	Gallop Swinging a partner Heel digs
We No Speak Americano	Yolanda Be Cool	"Pizza party"	Skipping Making pizza (rolling dough, cutting toppings, tossing and catching) Eating pizza Food fight!
Water Cycle	Rhythm, Rhyme, Results	Hip-hop and science	Side to side Funky walk Hip-hop poses Water waves
The Blue Danube	New 101 Strings Orchestra	Waltz	Swaying 3 walks and a bow Spins and jumps
The Sun	B-Tribe	Stillness and mindfulness	Still position Eyes closed Soft breathing Clear mind

2. Learn It

In this step, students learn the five foundational elements of dance, which give them the vocabulary they need in order to develop movement skills and begin creating their own dances. To help us remember the five elements, we can use the acronym DR BEST:

Dance is...
Relationship
Body
Energy

Space
Time

These elements are aligned with movement competencies and skills included in most HPE curricula. To teach the elements to your students, analyze and discuss with them the following topics for each element:

Definition. What is the element? Gather around a piece of chart paper and make notes with the students to define and describe the element. Try to elicit answers from the students by prompting them with suggestions and questions. Your students will refer to these notes as they create and explore.

Individual exploration. Prompt your students to kinesthetically explore the element in a creative manner throughout your space.

Group activity. Give students the opportunity to work with others in small groups. For primary students, use groups of 2 to 3 students and for intermediate students, use groups of 5 to 6 students. Show knowledge of the element through a small movement creation that they share with the class.

Reflection. Debrief, review, and either have students do a personal reflection or express thoughts after watching other groups share their creations from the group activity.

In addition to posting a piece of chart paper for each element, put up a poster with the DR BEST acronym showing all five elements.

Now, Let's explore some prompts and discussion topics for each of the five elements.

Body

Definition

- Shapes (e.g., curved, angular, symmetrical, asymmetrical)—both static and dynamic
- Body parts (e.g., head, shoulders, hands, hips, legs, feet)
- Body zones (e.g., right side, left side, upper body, lower body)
- Body bases (e.g., feet, back, knees)

Individual exploration

- Prompt students to spread out in the space.
- Ask them to create static shapes (frozen, like a statue) with their body: twisted, prickly, wavy, angular, curvy.
- Now ask them to create dynamic shapes (moving on a spot): shaking, swinging, exploding, melting, oozing, collapsing, freezing, swaying, suspending, crunching, being spongy.
- Ask them to explore symmetrical shapes (mirror image) and asymmetrical shapes (different on either side), both alone and then with a partner.

Group activity

- You'll need 8 to 10 images of shapes, as well as a music player (song suggestion: "Levels" by Avicii).

- Lay the images on the floor or ground and ask students to move around the space while you play the song suggestion. When the music stops, students create the shape shown in the image to which they are closest. Repeat the activity for a total of five times.
- Form groups of four or five, give each group an image, and instruct the groups to each generate a list of words describing their image. Prompt them by asking them to pretend they have a remote control and can make the image come to life.
- Each group then produces a movement creation meeting the following criteria: whole-group beginning shape, four or five different moves (each group member creates a move for each word from the list to facilitate accountability and acceptance), and a whole-group ending shape.
- Each group shares their creation with the rest of the class to the song suggestion.

Reflection

- Ask students the following question: When you watched the other groups, how did the group members use their bodies in creative ways?

Space

Definition

- Directions (e.g., forward, backward, sideways, diagonal)
- Levels (e.g., high, middle, low)
- Pathways (e.g., straight, curved, zigzag, spiral)

Individual exploration

- Gather the students at one end of the space, have them get into four or five squads, and have the squads each form a queue, all facing in the same direction. All of the students in a given line are referred to as a family.
- Prompt the families to walk down the room together. Now call out directions in which the families should travel, then levels, and then pathways. Then try a different locomotor movement instead of walking (e.g., skipping, jumping, galloping, running).

- Now ask students to leave their family lines and move throughout the space. Call out combinations of spatial elements (e.g., skipping backward in a zigzag, galloping sideways in a spiral) for students to perform.

Group activity

- You'll need blank paper and coloured markers for this activity. Students will work in groups of four or five to create visual treasure maps, each of which must have a starting point, a middle point, and an ending point.
- The teacher draws three circles anywhere on the piece of paper before handing it out to each group. The students write a nonlocomotor movement (e.g., punch, kick, wiggle, shimmy, march on the spot) in each circle. Each group then draws a pathway (e.g., zigzag, diagonal) to indicate how to travel from circle to circle (for added difficulty, they can indicate a level of movement as well).
- Each group then gives its treasure map to another group to figure out, practice, and share it with the rest of class.
- This activity is a great way to allow students to see possibilities for using space in more than just a lateral manner when creating.

Reflection

- Ask students the following question: When you watched another group share the treasure map created by your group, did you see anything they did that was surprising?

Time

Defintion

- Tempos (e.g., fast, slow)
- Rhythms (combinations of tempos, e.g., fast-fast-slow)
- Beat (connection to musical beat)

Individual exploration

- Clap different rhythms and have students respond in a call-and-answer style.
- Select various students to serve as the caller.
- Try using different body parts for clapping.

- Ask students to move around the room for eight claps and freeze for eight claps, then for four, and then for two.

Group activity

- Using chart paper or whiteboard, show the students a four-fruit pattern (e.g., pear, apple, pineapple, watermelon). Ask students how many syllables are in the word *apple*, then clap together and say *ap-ple* using two claps. Now clap and don't say the word.
- Next, say *ap-ple* and ask students to move their bodies using the two beats without saying the word or clapping. Encourage them to try moving different body parts. Explain that *ap-ple* is two beats and therefore supports two body movements.
- Repeat with *pear*, *pineapple*, and *watermelon*. Students now know four uses of time that show 1 to 4 syllables and beats (1 = pear, 2 = apple, 3 = pineapple, 4 = watermelon).
- Place students in groups of four and ask them to create a four-fruit pattern (using the fruit from the activity: *pear*, *apple*, *pineapple*, and *watermelon*). Each student then picks a fruit and creates a body movement to represent its number of beats and speed. For example, *pear* calls for one slow movement, whereas *watermelon* calls for four quick movements.
- Students then share with their group so that all group members know all of the fruit movements. They should be sure that the four movements flow from one into another with no breaks. Once ready, they share their sequence with the class.

Reflection

- Ask students the following question: How did the groups show unison, or working together as a unit?

Energy

Definition

- Quality (e.g., smooth, sharp, vibrating, fluid, twisted)
- Force (e.g., light, strong)
- Effort (e.g., pressing, gliding)

Individual exploration

- Ask students to walk through the space using different directions.
- Call out the following energy words to prompt students to change the look of their walk: flop, bounce, float, drip, pound, flick, soar, twitch, vibrate.

Group activity

- You will need a music player (song suggestions: "Cotton Eyed Joe," "Pirates of the Caribbean Krump Remix").
- Teach the students a very basic 24-count movement combination, such as the following:
  - Two jumping jacks (4 counts)
  - Four little two-feet jumps on the spot (4 counts)
  - Four steps forward (4 counts)
  - Four steps backward (4 counts)
  - Reach arms up then down and clap twice (4 counts)
  - Crouch down to the floor and jump up high and land with feet together (4 counts)
- At this point, ensure that students are not adding any expression. Play no music as they practice the sequence; move on only when the whole class gets it.
- Divide the class into groups of four and give the groups time to practice the combination again.
- Now play the following songs: "Cotton Eyed Joe" and "Pirates of the Caribbean Krump Remix." Ask the groups to discuss what each song sounds like and generate some words to describe the song's energy. Make it clear that the original movement combination is not changed—students are just modifying the same movements to suit the energy of the song.
- Give the groups time to work, then ask each group to share using the two song selections above.

Reflection

- Ask students the following question: How did the movements chosen by the groups reflect the music? Compare the groups' different interpretations of the same song.

Relationship

Definition

- To others (e.g., group formations, mirroring, physical connection)
- To props (e.g., scarves, ribbons, chairs, balls, clothing)
- To a theme (e.g., colours, emotions, animals, social justice)

Individual exploration

- Lead a mirroring activity in which students face each other and move together as if looking at a mirror image.
- Ask students to each find a partner with a similar height
- Ask students to start in a sitting position and move only their arms, then progress to standing.
- Each pair decides who will lead and who will act as the mirror. On your signal, they switch roles.
- Students should try to maintain eye contact and move slowly so that an observer would not know who is leading and who is mirroring. This synchronization shows close relationship to another person.

Group activity

- Create five stations, each of which has pieces of the same equipment (e.g., scoops, deck ring, beanbag, hoop, small ball).
- Place students in five groups, each of which starts at one of the stations. Give the groups one minute to explore and play with the equipment. Prompt them to make their movements and actions bigger, exaggerate it, add levels, and so on.
- For the second minute at the same station, ask the groups to use their imagination to make the equipment become something other than what it is used for in HPE class (e.g., treat the deck ring as a steering wheel) or to extend the skills used by adding rhythms, levels, and directions.
- Prompt the groups to rotate through the stations so that each group plays with all of the equipment.

■ Assign each student in the groups a piece of equipment (one per person) so each group member has a different object, and have each group member create a move with it. Ask students to apply their knowledge and movement vocabulary from exploring other elements (time, space, body, and energy).

■ Ask each group to share its moves.

Reflection

■ Ask students the following question: What did you notice about how other students were using the equipment?

3. Live It

In this final step, students use their knowledge of the foundational elements of dance to make a creation referred to as a dance recipe (see table 19.2). This recipe can then be used as your success criteria. Here are some tips for teaching this step:

■ Select group members ahead of time to facilitate effective communication, connection, and time on task.

■ When selecting music, keep it instrumental and global. Stay away from top 40 songs, which encourage students to mimic what they have seen in the media and thus hinder their creativity (and may also include inappropriate language and themes).

■ Have all groups use the same song for their dance creation. This approach allows you to maintain positive control of the practice since all groups can be in the same space.

■ When assessing and evaluating, you don't have to focus only on the final product. Observe students during the creative process; some students feel uncomfortable about sharing but apply themselves as leaders during group work.

■ Avoid giving them either too little or too much time to create their work; typically, it works well to allow two or three 40-minute blocks. If any groups seem done before the others, allow them to fulfill additional criteria.

■ When it is time to share, allow more than one group to go at a time and have them share more than once. This approach removes the pressure to make the final product a perfect performance.

■ Prompt the students who are watching (i.e., the audience) to be respectful in their body language, eye contact, and applause. After each round, invite peer feedback and share

■ **TABLE 19.2**

Dance Groove Recipe

Age group	Steps	Music suggestion
Primary (K-3)	In groups of 3 (K-1 whole class): Three Groove moves One move that travels One move that changes levels	"It Takes a Village" (Benjamin Bidlack)
Junior (grades 4-6)	In groups of 4: Beginning group shape Four Groove moves Fast and slow Locomotor and nonlocomotor Heavy and light	"Kicking the Flavour" (Geoff Bennett)
Intermediate (grades 7-8)	In groups of 5-8: Five Groove moves Clear beginning and ending Three group formations Two levels Movement in unison Moment with all group members connected Moment of stillness Two uses of time Vibration, floating, twisting	"Boroto" (Badenya—Les Freres Coulibaly)

your own feedback with the group. Provide two "glows" (what they did well) and one "grow" (something they could improve on when sharing again).

- Be sure that they are always creating. Don't make it about *you* as the teacher.
- Focus assessment not on skills and technical execution but on the success criteria developed earlier.
- Don't take yourself too seriously—keep it simple and have *fun*! Remember, you can't get it wrong!

Summary

I hope that you are now feeling excited and motivated to bring these activities and dance connections to your programming. The Groove philosophy—that students "can't get it wrong"—gives you a powerful tool for creating an environment in which all of your students feel accepted and safe in exploring ways to use their bodies. It is also important for you to jump and explore with them; when you do, you will see your students open up and try even more! The activities presented in this chapter are geared to inspire students to move in creative and expressive ways of their own, and you may find that the resulting self-confidence carries into other areas of the school day and beyond the walls of the classroom.

DISCUSSION QUESTIONS

1. In group work, how can you ensure that all students contribute meaningfully to the creation of dance pieces?
2. What does inclusive dance programming look like?
3. How will you represent a variety of cultures in your dance programming?
4. What will your class environment be like?
5. What do you need to consider as you set up your dance environment (e.g., music, sound system, chart paper, props and equipment, markers)?
6. How important is it for you to connect with your school community and with experts in the field of dance?
7. How can you prompt students to start talking about dance as they participate and provide feedback to their peers?

 Visit the web resource for ready-to-use dance activities and a Chance Dance template.

Voices From the Field

Courtesy of J. Moorhouse.

Adrian Xavier

Health and Physical Education Teacher (K-5), Ontario

As I often share with my students, "First we have fun, then we learn." Fun is specific to each of us, so it needs to be experienced in a variety of ways. Here are some examples:

- *Student choice and voice.* Students have a choice in what we learn, how we learn it, how we modify and adapt what we are doing, and how we express how we feel.

- *More play, less talk.* We establish intentions, expectations, and safety protocols at the beginning. We then explore through a process of doing or playing, then observing and analyzing, then more doing or playing, and then reflecting and sharing.

- *Finding what works for you.* There's more than one way to accomplish a task. Encourage students to use tools and techniques shared by you and by other students and make them their own. As the Groove philosophy says, you can't get it wrong!

- *Variety and integration.* Fun can be both the experience and the outcome. For instance, select a traditional sport and mix it up by modifying the equipment or the rules. Or implement the Teaching Games for Understanding (TGfU) model, which categorizes sports and games based on common game experiences (target, net and wall, striking-and-fielding, and territory). Connect students' learning experiences in the classroom with the HPE program; for example, if grade 5 students are reading a Harry Potter book in language class, play a variation of Quidditch or a territory game with a wizarding theme in physical education.

Imagination and analogies help foster learning in dance and movement education. A movement, skill, technique, or action comes to life when you make it meaningful, relevant, and perhaps humourous for your learners. If the intention is to promote and encourage movement and activity, then invite students into an experience where they can explore movement through characterization. Here are some examples of using imagination to teach fundamental movement skills:

- *Hopping.* Dare students to travel across hot rocks. As soon as one foot touches the stones, it burns, so they must immediately jump to the other foot. Encourage sound effects, such as "oooh," "eeeeee," and "aaaaaahhh."

- *Striking an object.* Sometimes we need to strike with force. Give each student an object and ask them to imagine that their arms are a volcano starting to brew and bubble from below. As they swing their arms up, the pressure builds, and the volcano bursts into eruption when they strike the object.

- *Squatting.* To help younger learners with form, have them practice by lowering onto a bench in order to learn the seated posture. As soon as their bums touch the bench, prompt them to "pop" or "bounce" up into a standing position. To add humour, refer to the movement as a "bum bounce" or "butt bounce."

My experience, both with young learners and with feedback from peers in education, has taught me that analogies and imagery can bridge the divide between the practical and the abstract, thus helping to make movements and techniques more inviting and engaging. For learners between the ages of three and eleven years, the "what" and the "how" of movement are likely more engaging than the "why." More often than not, students tend to greet me for PE class with the following question: "What are we playing today?" Once they know the answer, their next question is typically "How do we play?" or "What happens if . . . ?"

Certainly, the "why"—which likely acknowledges the benefits of technique or strategy—matters to some learners. However, when considering how to make learning inclusive and accessible to *all* learners, be mindful of the fact that the abstract can diminish both attention and enthusiasm among young learners. Fun comes first. As our learners experience the joy of playing, then we can begin to infuse and weave in the "why" in order to add value to the experience. In a sense, you are scaffolding the process to ensure that you achieve maximum inclusion at the onset and then build toward the higher level of critical thinking skills inherent in game play.

When assessing students in movement and dance education, look for the following elements:

- *Persistence.* Based on self-assessed level of success, the student continues to participate in the activity.

- *Engagement.* The student is smiling, consistently active, making it her or his own, encouraging others, and sharing positive or constructive peer assessment.

- *Curiosity.* The student explores alternative ways to succeed.

- *Extension.* The student may ask, "Can we try . . . ?" or "What if we . . . ?" or "I'm going to (I'd like to) . . . "

CHAPTER 20

Enhancing Teaching With Technology

Camille Rutherford

After studying this chapter, you will be able to

- integrate technology into your health and physical education (HPE) curriculum,
- use the SAMR model (substitution, augmentation, modification, redefinition) to guide technology use in order to enhance health and physical literacy, and
- create HPE learning opportunities that support the development of 21st-century competencies.

Although a number of provincial ministries of education have encouraged the integration of technology into school HPE programs, specific guidance has been lacking as to how to capitalize on the benefits of tech-enabled teaching to enhance learning. Thus, the goal of this chapter is to highlight how technology can be used to support the desired outcomes of health and physical education as promoted by Physical and Health Education Canada while also addressing the 21st-century competencies viewed as essential to the future success of our students.

Tech-Enabled HPE

Simply bringing technology into the classroom has frequently failed to exert a positive effect on students' learning (OECD, 2015). To ensure that technology use enhances HPE curriculum, we must focus on how students, not the teacher, will use the technology to support their learning. Toward this end, the SAMR model—substitution, augmentation, modification, redefinition—provides an excellent framework for ensuring that technology use does not simply replicate old practices (Puentedura, 2010). The SAMR model provides us with a guide to support professional reflection on how we integrate technology into instructional practice. The following SAMR stages document the progression of classroom technology integration.

- Substitution: The technological resource acts as a direct substitute for a traditional resource or practice with no functional change.
- Augmentation: The technological resource acts as a direct substitute for a traditional resource or practice with some functional improvement.
- Modification: The use of technology supports significant modification of a learning task.
- Redefinition: The use of technology supports the creation of new tasks that would not otherwise be possible.

Thus, when technology use fails to make a noticeable effect on student learners, the reason often lies in the fact that the technology is used merely as a substitution for a traditional activity. In contrast, when educators use the SAMR model to integrate technology and modify or redefine their lessons, the resulting lesson is more likely to enhance the learning experience. Table 20.1 provides a snapshot of a tech-enabled HPE activity and highlights the fact that changes in a lesson can affect how an activity is categorized according to the SAMR model.

When educators use the SAMR model to integrate technology and modify or redefine their lessons, the resulting lesson is more likely to enhance the learning experience.

This chapter explores detailed examples of how technology can be used to support HPE teaching and learning in ways that range from a limited functional change of typical activities to the complete redefinition of a traditional task. The examples progress from traditional HPE activities that even young students can complete with mini-

■ TABLE 20.1

Examples of Tech-Enabled Activities for Physical and Health Education

SAMR model	Tech-enabled teaching and learning examples
Substitution: The technological resource acts as a direct substitute for a traditional resource or practice with no functional change.	The teacher uses a camera to record a student gymnastics or dance routine, then reviews the video and provides written feedback.
Augmentation: The technological resource acts as a direct substitute for a traditional resource or practice with some functional improvement.	The teacher uses a video annotation app to provide detailed feedback on the video-recorded performance.
Modification: The use of technology supports significant modification of a learning task.	Students create a series of annotated videos to document their progress. They review the videos to self-assess and use video annotations to note specific improvements, as well as areas for growth.
Redefinition: The use of technology supports the creation of new tasks that would not otherwise be possible.	Students create annotated demonstration videos providing step-by-step guidance to help younger or less skilled students with a performance task.

mal need for technology to learning experiences that challenge older students to demonstrate both physical literacy and skilled use of technology.

To explore how the SAMR model can enhance learning in HPE, let's consider how it might be used to redefine a common practice in many physical education classes: performing a gymnastics or dance routine to demonstrate skill and understanding of specific movement elements. At the end of such a unit, the teacher often designates a specific time to watch and take notes as students perform their routines. During these evaluations, the teacher's attention must be closely focused on the task at hand; otherwise, crucial elements of the routine could be missed. As the teacher busily jots down notes, the rest of the class has to wait patiently for their turn be evaluated.

As a *substitution*, the teacher could use a video camera or smartphone to record the students' routines, then review the recordings and provide written feedback. Improvements in digital videography have shrunk digital video cameras to the point that $100 will buy one that can easily fit in a teacher's pocket. In addition, the availability of high-definition cameras in most smartphones has eliminated the need to purchase more sophisticated equipment. These advances have made it easier for teachers to simply use a smartphone or tablet to capture student performances. Again, this slight alteration in practice represents the *substitution* of technology for a traditional activity; there is no functional change in the teaching and learning process.

In contrast, the teacher could make a functional improvement, or *augmentation*, in the activity by using a video annotation app such as Coach's Eye instead of simply video-recording the performance. In addition to allowing both normal and slow-motion playback, these apps allow the user to add text or video comments, as well as drawings, to videos created on a smartphone or tablet. The functional improvement here results from enabling the student to hear and see the teacher's comments while watching the video.

Learning activities where the use of technology goes to either of the next two levels—that is, where it supports *modification* or *redefinition* of learning—is transformative. The first step in using technology to transform student learning is to *modify* or redesign the task. For example, instead of simply using technology as a summative assessment tool, an innovative teacher might assign students to use tablets to create a series of weekly Coach's Eye videos to document their progress.

The students would be provided with time to review the videos in order to self-assess and annotate their improvements and areas for additional work. This type of activity represents a dramatic shift from teacher-directed learning, in which only the teacher uses technology, to a student-centred approach in which the technology is put in the hands of students, who are given responsibility for assessing their own learning.

As profound as this transformation is, even more advancement is possible if the technology is used to support the creation of new tasks that would not otherwise be possible. For example, the teacher might *redefine* the task through which students demonstrate skill and understanding in regard to a gymnastics or dance element. Instead of simply recording the performances, students could use a video annotation app to create a series of videos including written, step-by-step guidance to enhance performance. When watching these performance videos, viewers would be provided with strategic tips to support successful execution of the task; moreover, instead of simply submitting the videos to the teacher, students could provide them to younger or less skilled students to support their acquisition of new skills and knowledge. This example highlights the capacity of technology to transform traditional HPE tasks if we invest the time to capitalize on the technological resources available to us.

> *The first step in using technology to transform student learning is to modify or redesign the task.*

Aligning HPE With 21st-Century Competencies

As the preceding section illustrates, using the SAMR model to support technology use in HPE constitutes an enhancement of traditional teaching and learning. Further progress is possible if we use tech-enabled HPE strategies to provide students with opportunities to develop essential competencies for future success. The 21st-century competencies are referred to as such because many people view them as necessary for success in the ever-changing and increasingly complex world in which we now live. These competencies can be generalized into five main categories of skill: collaboration, communication, creativity, critical thinking, and citizenship.

As with the future-oriented perspective of these 21st-century competencies, physical literacy as defined by Physical and Health Education Canada focuses on the future development of the whole person: "It is not just about the understanding and practice of physical activity, it also includes a child's knowledge and understanding of *why* physical activity is important and its resulting benefits, as well as the development of attitudes and habits to practice these skills on a regular basis" (Physical and Health Education Canada, 2010, p. 1). In keeping with this definition, physical literacy serves as an important foundation for many provincial HPE policies (Mandigo, Francis, & Lopez, 2009). Moreover, as noted in table 20.2, the alignment of physical literacy and 21st-century competencies highlights how these skill sets can be combined to support students' future success.

Although the development of these competencies does not depend on using technology, technological resources can be used to enhance learning. Thus, tech-enabled teachers who create learning opportunities that align the HPE curriculum with 21st-century competencies provide their students with a profound learning experience that can benefit them both now and in the future.

The rest of this chapter provides greater detail on each of the 21st-century competencies and how they can be integrated into HPE curriculum to foster physical literacy. Specific guidance is provided for using the SAMR model to design tech-enabled HPE activities that support the redefinition of health and physical education for the 21st century.

Collaboration

The ability to work positively and respectfully with others is vital to both academic and professional success. Thus, it is sensible for a health and physical education program to provide students with opportunities to learn how to build relationships, interact positively with others, and exhibit responsible personal and social behaviour during physical activities (Physical and Health Education Canada, 2010). When students participate in HPE tasks that help them develop the collaborative competencies needed for success in academic and workplace settings, they enhance their physical literacy while also preparing for future success in life. Table 20.3 demonstrates how to use technology to facilitate collaborative HPE activities.

> *The ability to work positively and respectfully with others is vital to both academic and professional success.*

∎ TABLE 20.2

Aligning Physical Literacy With 21st-Century Competencies

21st-century competencies	Physical literacy
Collaboration: ability to work positively and respectfully with others	• Students will display responsible personal and social behaviour during physical activity.
Creativity: ability to apply creative thought processes in order to create something new	• Students will "demonstrate a variety of movements confidently, competently, creatively, and strategically across a wide range of health-related physical activities" (PHE Canada, 2010, p. 1). • Students will understand that physical activity can support self-expression.
Communication: capacity to communicate using a variety of spoken, written, visual, and multimodal media and resources	• Students will "develop the motivation and ability to understand, communicate, apply, and analyze different forms of movement" (PHE Canada, 2010, p. 1). • Students will communicate information as a way to promote, maintain, and improve health in a variety of settings across the life-course.
Critical thinking: ability to interpret, analyze, synthesize, and evaluate information as a means to solve a problem	• Students will "consistently develop the motivation and ability to understand, apply, and analyze different forms of movement" (PHE Canada, 2010, p. 1).
Citizenship: Nurture respect for all, build a sense of belonging to a common humanity, and be responsible and active (United Nations Educational, Scientific and Cultural Organization, 2015).	• Students will display an understanding of and a respect for all people during physical activity. • Students "will make healthy, active choices throughout their life span that are both beneficial to, and respectful of their whole self, others, and their environment" (PHE Canada, 2010, p. 1).

Information from Physical and Health Education Canada 2010 and 2016

■ TABLE 20.3

Using the SAMR Model to Guide Tech-Enabled Collaboration

SAMR model	Tech-enabled teaching and learning examples
Substitution	Student pairs use a pedometer to collaboratively measure part of the distance around the school grounds or a community park. Then the class works together using spreadsheet software to calculate the overall distance.
Augmentation	Working in small groups, students use collaborative writing software (e.g., Google Docs, Office 365) to design fitness trail stations for the school grounds or a community park.
Modification	Students use 3-D modelling software (e.g., SketchUp) to create a replica of each station and the equipment needed. The sketch of the stations could also be added to a Google Earth map of the trail.
Redefinition	Students collaboratively create a website presenting the health benefits of using the fitness trail, tips and timing guides for using the trail, and video demonstrations of proper execution at each station. This information could be accessed by QR codes placed at the stations.

Even very young students can be presented with the task of estimating how many steps are required to complete a lap around the school grounds or around a local park. First, students work in pairs to count the steps required to complete a portion of the lap; then all students contribute to the final outcome by using the data from each pair to determine the overall distance in the number of steps covered. Without any functional change in the original activity, students can use pedometers to measure portions of the distance and spreadsheet software to calculate the total distance.

The activity can be augmented, enhancing the level of both collaboration and health and physical literacy, by providing students with examples of fitness trails and then challenging them to create one for their school or community. Working in small groups or pairs, students can use collaborative writing software (e.g., Google Docs, Office 365) to design fitness trail stations, then use a spreadsheet to calculate the overall distance covered when using the trail.

To further modify the activity, students can use 3-D modelling software (e.g., SketchUp) to create a model of each station and the equipment needed. To visualize what the trail would look like in person, the model of these stations can be added to a Google Earth map of the trail.

To completely redefine the original task—and require demonstration of a higher level of health and fitness knowledge—students can be challenged to collaboratively create a website that addresses the health benefits of using the fitness trail, tips and timing guides for using the trail, and video demonstrations of proper execution at each station. This information could be accessed by QR (quick-response) codes placed at each station.

(QR codes are barcodes that can be read by most smartphones and link quickly to specific websites; one app for creating them can be found at https://createqrcode.appspot.com.) The completion of this activity requires a high level of collaboration. Even though students may make different contributions to the overall product, they must work together to discuss and agree on the process, design, and final outcome of their work. This type of collaborative work closely approximates the collaboration skills that students will need in order to be successful in the future.

Creativity

In a rapidly changing world where innovations are often accompanied by new problems, we need creativity in order to find solutions. As a result, creativity has been highlighted as an essential skill for helping students prepare to cope with frequent and rapid changes. In response, as HPE educators, we need to be creative ourselves in order to provide students with opportunities to creatively demonstrate a variety of skills and movements across a wide range of physical activities (Physical and Health Education Canada, 2010).

Although it may not be possible to teach creativity, this competency may be enhanced by providing students with the opportunity to use creative thought processes to create something. We can do so in physical education by helping students understand that physical activity can support self-expression and encouraging them to engage in a variety of movements confidently, competently, creatively, and strategically across a wide range of health-related physical activities and skills (Physical and Health Education Canada, 2010). Allowing students to creatively

Although it may not be possible to teach creativity, this competency may be enhanced by providing students with the opportunity to use creative thought processes to create something.

demonstrate physical literacy also gives them an opportunity to personalize their learning experiences by addressing their individual interests, strengths, and talents. Table 20.4 highlights how technology can be used to facilitate creativity and physical literacy.

To support the development of creativity, learning tasks must require students to create a unique approach or solution that moves beyond the simple replication of prior learning. This approach can challenge both teachers and students because they may be unable to predict the final result. For instance, requiring students to develop a creative skipping routine or interval training station allows them to come up with a unique approach to the task. By integrating the use of technology into such activities, students can further develop their creativity while also being challenged to deepen their health and physical literacy.

Without any functional change to a typical cardio-building activity, students could be required to use tablets equipped with iTunes or Google Play Music to select energetic music for the class to use while completing a skipping or interval training activity. To augment these activities, students could use the tablets to create playlists of music to support transitions through the different stages of the skipping or interval training tasks. Even young students should be able to select appropriate music to demonstrate their understanding of the different levels of cardio exertion required during the warm-up, peak, and cool-down phases of the activity by selecting slow, upbeat, and calming

music, respectively. Using a class account on a free music-streaming service (e.g., Spotify, Google Play Music) would enable students to create their own playlists and share them with the rest of the class.

Additional technological resources could be used to further modify the original activity and challenge students to creatively demonstrate a variety of movements. For example, students could be asked to create unique skipping routines or interval stations and create soundtracks to guide performance of the activities. The soundtracks would be created by selecting creative-commons music (licensed for editing and free distribution) that is appropriately slow, fast, and calming and then using Audacity or GarageBand to sequence the music in appropriately timed intervals of high and low intensity.

To fully redefine the original activity in ways that would not be possible without the use of technology, students could add creative narration to their soundtracks. One of the highest-grossing health and fitness apps on Apple's App Store is an immersive running soundtrack called *Zombies, Run!*, which encourages running or walking by narrating a story in which the user is chased by zombies. The original app simply provided a narrated story about the survivor of a zombie apocalypse moving around a zombie-infested town while frequently being chased by zombies. By instructing the user to walk while looking for supplies or run to escape the grasp of a zombie, each 30- to 60-minute episode provided an interval training session. Students could use GarageBand or Audacity to create a similar soundtrack with a creative story line to scaffold the listener's performance of a sequence moving from warm-up to peak exertion to cool-down. This task would challenge students' creativity while prompting

■ TABLE 20.4

Using the SAMR Model to Guide Tech-Enabled Creativity

SAMR model	Tech-enabled teaching and learning examples
Substitution	Students use iTunes to create a playlist of energizing music for use while skipping or while working through interval training stations.
Augmentation	Students use Spotify or Google Play Music to create a playlist to support specific physical activities (e.g., slow, calming music for a warm-up; upbeat music for peak activity) that can be shared with others.
Modification	Students create a series of skipping routines or interval training stations, then use GarageBand or Audacity to create a workout soundtrack of creative-commons music that alternates fast and slow tracks at appropriately timed intervals.
Redefinition	Students use GarageBand or Audacity to create a timed exercise soundtrack that scaffolds the listener's performance—from warm-up to near-peak exertion to cool-down—by narrating an engaging story line that encourages the appropriate level of performance.

them to demonstrate their understanding of interval training. Their soundtracks could be shared via services (e.g., SoundCloud) that facilitate the sharing of original music created by DJs and musicians so that others beyond the classroom could experience health benefits.

Communication

Although the ability to communicate is an innate skill, the capacity to communicate effectively using a variety of spoken, written, visual, and multimodal media and resources must be developed. Physical educators can help students develop their communication ability by providing them with opportunities to discuss health topics that carry implications for their personal health and well-being; talking about different forms of movement; and using their communication skills to promote, maintain, and improve health in different settings throughout the life span.

Traditional assessment strategies such as testing—for instance, asking a student to execute a task (e.g., serving or spiking a volleyball) or write down the necessary steps for doing so—have always been ineffective at communicating students' understanding of movement concepts. Although performance tasks are obviously better suited to the purpose than are written assessments, not all students possess the refined skill and coordination required to adequately communicate the depth of their knowledge of the critical elements required to execute a complex sport skill. Conversely, a student with natural physical ability may lack the depth of understanding or the communication skills to analyze an intricate performance and provide useful feedback regarding proper technique. Consequently, HPE programs must support students' development of effective communication skills so that they can discuss health and fitness topics that affect their personal health and well-being while also being able to use different forms of movement to express their interests and perspectives (Physical and Health Education Canada, 2010).

In contrast to the technology-deficient classrooms of the past, current technology makes it easier for students to communicate the full depth of their knowledge by creating spoken, written, visual, and multimodal artifacts that exhibit their learning. The ability to use multimodal resources to communicate an idea or message can be considered essential for future success. Table 20.5 includes an example of how to use technology to support the development of communication skills as part of the HPE curriculum.

A tablet or digital camera could be substituted into the traditional volleyball performance task—without producing any functional change in the task—by having student pairs use a tablet or digital camera to video-record each other serving or spiking in order to demonstrate their knowledge of the required steps for completing the task. Students could then provide feedback to their partners about the execution of the task. Some functional improvement in the original task would result if students were required to use a tablet or digital camera to take pictures of each other serv-

In contrast to the technology-deficient classrooms of the past, current technology makes it easier for students to communicate the full depth of their knowledge by creating spoken, written, visual, and multimodal artifacts that exhibit their learning.

■ TABLE 20.5

Using the SAMR Model to Guide Tech-Enabled Communication

SAMR model	Tech-enabled teaching and learning examples
Substitution	Student pairs use a tablet or digital camera to video-record each other serving or spiking a volleyball in order to demonstrate knowledge of the required steps for completing the task, then provide feedback to each other.
Augmentation	Students use a tablet or digital camera to take pictures of each other serving or spiking a volleyball. The images are then used in conjunction with presentation software to create a guide to the steps required to serve or spike the ball.
Modification	Students use a GoPro or similar camera to create point-of-view video clips in addition to digital pictures, then create a guide to the steps required to serve or spike the ball during game play.
Redefinition	Students work collaboratively to create digital pictures, slow-motion and point-of-view video clips, and coaching annotations to produce a detailed instructional and game-play presentation or video to help younger or less skilled students learn how to play volleyball.

ing or spiking the ball and then load the images into Google Slides, Keynote, or PowerPoint and create a sequential guide to the steps required for completing the task.

The original task could be modified by having students use a GoPro or similar camera to create point-of-view video clips in addition to digital pictures for use as part of the sequential guide to the steps required for serving or spiking during game play. To further enhance the activity, students could work collaboratively to create digital pictures, slow-motion and point-of-view video clips, and coaching annotations to produce a detailed instructional and game-play presentation or video to help younger or less skilled students learn how to play. Students could also share these presentations or videos online for other students and the public to view, thus completely redefining the traditional task in a way that would not have been possible without the use of current technology.

Critical Thinking

Critical thinking involves the ability to interpret, analyze, synthesize, and evaluate information as a means of solving a problem. In order to enhance both critical thinking and physical literacy, students should be provided with opportunities to apply critical thinking processes to their own individual health and fitness data in order to improve their personal fitness. By fostering criti-

Critical thinking involves the ability to interpret, analyze, synthesize, and evaluate information as a means of solving a problem.

cal thinking, we enable students to consistently develop the motivation and ability to understand, apply, and analyze different forms of movement in their lives (Physical and Health Education Canada, 2010). As our world becomes increasingly complex, students must be able to think critically about available information in order to find solutions to the problems they encounter and make informed choices that support their health and physical well-being. Table 20.6 demonstrates how to use technology to foster critical thinking during an HPE lesson.

HPE curriculum lends itself to the integration of student-centred activities that challenge students to think critically about their individual health data in order to benefit their personal well-being. A traditional health education activity might ask students to document their caloric intake by creating a food diary. Thanks to the proliferation of smartphones and tablets, food diary apps and websites now reduce the burden of determining and documenting daily calorie consumption. Using these types of technology represents the simple substitution of technological resources for paper or text resources. A functional improvement of the original task is possible if students use pedometers or fitness trackers in addition to a food diary app to document both their caloric intake and their caloric output.

The task could be modified by asking students to use a heart rate app to measure their resting heart rate in order to document the effect of an activity on their heart rate. They could later analyze the effect of participating in activities that increase their heart rate on their daily caloric intake and output.

■ TABLE 20.6

Using the SAMR Model to Guide Tech-Enabled Critical Thinking

SAMR model	Tech-enabled teaching and learning examples
Substitution	Students use a food diary app or website to document caloric intake.
Augmentation	Students use pedometers or fitness trackers, in addition to the food diary app or website, to document caloric intake and output.
Modification	Students use a heart-rate-monitor app to measure their resting heart rate. They can then analyze how participation in activities that increase heart rate will affect their caloric intake and output.
Redefinition	Students use a heart-rate-monitor app to measure both their resting heart rate and their heart rate during physical activity to document the effect of the activity on their heart rate. Then they use a pedometer, fitness tracker, and food diary app to pursue healthy lifestyle goals (e.g., taking 10,000 steps per day, drinking more water, getting more sleep). After collecting data, students can analyze the effect of the lifestyle changes on their heart rate.

The original task of documenting caloric intake can be completely redefined by using a heart-rate-monitor app to document students' heart rates as they participate in a physical activity. This level of documentation would not have been possible without the widespread availability of current technological resources. It makes it possible for students to see the changes in their heart rate caused by participating in a variety of physical activities. With data gathered through the use of pedometers, fitness trackers, food diary apps, and a more detailed understanding of the effects of various activities on their heart rate and caloric output, students can establish specific lifestyle goals and then analyze the effect of their behaviours on their well-being.

Citizenship

Technological advances have served to shrink the globe and make it easier—and necessary—to interact with people of diverse backgrounds from around the planet. To prepare students to be responsible and active global citizens, the United Nations Educational, Scientific and Cultural Organization (2015) suggests providing them with opportunities to develop respect for all while building a sense that they belong to a common humanity. This notion resonates with fundamental principles of health and physical education—specifically, that students should develop understanding of how the process of living in a healthy, active manner is connected with the world around them and with the health of others (Ontario Ministry of Education, 2015) and that students should "make healthy, active choices throughout their life span that are both beneficial to and respectful of their whole self, others, and their environment" (Physical and Health Education Canada, 2010, p. 1). In this vein, challenging students to contemplate the local and global implications of what they learn in HPE class gives them the opportunity to use their knowledge to support the health and physical literacy of others and address real-world issues. Table 20.7 provides an example of an HPE activity that facilitates tech-enabled citizenship.

Students can support health and physical literacy by sharing the learning objects they create in HPE with other students or community members.

Students can support health and physical literacy by sharing the learning objects they create in HPE with other students or community members. For instance, a number of the learning activities already discussed in this chapter could be of great benefit to people outside of the classroom.

In another example—a project similar to the creativity task addressed earlier—students could create a playlist of energizing music for use at a community centre while people engage in physical activity, such as skating, swimming laps, and walking. In order for their playlists to be useful to community members, students would need to carefully consider the location and context of the physical activity.

Having learned the value of using current technologies to support health and physical literacy, students could share their newly acquired

■ TABLE 20.7

Using the SAMR Model to Guide Tech-Enabled Citizenship

SAMR model	Tech-enabled teaching and learning examples
Substitution	Students use iTunes to create a playlist of energizing music for use at a local community centre while people engage in physical activity (e.g., skating, swimming, walking).
Augmentation	Students work with senior citizens to demonstrate how to use pedometers, fitness trackers, and food diary apps to document the effect of physical activity on caloric intake and output.
Modification	Using the school website, students take turns sending daily nutritional tips, fitness reminders, and motivational messages to support their peers in pursuing healthy lifestyle goals (e.g., taking 10,000 steps per day, drinking more water, getting more sleep).
Redefinition	Students work collaboratively to create digital pictures, slow-motion and point-of-view video clips, and coaching annotations to produce detailed online instructional videos for young people with developmental delays who are training for the Special Olympics or a similar event.

knowledge with senior citizens by demonstrating the use of pedometers, fitness trackers, and food diary apps to document the effect of activity on caloric intake and output. To meet the needs of these community members, students would need to develop an understanding of the health needs and challenges experienced by senior citizens.

Students could also support the health literacy of the school community by organizing a school-wide health and fitness challenge. In this project, students would use the school website, email, or learning management system to send daily nutritional tips, fitness reminders, and motivational messages to support their peers in pursuing healthy lifestyle goals (e.g., taking 10,000 steps per day, drinking more water, getting more sleep) as part of a 30-day fitness challenge.

To take full advantage of technological resources while demonstrating knowledge of the HPE curriculum and 21st-century competencies, students could work collaboratively to create digital pictures, slow-motion and point-of-view video clips, and coaching annotations to produce detailed online instructional videos for young people with developmental delays who are training for the Special Olympics or a similar event. As with the other citizenship activities discussed, this project would require students to thoughtfully consider the unique abilities and needs of their audience. Consequently, the success of such activities would depend not only on students' health and fitness knowledge but also on their ability to empathize with their fellow citizens—a skill that will be of vital importance throughout their lives.

Summary

It should now be apparent that HPE curriculum provides educators with a wealth of opportunities to use technology to create engaging learning experiences while helping students develop the essential competencies of collaboration, creativity, communication, critical thinking, and citizenship. Supporting health and physical literacy while fostering these 21st-century competencies can make a profound difference in the future health and well-being of our students in ways that would not be possible without the merging of these areas.

DISCUSSION QUESTIONS

1. Brainstorm ways in which you could foster development of 21st-century competencies within the HPE curriculum.

2. What are some challenges to overcome when implementing tech-enabled HPE lessons? What are some suggestions for overcoming these challenges?

3. Reflect on how you have used technology in the classroom and how you would characterize that usage according to the SAMR model. What could be done to *modify* or *redefine* the activity?

4. How could technology have been used in one of your previous HPE lessons to support the development of 21st-century competencies?

 Visit the web resource for a complete activity guide to help students develop a physical activity video.

Voices From the Field

Lee Martin
French Immersion Teacher (Grades 3-8), Ontario

Courtesy of Ingrid Mudrazia

To make health and physical education fun and educational for all, I incorporate thematic pieces that enable students to connect things they enjoy in their personal lives with the content I am teaching. For example, students really buy in when they are invited to approach physical challenges by mimicking the characteristics of a favourite video game character or the hero of a favourite book. Helping students make real-world connections not only links the curriculum to their lives but also allows them to use their existing schemata to support understanding. For instance, class trips to a grocery store or local market help promote healthy living using familiar places in the community. This approach enables me to share my experiences of other cultures with students through foods and games enjoyed by kids from various places; it also enables me to integrate other subject areas, such as mathematics and literacy.

Recently, fitness has become a huge component of my program. Although many students in my community are involved in after-school sport programs, their level of physical fitness is often quite low. It is my hope that through promoting the practice of daily fitness routines, I can minimize the health risks faced by many students today. Given that technology has become a target for many people looking to find the cause of sedentary living among our children, the idea of using technology to support physical education seems only natural.

Here's one of my grade 3 lessons that uses technology to support fitness education. Before beginning the lesson, you'll need to contact a teacher from another school (possibly from another province or country) to plan several fitness challenges that both classrooms can participate in.

1. The warm-up portion of the lesson begins by Skyping (or using another video-chat program) the other classroom and displaying the video in your gym along with sound.

2. The challenge begins by having the teacher of the visiting classroom provide instructions and introduce the challenges they have created. It always helps to have this demonstration done both on the screen and by a student in your class. Students will understand that while they are completing the challenges, they are not only competing against themselves, but also against students from the other school. This friendly competition builds community among the members of the class and creates bonds that can be used for communication in other subjects, such as letter writing for literacy.

3. To provide additional guidance, QR codes can be placed around the gym that link to pictures or video examples of the fitness challenges that they will be doing. Students rotate through the stations and use a Wi-Fi-enabled tablet or smartphone to access the instructional picture or videos as they complete each challenge.

4. As the students complete the challenges, the local teacher can take anecdotal notes regarding the performance of both groups of students on an app (e.g., Notability) to enable both teachers to later share their assessments.

5. While the students complete these challenges, the local teacher can also use the Coach's Eye app to video-record them and then give instant feedback as we review the footage. The app allows me to really draw attention to mechanics and ways in which students can improve; it also enables me to reduce the likelihood of injury due to improper form.

6. The lesson concludes with both classrooms participating in a student-led cool-down routine that is projected on the gym screen.

I chose this lesson example to show the variety of ways in which technology can support both student success and teacher practice. The tools used are all mobile and for the most part free. The use of examples to aid assessment for learning is widely practiced in the classroom but often forgotten in the gym. These tools provide strategies to empower teachers and students alike; they also teach transferable technological skills.

(continued)

(continued)

Recommended technology resources:

- Skype: This program not only supports co-planning and co-teaching but also builds community among my students and their new friends from outside of our school. It also enables friendly competition among students.

- Notability: This program is a versatile notetaking tool that can be used for all subjects and enables teachers to capture assessment pieces such as conversations, observations, and products from their students.

- QR codes: This tool enables students to see the mechanics of movement before they try to do it. They can use the movement examples to understand how to perform the fitness challenge, overcome language barriers that may hinder them in learning from an informational poster, and take the fitness challenge with them to continue learning outside of school.

- Coach's Eye: This program allows you to give immediate feedback on student form and use examples to show subtle modifications that need to be made. It can also be used as a whole-group tool for assessment-as-learning by enabling students to look at examples and evaluate them in terms of success criteria or observe a peer's technique and provide useful feedback.

Here are some things to look for when using technology as an assessment tool:

- *Evaluation that assesses the process as well as the product.* The recording programs I use enable me to capture and review with students their growth throughout the process. This capability provides me with rich material to evaluate and gives a clear picture of the active student.

- *Involvement with feedback for active participation, not just performance.* The technological tools also enable teacher–student and student–student collaboration. Together, we are able to review the learning process; find individual and shared strengths; and produce timely feedback that is used to foster involvement, growth, and understanding.

- *Self-reflection, collective reflection, and collaboration about learning and the learning environment.* These tools enable students to step outside of themselves and review who they are as active learners, as teammates, and as members of our learning community. The technology helps them to learn both from themselves and through interactions with others.

If you want to use technology in your class to support HPE learning, consider the following tips:

- Let go of the idea that teaching with technology is done only in a computer lab. If technology is all around us in every area of our lives, then it can be integrated into every area of our teaching as well.

- Take risks! It is okay to *not* be a master of technology. The majority of technology that I use with my students is something we explore together. I bring good pedagogy and content knowledge, they bring technological familiarity, and together we create engaging learning opportunities for all of us.

- Find a model, such as SAMR or TPACK (technology, pedagogy, and content knowledge), that empowers you in planning to integrate technology into your practice. Always ask yourself, "How can I use this tool in my class?" or "How can I make this lesson better by integrating technology?" Also consider ways to turn high-tech tools into low-tech learning. For example, by mimicking the coding blocks used in programs such as Scratch (free software used to teach computer coding), I created laminated warm-up cards that students use to "program" steps for a partner to "run."

- Don't have the technology available that you would like? Start contacting your administration and IT department and get online. Money may be available for initiatives like the ones described here from your school district as well as hundreds of grants and companies looking to promote digital learning. Their support can help you acquire the tools you need. From such sources, I have raised more than $10,000, and it all started with asking people for their help to get educational technology in our school.

References

Chapter 1

Abels, J., & Bridges, J. (2010). *Teaching movement education: Foundations for active lifestyles.* Windsor, ON: Human Kinetics.

Begoray, D., Wharf-Higgins, J., & MacDonald, M. (2009). High school health curriculum and health literacy: Canadian student voices. *Global Health Promotion, 16*(4), 35-42.

Burrows, L., Wright, J., & Jungersen-Smith, J. (2002). "Measure your belly": New Zealand children's constructions of health and fitness. *Journal of Teaching in Physical Education, 22*(1), 29-38.

Canadian Public Health Association. (2008). *Media questions and answers on health literacy.* www.cpha.ca/uploads/portals/h-l/qa_e.pdf

Chang, C-P., Hsu, C-T., & Chen, I-J. (2013). The relationship between the playfulness climate in the classroom and student creativity. *Quality & Quantity, 47*(3), 1493-1510.

Cliff, K., Wright, J., & Clarke, D. (2009). What does a "sociocultural perspective" mean in health and physical education? In M. Dinan-Thompson (Ed.), *Health and physical education: Issues for curriculum in Australia and New Zealand* (pp. 165-182). Melbourne, Australia: Oxford University Press. http://ro.uow.edu.au/cgi/viewcontent.cgi?article=1097&context=edupapers

Common White Girl [GirlPosts]. (2014, June 11). PE is 5% exercise and 95% embarrassment [Tweet]. https://twitter.com/GirlPosts/status/476770348500021248

Forsberg, N., & Chorney, D. (2014). Physical education: Looking back, looking forward. In D. Robinson & L. Randall (Eds.), *Teaching physical education today: Canadian perspectives* (pp. 2-19). Toronto, ON: Thompson.

Freire, P., & Macedo, D. (1987). *Literacy: Reading the word and the world.* Westport, CT: Bergin & Garvey.

Gard, M. (2008). Producing little decision makers and goal setters in the age of the obesity crisis. *Quest, 60*(4), 488-502.

Halas, J., & Kentel, J. (2008). Giving the body its due: Autobiographical reflections and utopian imaginings. In G. Fenstermacher, R. Colvin, J. Wiens, & D. Coulter (Eds.), *Why do we educate in a democratic society?* (pp. 208-223). Malden, MA: National Society for the Study of Education and Blackwell Press.

Hellison, D. (2011). *Teaching personal and social responsibility through physical activity* (3rd ed.). Champaign, IL: Human Kinetics.

Kickbusch, I. (2006). Mapping the future of public health: Action on global health. *Revue Canadienne de Santé Publique, 97*(1), 6-8. http://journal.cpha.ca/index.php/cjph/article/viewFile/771/771

Lu, C., & McLean, C. (2011). School health education curricula in Canada: A critical analysis. *Physical and Health Education Nexus, 3*(2), 1-20.

Mandigo, J., Francis, N., Lodewyk, K., & Lopez, R. (2009). *Position paper: Physical literacy for educators.* Physical and Health Education Canada. http://69.90.163.107/sites/default/files/files/Archive/PHE%20Canada%20Position%20Paper%20Physical%20Literacy%20For%20Educators.pdf

McDermott, L. (2008). A critical interrogation of contemporary discourses of physical (in)activity amongst Canadian children: Back to the future. *Journal of Canadian Studies, 42*(2), 5-42.

Mental Health Commission of Canada (2013). Making the case for investing in mental health in Canada. www.mentalhealthcommission.ca/sites/default/files/2016-06/Investing_in_Mental_Health_FINAL_Version_ENG.pdf

Nutbeam, D. (2000). Health literacy as a public health goal: A challenge for contemporary health education and communication strategies into the 21st century. *Health Promotion International, 12*(3), 259–267.

Nutbeam, D. (2008). What would the Ottawa Charter look like if it were written today? *Critical Public Health, 18*(4), 435-441.

Partners in Planning for Healthy Living. (2014). *2012-2013 Manitoba youth health survey report.* http://partners.healthincommon.ca/tools-and-resources/youth-health-survey/

Physical and Health Education Canada. (n.d.). *Physical literacy.* www.phecanada.ca/programs/physical-literacy

Popik, B. (2013, September 24). PE doesn't stand for physical education, it stands for public embarrassment [Web log post]. The Big Apple [Web log]. www.barrypopik.com/index.php/new_york_city/entry/pe_doesnt_stand_for_physical_education_it_stands_for_public_embarrassment

Proyer, R.T., & Jehle, N. (2013). The basic components of adult playfulness and their relation with personality: The hierarchical factor structure of seventeen instruments. *Personality and Individual Differences, 55*, 811–816.

Public Health Agency of Canada. (2008). *What is health?* Ottawa, Canada: Public Health Agency of Canada. www.phac-aspc.gc.ca/ph-sp/approach-approche/qa-qr5-eng.php

Quennerstedt, M., Burrows, L., & Maivorsdotter, N. (2010). From teaching young people to be healthy to learning health. *Utbildning & Demokrati, 19*(2), 97-112.

Rail, G. (2009). Canadian youth's discursive constructions of health in the context of obesity discourse. In J. Wright & V. Harwood (Eds.), *Biopolitics and the "obesity epidemic."* New York, NY: Routledge.

Raphael, D. (Ed.). (2016). *Social determinants of health: Canadian perspectives* (3rd ed.). Toronto, ON: Canadian Scholars' Press.

Statistics Canada (2015). Directly measured physical activity of children and youth, 2012 and 2013. Ottawa: Statistics Canada. www.statcan.gc.ca/pub/82-625- x/2015001/article/14136-eng.htm

Tremblay, M., & Lloyd, M. (2010). Physical literacy measurement–The missing piece. *Physical and Health Education Journal, 76*(1), 26-30.

United Nations Educational, Scientific and Cultural Organization. (2004). *The plurality of literacy and its implications for policies and programmes.* http://unesdoc.unesco.org/images/0013/001362/136246e.pdf

United Nations Educational, Scientific and Cultural Organization. (2006). *Understandings of literacy.* www.unesco.org/education/GMR2006/full/chapt6_eng.pdf

Whitehead, M. (2001). The concept of physical literacy. *European Journal of Physical Education, 6*(2), 127-138.

Whitehead, M. (2007). Physical literacy: Philosophical considerations in relation to developing a sense of self, universality, and propositional knowledge. *Sports Ethics and Philosophy, 1*(3), 281-298.

Whitehead, M. (Ed.). (2010). *Physical literacy: Throughout the lifecourse.* New York, NY: Routledge.

World Health Organization. (1946). Preamble to the Constitution of the World Health Organization [Adopted by the International Health Conference, New York, June 19-22, 1946]. *Official Records of the World Health Organization, 2,* 100. www.who.int/about/definition/en/print.html

World Health Organization. (1986). *Ottawa charter for health promotion.* www.phac-aspc.gc.ca/ph-sp/docs/charter-chartre/pdf/charter.pdf

World Health Organization. (1995). *School and youth health: Global school health initiative.* www.who.int/school_youth_health/gshi/en/

Williams, N. (1994). The physical education hall of shame. *Journal of Physical Education, Recreation and Dance, 65*(2), 17-20.

Williams, N. (1996). The physical education hall of shame. *Journal of Physical Education, Recreation and Dance, 67*(8), 45-48.

Young J., Haas, E., & McGown, E. (2010). *Coyote's guide to connecting with nature.* Shelton, WA: Owlink Media.

Chapter 2

Alberta Education. (2008). *Daily physical activity survey report, 2008.* http://education.alberta.ca/media/756341/dpasurveyreport.pdf

Assessment Reform Group. (2002). *Assessment for learning: 10 Principles.* www.qca.org.uk/libraryAssets/media/4031_afl_principles.pdf

Barrett, J.M. (2011). *Teacher candidates' perceptions of the daily physical activity initiative and their emerging self-efficacy as daily physical activity instructors* (Doctoral dissertation). ProQuest Dissertations and Theses database. (UMI No. 3459116)

Barrett, J.M. (2014). *Beyond physical education: School-based physical activity programming.* In D. Robinson & L. Randall (Eds.), *Teaching physical education today* (pp. 274-292). Toronto, ON: Thompson Educational.

Barrett, J.M. (2015). School-based physical activity: Planning with student motivation in mind. *Teaching & Learning, 10*(1), 1-20.

Doolittle, S.P., Dodds, P., & Placek, J. (1993). Persistence of beliefs about teaching during formal training of preservice teachers. *Journal of Teaching in Physical Education, 12,* 355-365.

Earl, L.M., & Katz, M.S. (2006). *Rethinking classroom assessment with purpose in mind: Assessment for learning, assessment as learning, assessment of learning.* Western and Northern Canadian Protocol for Collaboration in Education. www.wncp.ca/english/subjectarea/classassessment.aspx

Gurvitch, R., & Metzler, M.W. (2009). The effects of laboratory-based and field-based practicum experience on pre-service teachers' self-efficacy. *Teaching and Teacher Education, 25,* 437-443.

Hill, G., & Brodin, K.L. (2004). Physical education teachers' perceptions of the adequacy of university coursework in preparation for teaching. *Physical Educator, 61,* 75-87.

Morgan, P. (2008). Teacher perceptions of physical education in the primary school: Attitudes, values, and curriculum preferences. *Physical Educator, 65,* 46-56.

Morgan, P., & Bourke, S. (2005). An investigation of pre-service and primary school teachers' perspectives of PE teaching confidence and PE teacher education. *ACHPER Healthy Lifestyles Journal, 52,* 7-13.

Morgan, P., & Hansen, V. (2008). Physical education in primary schools: Classroom teachers' perceptions of benefits and outcomes. *Health Education Journal, 67,* 196-207.

Ontario Ministry of Education. (2010). *Growing success: Assessment, evaluation, and reporting in Ontario's schools: Covering grades 1 to 12.* Toronto, ON: Author.

Ontario Ministry of Education. (2015). *The Ontario curriculum, grades 1-8: Health and physical education (Revised).* www.edu.gov.on.ca/eng/curriculum/elementary/health1to8.pdf

Whitehead, M. (2013). Definition of physical literacy and clarification of related issues. *ICSSPE Bulletin: Journal of Sport Science and Physical Education, 65,* 1.2.

Whitehead, M. (2016). Physical literacy definition. https://www.physical-literacy.org.uk/

Wiggins, G., & McTighe, J. (1998). *Understanding by design.* Alexandria, VA: Association for Supervision and Curriculum Development.

Wiggins, G., & McTighe, J. (n.d.). Backward design: Why "backward" is best. https://www.edutopia.org/pdfs/resources/wiggins-mctighe-backward-design-why-backward-is-best.pdf

Chapter 3

Barnett, T. A., O'Loughlin, J. L., Gauvin, L., Paradis, G., & Hanley, J. (2006). Opportunities for student physical activity in elementary schools: A cross-sectional survey of frequency and correlates. *Health Education and Behavior, 33*, 215-232.

Barnett, T. A., O'Loughlin, J. L., Gauvin, L., Paradis, G., Hanley, J., McGrath, J., & Boyle, S., Jones, G., & Walters, S. (2008). Physical activity among adolescents and barriers to delivering physical education in Cornwall and Lancashire, UK: a qualitative study of heads of PE and heads of schools. *BMC Public Health, 8*, 273-280.

Haug, E., Torsheim, T., & Samdal, O. (2008). Physical environmental characteristics and individual interests as correlates of physical activity in Norwegian secondary schools: The health behavior in school-aged children study. *International Journal of Behavioral Nutrition and Physical Activity, 5*, 47-56.

Lambert, M. (2009a). School opportunities and physical activity frequency in nine year old children. *International Journal of Public Health, 54*, 1-8.

Leatherdale, S. T., Manske, S. R., Faulkner, G., Arbour, K., & Bredin, C. (2010). A multi-level examination of school programs, policies and resources associated with physical activity among elementary school youth in the PLAY-ON study. *International Journal of Behavior, Nutrition and Physical Activity, 7*, 6-19.

Mahar, M., Murphy, S., Rowe, D., Golden, J., Shields, A., & Raedeke, T. (2006). Effects of a classroom-based program on physical activity and on-task behavior. *Medicine and Science in Sports and Exercise, 38*, 2086-2094.

Ontario Ministry of Education. (2015). *The Ontario curriculum, grades 1-8: Health and physical education (Revised).* www.edu.gov.on.ca/eng/curriculum/elementary/health1to8.pdf

Ontario Physical Education Association Safety Guidelines (2015). Retrieved October 7, 2015 from: http://safety.ophea.net

Chapter 4

Alexander, M., & Schwager, S. (2012). *Meeting the physical education needs of children with ASD.* Champaign, IL: Human Kinetics.

Boardmaker (software). Tobii Dynavox, 2100 Wharton St. Suite 400, Pittsburgh, PA 15203, Phone: 1 (800) 588-4548, Fax: 1 (866) 585-6260, Email: mjq@tobiidynavox.com, Web site: www.mayer-johnson.com.

Government of Ontario. (2009). *Ontario's equity and inclusive education strategy.* www.edu.gov.on.ca/eng/policyfunding/equity.pdf

Kasser, L., & Lytle, R. (2013). *Inclusive physical activity: Promoting health for a lifetime.* Champaign, IL: Human Kinetics.

Manitoba Education. (2010). *Student-specific planning—A handbook for developing and implementing individual education plans (IEPs).* Winnipeg, MB: Author.

Ontario Ministry of Education. (2004). *The individual education plan (IEP)—A resource guide.* www.oafccd.com/documents/IEP2004.pdf

Peel District School Board. (n.d.). *Character attributes in action: An educator's guide to promoting student wellness with physical activity, focused on character development.* www.peelschools.org/aboutus/safeschools/Documents/Character%20Attributes%20in%20Action%20-%20Activity%20Guide.pdf

Peel District School Board. (n.d.). *Special education programs and services.* www.peelschools.org/parents/specialed/Pages/default.aspx

Special Olympics Canada. (2014a). *Active start* (2nd ed.). http://www.specialolympics.ca/learn/special-olympics-programs/active-start

Special Olympics Canada. (2014b). *FUNdamentals: Program leaders guide* (2nd ed.). www.specialolympics.bc.ca/sites/default/files/FUNdamentalsGuide.pdf

Variety Village. (n.d.). About Variety Village. www.varietyvillage.ca/about-us/

Chapter 5

Adams, M., Bell, L., & Griffin, P. (Eds.). (2007). Teaching for diversity and social justice (2nd ed.). New York, NY: Routledge.

Cameron, E., Norman, M., & Petherick, L. (2016). Shifting Stories of Size: Disrupting Weight-Based Oppression in Physical Education through Critical Obesity Scholarship. In C. Ennis, K. Arour, A. Chen, A. Garn, E. Mauerberg-deCastro, D. Penny, S. Silverman, M. Solmon, & R. Tinning, *Routledge Handbook of Physical Education* (pp. 343-355). New York, NY: Routledge.

Cameron, E., Oakley, J., Walton, G., Russell, C., Chambers, L., & Socha, T. (2014). Moving beyond the injustices of the schooled healthy body. In I. Bogotch & C. Shields (Eds.), *International handbook of educational leadership and social (in)justice* (pp. 687-704). New York, NY: Springer.

Cameron, E., & Russell, C. (Eds.). (2016). *The fat pedagogy reader: Challenging weight-based oppression through critical education* (Vol. 467). Peter Lang.

Casey, C., Kentel, J., & Cameron, E. (2014). Diversities in physical education. In D. Robinson & L. Randall. *Teaching Physical Education Today: Canadian Perspectives* (pp. 123-136). Toronto, ON: Thompson Educational.

Campos, P. (2004). *The obesity myth: Why America's obsession with weight is hazardous to your health.* New York, NY: Penguin.

Darder, A., Baltodano, M., & Torres, R. (2009). Critical pedagogy: An introduction. In A. Darder, M. Baltodano, & R. Torres (Eds.), *The critical pedagogy reader* (2nd ed., pp. 1-20). New York, NY: Routledge.

Douglas, D., & Halas, J. (2008). Resistance? What resistance? Identifying racial inequities in faculties of physical education: Challenging the colour of domination. In *Unpublished conference paper)."To remember is to resist* (Vol. 40, pp. 1968-2008).

Fadiman, A. (2012). *The spirit catches you and you fall down: A Hmong child, her American doctors, and the collision of two cultures.* Macmillan.

Flintoff, A., & Scraton, S. (2004). Gender and physical education. In K. Green and K. Hardman (Eds.), *Physical education: Essential issues* (pp. 161-179). Thousand Oaks, CA: SAGE Publications.

Gard, M. (2011). *The end of the obesity epidemic.* London, England: Routledge.

Gard, M., & Wright, J. (2005). *The obesity epidemic.* London, England: Routledge.

Giroux, H. (1997). *Pedagogy and the politics of hope: Theory, culture, and schooling.* Boulder, CO: Westview Press.

Harvey, W. (2014a). Critical approaches to pedagogy. In D. Robinson & L. Randall (Eds.), *Social justice in physical education: Critical reflections and pedagogies for change* (pp. 191-206). Toronto, ON: Canadian Scholars' Press.

Harvey, W. (2014b). Adapted and inclusive physical education. In D. Robinson & L. Randall (Eds.), *Social justice in physical education: Critical reflections and pedagogies for change* (pp.137-152). Toronto, ON: Canadian Scholars' Press.

Harvey, W. (2016). Looking over our shoulders: Disability in physical education from a critical perspective. In D. Robinson & L. Randall (Eds.), *Social justice in physical education: Critical reflections and pedagogies for change* (pp. 122-138). Toronto, ON: Canadian Scholars' Press.

Kozub, F.M., Sherblom, P.R., & Perry, T.L. (1999). Inclusion paradigms and perspectives: A stepping stone to accepting learner diversity in physical education. *Quest, 51*(4), 346-354.

Kumashiro, K. (2009). *Against common sense: Teaching and learning toward social justice.* New York, NY: Routledge.

Meyer, D. K., & Turner, J. C. (2002). Discovering emotion in classroom motivation research. *Educational psychologist, 37*(2), 107-114.

Nieto, S., & Bode, P. (2012). *Affirming diversity: The sociopolitical context of multicultural education* (6th ed.). Boston, MA: Pearson Education.

Palmer, P.J. (2010). *The courage to teach: Exploring the inner landscape of a teacher's life.* New York, NY: Wiley.

Penney, D. (Ed.). (2002). *Gender and physical education: Contemporary issues and future directions.* Routledge.

Robinson, D., & Randall, L. (Eds.). (2016). *Social justice in physical education: Critical reflections and pedagogies for change.* Toronto, ON: Canadian Scholars' Press.

Sensoy, O., & DiAngelo, R. (2012). *Is everyone really equal? An introduction to key concepts in social justice education.* New York, NY: Teachers College Press.

Singleton, E., & Varpalotai, A. (Eds.). (2006). *Stones in the sneaker: Active theory for secondary school physical and health educators.* London, ON: Althouse Press.

Sykes, H. (2011). *Queer Bodies: Sexualities, Genders, and Fatness in Physical Education.* New York, NY: Peter Lang.

Tinning, R., Philpot, R., & Cameron, E. (2016). Critical pedagogy, physical education, and obesity discourse: More advocacy than pedagogy. In D. Robinson & L. Randall (Eds.), *Social justice in physical education: Critical reflections and pedagogies for change* (pp. 297-321). Toronto, ON: Canadian Scholars' Press.

Chapter 6

Battiste, M., & Youngblood Henderson, J. (2000). Ethical issues in research. In M. Battiste & J. Youngblood Henderson (Eds.), *Protecting indigenous knowledge and heritage: A global challenge* (pp. 132-144). Saskatoon, SK: Purich Press.

Brant Castellano, M. (2000). Updating Aboriginal traditions of knowledge. In G. Dei, B. Hall, & D. Rosenberg (Eds.), *Indigenous knowledges in global contexts: Multiple readings of our world* (pp. 21-36). Toronto, ON: University of Toronto Press.

Coalition for the Advancement of Aboriginal Studies (CAAS). (2002). *Learning about walking in beauty: Placing Aboriginal perspectives in Canadian classrooms.* Toronto, ON: Canadian Race Relations Foundation.

Halas, J. (2014). R. Tait McKenzie Scholar's Address: Physical and health education as a transformative pathway to truth and reconciliation with Aboriginal peoples. *Physical and Health Education Journal, 79*(3), 41-49.

Hall, M.A. (2013). Toward a history of Aboriginal women in Canadian sport. In J. Forsyth & Audrey Giles (Eds.), *Aboriginal peoples and sport in Canada: Historical foundations and contemporary issues* (pps. 64-94). Vancouver, BC: University of British Columbia Press.

Hampton, E. (1995). Towards a redefinition of Indian education. In M. Battiste & J. Barman (Eds.), *First Nations education in Canada: The circle unfolds* (pp. 5-46). Vancouver, BC: University of British Columbia Press.

Hart, M.A. (2002). *Seeking Mino-Pimatisiwin: An Aboriginal approach to helping.* Halifax, NS: Fernwood.

Heine, M. (2013). Performance indicators: Aboriginal games at the Arctic Winter Games. In J. Forsyth & Audrey Giles (Eds.), *Aboriginal peoples and sport in Canada: Historical foundations and contemporary issues* (pp. 160-181). Vancouver, BC: University of British Columbia Press.

Kalyn, B., Cameron, E., Arcand, Y., & Baker, J. (2013). Indigenous knowledge and physical education. In D. Robinson & L. Randall (Eds.), *Teaching physical education today: Canadian perspectives* (pp. 153-176). Toronto, ON: Thompson Educational.

King, T. (2012). Q&A: Thomas King [Television series episode]. In *8th Fire*. Toronto, ON: CBC. www.cbc.ca/8thfire/2012/02/thomas-king.html

Lane, P., Bopp, J., Bopp, M., & Brown, L. (2003). *The sacred tree: Reflections on Native American spirituality.* Lethbridge, AB: Four World International Institute for Human and Community Development.

Manitoba First Nations Education Resource Centre. (2008). *First Nations Teachings and Practices.* Winnipeg, MB: Author.

Robinson, D., Barrett, J., & Robinson, I. (2016). Culturally relevant physical education: Educative conversations with Mi'kmaw elders and community members. *In education, 22*(1).

Thomas, R.A. (2005). Honouring the oral traditions of my ancestors through storytelling. In L. Brown & S. Strega (Eds.), *Research as resistance: Critical, indigenous, and anti-oppressive approaches* (pp. 237-254). Toronto, ON: Canada Scholars' Press.

University of Manitoba. (n.d.). *Acknowledgement.* http://umanitoba.ca/admin/president/acknowledgement.html

Chapter 7

Alberta Education. (2002). Health and Life Skills K – Grade 9 (2002): Program rationale and philosophy. www.learnalberta.ca/ProgramOfStudy.aspx?lang=en&ProgramId=317413#355116

Barrett, J.M. (2015). School-based physical activity: Planning with student motivation in mind. *Teaching and Learning, 10*, 1-20.

Barrett, J.M., Robinson, D.B., & Ecclestone, K. (2016). Group experiences in health and physical education: Selection considerations for teaching practice. *Physical and Health Education Journal, 82*, 1-8.

British Columbia Ministry of Education. (2016, June 29). *Physical and health education: Goals and rationale.* https://curriculum.gov.bc.ca/curriculum/physical-health-education

Canadian Council on Learning. (2008*). Health literacy in Canada: A healthy understanding.* Ottawa, ON: Canadian Council on Learning. https://mips.ca/assets/healthliteracyreportfeb2008e.pdf

Canadian Mental Health Association, Alberta Division. (2011). *Mental health info: Statistics.* www.cmha.ab.ca/bins/ site_page.asp?cid=284-285-1258-1404&lang=1#6

Department of Education and Early Childhood Development of New Brunswick. (2016). *Personal wellness: Grades 3-5.* http://www2.gnb.ca/content/dam/gnb/Departments/ed/pdf/K12/curric/Health-PhysicalEducation/Personal-Wellness3-5.pdf

Kabat-Zinn, J. (2003). Mindfulness-based interventions in context: Past, present, and future. *Clinical Psychology: Science and Practice, 10*(2), 144–156.

Kilgour, L., Matthews, N., Christian, P., & Shire, J. (2015). Health literacy in schools: Prioritising health and well-being issues through the curriculum. *Sport, Education and Society, 20*(4), 485-500.

Lu, C. (2012). Integrating mindfulness into school physical activity programming. *Teaching and learning, 7*(1), 37-46.

Lu, C., & McLean, C. (2011). Health education curricula in Canada: A critical analysis. *Physical and Health Education Nexus, 3*(2), 1-20.

Lu, C., Tito, J., & Kentel, J. (2009). Eastern movement disciplines (EMDs) and mindfulness: A new path to subjective knowledge in Western physical education. *Quest, 61*(3), 353-370.

Manitoba Education and Training. (n.d.). Physical education/health education: Manitoba PE/HE curriculum overview. www.edu.gov.mb.ca/k12/cur/physhlth/c_overview.html

Maynard, B., Solis, M., Miller, V., & Brendel, K. (2017). Mindfulness-based interventions for improving cognition, academic achievement, behavior, and socioemotional functioning of primary and secondary school students. *Campbell Systematic Review 2017:5.* http://files.eric.ed.gov/fulltext/ED573474.pdf

Mitic, W., & Rootman, I. (2012). *An inter-sectoral approach for improving health literacy for Canadians: A discussion paper.* http://phabc.org/wp-content/uploads/2015/09/IntersectoralApproachforHealthLiteracy-FINAL.pdf

Newfoundland and Labrador Department of Education and Early Childhood Development. (2015). *Health 3: Curriculum guide 2015.* www.ed.gov.nl.ca/edu/k12/curriculum/guides/health/grade3/gr-3_health_curriculum_guide_2015.pdf

Northwest Territories Department of Education, Culture and Employment and Department of Health and Social Services. (1995, August). *Northwest Territories School Health Program: Grade three.* https://www.ece.gov.nt.ca/sites/www.ece.gov.nt.ca/files/resources/health_studies._grade_3.pdf

Nova Scotia Department of Education and Early Childhood Development. (2013). *Public school programs: 2013-2014.* https://www.ednet.ns.ca/files/curriculum/PSP2013-2014-Draft-Oct16-13.pdf

Nunavut Department of Education. (2016, September). *2016-2017 Nunavut approved curriculum and teaching resources.* https://www.gov.nu.ca/sites/default/files/introduction_3.pdf

Ontario Ministry of Education. (2014). *A parent's guide: Human development and sexual health in the health and physical education curriculum—Grades 1-6.* www.edu.gov.on.ca/eng/curriculum/elementary/HPEgrades1to6.pdf

Ontario Ministry of Education. (2015). *The Ontario curriculum grades 1-8: Health and physical education.* http://edu.gov.on.ca/eng/curriculum/elementary/health1to8.pdf

Ontario Ministry of Education. (n.d.). Promoting well-being in Ontario's education system. www.edu.gov.on.ca/eng/about/wellbeing2.html

Ontario Physical and Health Education Association (Ophea). (2010). Building health and physical literacy for schools and communities across Ontario. *Physical and Health Education Journal, 76*(2), 28-31.

Peirson, L., Fitzpatrick-Lewis, D., Morrison, K., Ciliska, D., Kenny. M., Usman Ali, M., &

People for Education. (2011). *Health and physical education.* www.peopleforeducation.ca/wp-content/uploads/2011/07/Health-and-Physical-Education-in-Schools-2011.pdf

Prince Edward Island Department of Education. (2007). *Prince Edward Island health curriculum: Grade 8.* https://www.princeedwardisland.ca/sites/default/files/publications/eelc_health_8.pdf

Public Health Agency of Canada. (n.d.). *What is health literacy?* www.phac-aspc.gc.ca/cd-mc/hl-ls/index-eng.php#tabs-2

Quebec Ministry of Education, Recreation and Sport. (2009). *Progression of learning: Physical education and health.* www1.education.gouv.qc.ca/progressionPrimaire/educationPhysique/pdf/edPhy_en_sectionCom.pdf

Rootman, I., & Gordon-El-Bihbety, D. (2008). *A vision for a health literate Canada: Report of the expert panel on health literacy.* Ottawa, ON: Canadian Public Health Association. http://citeseerx.ist.psu.edu/viewdoc/download?doi=10.1.1.541.7778&rep=rep1&type=pdf

Saskatchewan Ministry of Education. (n.d.). Aims & goals. https://sps.blackboard.com/webapps/moe-old_curriculum-BBLEARN/aimsgoals?view=goals&lang=en&subj=health_education&level=k

Statistics Canada. (2017). *Table 477-0025: Number of students in regular programs for youth, public elementary and secondary schools, by grade and sex, Canada, provinces and territories.* Retrieved from http://www5.statcan.gc.ca/cansim/a26?lang=eng&retrLang=eng&id=4770025&pattern=477-0025..477-0028&csid=

Yukon Education. (2017, December 13). *Curriculum.* www.education.gov.yk.ca/curriculum.html

Chapter 8

Anda, R.F., Butchart, A., Felitti, V., & Brown, D.W. (2010). Building a framework for global surveillance of the public health implications of adverse childhood experiences. *American Journal of Preventative Medicine, 39*(1), 93-98.

Canadian Alliance for Mental Illness and Mental Health. (2008, July). *National integrated framework for enhancing mental health literacy in Canada.* www.mooddisorderscanada.ca/documents/Publications/CAMIMH%20National%20Integrated%20Framework%20for%20Mental%20Health%20Literacy.pdf

Harvard Center on the Developing Child. (n.d.). *Toxic stress.* https://developingchild.harvard.edu/science/key-concepts/toxic-stress/

Keyes, C.L.M. (2002). The mental health continuum: From languishing to flourishing in life. *Journal of Health and Social Behavior, 43*, 207-222.

Kirby, M. (2013). Foreward. In A.W. Leschied (Ed.), *Everybody's children: Proceedings from the Western University Forum on School Based Mental Health* (pp. ii-iv). London, ON: Althouse Press.

Polanczyk, G.V., Salum, G.A., Sugaya, L.S., Caye, A., & Rohde, L.A. (2015). Annual research review: A meta-analysis of the worldwide prevalence of mental disorders in children and adolescents. *Journal of Child Psychology and Psychiatry, 56*(3), 345-65. doi:10.1111/jcpp.12381

Resnick, M.D., et al (1997). Protecting adolescents from harm: Findings from the National Longitudinal Study on Adolescent Health. *Journal of the American Medical Association, 278* (10), 823-832. doi:10.1001/jama.1997.03550100049038

Ungar, M. (2011). The social ecology of resilience: Addressing contextual and cultural ambiguity of a nascent construct. *American Journal of Orthopsychiatry, 81*, 1-17.

Waddell C., McEwan K., Shepherd C. A., Offord D. R., Hua J. M. (2005). A public health strategy to improve the mental health of Canadian children. Canadian Journal of Psychiatry, 50, 226-23.

World Health Organization. (2014, August). Mental health: A state of well-being. www.who.int/features/factfiles/mental_health/en/

Chapter 9

Ahmed, C. (2005). Bridging the gap between community health and K-12 schools. *International Quarterly of Community Health Education, 24*(2), 161-166.

Association for Supervision and Curriculum Development (ASCD). (2014). *Whole school, whole community, whole child: A collaborative approach to learning and health.* Alexandria, VA: Author. www.cdc.gov/healthyschools/wscc/wsccmodel_update_508tagged.pdf

Aston, J., Shi, E., Bullot, H., Galway, R., & Crisp, J. (2005). Qualitative evaluation of regular morning meetings aimed at improving interdisciplinary communication and patient outcomes. *International Journal of Nursing Practice, 11*, 206-213.

Butterfoss, F.D., Goodman, R.M., & Wandersman, A. (1993). Community coalitions for prevention and health promotion. *Health Education Research, 8*(3), 315-330.

Christian, D., Todd, C., Davies, H., Rance, J., Stratton, G., Rapport, F., & Brophy, S. (2015). Community led active schools programme (CLASP) exploring the implementation of health interventions in primary schools: Headteachers' perspectives. *BMC Public Health, 15*, 238.

Commission on the Social Determinants of Health. (2008). *Closing the gap in a generation: Health equity through action on the social determinants of health. Final report of the Commission on Social Determinants of Health.* Geneva, Switzerland: World Health Organization. http://whqlibdoc.who.int/publications/2008/9789241563703_eng.pdf

Corbin, J.H., & Mittelmark, M.B. (2008). Partnership lessons from the Global Programme on Health Promotion Effectiveness: A case study. *Health Promotion International, 23*(4), 365-371.

Coulter, K.S., & Coulter, R.A. (2003). The effects of industry knowledge on the development of trust in service relationships. *International Journal of Research in Marketing, 20*, 31-43.

Cuddapah, J.L., & Clayton, C.D. (2011). Using Wenger's communities of practice to explore a new teacher cohort. *Journal of Teacher Education, 62*(1), 62-75. doi:10.1177/0022487110377507

Davidson, A., Schwartz, S.E.O., & Noam, G.G. (2008, Winter). Creating youth leaders: Community supports. *New Directions for Youth Development, 120*, 127-37.

DeWitt, N., Lohrmann, K., O'Neill, J., & Clark, J. (2011). A qualitative analysis of success stories from Michiana Coordinated School Health Leadership Institute participants. *Journal of School Health, 81*(12), 727-732.

Emerson, K., Nabatchi, T., & Balogh, S. (2012). An integrative framework for collaborative governance. *Journal of Public Administration Research and Theory, 22*(1), 1-29.

Firth, N., Butler, H., Drew, S., Krelle, A., Sheffield, J., Patton, G., . . . the beyondblue project management team. (2008). Implementing multi-level programmes and approaches that address student well-being and connected-ness: Factoring in the needs of the schools. *Advances in School Mental Health Promotion, 1*(4), 14-24.

Flaschberger, E., Nitsch, M., & Waldherr, K. (2012). Implementing school health promotion in Austria: Experiences from a pilot training course. *Health Promotion Practice, 13*(3), 364-369.

Flook, L., Smalley, S.L., Kitil, J., Galla, B. M., Kaiser-Greenland, S., Locke, J., . . . Kasari, C. (2010). Effects of mindful awareness practices on executive functions in elementary school children. *Journal of Applied School Psychology, 26*(1), 70-95.

Freire, P. (1990). *Pedagogy of the oppressed.* New York, NY: Continuum Press.

Furnée, C.A., Groot, W., & Maassen van den Brink, H. (2008). The health effects of education: A meta-analysis. *European Journal of Public Health, 18*(4), 417-421.

Hawn Foundation. (2011a). *The MindUP curriculum, grades pre-K-2.* New York, NY: Scholastic.

Hawn Foundation. (2011b). *The MindUP curriculum, grades 3-5.* New York, NY: Scholastic.

Haydicki, J., Wiener, J., Badali, P., Milligan, K., & Ducha-rme, J.M. (2012). Evaluation of a mindfulness-based intervention for adolsecents with learning disabilities and co-occurring ADHD and anxiety. *Mindfulness, 3*, 151-164.

Inchley, J., Muldoon, J., & Currie, C. (2006). Becoming a health-promoting school: Evaluating the process of effective implementation in Scotland. *Health Promotion International, 22*(1), 65-71.

Jack, S.L. (2005). The role, use, and activation of strong and weak network ties: A qualitative analysis. *Journal of Management Studies, 42*(6), 1233-1259.

Jennings, P.A., Snowberg, K.E., Coccia, M.A., & Greenberg, M.T. (2011). Improving classroom learning environments by cultivating awareness and resilience in education (CARE): Results of two pilot studies. *Journal of Classroom Interaction, 46*(1), 37-48.

Kabat-Zinn, J. (2003). Mindfulness-based interventions in context: Past, present, and future. *Clinical Psychology: Science and Practice, 10*(2), 144-156.

Kaiser Greenland, S. (2010). *The mindful child: How to help your kid manage stress and become happier, kinder, and more compassionate.* New York, NY: Free Press.

Lloyd, R., Whitley, J., & Olsen, S. (2013, Summer). Promoting "Comprehensive school health" in teacher education: From consumers of knowledge to champions of health. *CAP Journal: The Canadian Resource for School Based Leadership*, pp. 14-20.

Lloyd, R.J., Garcia Bengoechea, E., & Smith, S.J. (2010). Theories of learning. In R. Bailey (Ed.), *Physical education for learning: A guide for secondary schools* (pp.187-196). London, UK: Continuum.

Maras, M.A., Weston, K.J., Blacksmith, J., & Brophy, C. (2015). Examining statewide capacity for school health and mental health promotion: A post hoc application of a district capacity-building framework. *Health Promotion Practice, 16*(2), 176-183.

Nyaradi, A., Foster, J.K., Hickling, S., Li, J., Ambrosini, G.L., Jacques, A., & Oddy, W.H. (2014). Prospective associations between dietary patterns and cognitive performance during adolescence. *Journal of Child Psychology and Psychiatry, 55*(9), 1017-1024.

Nyaradi, A., Li, J., Hickling, S., Foster, J., & Oddy, W.H. (2013). The role of nutrition in children's neurocognitive development, from pregnancy through childhood. *Frontiers in Human Neuroscience, 7*, 97.

Ontario Ministry of Education. (2010, October 4). *Policy/program memorandum no. 150.* ww.edu.gov.on.ca/extra/eng/ppm/ppm150.pdf

Ontario Ministry of Health Promotion. (2010, May). *School health guidance document.*www.health.gov.on.ca/en/pro/programs/publichealth/oph_standards/docs/guidance/schoolhealth_gr.pdf

Pan-Canadian Joint Consortium for School Health. (2016). *Mandate, mission, and vision.* www.jcsh-cces.ca/index.php/about/mandate-mission-vision

Pan-Canadian Joint Consortium for School Health. (n.d.). *What is a "comprehensive school health approach?"* www.jcsh-cces.ca/index.php/about/comprehensive-school-health/what-is-csh

Poulin, P.A., Mackenzie, C.S., Soloway, G., & Karayolas, E. (2008). Mindfulness training as an evidenced-based approach to reducing stress and promoting well-being among human services professionals. *Journal of Health Promotion and Education, 46*, 35-43.

Rothwell, H., Shepherd, M., Murphy, S., Burgess, S., Townsend, N., & Pimm, C. (2010). Implementing a social-ecological model of health in Wales. *Health Education, 110*(6), 471-489.

Senior, E. (2012). Becoming a health promoting school: Key components of planning. *Global Health Promotion, 19*(1), 23-31, 77, 91.

Staten, L.K., Teufel-Shone, N.I., Steinfelt, V.E., Ortega, N., Halverson, K., Flores, C., & Lebowitz, M.D. (2005). The school health index as an impetus for change. *Preventing Chronic Disease, 2*(1), A19.

Stewart, D. (2008). Implementing mental health promotion in schools: A process evaluation. *International Journal of Mental Health Promotion, 10*(1), 32-41.

Stolp, S., Wilkins, W., & Raine, K.D. (2015). Developing and sustaining a healthy school community: Essential elements identified by school health champions. *Health Education Journal, 74*(3), 299-311.

Thomas, M., Rowe, F., & Harris, N. (2010). Understanding the factors that characterise school-community partnerships. the case of the Logan Healthy Schools Project. *Health Education, 110*(6), 427-444.

Vassiloudis, I., Yiannakouris, N., Panagiotakos, D.B., Apostolopoulos, K., & Costarelli, V. (2014). Academic performance in relation to adherence to the Mediterranean diet and energy balance behaviors in Greek primary school-children. *Journal of Nutrition Education and Behavior, 46*(3), 164-170.

Viig, N.G., & Wold, B. (2005). Facilitating teachers' participation in school-based health promotion: A qualitative study. *Scandinavian Journal of Educational Research, 49*(1), 83-109.

Warwick, I., Aggleton, P., Chase, E., Schagen, S., Blenkinsop, S., Schagen, I., . . . Eggers, M. (2005). Evaluating healthy schools: Perceptions of impact among school-based respondents. *Health Education Research, 20*(6), 697-708.

Wenger, E. (1998). *Communities of practice: Learning, meaning, and identity.* Cambridge, UK: Cambridge University Press.

World Health Organization. (2003). Preamble to the Constitution of the World Health Organization [Adopted by the International Health Conference, New York, June 19-22, 1946]. *Official Records of the World Health Organization, 2*, 100. www.who.int/about/definition/en/print.html

World Health Organization. (2016). *The Ottawa Charter for Health Promotion.* www.who.int/healthpromotion/conferences/previous/ottawa/en/

World Health Organization. (n.d.). *School and youth health: WHO information series on school health.*www.who.int/school_youth_health/resources/information_series/en/

Chapter 10

CIRA Ontario. (1998). *Great gator games.* Ancaster, ON: Author.

Glover, D., & Anderson, L. (2003). *Character education: 43 fitness activities for community building.* Champaign, IL: Human Kinetics.

Midura, D., & Glover, D. (2005). *Essentials of team building: Principles and practices.* Windsor, ON: Human Kinetics

Chapter 11

Barnett, L., van Beurden, E., Morgan, P., Brooks, L, & Beard, J. (2010). Gender differences in motor skill proficiency from childhood to adolescence: A longitudinal study. *Research Quarterly for Exercise and Sport, 81*(2), 162-170.

Clark, J.E. (2007). *On the problem of motor skill development.* Speech delivered at the AAHPERD convention, Baltimore, MD.

Cleland Donnelly, F., Meuller, S., & Gallahue, D. (2017). *Developmental physical education for all children (5th ed.).* Champaign, IL: Human Kinetics.

Gallahue, D., Ozmun, J., & Goodway, J. (2012). *Understanding motor development: Infants, children, adolescents, adults* (7th ed.). New York, NY: McGraw-Hill.

Graham, G., Holt/Hale, S., & Parker, M. (2013). *Children moving: A reflective approach to teaching elementary physical education (9th ed.).* New York, NY: McGraw-Hill.

Haywood, K.M., & Getchell, N. (2011). *Life span motor development (5th ed.).* Champaign, IL: Human Kinetics.

Laban, R. (1948). *Modern educational dance.* London, UK: MacDonald & Evans.

Langston, T. (2007). Applying Laban's movement framework in elementary physical education. *Journal of Physical Education, Recreation & Dance, 78*(1), 17-24.

Logsdon, B., Barrett, K., Ammons, M., Broer, M., Halverson, L., McGee, R., & Robertson, M. (1984). Physical education for children: A focus on the teaching process. Philadelphia: Lea & Febiger.

PHE Canada (2011). *Fundamental movement skills, the building blocks for the development of physical literacy: An educator's guide to teaching fundamental movement skills.* Ottawa, ON: Physical and Health Education Canada.

Rovegno, I., & Bandhauer, D. (2013). *Elementary physical education: Curriculum and instruction.* Burlington, MA: Jones & Bartlett Learning.

SHAPE America. (2013) *National standards and grade-level outcomes for K-12 physical education.* Reston, VA: Author.

Stanley, S. (1977). *Physical education: A movement orientation* (2nd ed.). New York, NY: McGraw-Hill.

Stodden, D., Langendorfer, S., & Roberton, M. (2009). The association between motor skill competence and physical fitness in young adults. *Research Quarterly for Exercise and Sport, 80*(2), 223-229.

Wickstrom, R.L. (1983). *Fundamental motor patterns (3rd ed.).* Philadelphia, PA: Lea & Febiger.

Chapter 12

Allison, S., & Thorpe, R. (1997). A comparison of the effectiveness of two approaches to teaching games within physical education. A skills approach versus a games for understanding approach. *British Journal of Physical Education, 28*(3), 9-13.

Bright, G.W., Harvey, J.G., & Wheeler, M.M. (1979). Using games to retrain skills with basic multiplication facts. *Journal for Research in Mathematics Education, 10*, 103-110.

Bunker, D., & Thorpe, R. (1982). A model for the teaching of games in secondary schools. *Bulletin of Physical Education, 18*(1), 5-8.

Butler, J. (2014). TGfU—Would you know it if you saw it? Benchmarks from the tacit knowledge of the founders. *European Physical Education Review, 20*(4), 465-488.

Casey, A., & Hastie, P.A. (2011). Students and teacher responses to a unit of student-designed games. *Physical Education and Sport Pedagogy, 16*(3), 295–312.

Casey, A., Hastie, P.A., & Rovegno, I. (2011). Student learning during a unit of student-designed games. *Physical Education and Sport Pedagogy, 16*(4), 331-350.

Covey, S.R. (1998). *The 7 habits of highly effective people.* Provo, UT: Franklin Covey.

Deutsch, M. (1949). An experimental study of the effects of cooperation and competition upon group process. *Human Relations, 2*, 199-231.

Ellington, H., Gordon, M., & Fowlie, J. (1998). Using games & simulations in the classroom. London, UK: Kogan Page.

Griffin, L., & Butler, J. (Eds.). (2005). *Teaching games for understanding: Theory, research, and practice.* Champaign, IL: Human Kinetics.

Griffin, L., Mitchell, S., & Oslin, J. (1997). *Teaching sport concepts and skills.* Champaign, IL: Human Kinetics.

Henninger, M., & Coleman, M. (2008). Student success in physical education: Still busy, happy, and good? Poster presented at the annual convention of the American Alliance of Health, Physical Education, Recreation and Dance, Fort Worth, TX.

Hubball, H., Lambert, J., & Hayes, S. (2007). Theory to practice: Using the games for understanding approach in the teaching of invasion games. *Physical and Health Education Journal, 73*(3), 14-20.

Johnson, D., & Johnson, F. (2013). *Joining together: Group theory and group skills* (11th ed.). Boston, MA: Allyn & Bacon.

Johnson, D.W., Maruyama, G., Johnson, R., Nelson, C., & Skon, L. (1981). The effects of cooperative, competitive, and individualistic goal structures on achievement: A meta-analysis. *Psychological Bulletin, 89*, 47-62.

Launder, A. (2001). *Play practice: The games approach to teaching and coaching sport.* Champaign, IL: Human Kinetics.

Mackay, R.F. (2013) *Playing to learn: Panelists at Stanford discussion say using games as an educational tool provides opportunities for deeper learning* [Press release]. http://news.stanford.edu/news/2013/march/games-education-tool-030113.html

Mandigo, J., Butler, J., & Hopper, T. (2007). What is teaching games for understanding? A Canadian perspective. *Physical and Health Education Journal, 73*(2), 14-20.

Mandigo, J.L., & Holt, N.L. (2000). Putting theory into practice: How cognitive evaluation theory can help us motivate children in physical activity environments. *Journal of Physical Education, Recreation & Dance, 71*(1), 44-49.

Mandigo, J.L., & Holt, N.L. (2004). Reading the game: Introducing the notion of games literacy. *Physical and Health Education Journal, 70*(3), 4-10.

Marsh, H.W., & Peart, N. (1988). Competitive and cooperative physical fitness training programs for girls: Effects on physical fitness and on multidimensional self-concepts. *Journal of Sport and Exercise Psychology, 10*, 390-407.

McTighe, J., & Wiggins, G.P. (1999). *Understanding by design handbook.* Alexandria, VA: Association for Supervision and Curriculum Development.

Mitchell, S.A., & Oslin, J.L. (1999). An investigation of tactical transfer in net games. *European Journal of Physical Education, 4*(2), 162-172.

Muzurura, O. (2012). *Game based learning in primary education: Instance of English language spellings dictation.* Saarbrücken, SL, Germany: Lambert Academic.

Pill, S. (2012). Teaching game sense in soccer. *Journal of Physical Education, Recreation & Dance, 83*(3), 42-52.

Placek, J. (1983). Conceptions of success in teaching: Busy, happy, and good? In T. Templin & J. Olson (Eds.), *Teaching in physical education* (pp. 46-56). Champaign, IL: Human Kinetics.

Rink, J.E., French, K., & Tjeerdsma, B. (1996). Foundations for the learning and instruction of sport and games. *Journal of Teaching in Physical Education, 15*, 399-417.

Sleet, D.A. (1985). Application of a gaming strategy to improve nutrition education. *Simulation & Gaming, 16*(1), 63-70.

Stolz, S., & Pill, S. (2014). Teaching games and sport for understanding: Exploring and reconsidering its relevance in physical education. *European Physical Education Review, 20*, 36-71.

Tallir, I., Philippaerts, R., Valcke, M., Musch, E., & Lenoir, M. (2012). Learning opportunities in 3 on 3 versus 5 on 5 basketball game play: An application of nonlinear pedagogy. *International Journal of Sport Psychology, 43*, 420-437.

Whelan, M. (2011). *Effect of altering the number of players, the dimensions of the playing area and the playing rules on the number of selected technical skills performed, possession characteristics, physiological responses and levels of enjoyment and perceived competence during Gaelic football in prepubescent and adolescent boys.* Dublin, Ireland: Dublin City University Press.

Whitton, N., & Moseley, A. (2012). *Using games to enhance learning and teaching: A beginner's guide.* New York, NY: Routledge.

Yolageldili, G., & Arikan, A. (2011). Effectiveness of using games in teaching grammar to young learners. *Elementary Education Online, 10*(1), 219-229.

Chapter 13

Abels, K. & Bridges, J. (2010). *Teaching movement education.* Champaign, IL: Human Kinetics.

Balyi, I., Way, R., & Higgs, C. (2013). *Long-term athlete development.* Champaign, IL: Human Kinetics.

Chek, P. (2000). *Movement that matters.* Encinitas, CA: Chek Institute.

Dawes, J., & Mooney, C. (2006). *101 conditioning games and drills for athletes.* Monterey, CA: Coaches Choice.

Fahey, T., Insel, P., Roth, W., & Wong, I. (2013). *Fit and well: Core concepts and labs in physical fitness and wellness* (3rd Canadian ed.). Whitby, ON: McGraw-Hill Ryerson.

Howie, E., & Pate, R. (2012). Physical activity and academic achievement in children: A historical perspective. *Journal of Sport and Health Science, 1*(3), 160-169.

Johnston, K. (2013). *Skillfit: A blueprint for building physical skills youth ed.* San Bernardino, CA: CreateSpace.

Kemerly, T. (2011). *Acting like an animal: Playful strengthening and stretching activities for kid people.* Monterey, CA: Healthy Learning.

Lancaster, S., & Teodorescu, R. (2008). *Athletic fitness for kids*. Champaign, IL: Human Kinetics.

Physical and Health Education Canada (2011). *Fundamental movement skills: The building blocks for the development of physical literacy*. Ottawa, ON: Author.

Ratey, J., & Hagerman, E. (2008). *Spark: The revolutionary new science of exercise and the brain*. New York, NY: Little, Brown.

Spalding, A., & Kelly, L. (2010). *Fitness on the ball: A Core program for brain and body*. Champaign, IL: Human Kinetics.

Spicer, K. (2010a). *Functional fitness series: Elementary school level*. Victoria, BC: First Choice Books.

Spicer, K. (2010b). *Functional fitness series: Middle school level*. Victoria, BC: First Choice Books.

Statistics Canada. (2012). Overweight and Obesity in Children and Adolescents: Results from 2009-2011 Canadian Health Measures Survey. Health Reports: Vol 23(3). Statistics Canada.

Tremblay, M. (2012). Major initiatives related to childhood obesity and physical inactivity in Canada: The year in review. *Canadian Journal of Public Health, 103*(3), 164-169.

Whitehead, M. (2010). *Physical literacy throughout the life course*. New York, NY: Routledge.

Chapter 14

Butler, J. (2016). *Playing fair. Using student-invented games to prevent bullying, teach democracy, and promote social justice*. Champaign, IL: Human Kinetics.

Butler, J., & Griffin, L. (2010). *More teaching games for understanding: Moving globally*. Champaign, IL: Human Kinetics.

Griffin, L., & Butler, J. (2005). *Teaching games for understanding: Theory, research, and practice*. Champaign, IL: Human Kinetics.

Hastie, P. (2010). *Student-designed games: Strategies for promoting creativity, cooperation, and skill development*. Champaign, IL: Human Kinetics.

ParticiPACTION. (2016). *Results from the 2016 report card*. https://www.participaction.com/sites/default/files/downloads/2016%20ParticipACTION%20Report%20Card%20-%20Presentation.pdf

Chapter 15

Canadian Mental Health Association, Alberta Division. (2011). *Mental health info: Statistics*. www.cmha.ab.ca/bins/ site_page.asp?cid=284-285-1258-1404&lang=1#6

Creative Commons Licencing. (2016). *Interconnectedness*. http://firstnations pedagogy.ca/interconnect.html

Devis-Devis, J., & Sparkes, A. (1999). Burning the book: A biographical study of a pedagogically inspired identity crisis in physical education. *European Physical Education Review, 5*(2), 135-152.

Dyson, B. (2006). Students' perspectives of physical education. In D. Kirk, D. Macdonald, and M. O'Sullivan (Eds.), *The handbook of physical education* (pp. 326-346). Thousand Oaks, CA: Sage.

Gibbons, S., Wharf-Higgins, J., Gaul, C., & VanGyn, G. (1999). Listening to female students in high school physical education. *Avante, 5*(2), 1-20.

Grumet, M. (1980). Autobiography and reconceptualization. In W. Pinar (Ed.), *Contemporary curriculum discourses: Twenty years of JCT* (pp. 24-29). New York NY: Lang.

Hardman, K., & Marshall, J. (2000). The state and status of physical education in schools in the international context. *European Physical Education Review, 6*(3), 203-229.

Hart, M. (2008). Critical reflections on an Aboriginal approach to helping. In M. Gray, J. Coates, & M. Yellow Bird (Eds.), *Indigenous social work around the world: Towards culturally relevant education and practice* (pp. 59-70). Burlington, VT: Ashgate.

Health. (n.d.). *Online etymology dictionary*. www.etymonline com/index.php?search=health&searchmode=none

Hettler, B. (2015). *The six dimensions of wellness*. National Wellness Institute. www.national wellness.org/?page=Six_Dimensions

Humbert, L. (2006). Listening for a change: Understanding the experiences of students in physical education. In E. Singleton and A. Varpalotai (Eds.), *Stones in the sneaker: Active theory for secondary school physical and health educators* (pp. 155-181). London, ON: Althouse Press.

Kabat-Zinn, J. (1994). *Wherever you go, there you are*. New York, NY: Hyperion.

Kilborn, M. (2014). *(Re)conceptualizing curriculum in (physical) education: Focused on wellness and guided by wisdom* (Unpublished doctoral dissertation). University of Alberta, Edmonton.

Kilborn, M. (2016). *A curriculum of wellness: Reconceptualizing physical education*. New York, NY: Lang.

Kilborn, M., Lorusso, J., & Francis, N. (2016). An analysis of Canadian physical education curricula. *European Physical Education Review, 22*(1), 23-46.

Kindt, D. (2001). Yarn toss: A simple activity for demonstrating interconnectedness in language classrooms. *The Language Teacher, 25*(6), 54-55. http://jalt-publications.org/old_tlt/articles/2001/06/kindt

Kirk, D. (2010). *Physical education futures*. London, UK: Routledge.

Kirk, D. (2013). Physical education for the 21st century. In S. Capel & M. Whitehead (Eds.), *Debates in physical education*. London, UK: Routledge.

Kornfield, J. (2000). *After the ecstasy, the laundry: How the heart grows wise on the spiritual path*. London, UK: Rider.

MacDonald, D., & Hunter, L. (2005). Lessons learned . . . about curriculum: Five years on and half a world away. *Journal of Teaching in Physical Education, 24*, 111-126.

Pinar, W. (2012). *What is curriculum theory?* (2nd ed.). New York, NY: Rutledge.

Pura, T. (2002). *Stages: Creative ideas for teaching drama.* Winnipeg, MB: J. Gordon Shillingford Publishing, Inc.

Shannonhouse, L., Myers, J., Barden, S., Clarke, P., Weimann, R., Forti, A., . . . Porter, M. (2014). Finding your new normal: Outcomes of a wellness-oriented psycho-educational support group for cancer survivors. *Journal for Specialists in Group Work, 39*(1), 3-28.

Tinning, R. (2010). *Pedagogy and human movement: Theory, practice, research.* London, UK: Rutledge.

Welwood, J. (1992). *Ordinary magic: Everyday life as a spiritual path.* Boston, MA: Shambala.

Chapter 17

Alberta Education. (2007). *Primary programs framework—Curriculum integration: Making connections.* Edmonton, AB: Author.

Armstrong, T. (2000). *Multiple intelligences in the classroom* (2nd ed.). Alexandria, VA: Association for Supervision and Curriculum Development.

Bradford, B., & Schmidt, E. (2016, April/May). Making cross-curricular connections. *Canadian Teacher Magazine.* https://canadianteachermagazine.com/2016/04/17/making-cross-curricular-connections/

Drake, S.M., & Reid, J. (2010, September). *Integrated curriculum: Increasing relevance while maintaining accountability.* The Literacy and Numeracy Secretariat. www.edu.gov.on.ca/eng/literacynumeracy/inspire/research/WW_Integrated_Curriculum.pdf

Gardner, H. (1983). *Frames of mind: The theory of multiple intelligences.* New York, NY: Basic Books.

Heart and Stroke Foundation of Canada. (n.d.). *The benefits of physical activity: Physical activity can be a lifesaver—literally.* www.heartandstroke.ca/get-healthy/stay-active/benefits-of-physical-activity.

Heart and Stroke Foundation of Canada. (2000). *Jumping into the curriculum: Kindergarten to grade 3.* Ontario.

Mullender-Wijnsma, M.J., Hartman, E., de Greeff, J.W., Doolaard, S., Bosker, R.J., & Visscher, C. (2016, February). Physically active math and language lessons improve academic achievement: A cluster randomized controlled trial. *Pediatrics.* http://pediatrics.aappublications.org/content/early/2016/02/22/peds.2015-2743.full

National Association for Sport and Physical Education. (n.d.). *Integrating physical activity into the complete school day.* https://www.mhasd.k12.wi.us/cms/lib/WI01001388/Centricity/Domain/459/Movement-during-school-day.pdf

Raithby, A. (2016). *Counting on fun: Multiple games for sum fun.* Ancaster, ON: CIRA Ontario.

Raushenbach, J. (1996). Tying it all together: Integrating physical education and other subject areas. *Journal of Physical Education, Recreation and Dance, 67*(2), 49-51.

Rink, J., Hall, T., & William, L. (2010). *Schoolwide physical activity: A comprehensive guide to designing and conducting programs.* Champaign, IL: Human Kinetics.

Western Newfoundland and Labrador School District. *Daily physical activity program.* http://web.wnlsd.ca/student_health/DPA/Daily%20Physical%20Activity.htm

World Health Organization (WHO). (2017, February). Physical activity: Fact sheet. www.who.int/mediacentre/factsheets/fs385/en/

Chapter 18

Broda, H.W. (2007). *Schoolyard-enhanced learning: Using the outdoors as an instructional tool, K-8.* Portland, ME: Stenhouse.

Carlson, J. (2008). *Never finished . . . just begun: A narrative history of L.B. Sharp and outdoor education.* Edina, MN: Beaver's Pond Press.

Department of Education and Early Childhood Development (2015). Physical Education—Essential Learning Outcomes 2015–2016. https://www.ednet.ns.ca/files/curriculum/PhysEdP-3ProgressionChart-RevJuly30-2015.pdf

Foran, A. (2005). The experience of pedagogical intensity in outdoor education. *Journal of Experiential Education, 28*(2), 147-163.

Foran, A. (2008a). An outside place for social studies. *Canadian Social Studies, 41*(1).

Foran, A. (2008b). *Teaching outside the school.* Saarbrüchen, SL, Germany: VDM Verlag.

Foran, A., & Olson, M. (2012). Seeking pedagogical places. In N. Friesen, C. Henriksson, & T. Saevi (Eds.), *Hermeneutic phenomenology in education: Method and practice,* (pp. 177-200). Boston, MA: Sense.

Foran, A., Redmond, K., & Loeffler, T.A. (2016). *GO: Get outside—Winter activities for outdoor leaders.* Champaign, IL: Human Kinetics.

Foran, A., & Smith, B. (2011a). Cross-country skiing. In K. Lodewyk (Ed.), *Fundamental movement skills: Beyond the fundamentals—Alternative activities and pursuits,* (pp. 111-117). Ottawa, ON: Physical and Health Education Canada.

Foran, A., & Smith, B. (2011b). Snowshoeing. In K. Lodewyk (Ed.), *Fundamental movement skills: Beyond the fundamentals—Alternative activities and pursuits,* (pp. 118-125). Ottawa, ON: Physical and Health Education Canada.

Foran, A., Stewart Stanec, A., & Mwebi, B.M. (2009). Active outdoor living: Let's get out of the gym! *The Journal CAHPERD (Canadian Association Health, Physical Education, Recreation and Dance), 75*(1), 6–11.

Mannion, G., & Lynch, J. (2016) The primacy of place in education in outdoor settings. In B. Humberstone, H. Prince, & K.A. Henderson (Eds.), *International handbook of outdoor studies* (pp. 85-94). New York, NY: Routledge.

Redmond, K., Foran, A., & Dwyer, S. (2010). *Quality lesson plans for outdoor education.* Champaign, IL: Human Kinetics.

Chapter 19

Cone, S., & Cone, T. (2011). Assessing dance in physical education for the novice to the experienced assessor. *Strategies, 24*(6), 28-32.

Chapter 20

Mandigo, J., Francis, N., & Lopez, R. (2009). Physical and Health Education Canada - Position Paper Physical Literacy for Educators. http://www.phecanada.ca/sites/default/files/pl_position_paper.pdf

OECD. (2015). *Students, Computers and Learning: Making the Connection*, OECD Publishing, Paris. http://dx.doi.org/10.1787/9789264239555-en

Ontario Ministry of Education. (2015). *The Ontario Curriculum Grades 1-8: Health and Physical Education. 2015.* http://www.edu.gov.on.ca/eng/curriculum/elementary/health1to8.pdf

Physical and Health Education Canada. (2016, August 24). Physical Literacy | PHE Canada. http://www.phecanada.ca/programs/physical-literacy

Physical and Health Education Canada. (2010). What is the relationship between Physical Education and Physical Literacy? http://www.phecanada.ca/sites/default/files/PL_and_PE.pdf

Puentedura, R. (2010). SAMR and TPCK: Intro to advanced practice. http://hippasus.com/resources/sweden2010/SAMR_TPCK_IntroToAdvancedPractice.pdf

UNESCO. (2015). Global Citizenship Education: Topics and learning objectives. Paris, France. http://unesdoc.unesco.org/images/0023/002329/232993e.pdf

Index

Note: The italicized *f* and *t* following page numbers refer to figures and tables, respectively.

A
ABCs of information evaluation 77-78
ABC Tag 158*t*
ability, vs. disability 38, 51, 55
Ability in Action 48
Aboriginal peoples 62
academic achievement 144
accessibility, for disabled 57
accommodation (adaptation) 40, 40*f*, 41
accuracy, of health information 77
ACEs (adverse childhood experiences) 92-93
Active Start 48
activity selection, in PE-LRP process 17-18
adaptation (accommodation) 40, 40*f*, 41
adverse childhood experiences (ACEs) 92-93
advocacy, for policy change 98
Against Common Sense: Teaching and Learning Toward Social Justice (Kumashiro) 56
agility 145
amplitude (fitness variable) 148
animal activities 150
anxiety, in students 89, 91, 144
assessments
    criterion-referenced 15
    dance education 213
    inclusive education 44, 51
    learning-related 15
    movement education 125*f*, 126-127, 127*t*, 213
    outdoor education 178
    PE-LRP process 19-20
    stress management and 91
    tech-enabled 221-222, 221*t*, 226
    timing of 83
associative stage, of skill acquisition 148
atmosphere walks 174
augmentation (SAMR stage) 216, 217
authority, of information source 77
autism 39*t*
autonomous stage, of skill acquisition 148

B
backward design model
    game selection and design 136-137, 142
    long-range planning 16-17
Baker, Kellie 11-12
balance (dimension of self)
    activities for 174
    Medicine Wheel teachings 62, 63-64, 63*f*
    wellness approach 173
balance (physical skill)
    as fitness component 145
    teaching 125*f*, 128*t*, 129*t*
Barnyard Madness 115-116
basketball activity 33
beanbags, for team selection 44, 116
behaviour
    mental health and 88-89, 92
    outdoor expectations 192, 195
behaviour challenges (exceptionality) 39*t*
beliefs, teachers' 78-79
bias
    in health information 77
    teachers' 78-79
birthday month, for team selection 116
body (movement concept)
    dance education 208
    fitness activities 149*t*
    movement education 120, 121, 121*t*
body composition 145
body size 58
brainstorming, in PE-LRP process 17-18
bubbles activities 150
bucket drawing, for team selection 116
buddy programs 172-173
bullying, body-based 58
Bunker, David 137

C
camps, for outdoor education 199
cardiorespiratory endurance 145
Carpenter, Amy 65-66
Centers for Disease Control and Prevention (US) 77, 99
Charbonneau, Celine 154

checklists
    equipment 30*t*
    outdoor education 193, 194*t*
    safety 34*t*
Chek, Paul 146-147
Chester, Adele 167
Chicken Baseball 161*t*
childhood trauma 92-93
Chin, Andrew 118
circuit activities 150
circular world view
    Medicine Wheel teachings 65-66
    vs. squads 8
citizenship, tech-enabled 223-224, 223*t*
classroom models
    special needs 38, 38*f*
    traditional 180
clothing, for team selection 116
Coach's Eye 217, 226
cognitive challenges 39, 39*t*, 48. *See also* special needs students
cognitive factors
    in dance education 204
    as physical literacy domain 146
cognitive stage, of skill acquisition 148
collaboration, tech-enabled 218-219, 219*t*
communication
    tech-enabled 221-222, 221*t*
    verbal vs. whistle 8
communities
    as outdoor education setting 199
    role in resilience 88
communities of practice 99-100
community organization roles
    CSH partners 100-103, 100*t*
    health education partners 80
    inclusive education partners 47-48
    teacher support 78
compassion, teaching 172-173
competitive games 132-133
complexity (fitness variable) 148
comprehensibility, of health information 77-78
comprehensive school health (CSH)
    challenges 102-103
    communities of practice 99-100
    community partners 100-103, 100*t*

comprehensive school health (CSH)
(continued)
defined 96-97
exercise in 106-107
mindfulness in 103-106, 104*f*-105*f*
models of 97-99
readiness quiz 96
relational dimensions 96, 99
resources for 106
school buy-in 100, 101
teams in 96
concept map, in planning 17, 18, 19, 20
cool-downs 150
cooperative games
designing 157-158
as game type 133
coordination (physical skill) 145
Coulson, Danielle 82-83
counting, for team selection 116
Courchene, Mary 63-64
creativity
in team-building 115
tech-enabled 219-221, 220*t*
criterion-referenced assessment 15
critical thinking
in social justice education 55
in team-building 115
tech-enabled 222-223, 222*t*
cross-curricular teaching. *See* curricular integration
CSH. *See* comprehensive school health
cultural differences. *See also* Indigenous perspectives
dance and 205
as diversity issue 54
learning about 88
respect for 62-63
cultural norms, teachers' 78-79
currentness, of health information 77
curricular integration
benefits of 180-181
defined 180
to improve health literacy 76
in outdoor education 190
strategies and examples 181-184
curriculum
in outdoor education 188
rethinking 171
curriculum infusion. *See* curricular integration

D

dance education
assessments 213
benefits of 204-205
choreographed vs. student-centered 205-206
dance recipe (live it) 211-212, 211*t*
five elements of (learn it) 207-211
Groove method (move it) 206, 207*t*

teachers of 205
definition, vs. meaning 15
depression 144
designing games
backward design 136-137
cooperative games 157-158
misconceptions about 156, 157*t*
net and wall games 162*t*, 163*t*
striking-and-fielding games 161*t*
tag games 158, 158*t*
target games 160*t*
territory games 164*t*, 165*t*
TGfU approach 159. 159*t*
developmental disabilities 39*t*
DiAngelo, R. 56
differentiated instruction 40, 40*f*
digital game-based learning 132
disabilities. *See also* special needs students
vs. abilities 38, 51, 55
as diversity issue 57
diversity. *See also* inclusive education; Indigenous perspectives
adapting teaching to 60, 83
body size 58
disability 57
gender 57-58
race and ethnicity 56-57
social justice education and 55-56
sociocultural approach to 54-55
Downey, Kristen 60
DR BEST acronym 207-211
dual continuum model of mental health 87, 87*f*
dynamic balance
errors and solutions in 129*t*
poster 125*f*
progressions in 128*t*

E

educaching 199
effort (movement concept)
in fitness activities 149*t*
in movement education 120, 121, 121*t*
emotional challenges 39*t*
emotional domain
dance education and 204
in Medicine Wheel 64
emotional safety 28. *See also* safety
energy, in dance education 209-210
environment, for physical activity
modification of 46
outdoor settings 188, 191-192, 197-199
safe space and facilities 28-29, 29*f*
equipment
in game playability 136-137
modification of 46-47
for outdoor education 191, 195-196
safety and 29-30, 30*t*

equity
in health education 80
in social justice education 55
evaluation. *See* assessments
exclusion, of special needs students 38, 38*f*

F

fairness, in social justice education 55
families
role in resilience 88
stressors in 89
fat bullying 58
feedback
movement education 124, 126
team building 114-115
Feith, Joey 130
fight, flight, or freeze responses 89, 92
first aid, in outdoor education 192, 195, 196
First Nations 62. *See also* Indigenous perspectives
Fitts, Paul 148
flexibility 145
floor hockey
gated community activity 31-33, 32*f*
safe stick usage 30
Forte, Joseph 25
four directions 64
Foursquare 49, 49*t*
full-sided games 133-134
fun
in learning 185, 213
in successful games 135
functional fitness 152. *See also* physical fitness activities
fundamental movement development 123-124
fundamental movement skills
in fitness activities 146-147, 146*t*, 147*t*
imagination in teaching 213
in movement education 122-123, 122*f*, 130
primal patterns 145, 146-147, 147*t*
FUNdamentals 48
funding, for CSH 102, 103

G

game-based learning 132
games. *See also* designing games
defined 132
fitness activities as 150
Indigenous perspective 64-65, 68
modification of 48-50, 49*t*, 51
prevalence in physical education 132
selecting 136-137
student-designed 134-135, 156, 157*t*
successful 135

TGfU approach 40, 137-141, 138*f*, 154
types of 132-135, 138-139
Gardner, Howard 180
gated community activity 31-33, 32*f*
gender, as diversity issue 57-58
geocaching 199
giftedness 39*t*
Global School Health Initiative 97-98
goals for health education 73*t*-75*t*
government agencies, as information sources 77
Groove method 206, 207*t*
groups
    creating 44, 79-80
    managing outdoors 196-197, 197*t*
    outdoor gear for 195
guided visualization 174

H
Halas, Joannie 66-67
Handball Tennis 163*t*
hands-on outdoor activities 190
Hayes, Graham 142
health
    defining 4-5
    information sources 77-78
    in physical literacy context 6-7
    social determinants of 7, 91-92
    WHO definition 5, 97
    as wholeness 170, 171
health action teams 102
health behaviour, knowledge gap 5
Health Canada 77
health determinants 7-8, 91-92
health education. *See also* comprehensive school health; mental health
    goals and visions 73*t*-75*t*
    health literacy and 75-76
    reasons for teaching 72-75
    recommendations for 76-80
    sociocultural shift in 7-8, 9
    transfer effect of 76, 82
health literacy
    defining 4-5, 75
    health education and 75-76
    improving 76
health-promoting school (HPS) 5, 97-98
Health Promoting Schools Champion Award 98-99
health promotion. *See also* comprehensive school health
    emergence of 5
    Indigenous perspectives 66-67
    readiness quiz 96
health-related fitness 144-145
healthy school approach 97
holistic approach
    activities for 174
    Indigenous perspective 65, 66, 68

physical disabilities 57
physical education 170-171
physical literacy 5-6
honso ayinnai 62
Howlett-Mackay, Janice 201
HPS (health-promoting school) 5, 97-98

I
IEP (individual education plan) 39
inactivity health risks 181
inclusive education. *See also* diversity
    assessments in 44, 51
    classroom models 38, 38*f*
    community partners in 47-48
    environment modification 46
    equipment modification 46-47
    exceptionality types in 39, 39*t*
    game and sport modification in 48-50, 49*t*, 51
    instructional supports 39-41, 40*f*
    philosophy of 38
    sociocultural approach 54-55
    teaching methods 41-46
Indigenous peoples
    acknowledgment of 63, 66
    defined 62
Indigenous perspectives
    circular world view 65-66
    four directions 64
    games and activities 64-65
    health promotion 66-67
    oral traditions 63
    respect for 62-63
individual education plan (IEP) 39
individualistic games 133
individualized programming 40*f*, 41
information sources 77-78
instructional supports, for inclusive education 39-41, 40*f*
instructions
    for physical fitness activities 150
    for special needs students 42-44, 44*f*, 45*f*, 46*f*
integration
    curricular 76, 180-184, 190
    of special needs students 38, 38*f*
intellectual direction, in Medicine Wheel 64
interconnectedness 172-173
internalizing behaviours 92
Inuit peoples 62. *See also* Indigenous perspectives
inventive games. *See* student-designed games
Is Everyone Really Equal? (Sensoy, DiAngelo) 56

J
Joint Consortium for School Health (JCSH) 98

K
Keenliside, Nicki 185-186
Keep the Chicken 165*t*
Keyes, C.L.M. 87, 87*f*
kindness, teaching 172-173
kingpin 167-168
Krahn, Mandy 174
Kumashiro, K. 56

L
Laban, Rudolf 120, 148, 149*t*
LaMorre, Lindsay 51
language skills integration 181-184
large-sided games 133-134
leader gear, in outdoor education 195-196
leadership, for CSH 102
learning
    assessments of 15
    motor development and 123-124
    physical activity effects on 94, 144
    scope and sequence of 16
learning disabilities 39*t*
learning goals
    in backward design 16-17, 136-137, 142
    in PE-LRP process 19, 23
learning outcomes
    instructional supports and 39-41, 40*f*
    movement concepts in 121
    in outdoor education 190, 201
    in PE-LRP process 17, 22-23
    scope of learning in 16
    in successful games 135
learn it step, in dance education 207-211
Lewis, Carolyn 94
listening to the room activity 174
listening to your breath activity 174
literacy. *See also* health literacy; mental health literacy; physical literacy
    defining 4
    vs. health literacy 75
    physical activity integration 181-184
literacy terms, in movement education 125*f*, 126
live it step, in dance education 211-212, 211*t*
load (fitness variable) 148
locomotor skills 122, 147*t*
long-range planning
    backward design model 16-17
    key terms 15-16
    need for 14-15
    PE-LRP process 14*f*, 17-24
    teacher experience with 25
long-term athlete development (LTAD) 48, 150, 151*t*

M

manipulative skills 122, 147*t*

Martin, Lee 225

Math Challenge 183

math skills integration 181-184

McKinnon, Patrick 109

McTighe, J. 16-17, 136-137

meaning, vs. definition 15

Medicine Wheel. *See Mino' Pima-tisiwin*

mental health

    adverse factors in 91-93

    defined 87

    dual continuum model 87, 87*f*

    fitness activities and 144

    normalizing discussions of 93

    resilience and 87-88

    stress management 89-91

    teachers' role in 86, 88-89, 92-93

mental health literacy 86

mental illness 86, 88-89

metabolic disease 144

Métis peoples 62. *See also* Indigenous perspectives

mindfulness

    in CSH 103-106

    defined 79, 103, 171

    handout for parents, educators 104*f*-105*f*

    in health education 79

    in physical education 171-172

minigames 133-134

minobimaadiziwin 62

Mino' Pimatisiwin (Medicine Wheel)

    assessment of 67

    balance concept 62, 63-64

    circular world view 65-66

    four directions 63-64, 63*f*

    in health promotion 66-67

    play perspective 64-65

modification

    deciding to use 41

    described 40-41, 40*f*

    of environment 46

    of equipment 46-47

    of games and sports 48-50, 49*t*, 51, 137

    as SAMR stage 216, 217

motivator role, in team building 114

motor behaviour 146

motor development

    progressions in 127-129, 128*t*

    stages of 123-124, 124*f*, 126

move it step, in dance education 206, 207*t*

movement capacity 145

movement competence 145, 150-152

movement development

    fundamental 123-124, 146-147, 146*t*

    LTAD model 48, 150, 151*t*

motor development 123-124, 124*f*, 127-129, 128*t*

    running mechanics 152*t*

    through physical fitness activities 145-147

movement dysfunction 147, 150-151

movement education

    assessments 126-127, 127*t*, 213

    fundamental skills 122-123, 122*f*, 130

    layering in 130

    movement concepts 120-122, 121*t*

    movement skill posters 124, 125*f*, 130

    pioneer of 6, 120

    teaching method 124-129, 125*f*, 126*t*, 127*t*, 128*t*, 129*t*

movement missions activities 185-186

multiple intelligences 180

muscular endurance 145

muscular strength 145

N

Name Game 116

natural environment

    appreciation for 176-177

    for outdoor education 198-199

negative transfer 140

net and wall games

    described 138-139

    designing 162*t*, 163*t*

Notability app 226

Numbers Game 115

nutrition education 82

O

obesity 58, 144

oral traditions 63

organizer role, in team building 114

orthopedic problems 144

Ottawa Charter for Health Promotion 5, 97

outdoor education

    activities by setting 199

    checklist for 193, 194*t*

    deciding to use 188

    equipment for 191, 195-196

    goal of 189

    nature appreciation and 176-177

    planning and preparation 190-193

    risk management 194-195

    scope and benefits of 189-190

    seven "rights" 189

    site advantages, drawbacks 197-199

    site assessment 191-192

    student medical forms 193

    teacher experience with 178

    three "teachers" 188-189

P

Pan-Canadian Joint Consortium for School Health (JCSH) 98

parent engagement 78, 83

parks, for outdoor education 198-199

partnerships

    comprehensive school health 100-103, 100*t*

    health education 80

    inclusive education 47-48

    parent engagement 78

PDD (pervasive development disorder) 39*t*

PE-LRP process

    overview 14*f*

    steps in 17-24

performance indicators 124-126, 125*f*, 126*t*

personal responsibility for health 7

personnel changes, as CSH challenge 102

pervasive development disorder (PDD) 39*t*

PHE (Physical and Health Education) Canada 98-99

Phonic Dance 94

physical activity

    academic subject integration 181-184

    benefits of 181

    effect on learning 94, 144

    outdoor 176-177, 190

    as physical literacy domain 146

Physical and Health Education (PHE) Canada 98-99

physical direction, in Medicine Wheel 64

physical disabilities 39, 39*t*. *See also* special needs students

physical education. *See also* games; long-range planning; physical fitness activities

    challenges in 14

    curricular integration 76, 180-184, 190

    holistic approach. *See* holistic approach

    inclusive. *See* inclusive education; Indigenous perspectives

    rethinking 170-171

    sociocultural shift in 8-9

    sport-technique model 170

    sustainability in 177-178

    wellness approach 171-173, 172*t*

physical fitness

    components of 144-145

    as physical literacy domain 146

    skill acquisition 148

physical fitness activities

    benefits of 144

    dance as 204, 205

    design variables 148-150

    functional relevance 152

    implementing 145-148, 146*f*

incorporating into schedule 154
movement competence activities 150-152
movement development and 145-147, 150, 151*t*
outdoor. *See* outdoor education
student safety. *See* safety
team building 114-118
tech-enabled fitness challenge 225
types and elements of 150
used as punishment 144
physical literacy
  defining 5-6, 146
  domains of 146
  in LTAD model 48
  meaning in PE context 16
  21st-century competencies and 217-218, 218*t*
playability of games 135, 136-137
playfulness culture 9
playing cards, for team selection 44, 116
policy change advocacy 98
positive stress response 90
positive thinking, in teaching 41-42
Posner, Michael 148
potential of learners 55
power (physical skill) 145
primal patterns 145, 146-147, 147*t*
privilege
  in resilience 88
  in social identity 56
  white 57
problem-solving, in team building 115
professional development, in health education 76
provincial goals and vision statements 73*t*-75*t*
psychosocial factors, in physical literacy 146
Public Health Agency of Canada 77
public health organizations 77

Q
QR (quick-response) codes
  on movement skill posters 125*f*, 126
  in tech-enabled education 219, 226

R
race and ethnicity 56-57
reaction time 145
recorder role, in team building 114
redefinition (SAMR stage) 216, 217
relationship (movement concept)
  dance education 210-211
  fitness activities 149*t*
  movement education 120, 121, 121*t*
repetitions (fitness variable) 148
resilience 87-88

respect
  for cultural differences 62-63
  in team building 115, 117
Reverse Leader 118
risk management, in outdoor education 194-195
risk-taking, in team building 114-115
Robillard, Blair 64-65, 68
role modelling 28
roles, in team building 114
routines, for special needs students 42
rules
  to minimize what-ifs 140
  for safety 30-31
  in successful games 135
running mechanics 152*t*

S
safety
  checklist for 34*t*
  dimensions of 28
  equipment for 29-30, 30*t*
  in game playability 136
  in outdoor education 194-195
  role modelling 28
  rules for 30-31
  of space and facilities 28-29, 29*f*
SAMR model
  citizenship activities 223-224, 223*t*
  collaborative activity 218-219, 219*t*
  communication activity 221-222, 221*t*
  creative activities 219-221, 220*t*
  critical thinking activities 222-223, 222*t*
  stages of 216-217, 216*t*
scaffolding 54
school attendance, and mental health 89
school councils 102
school health
  models of 97-99
  policy change advocacy 98
School Health Guidance Document 106
school sites, for outdoor education 198, 199
scope of learning
  defined 16
  in PE-LRP process 17-18
Screaming Eagle 68
sedentary behaviour 144
segregation, of special needs students 38, 38*f*
self-awareness, of teachers 9
sensory overload 46, 47*t*
Sensoy, O. 56
sequence of learning
  defined 16
  in PE-LRP process 18-19
seven "rights" 189

shaking it out activity 174
silence, in dealing with students 92, 93
situational awareness, outdoors 197, 197*t*
skill-related fitness 144-145
Skype 226
small-sided games 133-134, 142
smoking effects activity 36
snowshoeing 199
soccer skill activity 28-29, 29*f*
social connections, in dance education 204
social determinants of health 7, 91-92
social identities 56
social justice education 55-56
social justice issues 56-58
social skills
  dance education and 205
  for special needs students 44-46
sociocultural approach
  curriculum shift to 7-8
  health literacy 4-5
  inclusive education 54-55
  physical literacy 5-6
  teaching practices for 8-9
sociocultural system 176
socioecological system 176
socioeconomics
  as health determinant 7-8
  physical activity, well-being and 176
space (environment)
  in game playability 136
  safety of 28-29, 29*f*
space (movement concept)
  dance education 208-209
  fitness activities 149*t*
  movement education 120, 121, 121*t*
special needs students
  classroom models for 38, 38*f*
  community support for 47-48
  game and sport modification for 48-50, 49*t*, 51
  instructional supports for 39-41, 40*f*
  teaching methods for 41-46
  types of 39, 39*t*
Special Olympics Canada 48
speed 145
spiritual direction, in Medicine Wheel 64
sports
  fundamental movement skills for 122*f*
  modification of 48-50, 49*t*, 51
sport-technique model 170
squads 8
stability (movement skill) 122-123, 147*t*
stakeholder engagement, in CSH 101
stereotypes, challenging 55

stress
 causes of 89, 91-92
 helping students manage 91, 92-93
 normal vs. toxic 90
 resilience and 88
 responses to 89-90
striking-and-fielding games
 described 138
 designing 161*t*
student-centred learning
 as teaching approach 80
 in technology use 217
student connections 188-189
student-designed games
 as game option 134-135
 introducing 156
 misconceptions about 156, 157*t*
student gear, in outdoor education 195, 196
substitution (SAMR stage) 216, 217
success criteria
 of games 135
 in PE-LRP process 19-20, 23
summarizer role, in team building 114
sustainability
 of CSH 103
 described 176
 physical education for 177-178

T
tag or chase activities
 designing 158, 158*t*
 in safe play 33
talking circles 65-66
target games
 described 138
 designing 160*t*
teacher training
 health education in 76
 long-range planning in 14-15
 teacher of 36
teaching cues 124-126, 126*t*
Teaching Games for Understanding (TGfU)
 designing games based on 159-165, 160*t*, 161*t*, 162*t*, 163*t*, 164*t*, 165*t*
 as differentiated instruction 40
 game categories and goals 159*t*
 game selection in 138-139
 implementing 139-141
 steps in 137-138, 138*f*
 teacher experience with 154
teaching methods
 to address diversity 56-58, 60
 movement education 124-129, 125*f*, 126*t*, 127*t*, 128*t*, 129*t*
 for special needs students 41-46

teaching personal and social responsibility (TPSR) 11-12
teaching time, in PE-LRP process 20-22
team building 114-115, 118
team pact, sample 117
team selection 44, 79-80, 115-116
teamwork, in dance education 205
technology use
 as assessment tool 221-222, 226
 recommended resources 226
 SAMR model 216-217, 216*t*
 tech-enabled fitness challenge 225
 tips for 226
 21st-century competencies and 218-224, 218*t*, 219*t*, 220*t*, 221*t*, 222*t*, 223*t*
tempo (fitness variable) 148
territorial goals and vision statements 74*t*-75*t*
territory games
 described 139
 designing 164*t*, 165*t*
TGfU. *See* Teaching Games for Understanding
Thorpe, Rod 137
Tic-Tac-Toe 160*t*
time, in dance education 209
timed sets (fitness variable) 148
time limitations, as CSH challenge 102
tobacco use effects activity 36
tolerable stress response 90
Tour du Canada 182
toxic stress response 90
TPSR (teaching personal and social responsibility) 11-12
transfer of learning
 in health education 76, 82
 in physical education 139-140, 142
Turtle Island (term) 62
21st-century competencies
 aligning with physical literacy 217-218, 218*t*
 citizenship 223-224, 223*t*
 collaboration 218-219, 219*t*
 communication 221-222, 221*t*
 creativity 219-221, 220*t*
 critical thinking 222-223, 222*t*

U
Understanding by Design (backward design)
 game selection and design 136-137, 142
 long-range planning 16-17
underwater mission activity 186
Ungar, Michael 87-88

United States Centers for Disease Control Prevention 77, 99
unit planning, in PE-LRP process 19, 20-24

V
Variety Village 48
verbal communication, vs. whistle 8
video games, in education 109
video recording, as teaching tool 216*t*, 217
vision statements for health education 73*t*-75*t*
visual aids
 activity instructions 42-44, 44*f*, 45*f*, 46*f*
 class schedule 42, 43*f*
visualization, guided 174
Vokes-Leduc, Lynne 36

W
warm-ups 150
weight bias 58
well-being
 adverse effects on 91-93
 in complex systems 176
 components of 87
wellness approach
 balance in 173
 characteristics of 171, 172*t*
 interconnectedness in 172-173
 mindfulness in 171-172
what-ifs 140
whistle use 8
Whitehead, Margaret 6, 146
white privilege 57
WHO. *See* World Health Organization
whole-person approach. *See* holistic approach
Whole School, Whole Community, Whole Child (WSCC) model 99
Wiggins, G. 16-17, 136-137
Winchar, Gavin 178
winter Olympics mission activity 185
World Health Organization (WHO)
 Global School Health Initiative 97-98
 health definition 5, 97
 as information source 77
 mental health definition 87
WSCC (Whole School, Whole Community, Whole Child) model 99

X
Xavier, Adrian 213

Z
Zombies, Run! 220

About the Editors

Courtesy of Kate Coulson.

Joe Barrett, EdD, is an associate professor in the department of teacher education at Brock University in Ontario. His research and service duties revolve around school health policy and health and physical education pedagogy. At Brock University, Dr. Barrett teaches a number of elementary and secondary undergraduate courses that focus on physical and health education curriculum and instruction, as well as graduate courses focused on physical and health education policy and curricula using problem-based learning pedagogies. He has served as the Ontario representative on the Physical and Health Education (PHE) Canada Board of Directors (2013-2015) and as co-chair (2010-2012) and chair (2012-2013) of the PHE Canada Research Council. He served a two-year term as the co-chair (2017-2019) of the PHE Canada National Research Forum.

Carol Scaini, MEd, is an instructor in the department of teacher education at Tyndale University College in Ontario and is an experienced health and physical education teacher with the Peel District School Board. At Tyndale University College, she teaches the physical and health education course for both primary/junior and junior/intermediate teacher candidates. She is well known in the field of health and physical education (HPE): She serves on a number of HPE committees, has taught HPE additional qualification courses at the Ontario Institute for Studies in Education at the University of Toronto, and has authored several health and physical education resources. She has earned numerous teaching awards, including the Prime Minister's Award for Teaching Excellence, the Ontario Teacher of the Year award, the Dr. Andy Anderson Young Professional Award from PHE Canada, the Ontario Association for the Support of Physical and Health Educators (OASPHE) Recognition Award and Advocacy Award, and an Award of Distinction from the Peel District School Board.

Courtesy of J. Bush.

About the Contributors

Courtesy of Erica Pratt.

Helena Baert, PhD, is an associate professor in the physical education department at the State University of New York College at Cortland. She is originally from Belgium and has also lived and taught in Manitoba, Canada. Baert teaches courses in movement education, elementary pedagogy, curriculum and instruction, technology in physical education, outdoor adventure education, and leadership in physical education. Her research interests include early childhood education and pedagogy, fundamental movement skill analysis, and effective technology-infused pedagogy. She enjoys kayaking and hiking in the summer and skiing and snowboarding in the winter. Along with Matthew Madden, Baert started the research team Making Movement Stick, which helps future physical education teachers develop skills in fundamental movement analysis. The group includes a host of undergraduate research assistants who work in collaboration with Baert and Madden. Its ultimate objective is to enhance the fundamental movement skills of preschool students.

© C. Scaini

Jeannine Bush, BEd, is an itinerant teacher focused on autism spectrum disorder with the Peel District School Board in Mississauga, Ontario. Her lifelong interest in special education led her to obtain degrees in psychology and education. After two of her children were diagnosed with autism, she obtained her honours certificate in autism and behavioural sciences. Her passion lies in connecting students, parents, and staff with community services in order to provide a wider base of support. She has presented at various conferences and organized parent networking evenings for families. She is an active member of the autism community and plans to continue her association with various autism-related charities.

Courtesy of Northern Ontario School of Medicine.

Erin Cameron, PhD, is an assistant professor in the human sciences division at the Northern Ontario School of Medicine. Her research centres on critical health education, promotion, and pedagogy. Cameron's research recognizes that interdisciplinary partnerships between health, education, recreation, and across the continuum of care, are essential to promoting health and wellness. As an education scholar, Cameron's most recent work explores the use of transformative pedagogies in educational settings to promote size diversity and inclusion so that everybody can feel supported to pursue healthy, active lives.

Courtesy of Alyssa Bird.

Amy Carpenter, MA, is a Métis woman from the Red River Region in Winnipeg. She is a public school administrator in the Seven Oaks School Division. Carpenter has taught grades 1 through 12 and recently took on the role of vice principal. In 2010, she completed her master's degree at the University of Manitoba. Her educational focus involves tapping into, nurturing, and celebrating the strong leadership capacity within Indigenous children, youth, and communities. Carpenter looks to family and community as her sources of strength, love, and interconnectedness.

©C. Casey

Catherine Casey, PhD, is an associate professor of studies in curriculum, teaching, and learning in the faculty of education at the University of Manitoba. Her areas of expertise include teacher development, child and adolescent physical activity levels, application of the Teaching Games for Understanding model, and experiential learning. The research projects in which she has been involved share the common thread of examining policies and programs that directly affect student achievement, learning experiences, and well-being. Casey is an award-winning scholar and teacher who has dedicated her career to enhancing the teaching and learning process as a teacher educator.

Photo by Joannie Halas.

Mary Courchene, BA, BEd, is a visionary educator who has built intercultural bridges between Indigenous and non-Indigenous educators throughout her life. Courchene is an Indian Residential School survivor whose contributions include teaching, counseling, and administration as dean of Indigenous Education at Red River College; cofounder of the Manitoba First Nations Educational Resource Centre and the Aboriginal Circle of Educators; and principal at Children of the Earth, the first Aboriginal-focused high school in Canada to introduce daily cultural programming. Courchene is currently Elder in Residence in the Seven Oaks School Division.

©Joanne G. de Montigny

Joanne G. de Montigny, PhD, earned her doctoral degree in population health from the Interdisciplinary School of Health Sciences at the University of Ottawa. While working in health promotion at Health Canada and the Public Health Agency of Canada, she pursued higher education in health administration and epidemiology (University of Ottawa). Her doctoral thesis, which was funded by the Canadian Institutes of Health Research and titled *Toward the Creation of Healthy Schools: Exploring Partnerships Across the Health and Education Sectors in Ontario*, generated knowledge about the development of partnerships between local public health units and school boards and shed light on the potential for widespread collaboration in creating healthy schools. She is currently a consultant in the areas of multisectoral partnerships, health equity, epidemiology, and social determinants of health.

Courtesy of Victor Pongetti.

Carolyn Evans, BEd, is a retired health and physical education teacher and teacher-librarian. She is co-author (with Carol Scaini) of *50 Games for Going Green*, a resource for physical education teachers, classroom teachers, and recreation leaders that teaches and promotes healthy environmental concepts through games and physical activities. Evans has presented workshops at various school, board, and provincial conferences and helped develop resources in health and physical education for not-for-profit and health and physical education organizations. In 2013, she received the Recognition Award from the Ontario Association for the Supervision of Physical and Health Education (OASPHE) for contributing to the "growth of the HPE community through sharing of innovative practice." Evans is a member of Physical and Health Education Canada and the Ontario Physical Health and Education Association. In her free time, she enjoys participating in fitness classes at the YMCA, playing pickleball, gardening, and being active in the great outdoors.

©Thomas Falkenberg

Thomas Falkenberg, PhD, is a professor in the faculty of education at the University of Manitoba. He is editor or co-editor of a number of books, including *Sustainable Well-Being: Concepts, Issues, Perspectives, and Educa-*

tional Practices. From 2011 to 2016, he served as coordinator of the interdisciplinary Education for Sustainable Well-Being Research Group at the University of Manitoba. More details about his research and academic background can be found at his professional website: http://home.cc.umanitoba.ca/~falkenbe/index.html.

Andrew Foran, PhD, is an associate professor at St. Francis Xavier University in Antigonish, Nova Scotia. He began his teaching career as a geography teacher and outdoor educator with the Halifax Regional School Board in Halifax, Nova Scotia. The focus of his teacher education practice is service learning, experiential applications within public school programs, and curriculum development in outdoor education primary–12. Foran's research examines teachers and students engaged in experiential courses and instruction outside of school settings. Foran has developed numerous teacher education programs, workshops, and courses, and has published nationally and internationally. Currently, he is leading a certificate program in outdoor education for physical education teachers through St. Francis Xavier University.

Joannie Halas, PhD, is a professor in the faculty of kinesiology and recreation management at the University of Manitoba. She received her doctorate from the University of Alberta. Her integrated teaching, research, and community service are focused on access to culturally relevant health and physical education for Indigenous and other underrepresented populations, including racialized minority youth. A seminal feature of her research has been the development of the Rec and Read Aboriginal Youth Mentorship Program for All Nations, which was awarded the international MacJannet Prize for exceptional university–community engagement in 2014.

Nathan Hall, PhD, is an associate professor at the University of Winnipeg, where he specializes in physical education teacher education. He teaches courses that focus on team activities, curriculum and assessment in health and physical education, outdoor education and recreation, and Teaching Games for Understanding. Hall's research interests include alternative environment physical education, physical literacy, and the benefits of using psychological skills to help teach physical education. He is a member of the Physical and Health Education Canada Research Council and serves on the board of directors for the Manitoba Physical Education Teachers Association. He is passionate about learning and sharing novel games and physical activities with teachers—for example, Hantis, Sabakiball, and Spikeball.

Kim Hertlein, BEd, BPEd, is a health and physical education educator at Ross Sheppard High School in Edmonton, Alberta. She graduated from the University of Alberta with a combined BEd and BPEd and was a member of the Pandas basketball team. After years of coaching basketball and teaching physical education, she decided to adopt a holistic approach to both her personal life and her career; as a result, she currently teaches holistic health, yoga, and psychology. She created her Holistic Health Option course in 2008 and has presented about her holistic approach to teaching at many local, provincial, and national conferences.

Michelle Hillier, BA, BEd, is a passionate educational presenter and consultant to school boards and teacher education programs across Canada. Hillier has shared her work and passion at national and international conferences including the Canadian Association of Principals Conference, International Physical Literacy Conference, Physical Health and Education Canada, Council of Ontario Dance and Drama Educators, and SHAPE America. She is also an instructional leader at York University in Toronto for a dance course and she is a member of the teaching faculty at the University of Ontario Institute of Technology in Oshawa, Ontario, in the teacher education program, where she inspires and equips future and current teachers with the tools to make movement and creativity accessible for all. When Hillier isn't inspiring others on the dance floor, she loves to try new fitness-related activities, travel, and spend time with her husband, Dave, and her 5-year-old son, James.

Jillian Janzen, MA, is an elementary health and physical education teacher for the District School Board of Niagara. She has an undergraduate degree in physical education, a master of arts degree in applied health science, and an honours specialist qualification for teaching in health and physical education through Brock University's continuing teacher education program. She is also a primary and junior HPE sessional instructor for the faculty of education at Brock University. In 2016, Janzen was the recipient of the Ophea Deb Courville Education Fund award that recognizes a young, new professional who is passionate for HPE. She has spent significant time volunteering in classrooms as well as traveling to Central America to learn, teach, and volunteer with schools in their HPE programs. Her previous research and involvement was focused on understanding the challenges and barriers teachers face in implementing quality HPE programming as well as the importance and benefits of teaching living skills through physical activity and sport settings. As a young professional, she is motivated to find innovative ways to promote and advocate for the importance of quality HPE and healthy school communities. Janzen enjoys being active, playing games, and cooking with friends and family.

Courtesy of Wenonah Justin.

Brian Justin, CEP, CSCS, is a kinesiology instructor at the University of the Fraser Valley in Chilliwack, British Columbia. He earned his master's degree (exercise physiology emphasis) and bachelor's degree (pedagogy and exercise physiology emphasis) from the University of British Columbia. He specializes in strength and conditioning, movement restoration, exercise physiology, and exercise testing and prescription. Justin is a Certified Exercise Physiologist (CEP) through the Canadian Society for Exercise Physiology and a Certified Strength and Conditioning Specialist (CSCS) through the National Strength and Conditioning Association. He is passionate about spreading the word regarding the benefits of physical activity for health, performance, and injury prevention.

©Michelle Kilborn

Michelle Kilborn, PhD, completed her doctorate at the University of Alberta and is currently an adjunct professor at Memorial University of Newfoundland and a researcher and health policy analyst for Alberta Health Services in Edmonton. Her research interests include reconceptualizing curriculum and pedagogy in physical education, health promotion, and wellness. In her 25-year career in education, she has taught elementary, junior, and high school physical education, as well as health education and outdoor education. She has also coordinated provincial programs for health and physical education in Alberta, and she continues to contribute to the field as a teacher educator in physical education programs.

©Brian Lewis

Brian Lewis, PhD, is a lecturer in health and physical education at the University of Regina. His research focuses on the experiences of urban Indigenous youth in an after-school wellness program. He also serves as a consultant, workshop facilitator, and resource developer. He has worked as both a physical education teacher and a curriculum consultant over the last 18 years. He sits on the board of directors for Physical and Health Education (PHE) Canada.

Michael Link, MEd, is a doctoral candidate and educational developer at the University of Manitoba. He served as an elementary school teacher for 13 years in Surrey and Abbotsford, British Columbia, and as an instructor for seven years in the Faculty of Education at the University of Manitoba. His research focuses on contemplative practice, well-being in education, and outdoor learning. He can be reached at michael.link@umanitoba.ca.

Rebecca Lloyd, PhD, is an associate professor in the faculty of education at the University of Ottawa. She promotes interdisciplinary thinking in her Function-2Flow-framed research and her teaching in the Comprehensive School Health cohort. She has chaired several conferences including the International Human Science Research Conference, Physical and Health Education Canada, and the physical education teacher education special interest group within the Canadian Society for the Study of Education. She has served as a keynote and invited speaker in the United Kingdom and Japan. Before becoming a professor, Lloyd was a full-time fitness educator and regularly presented at Canfitpro and the IDEA Health and Fitness Association. She continues to teach fitness classes in her local community, enjoys outdoor hikes with her sons, and competes in salsa dance at an international level.

Chunlei Lu, PhD, is a professor in the department of teacher education at Brock University. He obtained a BEd from Shandong Normal University in China, an MEd from Zhejiang University in China, an MSc from State University of New York at Brockport, and a PhD from the University of Alberta. He has a teaching certificate issued by the Ontario College of Teachers. Lu has taught at seven universities across the three countries. Based on these cross-cultural experiences, his research interests have concentrated on the overlapped areas of culture, education, and health. He has published two books, seven book chapters, and 60 academic articles.

Matthew Madden, PhD, is an associate professor in the physical education department at the State University of New York College at Cortland. He is experienced in teaching undergraduate and graduate physical education pedagogy courses in the areas of sport pedagogy, tactical games approaches, planning and instructional design, curriculum construction, and developmentally appropriate elementary activities. He has also supervised teacher candidates during student teaching as both a supervising and a cooperating teacher. His recent research focuses on preservice teachers' ability to analyze movement, teacher change, teacher development, and curriculum. He enjoys spending time outside and traveling with his partner and their three young children.

Greg Rickwood, PhD, is an associate professor in the School of Physical and Health Education at Nipissing University in North Bay, Ontario. He is a physical education teaching specialist with extensive teaching experience in secondary schools in Ontario and British Columbia. Recently, he has designed curriculum for Ontario's additional qualification courses in health and physical education and created learning modules for Hockey Canada's Sport Academy programs delivered nationally in secondary schools. Rickwood's research interests include the relationship between elementary and secondary school cultural systems and school-based physical activity opportunities.

Photo by Dusty Smarz.

Blair Robillard, BA, holds a bachelor of arts with a major in symbolic cultural anthropology from the University of Winnipeg. He has worked as a sessional instructor at the University of Manitoba for the past 17 years. His Aboriginal Games and Activities course incorporates cultural and historical components of holistic teachings from Indigenous knowledge keepers in Manitoba. He uses strengths-based capacity building as a fundamental component of his pedagogy.

©Daniel B. Robinson

Daniel B. Robinson, PhD, is an associate professor and chair of teacher education at St. Francis Xavier University. He teaches undergraduate courses in elementary and secondary physical education curriculum and instruction. He also teaches graduate courses in current research in curriculum and instruction, administration of inclusive schools, curriculum theory, and school and teaching effectiveness. His research focuses on culturally responsive physical education, gender and racialized minorities, service learning, and in-school health promotion programming.

Thomas Rodger.

Susan Rodger, PhD, CPsych, is a psychologist and associate professor in counseling psychology in the Faculty of Education at Western University. Also at Western, she is a research associate at both the Centre for School-Based Mental Health and the Centre for Research and Education on Violence Against Women and Children. Her research interests include barriers to mental health treatment; mental health literacy for teachers, teacher candidates, and foster care providers; and the influence on learning of exposure to violence. She is currently working on three national projects to develop resources for teacher wellness and to support child and youth mental health in schools.

Courtesy of Giulia Forsythe.

Camille Rutherford, EdD, is an associate professor of education at Brock University. As a former classroom teacher and university administrator, she works with teacher candidates, teachers, adult educators, and educational leaders to explore the use of technology to transform leadership and enhance teaching and learning.

Courtesy of Lakehead University.

Teresa Socha, PhD, is an associate professor and the chair of undergraduate studies in the faculty of education at Lakehead University. As a health and physical education teacher educator, she pursues research and teaching interests that include health and physical education, promotion, and pedagogy. She also explores how these practices can be understood through various theoretical frameworks, including critical obesity studies, fat studies, feminist and sociocultural theories, and anti-oppressive education for analysis.

Courtesy of University of Ottawa.

Jessica Whitley, PhD, is an associate professor in the faculty of education at the University of Ottawa. She teaches at the undergraduate and graduate levels in the areas of inclusive and special education and often draws on a Comprehensive School Health framework. Her research explores effective approaches to teacher preparation for inclusive and diverse classrooms and focuses in particular on social and emotional learning. She is past president of the Canadian Association for Educational Psychology and is a strong advocate for mental health literacy in K-12 schools and at the postsecondary level.